The Macintosh
iLife '09

by Jim Heid

Peachpit
Press

The Macintosh iLife '09
Jim Heid

Peachpit Press
1249 Eighth Street
Berkeley, CA 94710
510/524-2178
510/524-2221 (fax)
Find us on the Web at: www.peachpit.com
To report errors, please send a note to errata@peachpit.com

Peachpit Press is a division of Pearson Education.

Published by Peachpit Press.

Copyright © 2009 by Jim Heid

Editor: Barbara Assadi
Book Design and Illustration: Arne Hurty, BayCreative
Compositor and Layout Design: Jonathan Woolson, thinkplaydesign
Production Coordinator: Myrna Vladic
Indexer: Emily Glossbrenner, FireCrystal Communications
Cover Design: Arne Hurty, BayCreative

Portions originally appeared in *Macworld* magazine, ©Mac Publishing LLC.
Macintosh and iPod product photography courtesy Apple, Inc.

ISBN 13: 978-0-321-60134-6
ISBN 10: 0-321-60134-3
9 8 7 6 5 4 3 2 1
Printed and bound in the United States of America.

For Maryellen,
for my mother,
and in loving memory
of George Heid, my dad.
A master of the analog
hub, he would have
loved this stuff.

George Heid (right), recording direct to disc
on a moving train, in the early 1950s.

About the Author

Jim Heid describes himself as a poster child for iLife: he has been taking photos, making movies, and playing music since he was a kid.

He began writing about personal computers in 1980. As Senior Technical Editor of one of the first computer magazines, *Kilobaud Microcomputing*, he began working with Mac prototypes in 1983. He began writing for *Macworld* magazine in 1984, and is now a Senior Contributor. He has also written for *PC World, Internet World,* and *Newsweek* magazines, and was a technology columnist for the *Los Angeles Times.*

In 2007, Apple approached Jim to help develop the iLife video tutorials that are available at Apple's Web site. He also develops the curricula for the iLife Apple Camp workshops that take place at Apple retail stores worldwide.

Jim is a popular speaker at user groups, conferences, and other events. He has taught at the Kodak Center for Creative Imaging in Camden, Maine, at the University of Hawaii, and at dozens of technology conferences in between. He's also an obsessed amateur photographer whose photos have been featured in the *San Francisco Chronicle.*

Jim and his standard poodle and mascot, Sophie, divide their time between San Francisco and the rugged coast of Mendocino, California.

Acknowledgements

This book wouldn't exist if it weren't for Arne Hurty and Barbara Assadi. It's that simple, and I thank you both.

Jonathan Woolson, principal of thinkplaydesign, crafted the layouts in Adobe InDesign. I'm hugely grateful for the aesthetics, precision, and attention to detail that you bring to the table.

My thanks also go to Jeff Carlson for expertly revising the iMovie chapter—no small task this time around.

Thanks also to the Apple engineers and product managers behind iLife '09, and to everyone at Peachpit Press. The best computer platform and the best publisher: what more could a geek author want?

My dear friend Cynthia took a great author photo—and takes great photos, in general (see cynthiawoodphoto.com). Thanks also to Mitch and everyone at MCN; to Chuck Wilcher; to Judy, Terry, Mimi, Pierre, Laura, Rennie, Hope, Bob, Doug, Stephanie, and Marley; and to Sophie, my sweet iPoodle.

Finally, my love and my thanks to Toby, for more reasons than I can say. Like the man said, you are special.

Jim Heid

Table of

Contents

Read Me First

How the Book Works

This book devotes a separate section to each of the iLife '09 programs: iPhoto for photography; iMovie for video editing; iDVD for creating DVD-Video discs, GarageBand for making music and podcasts, and iWeb for creating Web sites. Each section is a series of two-page spreads, and each spread is a self-contained reference that covers one topic.

Most spreads begin with an introduction that sets the stage with an over-view of the topic.

Many spreads refer to this book's companion Web site, where you can get updates and more information.

The Book, the Web Site

There's just one thing this book doesn't cover: tomorrow. The iLife scene is always evolving as new programs and new develop-ments change the way we work with digital media.

That's why this book also has a companion Web site: www. macilife.com. At this site, you'll find links to the products dis-cussed in the book as well as tips and news items, updates, and reviews of iLife-related products.

You'll also find convenient links to the video tutorials that I discuss on the opposite page.

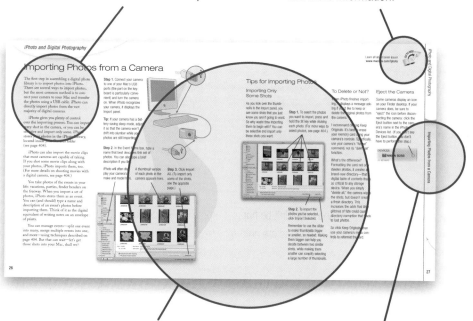

Here's the main course of each spread, where you'll find instructions, background information, and tips.

The section and spread names appear on the edges of the pages to allow you to quickly flip to specific topics.

Read the Book, Watch the Movies

You can't beat the printed page for delivering depth and detail, but some people learn best by watching. If you're in this second group, head to Apple's iLife Web site, www.apple.com/ilife.

There, you'll find a collection of video tutorials. For the big picture, watch the iLife '09 Guided Tour movie. iPhoto, iMovie, GarageBand, and iWeb each have their own "Getting Started" movie, too.

To drill into specific topics, head directly to www.apple.com/ilife/tutorials, where over 100 video tutorials await. They'll help you get up to speed with iLife and set the stage for the details that you'll read in these pages.

Tip: You can also get to the video tutorials using each iLife program. Just head up to the Help menu and choose the Video Tutorials command. If you're working in one of the iLife programs and want to see a feature in action, that command is your fastest path to the movie theater.

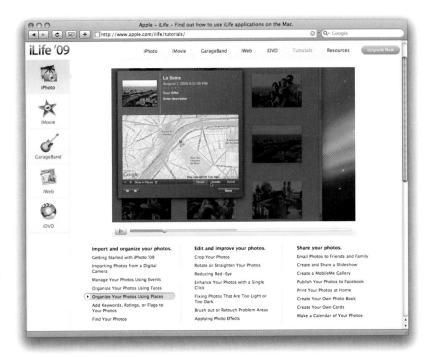

A Short History Lesson

The Macintosh iLife '09 is the seventh edition of a book that was originally called *The Macintosh Digital Hub*. The first edition contained about 120 pages and debuted in 2002—before Apple brought iTunes, iPhoto, iMovie, and iDVD under the iLife umbrella. When that happened, in January

2003, the second edition, renamed *The Macintosh iLife*, appeared.

Since then, a new version of iLife—and a new edition of this book—have become an almost-annual adventure. The book has grown to over 400 pages and become the best-selling book on iLife.

And I couldn't be happier. Apple and the Mac are on a roll, thanks in part to the iLife programs. And I get to spend a healthy (okay, sometimes unhealthy) part of each day listening to music, playing music, taking photos, and making movies: things I've loved since I was a kid.

If you've bought previous editions of this book, thank you and welcome back. If you're new to iLife, you're in for a treat. Watch the video tutorials, dig into the book, check out my Web site, and have *fun*.

Welcome to *The Macintosh iLife '09*.

Introducing iLife

The Macintosh
iLife '09

Personal Computers Get Personal

Music, photographs, and movies can inspire, amuse, persuade, and entertain. They're time machines that recall people and places. They're vehicles that carry messages into the future. They're ingrained in infancy and become intensely personal parts of our lives. And they've all gone digital.

It's now possible to carry a music library in your pocket, to take photos without film, and to edit video in your den—or on a cross-country flight. It's easier than ever to combine music, images, and video. And it's easy to share your finished product, whether with loved ones in the living room, clients in a conference room, or a global audience on the Internet.

Behind this digital age are breakthroughs in storage technologies, processor speed, chip design, and even in the types of connectors and interfaces used to attach external gear. In the past, personal computers weren't powerful enough to manage the billions of bits that make up digital media. Today, they are.

You might say that personal computers have finally become powerful enough to become truly personal.

Audio

1972	1979	1982	1988	1989
Nippon Columbia Company begins digitally recording master tapes.	Sony's Walkman is the first portable music player.	Billy Joel's *52nd Street* is the first album released on CD.	CDs outsell vinyl albums for the first time.	MP3 audio compression scheme is patented.

Imaging

1969	1991	1994	1997	1998
Bell Labs researchers invent the charge-coupled device (CCD).	Kodak adapts Nikon F-3 camera with 1.3-megapixel CCD.	Apple's QuickTake 100 camera debuts at $699.	The Associated Press switches to digital photography.	1-megapixel cameras proliferate. Online photo sites offer prints and other services.

Video

1956	1967	1975	1983	1991
First videotaped TV program is broadcast.	Sony delivers first portable videotape recorder.	Bell Labs demonstrates CCD TV camera. Sony Betamax debuts.	Sony's Betamovie is the first one-piece camcorder.	Apple's QuickTime 1.0 brings digital video to the Macintosh.

Storage

1956	1973	1980	1984	1992
IBM disk system holds 5MB and uses disks two feet wide.	First hard disk: 30MB on an 8-inch disk platter.	Philips and Sony develop the compact disc standard.	First Mac hard disks store 5MB and cost over $2500.	Apple includes CD-ROM drives with Macs.

1996
Fraunhofer releases MP3 encoder and player for Windows PCs.

1999
Napster and other Internet services enable swapping of MP3 files.

2001
Apple introduces iPod. First copy-protected audio CDs appear amid controversy.

2003
iTunes Store debuts for Macs and Windows.

2004
Internet radio shows called podcasts begin to proliferate.

2005
iTunes Store ranks among the top ten music retailers for the first time.

2008
Apple passes Wal-Mart to become the top music retailer in the United States.

Truly Personal Computing

1999
2-megapixel cameras, led by Nikon's $999 Coolpix 950, are the rage.

2000
3-megapixel cameras add movie modes. Digital cameras represent 18 percent of camera sales.

2001
Consumer cameras hit 4 megapixels. Digital cameras comprise 21 percent of camera market.

2002
Apple introduces iPhoto. Consumer cameras reach 5 megapixels.

2004
8-megapixel cameras appear as digital cameras outsell film cameras for the first time.

2006
Consumer cameras reach 10 megapixels. Nikon discontinues most of its film cameras.

2008
Apple's iPhone tags photos with geographic location—ideal for iPhoto '09.

1994
miniDV format debuts: digital audio and video on 6.3 mm wide tape.

1995
FireWire, invented by Apple in the early 90s, is adopted as industry standard.

1999
Apple builds FireWire into Macs and releases iMovie 1.0.

2003
Sony, Canon, and others announce HDV high-definition standard.

2005
iPod gains video playback. Apple sells videos through iTunes.

2006
Google buys online video site YouTube for $1.65 billion.

2009
Tapeless camcorders begin to dominate the market.

1993
A 1.4GB hard drive costs $4559.

1995
DVD standard is announced.

1999
IBM MicroDrive puts 340MB on a coin-sized platter.

2001
5GB Toshiba hard drive uses 1.8-inch platter; Apple builds it into the new iPod.

2001
Apple begins building SuperDrive DVD burners into Macs.

2005
Some Macs include dual-layer SuperDrives capable of burning over 8GB.

2009
The iPod classic packs a 120GB hard drive and one-terabyte drives become popular.

A Sampling of the Possibilities

This technological march of progress is exciting because it enables us to do new things with age-old media. I've already hinted at some of them: carrying a music library with you on a portable player, shooting photographs with a digital camera, and editing digital movies.

But the digital age isn't about simply replacing vinyl records, Instamatic cameras, and Super 8 movies. What makes digital technology significant is that it lets you combine various media into messages that are uniquely yours. You can tell stories, sell products, educate, or entertain.

And when you combine these various elements, the whole becomes greater than the sum of its parts.

Go Digital

Pictures That Move

The latest digital video formats have transformed video for amateurs and professionals alike. Shoot sparkling video with stereo sound using a camcorder that fits in the palm of your hand. Transfer your footage to the Mac, then edit to tell your story.

Forget Film

Digital cameras provide convenience that film can't touch. Review your shots instantly. Delete the ones you don't want. Transfer the keepers to your Mac, and then share them—through the Internet, through CDs and DVDs, and much more.

Bring It All Together

Preserve the past.
Relive a vacation
with pictures, video,
and sound.

Create for the future.
Produce a book that
commemorates a baby's
first year.

Make gifts.
Create books, calendars, and
greetings cards that contain
your own photos.

Start a show.
Create an audio or video
podcast containing rants,
raves, business tips—
you name it.

Educate.
Create a training
video that teaches
a new skill or lets
people see your
product in action.

Tell a story.
Interview relatives and
create a multimedia
family history.

Promote yourself.
Create a DVD or
Web portfolio of your
design work or
photography.

Create a journal.
Publish a blog
containing ongoing
opinions, tips, or
vacation dispatches.

Compose yourself.
Record your own
original music, then
use it in your video and
DVD productions.

Gather 'round.
Share photos,
videos, and ideas on
social networking
Web sites, such as
YouTube, Facebook,
and Flickr.

Tell the world.
Create a Web site
about your family,
company, vacation,
or favorite cause.

Where the Mac Fits In

All of today's personal computers have fast processors, fat hard drives, and the other trappings of power. But powerful hardware is only a foundation. Software is what turns that box of chips into a jukebox, a digital darkroom, a movie studio, a recording studio, and a soapbox with a global audience.

Software is what really makes the Macintosh digital hub go around. Each of Apple's iLife programs—iPhoto for photography, iMovie for video editing, iDVD for creating DVDs, GarageBand for recording music, iWeb for creating Web sites—greatly simplifies working with, creating, and combining digital media.

Similar programs are available for PCs running Microsoft Windows. But they aren't included with every PC, and they lack the design elegance and simplicity of Apple's offerings. It's simple: Apple's iLife has made the Mac the best personal computer for digital media.

And then there's iTunes and its sidekicks, the iPod and iPhone. While this i-ware isn't part of iLife, they work together beautifully. Use music from your iTunes library in your movies and other iLife projects, and view photos, play GarageBand tunes, and watch iMovie flicks on an iPod or iPhone. Connect your portable theater to a big-screen set—or add an Apple TV—and live iLife through your home entertainment system. Go from consuming media to producing your own, with your Mac at the center of it all.

iPhoto

· Import photos from digital cameras
· Organize photos into albums—or let iPhoto organize them based on events, faces, and places
· Crop, modify, and print photos
· Order prints, calendars, cards, and books
· Create slide shows, and share photos online

iMovie

· Import and organize video from camcorders
· Edit video and create titles
· Add music soundtracks from iTunes
· Enhance video and add special effects
· Add photographs from iPhoto
· Share video through DVDs, or the Web
· Export video for viewing on iPod, iPhone, or Apple TV

iWeb

· Create Web sites and publish them on Apple's MobileMe service
· Publish photo albums from iPhoto
· Publish movies from iMovie
· Create and maintain Web journals (blogs)
· Publish podcasts from GarageBand

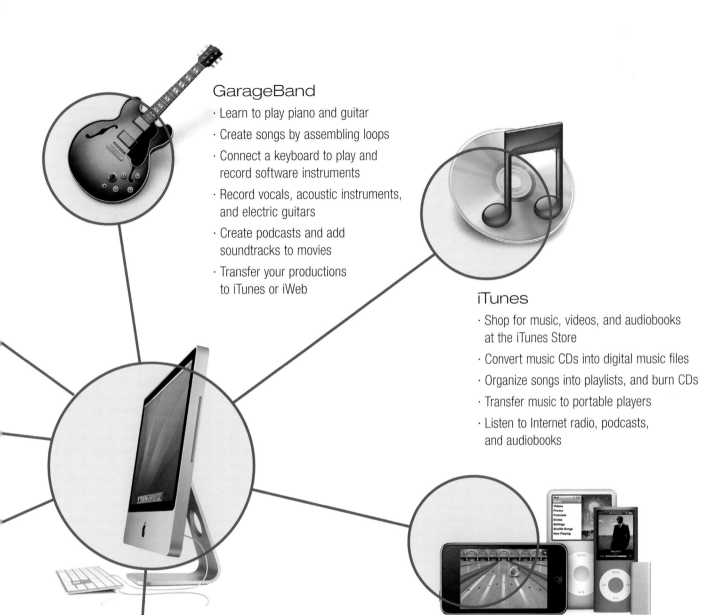

GarageBand

· Learn to play piano and guitar
· Create songs by assembling loops
· Connect a keyboard to play and record software instruments
· Record vocals, acoustic instruments, and electric guitars
· Create podcasts and add soundtracks to movies
· Transfer your productions to iTunes or iWeb

iTunes

· Shop for music, videos, and audiobooks at the iTunes Store
· Convert music CDs into digital music files
· Organize songs into playlists, and burn CDs
· Transfer music to portable players
· Listen to Internet radio, podcasts, and audiobooks

iPhone and iPod Family

· Carry your favorite songs with you
· Synchronize with your iTunes library
· Connect to stereo system, TV set, or car audio adapter
· Store contacts, calendars, photos, video, and more
· Use your iPhone or iPod touch to shop at the iTunes Store

iDVD

· Create slide shows from your iPhoto library
· Add music soundtracks from iTunes
· Present video created in iMovie
· Distribute files in DVD-ROM format

No Medium is an Island

Combining multiple media is a key part of audio-visual storytelling—even silent films had soundtracks played on mighty Wurlitzer theater organs.

Combining media is easy with the iLife programs. There's no need to plod through export and import chores to move, say, a photograph from iPhoto into iMovie. That's because the iLife programs have *media browsers* that make it easy to access your music, photos, and movies. The media browsers also have Search boxes to help you find the music track, photo, or movie you want.

You can also move items between programs by simply dragging them. Drag a photo from iPhoto into iMovie, iWeb, GarageBand, or iDVD. Drag a music track from iTunes into iPhoto, iMovie, or iDVD. And when you've finished a hot tune in GarageBand, add it to your iTunes music library with a click of the mouse.

These lines of communication extend beyond iLife, too. For example, Apple's iWork programs also provide media browsers that make it easy to add photos, music, and movies to documents and presentations.

The iLife programs work together in other ways, which I'll describe as we go. In the meantime, think about ways to marry your media and tell a stronger story.

Feel free to browse.
With the media browser (iWeb's is shown here), it's easy to access— and combine—music, photos, and movies.

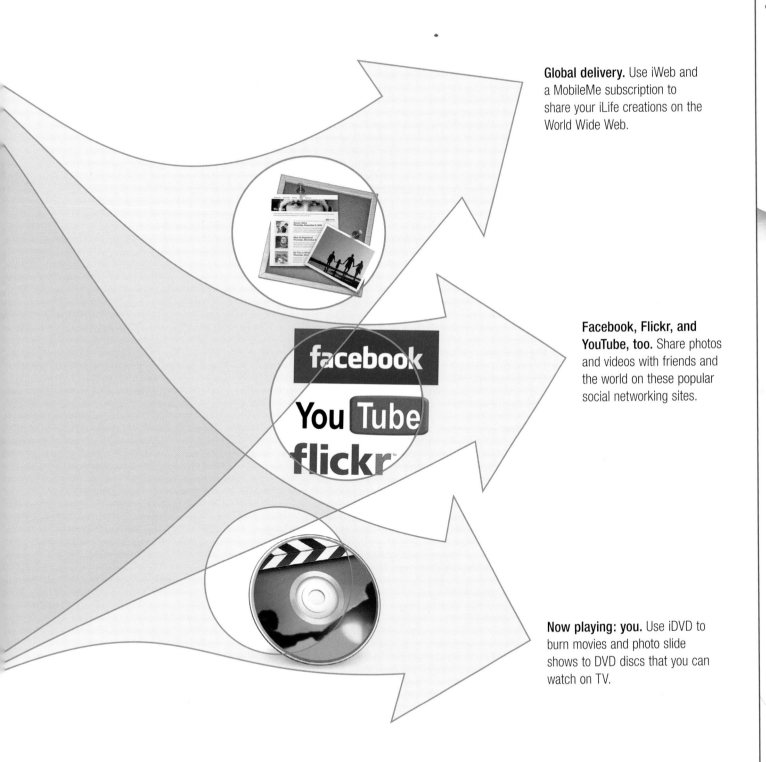

Global delivery. Use iWeb and a MobileMe subscription to share your iLife creations on the World Wide Web.

Facebook, Flickr, and YouTube, too. Share photos and videos with friends and the world on these popular social networking sites.

Now playing: you. Use iDVD to burn movies and photo slide shows to DVD discs that you can watch on TV.

iLife Keeps You Connected

It's no secret that the Internet is a great way to stay current—with news, family, and anything else you find interesting.

A relatively new Internet technology makes it even easier to stay current with subjects of interest. It's called *RSS*, and it allows you to *subscribe* to information, called *feeds*, from Web sites and other Internet sources.

Say your hometown newspaper is called *The Banner*, and you're interested in keeping tabs on it. If the newspaper provides an RSS feed, you can subscribe to the feed using the latest versions of Apple's Safari browser, Mail program, or a separate *news-reader* program, such as NetNewsWire (www.newsgator.com).

After you've subscribed to a feed, it's updated at regular intervals—for example, every 30 minutes in Safari. Want to see what's new in the hometown? There's no need to go *The Banner*'s home page. Simply check your RSS feed in Safari. RSS brings the news to you.

What does all this have to do with iLife? Apple has built RSS into several of the iLife programs. As a result, you can subscribe to audio content, you can publish and subscribe to photos, and you can create Web journals (called *blogs*) to which others can subscribe.

I'll cover the details behind RSS and how it relates to iLife '09 throughout this book. Here's an overview of how iLife '09 and RSS work together to keep you current.

 ## Subscribe to Podcasts

iTunes is your gateway to thousands of *podcasts*—Internet radio programs that cover every imaginable subject (and some unimaginable ones). When you subscribe to a favorite podcast, iTunes downloads new episodes for you whenever they become available.

Use Safari RSS or a newsreader program? Don't forget to subscribe to the feed for this book's companion site at **www.macilife.com**

Tap Into Social Networks

Publish photos on Flickr or Facebook? Remind your friends that they can subscribe to your posted items to keep tabs on you—both Flickr and Facebook provide RSS feeds.

Publish and Subscribe to Web Galleries

Keep friends and family current with your favorite photos and movies by publishing Web galleries and photo albums. Use an optional password to keep your photos private if you like. You can even allow other people to add their own photos, turning your gallery into a collaborative adventure.

Know someone who's published a Web gallery? Use iPhoto to subscribe to it. The remote photos appear in your iPhoto library, and when the gallery is updated, the latest photos appear in your iPhoto. It can be a lot more fun than emailing photos back and forth.

Publish Audio and Video Podcasts

Use GarageBand and iMovie to create audio or video podcasts, then use iWeb to publish them via Apple's MobileMe service so that others can subscribe to them.

Share Video on YouTube

Use iMovie to edit video, then share the final product on YouTube. Your biggest fans can subscribe to your movies.

Create Your Own Blog

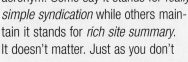

Publish an online journal: a vacation travelogue, a diary, or daily tips for your business clients. Create it in iWeb, then publish it via Apple's MobileMe Internet service. iWeb automatically creates an RSS feed for you, enabling others to subscribe to your blog.

What Does RSS Stand For?

RSS is YACA: yet another computer acronym. Some say it stands for *really simple syndication* while others maintain it stands for *rich site summary*. It doesn't matter. Just as you don't need to know what DVD stands for in order to create or play one, you don't need to know what RSS stands for to enjoy its benefits.

11

Putting the Pieces Together

Software is important, but so is hardware. Several aspects of the Mac's hardware make it ideally suited to digital media work. All Macs contain fast processors and copious hard drives—essential ingredients for storing and manipulating digital media.

Another factor in the hardware equation is ports: the connection schemes used to attach external devices, such as portable music players, digital cameras, camcorders, printers, and speakers. Every Mac contains all the ports necessary for connecting these and other add-ons.

And finally, the Mac's hardware and software work together smoothly and reliably. This lets you concentrate on your creations, not on your connections.

Here's a quick reference to the ports and connectors you'll use in your journey through iLife.

Audio Line Out

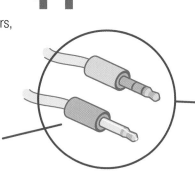

Standard 3.5 mm stereo minijack connects to headphones, amplifiers, and other audio equipment.

On all current Macs, this connector also provides optical digital audio output for connection to home theater and stereo systems (see page 16).

Universal Serial Bus (USB)

Connects to iPods and iPhones, digital cameras, some camcorders, some hard drives, microphones, printers, some music keyboards and interfaces, and other add-ons.

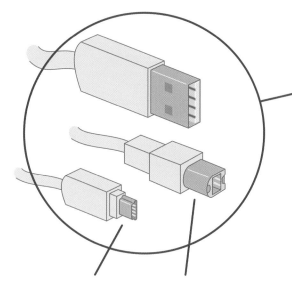

Many digital cameras use this miniature USB connector.

Many printers, scanners, and USB hard drives use this type of connector.

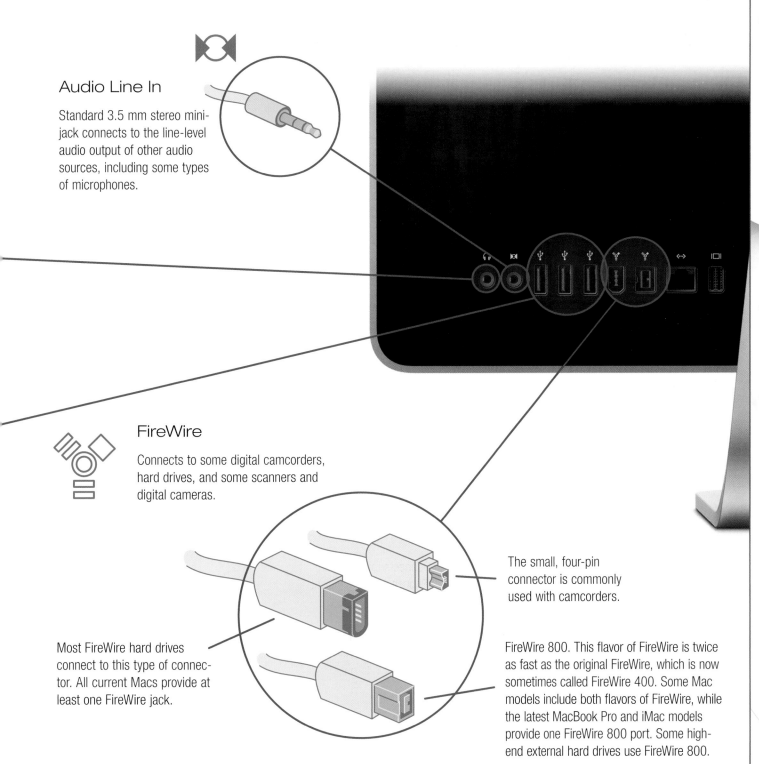

Audio Line In

Standard 3.5 mm stereo mini-jack connects to the line-level audio output of other audio sources, including some types of microphones.

FireWire

Connects to some digital camcorders, hard drives, and some scanners and digital cameras.

The small, four-pin connector is commonly used with camcorders.

Most FireWire hard drives connect to this type of connector. All current Macs provide at least one FireWire jack.

FireWire 800. This flavor of FireWire is twice as fast as the original FireWire, which is now sometimes called FireWire 400. Some Mac models include both flavors of FireWire, while the latest MacBook Pro and iMac models provide one FireWire 800 port. Some high-end external hard drives use FireWire 800.

Outfitting Your Mac for Digital Media

The digital lifestyle is many things, but inexpensive is not one of them. iPods, cameras, camcorders, music keyboards, microphones, accessories of all kinds—spending opportunities abound. Just ask my credit cards.

I explore many of these buying opportunities throughout this book. But first, it's important to ensure that your Mac is well equipped for your iLife endeavors.

With their built-in USB and FireWire ports, today's Macs are able to connect to cameras, portable music players, camcorders, and other digital devices.

But there's always room to grow, especially where digital media are concerned. To get the most out of iLife, consider upgrading several key components of your Mac. At right is a shopping list.

And if you're outfitting an older Mac for iLife '09, you may need to throw in a copy of Mac OS X 10.5 (Leopard), or a later version, if available. The iLife '09 programs aren't compatible with older versions of Mac OS X, such as 10.4 (Tiger).

To learn more about the latest version of Mac OS X, see www.apple.com/macosx.

Storage in Two Flavors

Digital media takes up space—lots of it. Upgrading your Mac's storage capacity is an essential first step in outfitting it for digital media.

Memory Upgrade. Adding memory is a great way to boost any Mac's overall performance. On a Mac with insufficient memory, programs run slowly, particularly if you're trying to run several at once. Each of the iLife programs can benefit from plenty of memory, but GarageBand in particular will appreciate it.

With all current Mac models, you can install a memory upgrade yourself. If you have a Mac mini, Apple recommends having memory installed by a qualified technician. But if you have dexterous hands and a modicum of bravery, you can do the job yourself.

How much memory should you add? As much as you can afford. A gigabyte (1GB) or more is ideal. Memory is relatively inexpensive, especially compared to the performance benefits it provides—not just in iLife, but in other programs, too.

Hard Drive. All digital media eat up disk space—except for video, which utterly devours it. If you're serious about digital media, you'll want to expand your Mac's storage.

It's easy to do. If you have a tower-style Mac, you can install a second hard drive inside the Mac's case. For iMacs, Mac minis, and laptops, you can connect an external FireWire or USB hard drive—or several of them, if you like.

External hard drives are available in a wide range of capacities and case sizes. Portable drives are particularly convenient: they fit in a shirt pocket and can draw power from the Mac—no separate power supply needed. On the downside, though, portable drives cost more than conventional external drives, and they tend to be slower—a big drawback for iMovie and GarageBand, both of which greatly benefit from a fast hard drive.

Digital Hubs

The Mac's FireWire connectors are durable, but they aren't indestructible. All that plugging and unplugging of camcorders, hard drives, and other doodads can take its toll. What's more, some Macs have just one FireWire connector, limiting the number of devices you can connect directly to the Mac.

A FireWire hub is an inexpensive add-on that addresses both issues. A hub is to FireWire what a power strip is to a wall outlet: it provides more jacks for your devices. After connecting the hub to your Mac, you can connect several devices to the hub.

You can also buy USB hubs that provide the same expansion benefits for USB devices. Belkin (www.belkin.com) is a major supplier of hubs and accessories of all kinds.

The Right Accounts

To order prints and more with iPhoto (and to buy from the iTunes Store), you'll want an Apple account. You can set one up with a few clicks using iTunes or iPhoto.

If you're serious about living the iLife, take the next step and subscribe to Apple's MobileMe service. Currently $99 per year, MobileMe enables you to publish Web galleries with iPhoto as well as Web sites with iWeb. You'll also be able to access Apple's iDisk remote storage service.

To sign up, go to www.me.com. Unsure whether MobileMe is for you? Sign up for a free trial membership.

Sounding Better: Speaker Options

Alfred Hitchcock once said, "In radio, sound is a rather important element." That understatement also applies to iLife. Whether listening to music or creating a narration for a movie, you'll want to hear more sound than your Mac's built-in speaker can reproduce.

You have options aplenty. If your Mac and stereo system are close to each other, you can connect them with a cable and listen through your speakers. You can also use Apple's AirPort Express

Base Station or Apple TV to wirelessly beam audio to your stereo. For details on these options, see the following pages.

When working at your Mac, you'll want speakers that are directly adjacent to your display. This delivers the most realistic stereo field—and that's essential whether you're mixing a song in GarageBand or just wanting to enjoy your favorite tunes while you type.

Several companies sell speaker systems designed for use with

computers. Harman Multimedia (www.harman-multimedia.com) sells a large selection under the venerable Harman/Kardon and JBL names. Another highly regarded audio brand, Bose (www.bose.com), also sells speaker systems designed for computers and portable music players. Most systems include a *subwoofer* that sits under your desk and provides a deep, gut-punching bass.

If you're a GarageBand musician, you might prefer a set of

monitor speakers, whose frequency response is superior to that of typical computer speakers. For my GarageBand setup, I use a pair of Yamaha MSP5 monitors. At about $500 a pair, they're pricey by computer speaker standards, but inexpensive by studio monitor standards. And they sound great—beefier and truer than a pair of inexpensive computer speakers and a subwoofer. For reviews of numerous monitor speakers, see www.emusician.com/speakers.

The Mac and Your Stereo

Buying a separate set of speakers has its advantages—foremost among them, the ability to place the speakers directly on either side of your display to get the best stereo mix as you use your Mac.

But if you have a good stereo system, you might prefer to use the gear you already have. Listen to iTunes and streaming Internet radio through your stereo. Watch your iPhoto slide shows, iMovie projects, and iTunes videos on the Mac, but with home-theater sound.

The journey from Mac to stereo system has several possible paths; the best one for you depends on the distance between your computer and your audio system, the specific Mac model you have, and your listening goals. Here's a roadmap of some popular routes. And if you want to also view iTunes videos on your TV, turn the page to learn about Apple TV.

Three Ways to Connect

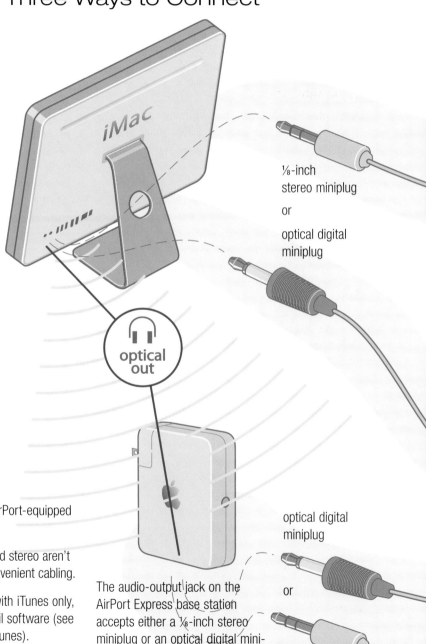

⅛-inch stereo miniplug

or

optical digital miniplug

optical out

AirPort Express

Connect an AirPort Express base station to your stereo, and you can transmit music from any AirPort-equipped Mac within range. In iTunes, simply select the base station from the pop-up menu.

Works with: Any AirPort-equipped Mac.

Best when: Mac and stereo aren't close enough for convenient cabling.

Downside: Works with iTunes only, unless you use Airfoil software (see www.macilife.com/itunes).

optical digital miniplug

or

⅛-inch stereo miniplug

The audio-output jack on the AirPort Express base station accepts either a ⅛-inch stereo miniplug or an optical digital miniplug (it's the same type of jack provided by all current Macs).

Analog Direct Connection

You can connect any Mac to a stereo system by plugging a cable into the Mac's headphone jack.

Works with: Any Mac.

Best when: Mac and audio system are relatively close together.

Downside: Audio is less pristine than with digital connections, although most ears will never notice.

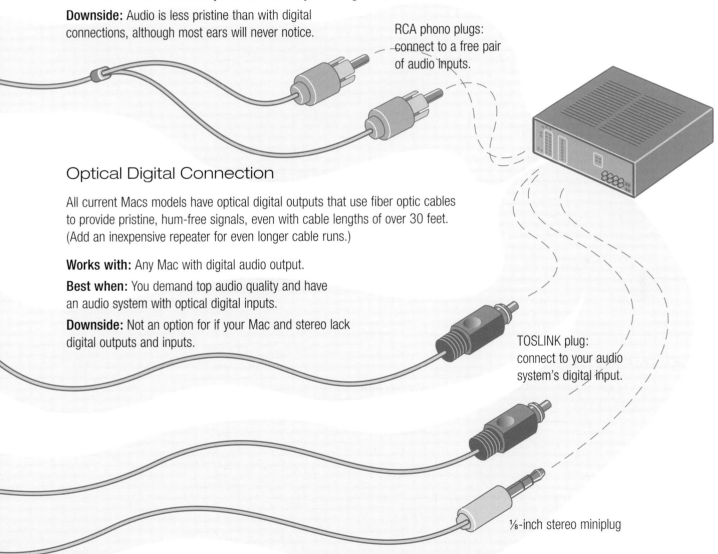

RCA phono plugs: connect to a free pair of audio inputs.

Optical Digital Connection

All current Macs models have optical digital outputs that use fiber optic cables to provide pristine, hum-free signals, even with cable lengths of over 30 feet. (Add an inexpensive repeater for even longer cable runs.)

Works with: Any Mac with digital audio output.

Best when: You demand top audio quality and have an audio system with optical digital inputs.

Downside: Not an option for if your Mac and stereo lack digital outputs and inputs.

TOSLINK plug: connect to your audio system's digital input.

⅛-inch stereo miniplug

Apple TV: The Mac and Your TV

A high-definition TV set is a great place to watch your iPhoto slide shows and your iMovie films. Connect an Apple TV to your set, and you can do these things and more.

Apple TV is a bridge between iTunes and your TV set and stereo system. Synchronize part or all of your iTunes library with Apple TV: iTunes copies items to the Apple TV's hard drive via AirPort wireless networking or an Ethernet cable.

Once that's done, use the Apple TV's remote control to navigate your library, watch videos, listen to music and podcasts, and view photos from your iPhoto library or Flickr.

It gets better. Apple TV also lets you search for and view videos on YouTube, and view photos on Flickr. You can also buy and rent items from the iTunes Store. And if you have additional Macs or Windows PCs in your house, they can stream music and videos to the Apple TV—much as you can share iTunes and iPhoto libraries between computers (page 120).

Tuning In to Apple TV

Step 1. Set up.

Connect your Apple TV to your TV and stereo. You have several options, depending on the kind of video- and audio-input jacks your TV and stereo provide. (For some advice, see the preceding pages—connecting an Apple TV to a stereo is a lot like connecting your Mac to one.)

You'll also need to provide a way for your Mac and the Apple TV to communicate. An AirPort wireless network is ideal—no need to string more wires into your TV cabinet. You can also run an Ethernet cable from your Mac to the Apple TV.

Next, configure the Apple TV. This involves connecting to your wireless (or wired) network and specifying some video options. Finally, a five-digit passcode appears on your TV screen.

Tip: On the latest Macs, Ethernet transfers data much faster than AirPort. If you're syncing a large library, consider connecting your Mac directly to the Apple TV using an Ethernet cable. After the first sync, you can switch to AirPort wireless syncing for subsequent updates.

Step 2. Connect to iTunes and sync.

Sit down at your Mac and launch iTunes. Your Apple TV appears in the Devices list. Select it, and then type the passcode that appeared on your TV.

This step pairs your Mac's copy of iTunes with your Apple TV. iTunes then begins syncing: copying your iTunes library to the Apple TV's hard drive. A status message appears in iTunes.

If you don't want to sync everything in your library, take the reins yourself: click the Apple TV item in the Devices list, then use the tabs to specify what you'd like to sync.

Step 3. Enjoy and repeat.

Crack open a Dr. Pepper and start watching or listening. Use the Apple TV's remote control to navigate and choose options from the menus on your TV. Explore your iTunes library, or detour to YouTube or Flickr if you'd like.

Sync or Stream? Or Both?

The Apple TV works best when you've copied your iTunes library to the Apple TV's hard drive, as described here. Syncing enables you to use the Apple TV without your Mac having to be up and running.

But as I mentioned on the opposite page, you can also stream music and videos to the Apple TV. Streaming has the advantage of not using up disk space on the Apple TV. If your iTunes library is larger than will fit on the Apple TV's hard drive, streaming is an excellent option.

Up to five Macs or Windows PCs can stream to a single Apple TV. If everyone in the house has his or her own computer, each person can tap into his or her copy of iTunes and watch videos and listen to music.

You can also combine syncing and streaming with a single library. Maybe you have a slower AirPort network—you have a base station that uses the original, 801.11b standard—and video playback is choppy when streaming. Solution: Sync your videos to the Apple TV, but stream the music.

Streaming downsides. Streaming has some limitations. To state the obvious, the computer from which you're streaming must be up and running; put it to sleep, and the stream dries up.

Setting it up. To set up streaming on the Apple TV, select Settings > Computers > Add Shared iTunes Library. A passcode appears; peck it into iTunes, just as you did when setting up for syncing. Your Apple TV connects to the remote iTunes library, and you're off and running—just add Pringles.

iPhoto and Digital Photography

iPhoto at a Glance

Millions of photographs lead lives of loneliness, trapped in unorganized boxes where they're never seen. Their digital brethren often share the same fate, exiled to cluttered folders on a hard drive and rarely opened.

With iPhoto, you can free your photos—and organize, print, and share them, too. iPhoto simplifies the entire process. You begin by *importing* images from a digital camera, your hard drive, a CD from a photofinisher, or another source. Then take advantage of iPhoto's ability to organize photos according to the events, the places, and even the faces you've photographed.

Along the way, you might also use iPhoto's editing features to make your photos look better. And you might use iPhoto's organization and searching features to help you file and locate images.

When you've finished organizing and editing photos, share them. Order prints or make your own. Design gorgeous photo books, arranging photos on each page and adding captions. Design calendars and greeting cards. Create slide shows, complete with music from iTunes, and then watch them on the Mac's screen, burn them to DVDs, or transfer them to an iPod or Apple TV.

Prefer to share over the Internet? Email photos to friends and family. Share photos on Facebook and Flickr, and create Web galleries on Apple's MobileMe service.

Welcome to the Photo Liberation Society.

Beyond the Shoebox

You can't enjoy photos if you can't find them. Use iPhoto's tools to organize and find your shots.

Organize

By faces. iPhoto can learn to recognize the people in your life (page 40).

By places. View your photos on a map (page 46).

And more. Add descriptions (page 38), create albums (page 58), and assign keywords for fast searching (page 54).

Find

Use the Search field to locate photos.

By text. Search for photo names and descriptions (page 56).

By date. Locate photos by when you took them (page 57).

And more. Search for keywords and ratings you've added (page 56), and create smart albums that search on multiple criteria (pages 62–65).

Your eventful life: iPhoto stores each set of photos you import as an *event*. You can create new events, combine events, and much more (page 36).

Skim and browse: To preview the photos in an event, skim the mouse pointer over the event (page 34). There isn't a faster way to browse.

People and places: iPhoto also helps you organize photos by faces (page 40) and locations (page 46).

To see the most recent photos you imported, click Last Import.

You can share photos with other Macs on your network (page 120).

Use albums to organize related photos—before creating a book or slide show, for example (pages 58–61).

Share photos online with Web galleries (page 108).

The Keepsakes area holds books, greeting cards, and calendars (pages 130–147).

Create and display slide shows (pages 94–105).

View and edit photo names and captions (page 38).

Create a new album, Web gallery, slide show, or print project.

Search for photos (opposite page).

View a photo in full-screen view (page 84).

Play an instant slide show (pages 28 and 94).

Use these buttons to manage events, view slide shows, create print projects, and share photos.

To change the size of photo thumbnails, drag the slider. The slider works in other areas of iPhoto, too—for example, to zoom in on book pages.

The Essentials of Digital Imaging

Like any specialized field, digital imaging has its own jargon and technical concepts to understand. You can accomplish a lot in iPhoto without having to know these things, but a solid foundation in imaging essentials will help you get more out of iPhoto, your digital camera, and other imaging hardware.

There are two key points to take away from this little lesson. First, although iPhoto works beautifully with digital cameras, it can also accept images that you've scanned or received from a photofinisher. You can even save your favorite images from Web sites that you visit and from emails that you receive (page 31).

Second, the concept of resolution will arise again and again in your digital imaging endeavors. You'll want big, high-resolution images for good-quality prints, and small, low-resolution images for convenient emailing to friends and family. As described on page 106, you can use iPhoto to create low-resolution versions of your images.

Where Digital Images Come From

iPhoto can work with digital images from a variety of sources.

Digital Camera

Digital cameras are more capable than ever. One key factor that differentiates cameras is *resolution*: how many *pixels* of information they store in each image. Even inexpensive digital cameras now provide resolutions of between 8 and 10 megapixels—more than enough to make large prints.

Most digital cameras connect to the Mac's USB port. Images are usually stored on removable-media cards; you can also transfer images into iPhoto by connecting a *media reader* to the Mac and inserting the memory card into the reader (page 32).

Scanner

With a scanner, you can create digital images from photographs and other hard-copy originals.

Scanners also connect via USB, although some high-end models connect via FireWire. Film scanners are a bit pricier, but can scan negatives and slides and deliver great image quality (page 154). Save your scanned images in JPEG format, and then add them to iPhoto by dragging their icons into the iPhoto window (page 31).

For tips on getting high-quality scans, visit www.scantips.com.

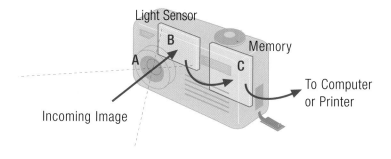

Light Sensor

B

Memory

A

C

Incoming Image

To Computer or Printer

In a digital camera, the image is focused by the lens (**A**) onto a sensor (**B**), where tiny, light-sensitive diodes called photosites convert photons into electrons. Those electrical values are converted into digital data and stored by a memory card or other medium (**C**), from which they can be transferred to a computer or printer.

Compact Disc

So *you're* the person who's still shooting film? Good news: for an extra charge, most photofinishers will burn your images on a compact disc in Kodak Picture CD format. You get not only prints and negatives, but also a CD that you can use with the Mac.

To learn more about Picture CD, google the phrase *picture cd*.

Internet

Many photofinishers also provide extra-cost Internet delivery options. After processing and scanning your film, they send you an email containing a Web address where you can view and download images. After downloading images, you can drag their icons into iPhoto's window.

A Short Glossary of Imaging Terms

artifacts Visible flaws in an image, often as a result of excessive *compression* or when you try to create a large print from a low-resolution image.

CompactFlash A removable-memory storage medium commonly used by digital cameras. A CompactFlash card measures 43 by 36 by 3.3 mm. The thicker *Type 2* cards are 5.5 mm wide.

compression The process of making image files use less storage space, usually by removing information that our eyes don't detect anyway. The most common form of image compression is *JPEG*.

EXIF Pronounced *ex-if*, a standard file format used by virtually all of today's digital cameras. EXIF files use JPEG

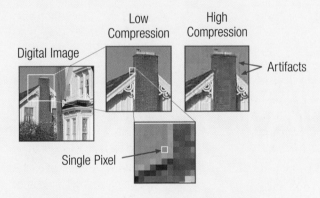

Low Compression High Compression

Digital Image

Artifacts

Single Pixel

compression but also contain details about each image: the date and time it was taken, its resolution, the type of camera used, the exposure settings, and more. iPhoto retrieves and stores EXIF information when you import images. EXIF stands for *Exchangeable Image File*.

JPEG Pronounced *jay-peg*, the most common format for storing digital camera images. JPEG is a *lossy* compression

format: it shrinks files by discarding information that we can't perceive anyway. There are varying degrees of JPEG compression; many imaging programs enable you to specify how heavily JPEG images are compressed. Note that a heavily compressed JPEG image can contain *artifacts*. JPEG stands for *Joint Photographic Experts Group*.

megapixel One million pixels.

pixel Short for *picture element*, the smallest building block of an image. The number of pixels that a camera or scanner captures determines the *resolution* of the image.

raw An image containing the data captured by the camera's light sensor, with no additional in-camera image processing applied (see page 88).

resolution **1.** The size of an image, expressed in pixels. For example, an image whose resolution is 640 by 480 contains 480 vertical rows of pixels, each containing 640 pixels from left to right. **2.** A measure of the capabilities of a digital camera or scanner.

SmartMedia A commonly used design for removable-memory storage cards.

Importing Photos from a Camera

The first step in assembling a digital photo library is to import photos into iPhoto. There are several ways to import photos, but the most common method is to connect your camera to your Mac and transfer the photos using a USB cable. iPhoto can directly import photos from the vast majority of digital cameras.

iPhoto gives you plenty of control over the importing process. You can import every shot in the camera, or you can be selective and import only some. iPhoto stores your photos in the iPhoto Library, located inside your Pictures folder (see page 31).

iPhoto can also import the movie clips that most cameras are capable of taking. If you shot some movie clips along with your photos, iPhoto imports them, too. (For more details on shooting movies with a digital camera, see page 245.)

You take photos of the events in your life: vacations, parties, fender benders on the freeway. When you import a set of photos, iPhoto stores them as an event. You can (and should) type a name and description of an event's photos before importing them. Think of it as the digital equivalent of writing notes on an envelope of prints.

You can manage events—split one event into many, merge multiple events into one, and more—using techniques described on page 36. But that can wait—let's get those shots into your Mac, shall we?

Step 1. Connect your camera to one of your Mac's USB ports (the port on the keyboard is particularly convenient) and turn the camera on. When iPhoto recognizes your camera, it displays the Import panel.

Tip: If your camera has a battery-saving sleep mode, adjust it so that the camera won't drift into slumber while your photos are still importing.

Step 2. In the Event Name box, type a name that best describes this set of photos. You can also type a brief description if you like.

iPhoto will often display your camera's make and model here.

A thumbnail version of each photo in the camera appears here.

Step 3. Click Import All. (To import only some of the shots, see the opposite page.)

Tips for Importing Photos

Importing Only Some Shots

As you look over the thumbnails in the Import panel, you see some shots that you just know you aren't going to want. So why waste time importing them to begin with? You can be selective and import only those shots you want.

Step 1. To select the photos you want to import, press and hold the ⌘ key while clicking each photo. (For more ways to select photos, see page 59.)

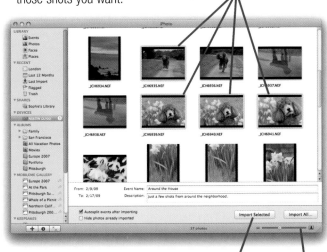

Step 2. To import the photos you've selected, click Import Selected.

Remember to use the slider to make thumbnails bigger or smaller, as needed. Making them bigger can help you decide between two similar shots, while making them smaller can simplify selecting a large number of thumbnails.

To Delete or Not?

When iPhoto finishes importing, it displays a message asking if you'd like to keep or delete the original photos from the camera.

I recommend clicking Keep Originals. It's best to erase your memory card using your camera's controls. Specifically, use your camera's "format" command, not its "delete all" function.

What's the difference? Formatting the card not only deletes photos, it creates a brand-new directory—that digital table of contents that's so critical to any storage device. When you simply "delete all," the camera wipes the shots, but doesn't create a fresh directory. This increases the odds that little glitches of fate could cause directory corruption that leads to lost photos.

So click Keep Originals, then use your camera's menu controls to reformat the card.

Eject the Camera

Some cameras display an icon on your Finder desktop. If your camera does, be sure to "eject" the icon before disconnecting the camera: click the Eject button next to the camera's name in the iPhoto Devices list. (If you don't see the Eject button, you don't have to perform this step.)

After the Import

What happens after iPhoto imports a set of photos? That's up to you. Admire your shots. Start filing and organizing them. Email a few favorites to a friend.

If you're like me, you'll want to check out your shots right away. A couple of clicks gives you a full-screen slide show, complete with music—perfect when you have a circle of eager friends and family watching over your shoulder. Or be selective: display thumbnails of your new photos, then take a close-up look at the best of the bunch.

Some housekeeping may await, too. Delete the shots you don't want. Rotate vertically oriented shots, if necessary. As you tidy up, you'll probably start getting ideas for sharing the photos. Email, prints, books, calendars, cards, Web galleries, DVDs, Facebook, Flickr, YouTube: if you like to share images, this is a great time to be alive.

And along the way, you'll want to celebrate your inner librarian. Organize your photo library with events, titles, captions, keywords, and albums. Trust me: you'll accumulate thousands of photos in no time. A few simple steps will make them easier to find.

But filing can wait. We have some fresh photos to explore.

Viewing Your Shots

Start by clicking the Last Import item in the Library area. This is the fastest way to access the most recent set of shots.

Selective viewing. Adjust the size of the photo thumbnails to your liking: jump down to the lower-right corner and use the size slider.

To magnify a photo so that it fills the iPhoto window, double-click its thumbnail, or select the photo and press the spacebar. **Tip:** Maximize your viewing area: choose Window > Zoom or click the green zoom button in the upper-left corner.

To return to thumbnails, click the mouse or press the Esc key.

Full-screen variation. To fill the entire screen with a photo, click . To return to the thumbnails, double-click the mouse or press Esc. (For more about full-screen view, see page 84.)

Tip: To move to the next or previous photo in either magnified view, press your keyboard's right- or left-arrow key.

Instant slide show. To screen your photos with more style, display a slide show. Click the Slideshow button, then click the Play button in the settings panel that appears next. To learn all about slide shows, see pages 94–105.

Notes and Tips

Rotate Verticals

Some cameras automatically rotate photos taken in vertical orientation. If yours doesn't, the job is yours. Select the photo or photos and then click the Rotate button or press ⌘-R (to rotate counterclockwise). To rotate clockwise, Option-click the Rotate button or press ⌘-Option-R.

Tip: If you find yourself doing a lot of clockwise rotation, you can tweak iPhoto preferences to eliminate having to press Option while clicking Rotate. Choose iPhoto > Preferences, click the General button, then click the leftmost Rotate option:

Now you can rotate clockwise by simply clicking the Rotate button.

Delete the Dregs

See a photo that you know you don't want to keep? Trash it. To delete a photo, select it (click it once), then press the Delete key. You can also delete a photo by dragging it to the Trash on the left side of the iPhoto window.

When you put a photo in the Trash, iPhoto doesn't actually erase the photo from your hard drive; that doesn't happen until you choose Empty Trash from the iPhoto menu. If you change your mind about deleting a photo, click the Trash item in the library list, select the photo you want to keep, and choose Photos > Restore to Photo Library (keyboard shortcut: ⌘-Delete.)

Playing Movies

If your last import included a movie clip, you can play it by double-clicking its thumbnail. iPhoto starts the QuickTime Player program, which loads the movie. To play the movie, press the spacebar or click the Play button.

Customizing iPhoto's Appearance

As the tip above described, the Preferences dialog box is the key to customizing how iPhoto's Rotate button works.

The Preferences dialog box is also the gateway to many other iPhoto settings, which we'll explore as we go along. But you might want to begin by exploring the options in the Appearance pane—they let you tweak how iPhoto looks.

Choose iPhoto > Preferences, then click Appearance.

Want to see your thumbnail photos against a dark gray background? Drag the Background slider to the left.

With the Border options, you can turn off the shadow effect that iPhoto puts behind each photo, and display a thin border around each photo.

If you'd prefer larger text in the Library area of the iPhoto window, choose Large from the Source Text pop-up menu.

Event customizing. With the Events pane of the Preferences dialog box, you can fine-tune how iPhoto displays events. For more details, see page 37.

Window customizing. You can adjust the width of the Library area of the iPhoto window. Position the mouse pointer over the vertical line that separates the Library area from the rest of the window. It changes into a double-headed arrow: ↔ . Drag left and right to adjust the width. A thinner Library area gives you more room for photo thumbnails, as well as a larger canvas for magnified views.

More Ways to Import Photos

Most people import photos directly from a camera using the technique I described on the previous pages. But you have more than one way to get photos into iPhoto.

A media reader is a great way to import photos from a camera's memory card. Plug the reader into your Mac, then insert the memory card into the reader. Because you aren't using your camera to transfer photos, its battery charge will last longer.

Be sure to get a reader that supports the type of memory cards your camera uses. Or get a multi-format reader that supports several types of memory cards.

You can also import images by dragging their icons into the iPhoto window. If you've scanned a batch of images, you can use this technique to bring them into iPhoto. You can also use this technique to save photos that people email to you or that you find on Web sites.

Using a Media Reader

Here's the photo-importing technique I use most often.

Step 1. Connect the media reader to your Mac.

Step 2. Be sure your camera's power is off, then remove the memory card from the camera and insert it into the reader. iPhoto recognizes the card and displays the Import panel shown on page 26.

Step 3. Type a name and description for the photos you're about to import, then import all or some of the photos, as described on the previous pages.

Step 4. After iPhoto has imported the photos, click the Eject button next to the memory card's name in the Devices list. Finally, remove the memory card from the reader, return the card to your camera, and then erase the card.

Laptop media readers. Media readers are also available for the ExpressCard/34 slot provided by the MacBook Pro laptops. Unfortunately, the ExpressCard/34 slot is too small to accommodate a Compact Flash card, requiring you to use an awkward adaptor. If you use Compact Flash cards and own a MacBook Pro, you're probably better off with an external FireWire or USB 2.0 reader.

Still using a PowerBook G4? You can also buy a media reader that plugs into the PC Card slot of a PowerBook. If you're traveling with a PowerBook, a PC Card-based reader is a compact alternative to a FireWire or USB reader.

To see some laptop media readers, visit www.macilife. com/iphoto.

Importing from the Finder

To import an entire folder full of images, drag the folder to the Photos item or into the photo area.

iPhoto gives the new event the same name as the folder from which its images came. You can rename the event using the techniques described on page 34.

To import only some images, select their icons and then drag them to the Photos item or into the iPhoto window.

Note: When you import images that are already stored on your hard drive, iPhoto makes duplicate copies of them in your iPhoto library. You can change this using the Preferences command; see "File it Your Way" on page 33.

Importing from Email and Web Pages

A friend has emailed some photos to you, and you want to add them to your iPhoto library. If you're using Mail, the email program included with Mac OS X, simply drag the photos from the email message into the iPhoto window. If the email message contains several photos, Shift-click on each one to select them all before dragging. As an alternative to dragging, you can also choose Add to iPhoto from the little Save pop-up menu that appears near the top of an email message.

If you use Microsoft Entourage, your job is a bit more difficult. First, save the photos on your Mac's desktop. Next, drag them into the iPhoto window as shown at left. Finally, delete the photos from your desktop.

To save a photo that's on a Web page, just drag the photo from your Web browser into the iPhoto window. In Apple's Safari browser, you can also Control-click on a photo and choose Add Image to iPhoto Library from the shortcut menu.

Importing from Picture CDs and PhotoCDs

iPhoto can also import images saved on a Kodak PhotoCD or Picture CD. (PhotoCD is an older format that you aren't likely to see too often. Picture CD is a newer format that most photo finishers use.)

Picture CD. Choose Import to Library from iPhoto's File menu, locate the Picture CD, and then locate and double-click the folder named Pictures. Finally, click the Import button. Or, use the Finder to open the Pictures folder on the CD and then drag images into iPhoto's window.

PhotoCD. Simply insert the PhotoCD in your Mac's optical drive. iPhoto launches and displays its Import panel. Type a name and description for the photos, then import some or all of the photos, as described on the previous pages.

Where iPhoto Stores Your Photos

When you import photos, iPhoto stores them in the iPhoto Library, located inside the Pictures folder. (If you like, you can store your iPhoto Library elsewhere, such as on an external hard drive. For details, see page 153.)

Get in the habit of frequently backing up your iPhoto Library to avoid losing your images to a hardware or software problem.

You can use iPhoto's disc-burning features to back up photos (page 150), or you can copy your iPhoto Library to a different hard drive. For advice on backing up your photos, see page 153.

For more details on the iPhoto Library, see page 156.

Importing Tips

iPhoto gives you plenty of control over the importing process. Do you want iPhoto to automatically split up the photos into numerous events? If so, what time interval do you want to use?

If you're adding photos by dragging them from folders on your hard drive, where do you want iPhoto to store the photos?

If questions like these burn in your brain, your fire extinguisher has just arrived. Otherwise, feel free to skip on. You can always return here when the embers begin to glow.

Hiding Shots You've Already Imported

You wisely took my advice and told iPhoto to not delete photos from your camera after an import (see page 27). But you forgot to erase the card before shooting another two-dozen shots.

No problem. When you connect your camera and switch to iPhoto's Import panel, check the box labeled Hide Photos Already Imported. Photos you've already imported will disappear from the Import panel, making it easy to import some or all of the new shots.

Dealing with Duplicates

Even if you forget to check the aforementioned box, iPhoto has you covered. If you try to import a photo that already exists in your library, iPhoto asks if you really want to import the duplicate.

To cancel the import session, click Cancel.

To have iPhoto apply your choice to all duplicates it finds during this import session, click Apply to all duplicates.

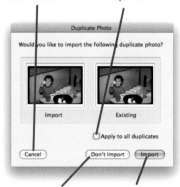

To not import the duplicate, click Don't Import.

To import the duplicate displayed, click Import.

Adjusting Event Settings

As I mentioned on page 26, iPhoto stores imported shots as events. When you import photos from a camera, iPhoto automatically splits them into events (unless you uncheck the Autosplit Events After Importing box in the Import pane).

Normally, iPhoto considers one day's worth of photos to represent an event. For example, if you import some shots taken over a weekend, you'll have two events: Saturday's photos and Sunday's.

Using the Preferences command, you can change the interval of time iPhoto uses when splitting photos into events. Choose iPhoto > Preferences, then click Events. You have three additional choices.

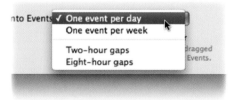

One event per week. iPhoto creates a new event for each seven-day period. Take a two-week vacation, import all your shots, and you'll have two events.

If you don't care to divide your time into small chunks, this is a reasonable option—although if you take as many shots as I do, you may end up with events containing a cumbersomely large number of photos.

Two-hour gaps. iPhoto creates a new event every two hours. Say you do a day's worth of shooting: a sunrise hike at 6:00 a.m., a brunch with friends at 10:00 a.m., and a party at night. Import the shots, and iPhoto will create three events.

When you shoot a lot of shots throughout a day, this option can help corral them into manageable (and related) chunks. Surviving the busy day is your problem.

Eight-hour gaps. iPhoto creates a new event every eight hours. In the busy-day example above, you'd end up with two events: the first containing the hike and brunch photos, and the second containing the party pix.

Eventful advice. Before you import a set of photos, think about what kind of time intervals the photos represent, then consider tweaking the interval preference to match.

Or don't bother. You're never locked into the way iPhoto divvies up your life. You can move photos between events in whatever way you like, and you can have iPhoto autosplit events for you *after* you've imported photos. Pages 36–37 have all the details.

Events and Imports from the Finder

When you import photos from the Finder—by dragging their icons into iPhoto, as described on page 31—iPhoto does not split the photos into events. That makes sense when you think about it: if you're importing a dozen scanned images of photos that are decades old, how would iPhoto know how to divvy them up?

But in some circumstances, you might want iPhoto to automatically split photos imported from the Finder. For example, maybe you're about to import a CD's worth of digital photos that a friend burned for you.

For times like these, return to the Events portion of the Preferences dialog box, and check the box labeled Imported Items From Finder.

File it Your Way

Since the dawn of time—well, since the dawn of version 1.0—iPhoto has always stored images in the iPhoto Library. Generally, that's exactly what you want: when you copy photos from a camera or memory card, you want them stashed safely in your iPhoto Library.

But under some circumstances, iPhoto's "do things my way" approach to organization can work against you. When you add photos that are already stored on your hard drive—for example, images that you've scanned and saved—iPhoto makes additional copies in the iPhoto Library.

After adding photos to your Library that are already on your hard drive, you need to delete the originals. That isn't exactly a sweat-breaking chore, but it does take time. And you might prefer to stick with your existing filing system.

You have the option to not copy image files to the iPhoto Library. If you have a large library of meticulously filed scanned images on your hard drive, you might want to take advantage of this option. You won't have duplicate photos to delete, and you won't have to change the filing system you've developed for your scanned images.

To activate this option, choose iPhoto > Preferences, click the Advanced button, and then uncheck the box labeled Copy Items to the iPhoto Library.

From now on, when you add items from your hard drive to your iPhoto library, iPhoto simply creates aliases for each item. (In Mac OS parlance, an alias is a small file that simply points to an existing file.) If you edit an image, iPhoto stores the edited version in your iPhoto Library.

And by the way, unchecking this option does not change how iPhoto stores photos that you're importing from a camera or media reader. Photos that you import from a location other than a hard drive are always stored in your iPhoto Library.

Browsing Your Photo Library

Unlike any shoebox, iPhoto gives you several ways to browse and explore your photo library. Use Events view to get an at-a-glance look at your library. Forget which photos are in an event? Move your mouse pointer across the event thumbnail, and its photos flash before your eyes.

Events view is the most convenient way to work with your photo library, and chances are it's the view you'll use most of the time. But there's another way to see your shots. Click the Photos item in the Library list, and iPhoto displays your events in a different format—one that you may find useful for some browsing and photo-management tasks.

(If you're an iPhoto veteran, you'll recognize the Photos view—it's similar to the "film rolls" view provided by earlier versions of iPhoto.)

In both views, iPhoto provides little conveniences that help you home in on the photos you seek. For example, as you scroll the iPhoto window, semi-transparent *scroll guides* appear that show the date and title of each event.

Knowing the basics of photo browsing is important—the faster you can get around in your photo library, the greater the chances that you'll explore and enjoy your photos. And once you're familiar with those basics, you may want to investigate the ways iPhoto lets you organize and explore your photos by faces and places.

Here's an overview of the ways iPhoto lets you browse.

Basic Event Techniques

Here are the basic techniques you'll use when working with events.

Skimming thumbnails. Pass your mouse pointer over the event without clicking. **Tip:** You can also skim by combining the mouse and keyboard: point to an event, then press the left- or right-arrow keys. I like to use this technique when an event has a lot of photos in it, or when I've used the size slider to make the event thumbnails small.

Changing an event's name. Click the event's name, then type a new name and press Return.

Accessing an event's photos. Double-click the event thumbnail. Or select the event (click it once) and press the Return key. To return to Events view, click the All Events button (All Events) above the thumbnails, or press the Esc key.

Tips: Want to browse using just the keyboard? First, be sure the mouse pointer isn't over an event. Then, use the arrow keys to select an event. Press Return to see its thumbnails. Press Esc to return to Events view, then arrow-key your way to a different event and repeat.

When you're viewing an event's photos, you can jump to the previous or next event by clicking the arrows in the upper-right corner of the iPhoto window.

Setting the key photo. Each event is represented by one photo, called the key photo or the poster photo. You can change the key photo to one that best represents the event. Skim across the event, and when you see the photo that you want to be the new key photo, press the spacebar. You can also Control-click on the photo and choose Make Key Photo from the shortcut menu. (This latter technique also works in Photos view.)

More Ways to Display Events

Detail view. Sometimes, you need to view the photos of more than one event at once. Maybe you're organizing some recent imports and you want to work on multiple events at the same time—to move some photos from one event to another, for example.

To open more than one event, select each event (click it once), then double-click one of the selected events or press Return. iPhoto opens each selected event.

To return to Events view, click All Events or press Esc.

Separate event window. You can also open an event in its own window: select the event, then choose Events > Open in Separate Window. A new window opens containing the event's photos.

The separate window is a great way to focus in on the shots in one event while retaining quick access to the rest of your library. The window provides its own size

slider for adjusting the size of photo thumbnails. You can even zoom the separate window to fill your screen or a second display, if your Mac has one: choose Window > Zoom.

The following pages describe more uses for the separate event window.

Another Way to Look: Photos View

The Events view is so efficient and versatile that you'll probably spend most of your time there. But there's another option: Photos view. To use it, click the Photos item in the Library area.

The Photos view can be handy for moving photos between events and for combining and splitting events, though as the

following pages describe, you can do all of these tasks in Events view, too.

To open an event, click its triangle. **Tip:** To expand every event in your library, press the Option key while clicking any closed event's triangle. Conversely, to close every event, press Option while clicking any open event's triangle.

To rename an event in this view, click the title, then type the new name.

Tips for Working with Events

Anxious to start having fun with your photos? Go ahead and skip to page 40, where you can learn about iPhoto's faces and places features; or to page 58, where you can learn about creating photo albums and much more.

Eventually, you'll want to learn about the power tools that iPhoto provides for managing photos and events. These maneuvers can help you organize your iPhoto Library and make it easier to corral photos prior to sharing them.

Hiding Photos

A lot of photos fall into that middle ground between bad and beautiful: not awful enough to trash, not good enough to look at all the time. iPhoto lets you hide those mediocre shots to tidy up an event, but bring them back whenever you like.

Hiding photos is also a good strategy when you've taken several nearly identical shots—some portraits, each with a different smile. Pick the best, hide the rest.

To hide a photo, select it and click the Hide button (or press ⌘-L). The photo vanishes, and adjacent photos snuggle in to fill the void.

Bringing them back. When you're viewing an event, iPhoto lets you know if any of its photos are hidden.

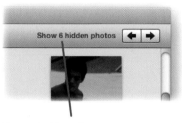

To see hidden photos, click the message. A photo marked as hidden has an X on its corner.

To hide the photos again, click the message again. To unhide a photo, select it and click Unhide or press ⌘-L.

Splitting and Merging

You can split one event into two. Say you have an event containing a hundred shots from an afternoon bike ride and an evening dinner. You may prefer to split the event into two separate, more manageable ones.

To split an event, open it to display its thumbnails. Then, select the photos you want to split off (the dinner shots, for example), and click the Split button. Finally, name the new event.

Merging events. You can also combine two or more events into one. Maybe you fired off some shots at a party, imported them so everyone could see, then took some more. You want all the party shots to be in one event. Easy: drag one event to the other.

You can also merge more than two events: Shift-click or ⌘-click on each event, then drag them to another event. Or select all the events, then click the Merge button.

Moving Photos Between Events

Sometimes, your life as an event planner requires you to move individual photos between events. Maybe you want to fine-tune the way iPhoto autosplit an event. Or maybe a travel companion emailed you some shots that she took, and you want to add a few of them to your vacation event.

There are moving plans aplenty.

Dragging. Open the events in detail view: select them and double-click one of them (page 35). Now drag thumbnails from one event to another. To give yourself more dragging room, zoom the iPhoto window (Window > Zoom) and make the thumbnails smaller (drag the size slider).

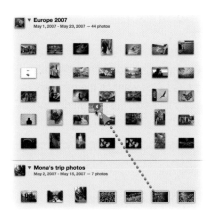

The separate event window, described on page 35, can be handy when dragging photos between events, especially if the events aren't near each other in your library.

Cut and paste. Select the photos you want to move, and choose Edit > Cut. Select the event where you want them, then choose Edit > Paste. When dragging seems like too much work—too many photos, too many events—this is an efficient alternative.

Flagging. This can be the most powerful way to move photos, and it's described at right.

A New Event

You can create a new, empty event and then add photos to it. Be sure no events are selected, then choose Events > Create Event.

(You can also use Create Event to merge events or split photos off into their own

event: Select the events or individual photos, then choose Create Event.)

Flagging Photos

Flagging is like attaching a sticky note to a photo. Trying to decide which shots to add to a book? Flag the best candidates, and you can return to them in a flash.

To flag a photo, select it and click the Flag button or press ⌘-period. A flag badge appears on the photo's thumbnail.

You can flag multiple photos at once—select them first, then click Flag—and you can flag as many shots as you like. To quickly see the shots you've flagged, click the flagged item in the Recent area of the Library list.

You've flagged some shots. Then what?

Move them to an existing event. After flagging the shots, return to Events view. Select the event where you want to move the photos, then choose Events > Add Flagged Photos to Selected Event. If you need to move some shots that are scattered throughout your library, this is the best way to do it.

Move them to a new event. To move flagged photos into a new event of their own, choose Events > Create Event From Flagged Photos. Keep in mind, though, that iPhoto will move those photos from their original events.

Work with them. Select the Flagged item in the Library area. The flagged shots lurk there, ready to be edited, shared—whatever you like.

Lower the flags. Done working with some flagged photos? Here's the easiest way to unflag them all: click the little number next to the Flagged item in the Library area.

Setting Event Preferences

Normally, when you double-click an event thumbnail, you see the event's photos. With this trick, you can double-click to magnify whichever photo is visible under the mouse pointer. Skim across an event, see a photo you want to magnify, and double click.

Choose Preferences > iPhoto, click Events, then choose the Magnifies Photo option.

You can also tweak iPhoto so that a double click opens a photo in edit view (page 66)—the way earlier iPhoto versions worked. Choose iPhoto > Preferences, click General, and choose the Edits Photo option.

Creating Titles and Captions

iPhoto forces some organization on you by storing each set of imported images as a separate event. Even if you never use iPhoto's other organizational features, you're still ahead of the old shoebox photo-filing system: you will always be able to view your photos in chronological order.

But don't stop there. Take the time to assign *titles* and *descriptions* to your favorite shots. By performing these and other housekeeping tasks, you can make photos easier to find and keep your library well organized.

Titles are names or brief descriptions that you assign to photos and events: Party Photos, Mary at the Beach, and so on. iPhoto can use these titles as captions for its Web photo albums and books. Using the View menu, you can have iPhoto display titles below each thumbnail image. You can also search for photos by typing title or description text in the Search box (page 56).

There's one more benefit to assigning titles to photos: when you're working in other iLife programs, you can search for a photo by typing part of its title in the photo media browser's Search box.

Of course, you don't have to type titles and descriptions for every photo in your library. But for the ones you plan to share in some way—or that you'll want to search for later—it's time well spent.

Using the Information Pane

When you want to give photos titles and descriptions, turn to the Information pane. To display the Information pane, click the [◉] button.

Step 1. Select the photo to which you want to assign a title and/or description.

Step 2. Click in the Title or Description area of the Information pane, then type the title or description.

Keep your titles fairly short.

Think of a description as the text you'd normally write on the back of a photo.

Information

title Twilight Walk
date 5/1/2007
time 9:49:18 PM
rating · · · · ·
keyword
kind JPEG Image
size 3837 × 2539
3.6 MB

Along the canals of Amsterdam, the Netherlands.

Tips

On a roll. Want to quickly title (or describe) one photo after another? Press ⌘-] after typing a title or description, and iPhoto selects the next photo and highlights its title or description field so you can immediately begin typing. To move to the previous photo, press ⌘-[. And to keep your hands on the keyboard, press Tab and Shift-Tab to jump from one field to the next in the Information pane.

Check your spelling. Want to check the spelling of your titles and descriptions? Select the text you want to proofread, then choose Edit > Spelling > Check Spelling. Or select the text you want to proofread and press ⌘-;.

Many at once. To change information for many photos at once, select them and choose Photos > Batch Change (see the opposite page). If you're like me and are often too lazy to assign titles and descriptions to individual photos, this can be a good compromise: assign a phrase to a set of related photos, and you can search for that phrase later.

Editing Photo Information Directly

The Information pane is a great place to view and change all kinds of details: a photo's title, its description, the date and time it was taken, and more.

But there's another way to edit photo information, and it's often more convenient than opening the Information pane. Simply click the title beneath a photo's thumbnail, and start typing:

Bethany and Grimmy

(If you don't see titles beneath your photo thumbnails, choose View > Titles.)

The keyboard-shortcut tips described at at left work here, too: type a title, and press ⌘-] to jump directly to the title field of the next photo. Or move the next and previous photo by pressing Tab and Shift-Tab.

Note: You can also type photo titles and descriptions when specifying location information for a photo (page 46). And you can also assign keywords and ratings by working directly beneath photo thumbnails (page 54).

Changing the Date

Time is important. The date stored along with a photo determines how iPhoto sorts the photo. Accurate dates also simplify searching and organizing your library.

All digital cameras store date and time information along with the image (see the sidebar on page 157). But what if your camera's clock is off? Maybe you forgot to adjust its time zone when you flew to Hawaii.

Or maybe you've scanned some old family photos and you want their dates to reflect when they were *taken*, not scanned. That Aunt Mary photo is from 1960, not 2009.

Time travel is easy in iPhoto. You can edit the date of an event, a selection of images, or just one photo. The steps differ depending on what you want to change.

An event. Select the event, choose Photos > Adjust Date & Time.

More than one photo. Select the photos, and choose Photos > Batch Change.

Just one photo. Select the photo, open the Information pane, and type new dates and times.

Tip: Of all these techniques, only one has a keyboard shortcut: Batch Change (⌘-Shift-B). If you're a keyboard jockey, you might find it's actually the *fastest* way to change the date of just one photo—a batch of one.

Choose Date from the pop-up menu.

Type the date and time, pressing Tab to move from one value to the next.

To aid sorting, you can have iPhoto add a time increment between each photo.

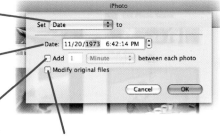

If you check this box, iPhoto records the modified date in the image file itself. (Otherwise, iPhoto simply notes the changed time in its internal database, leaving the original image unchanged.) You might choose this option if you plan to export the image for use in another image-management program, such as Apple's Aperture or Adobe Bridge or Lightroom.

Faces at a Glance

Chances are you take a lot of photos of the people in your life. With the Faces feature, new in iPhoto '09, you can explore your photo library by face: "Show me all the photos of Suzanne," or "Show me every photo containing both Suzanne and Bethany."

Start by "introducing" iPhoto to someone: select a photo of Suzanne and type her name. iPhoto displays more photos that may contain her. Confirm the ones that include Suzanne, reject the ones that don't. The more photos you confirm, the better iPhoto gets at recognizing Suzanne. When you import new photos of her, iPhoto recognizes them. It's futuristic facial-recognition technology—applied to the people you love.

Once you've built up a collection of faces, you can bring iPhoto's other talents to bear. View a slide show. Make a book. Or just browse your favorite mugs. And unless you tell it to, iPhoto never forgets a face.

Upgrading for Faces

Just upgraded to iLife '09? The first time you start iPhoto, it scans your library for photos containing faces. For a library of thousands of photos, this process could take an hour or more, and it slows your Mac down just a bit. If you'd rather postpone scanning— until you're away from your Mac, for example—click the Faces item in the Library list, then click the Pause button. (This scanning also occurs when you import new photos but because it happens *while* iPhoto is importing, you won't notice a slowdown.)

Naming a Face

When iPhoto scans your photos for faces, it's simply identifying photos that it thinks contains eyes, noses, and mouths. It's up to you to tell iPhoto who those folks are—a process called *naming a face.*

Step 1. Select a photo containing a face you want to name.

You can select a photo's thumbnail, or double-click the photo to display a larger version.

Step 2. Click the Name button.

The photo appears with a box enclosing each face.

Step 3. Click the *unnamed face* text, type the person's name, and then press the Return key. If the photo contains additional unnamed faces, repeat this step to name each face.

To move to different photos and name the faces they contain, click the arrow buttons.

Are you all done naming? Click Done.

Notes and Tips

Name suggestions. As you type a name, iPhoto may display suggestions based on similarly spelled names that you've already provided.

To take one of these suggestions, click it. Or just ignore the suggestion and continue typing a name.

Forget a face. Say you have a group shot containing some faces you don't want to track. To have iPhoto forget a face, as it were, point to the face and then click the X that appears in the box.

More of the Same

You probably have more than one photo of someone you've named. Now it's time to let iPhoto know that. iPhoto helps by suggesting photos that may contain that named person. The more photos you positively identify, the better iPhoto gets at recognizing someone's face.

Step 1. If you've just finished naming a face, click the right-pointing arrow next to the person's name. If you're viewing the corkboard (see below), double-click a tile.

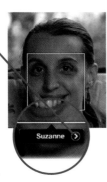

iPhoto displays photos that may contain that person.

Step 2. Click the Confirm Name button, then confirm photos as shown here.

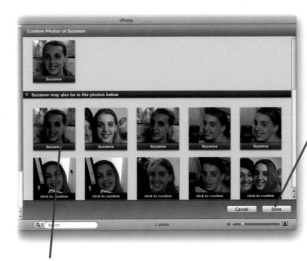

Right person? Click each correctly identified photo. **Tip:** To quickly confirm numerous photos, drag a selection box around them.

Wrong person? If iPhoto misidentified a person, click the photo twice (or press Option while clicking the photo). The text *Not [name]* appears below the photo.

Step 3. When you're finished, click Done.

Even more of the same. After you click Done, iPhoto may display additional photos that it suspects contain that person—proof that iPhoto gets better at recognizing people as you confirm photos of them. Repeat the above steps to confirm or reject photos.

Tip: If iPhoto misidentified a number of photos, press Option while dragging across the photos to quickly reject them.

Introducing the Corkboard

iPhoto displays your collection of faces on the *corkboard*. To see the corkboard, click the Faces item in the Library list. Each person appears on his or her own *tile*.

You can work with the faces tiles using many of the same techniques that you use when working with events (page 34). To

make the tiles larger or smaller, drag the size slider. To see someone's face flash before your eyes, skim the mouse pointer across his or her tile. (It's fun!) To set a key photo for a tile, skim across the tile until you see the photo you want, then press the spacebar. To rename a tile, click its name, then start typing.

For more tips, see the following pages.

41

Working with Faces

Adding a Missing Face

Sometimes, iPhoto isn't able to recognize that a face is a face. This can happen if face is in profile, if someone's head was tilted significantly, or if the photo was taken in poor or unusually colored light. (To appreciate why iPhoto can miss faces in these circumstances, see page 44.)

The solution: add the face by hand.

Step 1. Click Add Missing Face.

Here, my sister Jeanné's jaunty head tilt has stumped iPhoto.

Step 3 (optional). Customize the size of the box by dragging its corners.

The box's size isn't critical—it simply determines how that occurrence of the face appears on the corkboard. In general, a "tighter" crop is better.

A box appears in the center of the photo.

Step 2. Drag the box so that it encloses the face.

Step 4. Click Done.

Step 5. Type that person's name and press Return.

Notes and Tips

For your convenience only. Adding a missing face won't help iPhoto recognize that person's face in the future. Put another way, iPhoto never considers a manually added face as the "seed" for further recognition. Adding a missing face is simply a way to ensure that a particular photo is included in someone's corkboard tile.

Back-of-the-head shots. You have a romantic shot of a couple walking away from the camera on a country road. In the interest of thorough filing, you want that shot in their respective corkboard tiles—but iPhoto obviously can't recognize the back of someone's head. The solution: add their "faces" manually. That way, this photo will appear in their corkboard tiles.

Group challenges. In group photos, faces tend to be on the small side, and that can cause iPhoto to miss a face, particularly with fairly low resolution photos. iPhoto just doesn't have enough pixel data to perform facial analysis. Again, the solution is to manually add faces that iPhoto missed.

Working in Face View

When you double-click a person's corkboard tile to view photos of him or her, a set of thumbnails appears—much as it does when you double-click an event. And as with the event view, a row of buttons lets you do things with those thumbnails—edit, hide, and flag photos; display a slide show; create print projects; and share photos online. These buttons are a convenient way to immediately start showcasing a favorite person.

But face view contains some unique elements, too—things you don't see when viewing event thumbnails.

More matches. If you've imported new photos—or if you never did finish confirming every suspected match—you may see more thumbnails below the *[name] may also be in the photos below* dividing line described on page 41. (You may have to scroll the iPhoto window to see them.)

Tip: If you'd like to confirm or reject those suspected matches now, you can click the Confirm Name button. But if you just want to confirm some photos, simply drag their thumbnails up above the dividing line. This handy drag-and-drop trick isn't available in the Confirm Name view.

The Confirm Name button. As you already know, you can click this button to confirm or reject photos. If you've accidentally confirmed a photo of the wrong

person, click Confirm Name, then click the wrong photo so that its label reads *Not Suzanne* (for example).

Face view buttons. With the View buttons, you can switch between viewing the full thumbnail or just the person's face. When the leftmost button is active, the full thumbnail appears. Here's a group shot containing my mom:

When you click the rightmost button, each thumbnail shows only the face of the person whose photos you're viewing. Here's the identical group shot in this face-detail view:

Tip: Face-detail view is a great way to rediscover photos. That cute facial expression someone was wearing in a group shot may have gotten lost in the crowd. By focusing your attention on just that one person, face-detail view lets you see your photos in a new way.

Working with Corkboard Tiles

When you point to someone's tile on the corkboard, a small *i* button appears in its lower-right corner. Click this button, and the tile "flips over" to reveal a panel where you can do a few things.

Bethany
1/1/98-8/12/07
64 photos

Bethany Dugdale
betka@betka.net

Click to set key photo

Done

To view the information panels for other people, click the arrow buttons.

To set the key photo for this person, skim across the thumbnails, then click the photo you want.

To rename this person, click the name and type. (You can also rename tiles directly on the corkboard; see page 41.)

Optional: You can type the person's full name and email address here. **Important:** If you plan to share photos of this person on Facebook, be sure to type the full name and email address under which that person is registered on Facebook. For details, see page 115.

Tips for Faces

How Face Recognition Works

You obviously don't have to understand how iPhoto recognizes faces in order to use the faces feature. Still, you might be curious. What's more, understanding how iPhoto recognizes faces can help explain why it sometimes fails to, as described on the previous pages.

C. Tilt! If your subject's head is tilted more than approximately 30 degrees in either direction, iPhoto may miss that face.

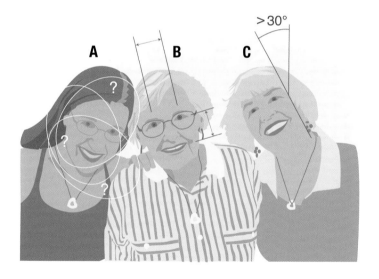

A. Is that a face? iPhoto searches for patterns of light and dark that are common in a face. This is why iPhoto may miss a face that's in profile or poorly lit. iPhoto also checks to see if the area's color is within the range of common skin tones. Photograph someone under a blue neon light, and iPhoto is likely to miss that face.

B. Is it a named face? Once iPhoto determines that it has found a face, it compares the face to other faces you've already named. This process involves assessing characteristics such as the distance between the eyes, the distance between the eyes and mouth, and more.

Improving Recognition

Variety matters. As I've mentioned, the more photos of a specific face that you confirm, the better able iPhoto is to identify additional photos containing that face.

But quantity isn't the only factor; variety is critical, too. Confirming one photo can sometimes unlock the door to iPhoto suddenly recognizing many more photos of that person. This is most likely to happen when that photo depicts the person in a slightly different way—with his or her head tilted or in partial profile, for example.

The value of rejection. When you tell iPhoto that a photo *isn't* of a specific person, you don't help iPhoto identify future photos of that person. Still, rejection has its place: by confirming who *isn't* in a photo, you prevent the misidentified photo from showing up in future naming sessions for that person.

The cream rises. Just as Google puts the most relevant search results at the top of the list, iPhoto puts the most likely facial matches at the top of its confirmation view. Photos that match more loosely appear farther down.

Gene recognition. iPhoto sometimes mistakes family members for one another. (It often confuses my mom and my aunt—something I once did when I was a toddler.) It's no wonder: family members often look alike, and as the illustration at left shows, part of iPhoto's facial recognition technology involves measuring features that make one face different from another.

There's no tip here, except maybe a tip of the hat to the beauty of genetics. And a reminder that the more photos you confirm, the better iPhoto gets at telling everyone apart.

Another Way to Confirm

As you work with faces, you may occasionally see an inquiry like this one:

iPhoto displays this query when you're looking at a photo containing a face that iPhoto thinks it recognizes, but that you haven't yet confirmed.

To confirm iPhoto's suspicions, click the check mark. If iPhoto misidentified the person, click the X.

This process is simply a convenient alternative to switching into the Confirm Name mode and confirming or rejecting the photo there. It's iPhoto's way of saying, "Hey, as long as you're here, maybe you want to confirm this person's identify."

Forgetting a Face

The time may come when you want to remove someone's tile from your corkboard. (And that, I assure you, is the most interesting euphemism for "break up" that you'll read in this book.) It's easy: select the person's tile, then press ⌘-Delete. iPhoto asks if you really want to delete that person from your list of faces. To confirm the deed, click Delete Face.

Besides a parting of the ways, there are other reasons why you might delete a face. Maybe you accidentally confirmed a bunch of misidentified photos, and you want to start over. And incidentally, you can delete multiple faces tiles in one fell swoop: Shift-click on each one or enclose them in a selection rectangle, then press ⌘-Delete.

Note: Deleting a face does *not* delete the photos of that person from your iPhoto library.

No Pets, Please

It was a common question when iPhoto '09 debuted: does the faces feature recognize pets? The answer is no. And armed with the background into how facial recognition works, you can understand why: a cat's color is not usually going to be a skin tone, nor will your poodle's facial geometry match that of a human face—even if your friends claim you two look alike.

iPhoto may occasionally recognize an animal's face, but consider those incidents happy accidents. And keep in mind that if you want to create a corkboard tile for your critters, you can always manually add their faces, as described on page 42.

Faces and Smart Albums

The smart albums feature lets you quickly search for and view photos that meet very specific criteria. And it works beautifully with faces; for details, see page 64.

Beyond the Corkboard

As I describe later in this chapter, iPhoto's facial smarts extend beyond the faces feature. When positioning photos in slide shows, iPhoto looks for faces and tries to position a photo so that faces aren't cut off. Similarly, in iPhoto's edit view, the red-eye removal feature as well as some color controls are smart enough to detect faces.

The bottom line: whether you're organizing, enhancing, or sharing photos, iPhoto knows a face when it sees one.

Places at a Glance

You and your camera, you go places. When you return home, you tell iPhoto where you've been.

That's the idea behind iPhoto's *places* feature, which lets you associate geographical locations with your photos—and then explore your library using maps and more.

Some digital cameras include or accept optional Global Positioning System (GPS) receivers that record your location as you shoot, a process called *geotagging*. Apple's iPhone 3G can also go along for the ride, thanks to its built-in GPS and camera.

A camera with GPS is a fine traveling companion, but is by no means essential. You can use iPhoto to geotag your shots —doing so takes just a few clicks, and you can be more precise than GPS allows.

What does geotagging get you? For starters, the ability to explore your library by place. View a Google map directly within iPhoto, with little pushpins indicating where you've snapped the shutter. Browse and search for photos based on their location. Add beautiful travel maps to your iPhoto book projects.

You don't have to geotag photos, but doing so does give you another way to explore and organize your library. And for those shots where locations are particularly memorable and relevant—a vacation, a honeymoon, an amusement park outing, a family barbecue in the back yard—geotagging adds something important to your photos: a sense of place.

Getting Around

When your library contains geotagged photos, you can explore them in a few different ways.

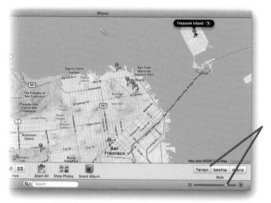

Read the map. Use a built-in Google map to see where you've been (page 51). Zoom in, pan around, even switch to a satellite view.

Browse. Use the location browser to explore. iPhoto even understands how places relate to each other—showing, for example, cities within states within countries (page 50).

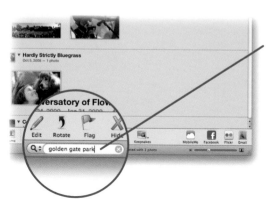

Search. Type a place name and immediately view shots taken there (page 56). You can also create smart albums that collect photos taken in specific locations (page 65).

Assigning a Location to an Event

You can add a location to an entire event or to individual photos. The following pages contain full driving directions and some sightseeing tips. Here's the fastest way to add the same location to all the photos in an event.

Step 1. Select the event, then click the **ⓘ** button in the lower-right corner of the event thumbnail.

The event flips over to reveal an information panel.

Step 2. Type a location in the *Enter event location* field.

iPhoto is aware of thousands of places (see the sidebar, below). As you type a location, a list of places appears. You can click one to choose it, or just keep typing.

You can customize a place or add an entirely new one (page 48).

Step 3. Click Done.

The information panel displays a map of the location.

Notes and Tips

All or one? If you took all an event's photos in one place, it's fine to assign one location to all the photos in the event. But you can also assign a location to individual photos. The steps are almost identical to those at left. Select the photo, click its **ⓘ** button, then specify the location.

Several at a time. To specify the same location for a few photos, select the photos (see page 59 for selection tips), then click the **ⓘ** button for any one of them. In the location information panel, click the check box labeled *Enter location of photos*, then specify the location.

Beyond Cities: Points of Interest

iPhoto's built-in database of locations includes not only cities and towns, but also popular points of interest: the Grand Canyon, the Space Needle in Seattle, Wrigley Field in Chicago, the Eiffel Tower in Paris, even the Pyramid of Cheops in Egypt.

If you took photos at a famous landmark, try typing the landmark's name when specifying the location. iPhoto may know about it.

If iPhoto doesn't know about that landmark, add it as described on the following pages. Because iPhoto "understands" geography and the hierarchical relationship between places, the photo will still be searchable by city and other

criteria. For example, iPhoto knows that Wrigley Field is in Chicago, in Illinois, in the United States.

Tip: When using points of interests as locations, keep in mind that you're telling iPhoto where the photo was taken, not what the photo contains. If you took a photo of the Space Needle from your Seattle hotel room window, don't specify

Space Needle as that photo's location. Conversely, if you took a close-up of your kids while at the Space Needle, specify Space Needle—even if the Needle doesn't appear in the photo at all.

Remember: when it comes to places, it's all about where you were when you snapped the shutter—not about what appears in the photo.

Adding a New Place

iPhoto knows about a lot of places, but it doesn't know about *every* place. New Hampshire's beautiful Mount Monadnock isn't in its database. Nor is PNC Park, home of the Pittsburgh Pirates. Nor is your back yard.

Now, you could simply place that mountain photo in Dublin, New Hampshire. Or that Pirates photo in Pittsburgh. Or those back-yard barbecue shots in Your Town, USA.

But you can also be specific and add the place to iPhoto's database. Adding a place takes just a few steps, and if you enjoy playing with Google maps as much as I do, you'll find it fun. But most important, you'll place your photos with precision.

Step 1. Select an event or one or more photos, then click the 🛈 to flip over to the location information panel.

Step 2. Click in the *photo place* field, then click Find on map.

The Add New Place dialog box appears.

Step 3. In the search box, type what you're looking for (for example, an address or a landmark name; see the tips below), then press the Return key.

Step 4. A few potential locations may appear. Select the most relevant, then click Assign to Photo (or Assign to Event, as appropriate).

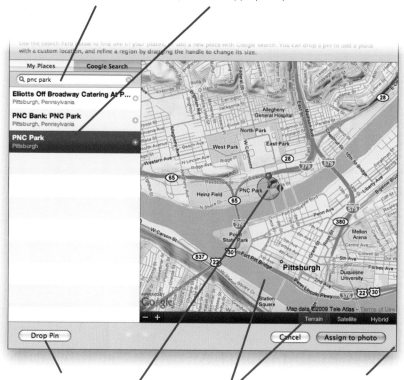

Want to create a personalized location? Drop a pin, then fine-tune it (see opposite page).

A Google map of the location appears, and a *marker pin* appears at the spot. To fine-tune the marker pin's location, drag it. You can also change the vicinity covered by the location (see "Fine-tuning a Location," opposite).

To pan the map, drag within it. To zoom out, zoom in, and switch between terrain and/or satellite views, click the buttons. **Shortcut:** To zoom in, double-click within the map.

The location appears in the place information panel.

Tip: For a bigger map, enlarge the dialog box by dragging its lower-right corner.

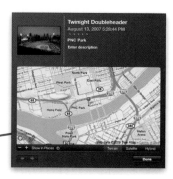

Searching Tips

You can search for towns (*Albion*), street addresses (*52 Grove St, Peterborough, NH*), landmarks (*Mount Monadnock*), ZIP codes (*94133*). You can also search for business names: *North Beach Pizza.* And you can mix and match: *701 Washington Rd., 15228* or *Joe's Diner, St. Louis.*

Because iPhoto uses Google maps, the best place to learn about searching options is Google. Go to www.google.com/maps, then click the Help link.

Tips for Adding Places

Fine-tuning a location. When iPhoto locates a place through a Google search, the location's pin may not be where you were when you snapped the shutter. Say you spent an afternoon on the beach at San Francisco's Chrissy Field. You want to geotag some photos you took in the shadow of the Golden Gate Bridge, but the pin that iPhoto dropped is located at the Chrissy Field main entrance—not where you were standing.

The solution: drag the pin to the correct spot.

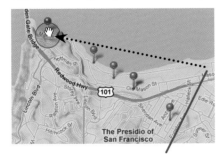

Google places Chrissy Field here, at its main entrance. To fine-tune the location, drag the pin to the desired spot.

Changing a place's vicinity. The blue circle that surrounds a marker pin denotes the *vicinity* of that location: if you take a photo anywhere within that shaded area, iPhoto considers the photo to have been taken at that location. You can make that vicinity region larger or smaller by dragging the arrows on its right side.

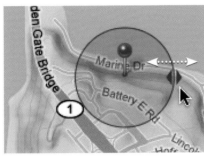

You might want a very small vicinity if you want to define a very precise location: a favorite restaurant, for example.

Conversely, you might want to enlarge a vicinity to encompass a larger area, such as the neighborhood around your house.

A location's vicinity also comes into play as you add to your iPhoto library. For example, say you later import photos that were taken with a GPS camera or an iPhone 3G. If those photos' geotag coordinates are within an existing location's blue region, iPhoto places those new photos at that location.

Dropping a pin. Google doesn't know about locations that are meaningful only to you: the camping spot where you pitched your text, or the mountain trail where you had a picnic.

To create personalized locations, drop a pin. In the Edit My Places dialog box, do a Google search to home in on the approximate location—for example, the state park where you camped. Next, click the Drop Pin button, then drag the pin to the appropriate location, fine-tuning its vicinity at the same time, if you like.

Finally, click the pin's place name and type the name of the custom location.

By dropping a pin to create a personalized place, you can let iPhoto know about places that are important to *you*, not just to Google maps. And again, because iPhoto understands how places relate to each other, you can still search for the photo using related criteria. In the example above, iPhoto knows that Our Camp Site is located in Raccoon State Park, in Hookstown, PA, in the United States.

For a few ideas of ways to use personalized places, see "A Cookbook of Custom Places" on page 52.

Never forgets a place. Once you create a new place, it joins the list of thousands of places iPhoto already knows about. That means you can assign that place to new photos and events: flip over an event or photo, then start typing the place name (page 47).

Exploring and Browsing Places

The real payoff to specifying locations for your photos comes later—when you want to browse and search for photos. By clicking the Places item in the Library list, you can explore your world in a couple of ways. Use the *map view* to display a Google map that contains marker pins showing where you've taken photos. Zoom in to see a street-by-street view, or zoom out for the big picture. Want to see the photos that you took at a particular place? Click its pin.

You can also use *browser view* to browse your geotagged photos by category. Step back for the big picture: "show me all the photos I've taken in California." Or drill down to a specific area: "Let's see the photos I've taken in San Francisco's North Beach neighborhood."

Browser view is an excellent way to appreciate iPhoto's "smarts" when it comes to geography. The columns in the browser view show how places relate to each other: for example, the North Beach neighborhood is in San Francisco, which is in California, which is in the United States.

As I described on page 46, you can also search for places using the Search box. And as I'll show on page 64, you can also use smart albums to search for places in some powerful ways.

Here's a close-up look at the map and browser views.

Exploring with Browser View

Browser view is a great way to quickly browse the places you've been.

Step 1. In the Library list, click Places, then click the Browser View button.

The column browser appears, with the thumbnails of geotagged photos below it.

States, provinces, prefectures, and similar *subnational* regions.

Specific neighborhoods, places of interest, and places you've created.

Countries.

Cities and towns.

Step 2. Click the items in the columns to focus in on specific locations.

iPhoto displays only those photos taken at the location whose name you clicked.

Notes and Tips

Changing columns. The locations in the columns change to reflect the country, region, or state you've selected. In the example above, selecting Netherlands causes iPhoto to display only regions in that country where you've taken photos.

Taller or shorter columns. To resize the column browser, point to the dividing line at its bottom and then drag up or down.

Combining browser and map views. The browser and map views team up nicely: you can use browser view to quickly home in on a specific region that you then display on the map. For example, to quickly see a map of your Pennsylvania photos, click Pennsylvania in browser view, then click the Map View button to switch to map view.

Exploring with Map View

To use Map View, your Mac must be connected to the Internet. If you're camping in the wilderness, use browser view instead. Better yet, just enjoy the wilderness.

Step 1. In the Library list, click Places, then click the Map View button.

Step 2. Use the controls to navigate the map, switch between terrain and/or satellite views, and view photos.

When you're zoomed out, iPhoto may use just one marker pin to represent locations that are close to each other. To see individual places, zoom in.

Point to a marker pin, and iPhoto displays the location or locations that it represents. To see photos taken there, click the ● next to the place name.

Switch between views, and zoom in and out. **Shortcuts:** To zoom in on an area, double-click it. To zoom out, press Control and double-click.

Zoom all the way out and see marker pins for all your geotagged photos.

View the photos for the places visible in the current map zoom setting. For example, if you're zoomed in on Northern California, clicking Show Photos displays thumbnails of all photos taken there.

Do you view a particular area frequently? Zoom in to display that area, then click Smart Album (see page 65).

Places in the Event Information Panel

The event information panel—that panel that appears when you flip an event over—provides a few location-related niceties.

The map in the panel shows marker pins for each geotagged photo in that event. But here's a detail you may not have noticed:

skim over the event's thumbnails, and the marker pin for the currently visible thumbnail highlights in blue. It's fun to watch the pins light up as you skim through the thumbnails.

Near the bottom of the event information panel is an arrow

labeled Show in Places. Click this arrow, and iPhoto switches to map view, with the map zoomed to match its counterpart in the event information panel. It's a handy way to jump to map view for further exploration.

Tips for Places

Managing Your Places

Sometimes you need to clean up your place. And sometimes you need to clean up your places. Maybe you want to change the name of a place—for example, iPhoto inaccurately calls San Francisco's AT&T Park *At Park*. Or maybe you'd like to refine a place's exact location and vicinity. Or maybe you need to delete a place you no longer want.

To search for one of the places you've created, type in the box.

Want to create a new place? Click Drop Pin, then follow the instructions on page 49.

(That smells like another euphemism for "breakup.")

To manage your places, choose Window > Manage My Places. Doing so displays the Edit My Places dialog box, which is covered in detail on the previous pages. But now, the My Places button is active, and the dialog box lists the places you've added.

You can also refine a place's location and vicinity, as described on page 49.

To rename a place, double-click its name, then type. To delete a place, click the little minus sign. **Note:** Deleting a place doesn't delete photos you took there; it simply removes the geotagging from those photos.

Map Options: Terrain or Satellite?

When you're viewing a Google map in iPhoto—whether in the Edit My Places dialog box or in Map view—you can choose between terrain view, satellite view, or a hybrid of both.

Many times, the choice is one of personal preference. Choose terrain if you like viewing maps that look like folding road maps (kids: ask your parents). For an added coolness factor, go satellite.

But there are some circumstances that recommend one view over the other.

Terrain: for addresses. When you want to add or refine a place with a street address, a terrain map is often easier to read.

Satellite: for close-ups. You can zoom in for a much closer look by using satellite view. That's particularly handy when you want to precisely position a marker pin or its region. Here, I've very precisely defined the location: the right-field bleachers at AT&T Park in San Francisco. In terrain view, you can't zoom in to this degree.

Find more GPS products and geotagging ideas.
www.macilife.com/iphoto

Web Sharing: Privacy Matters

When you export a photo from iPhoto —to share it on a MobileMe Web gallery or your Flickr account, for example— iPhoto does *not* include the location information with the photo. That's to protect your privacy: you might not want just anyone to know exactly where your kids play, for example.

But if you do want to include location information, it's easy: choose iPhoto > Preferences, click Web, then check the box labeled *Include location information for published photos.*

Note: To have your geotagged photos show up on your Flickr map, you have another step to perform; see page 118.

A Cookbook of Custom Places

As I've already mentioned, by dropping a pin and then refining its location and vicinity, you can create your own custom places. Here are a few ideas.

Custom Place Ideas	
Place	Technique
A camp site	Google-search to find the campground or park. Drop a pin. Drag the pin to the camp site's location, then adjust the size of its vicinity to encompass the camp site.
Your neighborhood	Google-search to find your address. Drop a pin. Drag the pin and resize its vicinity to encompass the area you consider to be "your neighborhood."
Your back yard	Same as above, but resize the pin's vicinity to encompass your back yard.
A favorite restaurant	Google-search the restaurant name or address. Drop a pin. Drag it to the exact address, then make the vicinity very small.
Your seats in the bleachers	Google-search the ballpark, then drop a pin. Switch to satellite view, then zoom in on the map. Position the pin where you were sitting, then make its vicinity small.

The GPS Angle

If your camera has a GPS receiver or you're using an iPhone 3G, you've already arrived: every photo you take contains location information. iPhoto reads this data when you import photos, adding those photos to your map.

At this writing, only one consumer-oriented digital camera, Nikon's Coolpix P6000, has a built-in GPS receiver. Many single-lens reflex (SLR) digital cameras accept optional GPS receivers. Shown here: the oddly named Promote GPS, which works with

many Nikon and Fuji digital SLRs and costs about $150.

If your camera can't accept a GPS add-on, there's ATP's Photo Finder. It takes a clever approach to geotagging. Synchronize your digital camera's built-in clock with the Photo Finder's clock, then go shooting. When you get home, insert your camera's memory

card into the Photo Finder, and it adds locations to each shot.

Should you bother? Before investing in GPS camera gear, try geotagging in iPhoto. It's easy and actually allows for more precision than GPS, which can be inaccurate (and generally doesn't work at all indoors).

Assigning Keywords and Ratings

Chances are that many of your photos fall into specific categories: baby photos, scenic shots, and so on. By creating and assigning *keywords*, you make related images easier to find.

Keywords are labels useful for categorizing and locating all the photos of a given kind: vacation shots, baby pictures, mug shots, you name it.

iPhoto has several predefined keywords that cover common categories. But you can replace the existing ones to cover the kinds of photos you take, and you can add as many new keywords as you like.

You can assign multiple keywords to a single image. For example, if you have a Beach keyword, a Dog keyword, and a Summer keyword, you might assign all three to a photo of your dog taken at the beach in July.

Keywords are one way to categorize your photos; ratings are another. You can assign a rating of from one to five stars to a photo—rank your favorites for quick searching, or mark the stinkers for future deletion.

As with many iPhoto housekeeping tasks, assigning keywords and ratings is entirely optional. But if you take the time, you can use iPhoto's search and Smart Albums features to quickly locate and collect photos that meet specific criteria.

Creating and Editing Keywords

Step 1. Choose Window > Show Keywords (⌘-K).

Step 2. Click the Edit Keywords button.

Step 3. Edit keywords as shown below, then click OK.

Use the checkmark keyword (or not) however you like—to mark some photos for future use, for example.

Creating a new keyword. Click the plus sign, then type the keyword and press Return.

Deleting a keyword. Don't want to use a certain keyword any more? Select it, then click the minus sign. **Note:** The keyword is removed from any photos to which you'd assigned it.

Editing a keyword. Select the keyword, click Rename, then type the new name. Or simply double-click directly on the keyword.

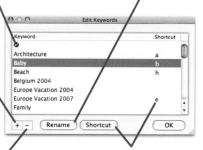

Use certain keywords often? Give them one-key shortcuts (see the opposite page). To create or edit a shortcut, select the keyword and click Shortcut, or simply double-click on that keyword's shortcut area.

Tips

Displaying keywords. To have iPhoto display keywords beneath photo thumbnails, choose View > Keywords.

Creating a keyword directly. When viewing keywords beneath thumbnails, you can create a new keyword by simply typing it beneath a photo thumbnail. Point beneath the thumbnail until the text *add keywords* appears.

Click this text, then type a keyword and press Return. This both creates the keyword and assigns it to the photo.

Assigning Keywords

You have a few ways to assign keywords.

The Keywords window. Choose Window > Show Keywords. Select the photo(s), then click one or more keywords.

The keyboard. If you assigned a keyboard shortcut to the keyword, reap your reward now. Select the photo(s), and tap the shortcut key.

If you have to assign various keywords to a set of photos, combine shortcut keys with the arrow keys. Select a photo, tap a key, tap an arrow key to move to a new photo, tap a key. There's no faster way to assign keywords in iPhoto.

Directly beneath the thumbnail. See the tip on the opposite page, at lower left.

Keyword Tips

Removing a keyword. To remove a keyword from a photo, select the photo and click the keyword in the Keywords window, or tap the keyword's keyboard shortcut, if you created one. If you're viewing keywords beneath photo thumbnails (View > Keywords), you can also simply select the keyword and press the Delete key.

Keywords window tips. Here are a few tips for the Keywords window.

Keywords for which you've created keyboard shortcuts appear in this area, along with their shortcuts.

Just working with keyboard-shortcut keywords? Hide the rest of your keywords.

Want to add a shortcut to an existing keyword? No need to click Edit Keywords: simply drag the keyword into the Quick Group area. Similarly, to remove a shortcut from a keyword, drag the keyword down to the Keywords area.

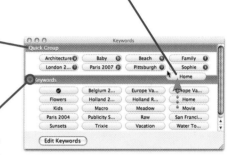

Art Critic: Rating Your Photos

You can assign a rating of from one to five stars to a photo, and there are a few ways to do it.

The Photos menu. Choose a rating from the My Rating submenu.

The keyboard. Press ⌘ along with 0 (zero) through 5. This shortcut pairs up nicely with the arrow keys: rate a photo, press an arrow key to move to the next photo, and repeat.

The shortcut menu. Control-click on a photo and choose a rating from the My Rating submenu.

In one fell swoop. Want to give a bunch of photos the same rating? Select them, then use one of the previous techniques.

With the Information pane. Select a photo and then click the stars in the Information pane.

With the Places panel. When specifying a photo's location, you can rate it, too (page 46).

Ratings Tips

To see ratings beneath your photo thumbnails, choose View > Rating (Shift-⌘-R). When ratings are visible, you can change them by clicking the stars and dots.

The Encounter
★★★★★

Veiled
★★★

Searching for Photos

Browsing is fun, but not when you're looking for something specific. When you're on the hunt, you want help: directions from your car's navigation system, a directory in a shopping mall, or a search feature in your digital photography program.

iPhoto lets you search in several ways. For quick searches, jump down to the Search box and start typing. As you type, iPhoto narrows down the photos it displays—much as iTunes does during song searches. The more time you spend giving titles and descriptions to your best shots (page 38), the better the search feature works.

Next to the Search box, a pop-up menu lets you search in more specific ways. Look for photos taken on certain dates. Or photos with a four-star rating, or with certain keywords.

And when your searching needs are *very* specific—show me the four-star photos of the dog taken before noon at the  beach with my Nikon camera during the month of July in San Francisco—iPhoto can accommodate. Just create a smart album (page 62).

So go ahead and browse when you want to relive random memories. But when you're on a mission? Search.

Search Box Basics

No matter what kind of search you perform, keep this in mind: iPhoto searches whatever item you've selected in the Library list. If you want to search your entire library, be sure to click Events or Photos. To search the last year's worth of photos, click Last 12 Months. To search for a specific face or place, click Faces or Places, respectively. To search a specific album, click the album. You get it.

Step 1. Click in the Search box or press ⌘-F.

Step 2. Type something. iPhoto searches photo filenames, event names, titles, descriptions, faces, places, and keywords.

Step 3. To clear a search (displaying everything again), click ⊗ in the Search box.

Variations

Searching by rating. From the Search box pop-up menu, choose Rating. Click the dots to specify a minimum number of stars a photo must have.

Note: Higher-rated photos also appear: if you click three stars, four- and five-star photos also appear. To find *just* three-star  photos, for example, create a smart album.

Searching by keyword. From the Search box pop-up menu, choose Keyword, then click one or more keywords. (For tips on keyword searching, see the opposite page.)

Searching by date. From the Search box pop-up menu, choose Date, then specify a date or range of dates (see the opposite page).

Searching By Date

Even if you never give a photo a title, description, or keywords, you can always search by date, since your camera records the date and time when you take a photo.

And remember, you can use iPhoto to adjust the dates of your photos to make date searches as accurate as possible (page 39).

The Big Picture

When you display the Calendar panel, it shows the current year.

Display the previous or following year.

Switch between viewing by year or by a specific month.

Months in which you've taken photos appear in bold. To see photos from a specific month, click that month. To select more than one month, drag across months, Shift-click, or ⌘-click.

Narrow Your View

To explore a specific month, double-click its name.

Display the previous or following month.

Return to year view.

Days on which you've taken photos appear in bold. To see photos from a specific day, click the day. To see photos from a range of days, drag across the days. To see photos from discontinuous days (for example, every Saturday), ⌘-click the days.

Tip: If you point to a month or date without clicking, iPhoto tells you how many photos you took during that month or on that date, as shown here.

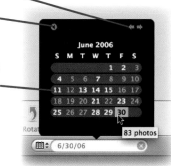

Advanced Keyword Searches

When you click multiple keywords, iPhoto puts an *and* between each one: "find all photos with the keywords Sophie *and* Beach."

Sometimes, *and* isn't what you want.

Excluding a keyword. To exclude a keyword, press Option while clicking it. Say you want to find all Sophie photos that *weren't* taken at the beach. Click the Beach keyword, then Option-click the Beach keyword. Notice the Search box: it reads *not Beach and Sophie.*

Either/or. To search for photos with one keyword or another, press Shift while clicking keywords. For example, to find all photos of the baby *or* the dog, Shift-click the Baby and Dog keywords.

Combinations thereof. By combining the Shift-click and Option-click variations, you can conduct some fairly complex searches, though it can be confusing to figure out which key sequences to use. For very specific searches, smart albums are easier.

Creating Albums

Getting photos back from a lab is always exciting, but what's really fun is creating a photo album that turns a collection of photos into a story.

An iPhoto album contains a series of photographs sequenced in an order that helps tell a story or document an event. Creating an album is often the first step in sharing a set of photos. For example, before creating a slide show or book, you'll usually want to create an album containing the photos you want to use.

Creating albums in iPhoto is a simple matter of dragging thumbnail images. You can add and remove photos to and from albums at any time, and you can sequence the photos in whatever order you like. You can even include the same photo in many different albums.

The photos in an album might be from one event, or from a dozen different events. If you've used iTunes to create playlists, you're well on your way to understanding albums: just as an iTunes playlist lets you create your own music compilations, an iPhoto album lets you create your own image compilations.

You don't have to create albums for every set of photos you import. But when you want to combine photos from different events, particularly when you're planning to share the photos in some way, albums are the answer.

Step 1. Choose File > New Album

You can also use the ⌘-N keyboard shortcut, or click the ⊕ button and then choose Album in the subsequent dialog box.

Step 2. Type a name, then click Create or press Return.

Tip: To create an album and add photos to it in one step, select the photos *before* choosing New Album (page 60).

Step 3. Add photos.

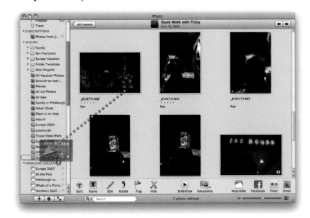

After you've created the album, begin dragging photos into it. You can drag photos one at a time, or select multiple photos and drag them in all at once.

As you drag, iPhoto indicates how many photos you've selected.

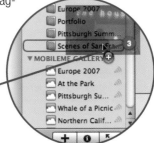

Organizing an Album

The order of the photos in an album is important: when you create slide shows, books, or Web photo galleries, iPhoto presents the photos in the order in which they appear in the album.

Once you've created an album, you may want to fine-tune the order of its photos.

To edit an album's name, double-click it or use the Information pane.

To move an album to a different location in the Albums area, drag it up or down. As the following pages describe, you can also create folders to organize related albums.

To change the order of the photos, drag them. Here, the nighttime skyline photo is being moved so it will appear after the other nighttime shot.

Removing a photo. Don't want a photo in an album after all? Select it and press the Delete key. This removes the photo from the album, but not from your hard drive or photo library.

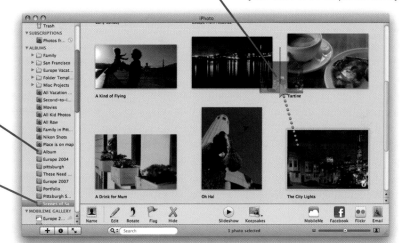

Tips for Selecting Photos

Selecting photos is a common activity in iPhoto: you select photos in order to delete them, add them to an album, move them around within an album, and more.

When working with multiple photos, remember the standard Mac selection shortcuts: To select a range of photos, click on the first one and Shift-click on the last one. To select multiple photos that aren't adjacent to each other, press ⌘ while clicking on each photo.

As the screen below shows, you can also select a series of pictures by dragging a selection rectangle around them.

Tips for Working with Albums

Albums are Optional

You don't *have* to create an album in order to share photos: you can create slide shows, books, calendars, and Web pages by simply selecting photos in your library, and then using the appropriate button or command. And by hiding less-than-perfect photos (page 36), you can "edit" an event to contain only those photos you want to use in a project.

Still, when you're about to create a photo project of some kind, it's better to create an album first. Albums give you the ability to change the sequence of photos. You can resequence photos while creating slide shows, books, and the like, but creating these items is easier when you start with photos that are in roughly the final order that you plan to use.

Album Shortcuts

You can create an album and add images to it in one step. Select one or more images and choose File > New Album. In the dialog box that appears, check the box labeled Use Selected Items in New Album. Or select some photos, then choose File > New Album from Selection (Shift-⌘-N).

You can also drag the images into a blank spot of the Library area. When you use this technique, iPhoto gives the new album a generic name, such as *untitled album*. To rename the album, double-click its name and type a new name.

If you have photos on a storage device—your hard drive, a Picture CD, or a digital camera's memory card—you can import them into iPhoto *and* create an album in one fell swoop.

Simply drag the photos from the Finder into a blank area of the Library list. iPhoto imports the photos, storing them in their own event. iPhoto also creates an album and adds the photos to it.

Tip: As your collection of albums and other items grows, you may find that you no longer have a "blank area" at the bottom of the Library list. To create one, close some of the items in the Library list—for example, close the Albums list by clicking its triangle.

Albums and flagging. iPhoto's flagging feature (page 36) teams up nicely with albums. Want to create an album of shots that are scattered throughout your library? Flag the shots, then select the Flagged item in your Library list. Next, choose Edit > Select All, then choose File > New Album from Selection.

From Album to Event

You've created an album containing the best photos of a friend's wedding. The photos are from various events; indeed, some were emailed to you from other attendees.

You'd prefer that the photos were in an event of their own. Easy. Select the album, choose Edit > Select All, then choose Events > Create Event. iPhoto creates a new event, and moves the photos in the album into the event. Note, however, that the photos are removed from the events where they originated.

Photo Count

You can have iPhoto display the number of photos in each album next to each album's name. In the Preferences dialog box, click General, then check the Show Item Counts box.

To Experiment, Duplicate

You have a photo that appears in multiple albums, but you want to edit its appearance in just one album, leaving the original version unchanged in other albums. Time for the Duplicate command: select the photo and choose Duplicate from the Photos menu (⌘-D). Now edit the duplicate.

Duplicating an album. There may be times when you'll want several versions of an album. For example, you might have one version with photos sequenced for a slide show and another version with photos organized for a book. Or you might simply want to experiment with several different photo arrangements until you find the one you like best.

iPhoto makes this kind of experimentation easy. Simply duplicate an album by selecting the album and choosing Duplicate from the Photos menu. iPhoto makes a duplicate of the album, which you can rename and experiment with.

You can make as many duplicates of an album as you like. You can even duplicate a smart album—perhaps as a prelude to experimenting with different search criteria. Don't worry about devouring disk space. Albums don't include your actual photos; they simply contain "pointers" to the photos in your library.

Albums and iLife

Another good reason to create albums surfaces elsewhere in iLife: iMovie, iDVD, GarageBand, and iWeb all display iPhoto albums in their photo media browsers.

Have a batch of photos you want to use in another iLife program? Rather than searching through your library using those programs' media browsers, first stash the photos in an album. Then, choose that album in the other iLife program.

iPhoto album support is also built into other programs, including Mac OS X's screen saver and Apple's iWork programs. And you can choose to share or sync only certain albums to an iPod or Apple TV (page 120).

Organize Your Library with Folders

As you create albums, slide shows, and books, your Library list may become cluttered. iPhoto helps a bit by providing separate areas for albums, slide shows, projects, and other items. But you can do your part, too. Take advantage of the ability to create folders in the Albums area of the Library list.

Folders in iPhoto have the same benefit that they have on your hard drive: they let you store related items. And as with the documents on your hard drive, the definition of "related items" is up to you.

Filing strategies. You can use folders in any way you like. You might want to set up a project-

based filing system: create a folder for a project, then stash albums, books, and slide shows in that folder.

▼ 🗀 Europe Vacation
  ▼ 🗀 Albums
    🟦 Holland
    🟦 Paris
    🟦 Belgium
    🟦 London
  🖼 Paris Book
  📇 Belgium Card
  🎞 Paris Slideshow
  🎞 London Slideshow

Or you might prefer an object-oriented filing system: stash all your albums in one folder, all your slide shows in another, and all your books in yet another.

You might want to mix and match these approaches or

come up with something completely different. What's important is that you create a filing scheme that helps you quickly locate items.

Creating a folder. To create a folder, choose New Folder from the File menu. Or, Control-click on a blank area of the Library list and choose New Folder from the shortcut menu. iPhoto names a new folder *untitled folder*, and selects its name. To rename the folder, just start typing.

Working with folders. To move an item into a folder, simply drag it to the folder until you see a black border around the folder.

To close or open a folder, click the little triangle to the left of its name.

Like folders in the Mac's Finder, iPhoto folders are "spring loaded"—if you drag something to a closed folder and pause briefly, the folder opens.

Folders within folders. You can create folders inside of folders. You might use this scheme to store all the albums, books, and slide shows that relate to a specific event or theme.

To open a folder and all the nested folders within it, press Option while clicking on the folder's triangle.

Creating Smart Albums

iPhoto can assemble albums for you based on criteria that you specify. Spell out what you want, and iPhoto does the work for you.

A few possibilities: Create an album containing every shot you took in the last week. Or of every photo you took in November 2002. Or of every November 2002 photo that has *Sophie* in its title. Or of every photo from 2008 that has *Paris* as a location, *croissant* in its title, *food* as a keyword, and a rating of at least four stars.

If you've taken the time to assign titles, comments, faces, places, and keywords to your photos, here's where your investment pays off. You can still use smart albums if you haven't assigned this kind of information to photos; you just won't be able to search on as broad a range of things.

You can also create smart albums that have criteria based on information that your camera stores with each photo (see page 157). Create one smart album that corrals all the shots you took with your Sony camera, and another that collects all your Canon shots. Or create a smart album of all your photos shot at a high ISO speed (page 162), or at a fast shutter speed, or with a telephoto lens.

As described on page 64, smart albums also team up beautifully with the places and faces features.

Smart albums are a great way to quickly gather up related photos for printing, backing up, browsing, emailing—you name it.

Creating a Smart Album

Step 1. Choose New Smart Album from the File menu (Option-⌘-N).

You can also create a new smart album by pressing the Option key and clicking on the ⚙ button in the lower-left corner of the iPhoto window. And you can create one by choosing File > New, then clicking the Smart Album option.

Step 2. Specify what to look for.

Type a name for the smart album.

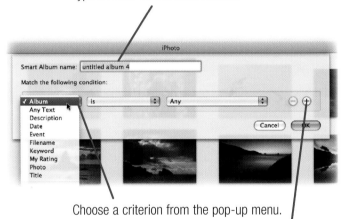

Choose a criterion from the pop-up menu.

To add another criterion, click the ⊕ button (see opposite page).

Step 3. Click OK or press Return.

In the Albums area, iPhoto indicates smart albums with a special icon: ⚙ .

Changing a Smart Album

To modify a smart album, select it in the Albums area and choose File > Edit Smart Album.

Get more smart album ideas.
www.macilife.com/iphoto

Be More Specific: Specifying Multiple Criteria

By adding additional criteria, you can be very specific about what you want to find.

Normally, iPhoto locates photos that meet all the criteria you specify. To have iPhoto locate a photo that meets any of the criteria, choose any.

To delete a criterion, click the ⊖ button. To add a criterion, click the ⊕ button.

Tips for Smart Albums

They're alive. iPhoto is always watching. If you import photos that meet a smart album's criteria, iPhoto adds those photos to the album. iPhoto may also add to a smart album when you edit photo information. For example, if you change a photo's title to *Beach picnic*, iPhoto adds the photo to any smart album set up to search for *beach* in the title.

From smart to dumb. You can't turn a smart album into a static one (unlike iTunes, iPhoto doesn't provide a Live Updating check box). Here's a workaround. Click the smart album in the Albums list, then select all the photos in the

album. (Click one photo, then press ⌘-A.) Next, choose New Album from Selection from the File menu. This creates an album containing the photos currently in the smart album.

Deleting photos. To delete a photo from a smart album, select it and press ⌘-Option-Delete. Note that this also deletes the photo from your library and moves it to the iPhoto Trash.

Smart Album Suggestions

For a Compilation of	Specify These Criteria
All your movies	Photo is Movie
All your raw-format photos	Photo is Raw
All flagged or hidden photos	Photo is Flagged or Photo is Hidden
Recent favorites	Date is in the last 1 month (for example) and My Rating is greater than three stars
All your Winter photos	Date is in the range 12/21/2008 to 3/20/2009
All photos that aren't in any album	Album is not Any
Photos from a specific camera	Camera Model is *model*
Photos from the second-to-last event you imported	Event is not in the last 1 event and Event is in the last 2 events
Photos from two weeks ago	Date is not in the last 1 week and Date is in the last 2 weeks
Photos taken with a telephoto lens	Focal Length is greater than 150 (for example)

Smart Albums, Faces, and Places

Smart albums team up beautifully with the Faces and Places features—so much so that you'll find a Smart Albums button in the iPhoto toolbar when you're using Faces and Places.

By creating a smart album for one or more faces, you can easily corral photos of specific people: Show me every photo of Mimi that I took at the beach last July. Show me every photo in which mom and I appear.

For Places, smart albums provide a few benefits. Gather photos taken at a certain location: Show me the photos I took in San Francisco last summer. Show me the San Francisco photos that have Sophie in them. Show me the nighttime Eiffel Tower photos that I took with my Nikon's telephoto lens. Smart albums even give you a convenient way to save a specific view of the Places map.

As I mentioned on the previous pages, iPhoto updates the contents of a smart album as you add to your library. So each time you add a photo containing a face you've named or containing a geotagged location, iPhoto adds that photo to any appropriate smart albums.

As always, the more criteria you specify in a smart album, the more searching power you have. But even with just a single criterion, a smart album gives you quick access to a favorite person or a favorite place. What's not to like about that?

Smart Albums and Faces

You can create a smart album that collects photos of a specific person in a couple of ways.

Step 1. On the Faces corkboard, select someone's tile.

Step 2. Click the Smart Album button.

Other ways. You can also create a smart album for a person by simply dragging that person's tile over to the Library area. And you can include a Face criterion when building a smart album. Set up the pop-ups in the smart albums dialog box to read Face is *name of person.*

Notes and Tips

To create a smart album that gathers photos in which two people appear *together*, select both of their corkboard tiles (click one, then Shift-click the other), then click the Smart Album button.

Next, in the Albums list, select the smart album you just created and choose File > Edit Smart Album. In the smart album dialog box, change the Match pop-up to read All.

To gather photos that contain more than two people, just Shift-click each person's face tile before creating the smart album.

Here are more face-related smart album ideas.

Faces and Smart Albums

For a Compilation of	Specify These Criteria
All members of the Polk family	Face ends with *Polk* (requires that you use first and last names in tiles)
All the women in your library	Face starts with *Ms.* (requires that you use honorifics in names)
Photos that don't contain Bill	Face does not contain *Bill*
All photos containing Toby and Josh, whether they're together in a photo or not	Face is *Toby* and Face is *Josh*, with the pop-up set to Any

Smart Albums and Places

A Smart Album for a Region

Maybe you'd like to create a smart album that collects photos created in a region, such as the San Francisco Bay Area or greater Paris. The technique at right won't do the job—if you specify *San Francisco*, iPhoto won't find photos taken in Sausalito.

Here's where map view helps.

Notes and Tips

When you create a smart album in this way, iPhoto gives it the name of the region it encompasses. In the above example, the album gets the name *California*. You can change its name—to *San Francisco Bay Area*, for example.

If you edit the smart album, you'll notice its criterion reads *Place is on map GPS values from map*.

Here are a few more place-related smart album ideas.

Step 1. Use the map view in Places to zoom and pan so that the region whose photos you want are visible.

Step 2. Click the Smart Album button.

A Smart Album for a Specific Place

Here's how to quickly gather all the geo-tagged photos taken in a certain location.

Step 1. Create a new smart album (see page 62).

Step 2. Set up the pop-up menus to read Place is *location name*.

Be sure to type the location exactly as it appears in Places, lest iPhoto not find it.

Places and Smart Albums

For a Compilation of	Specify These Criteria
Photos that are not geotagged	Photo is not tagged with GPS
Photos taken in a few different places	Place is *place name* (repeat for each location and change Match pop-up to All)
Photos that were not taken in a specific region	Place is not GPS values from map (create the smart album as above, then edit it and change *is on map* to *is not*)

Basic Photo Editing

Many photos can benefit from some tweaking. Maybe you'd like to crop out that huge telephone pole that distracts from your subject. Maybe the exposure is too light, too dark, or lacks contrast. Or maybe the camera's flash gave your subject's eyes the dreaded red-eye flaw.

iPhoto's edit view can fix these problems and others. And it does so in a clever way that doesn't replace your original image.

When you edit a photo, iPhoto keeps a list of the changes you made. If you reopen an edited image and make more changes, iPhoto applies your entire list of changes to the *original* version of the photo. It's called *non-destructive* editing, and the result is fewer passes through the evil JPEG-compression meat grinder—and better photo quality. (For more about iPhoto non-destructive editing, including an important caveat, see page 157.)

As you get accustomed to iPhoto editing, you might want to experiment with full-screen editing (page 84), the separate editing window (page 86), and the ability to tweak some editing preferences (pages 86 and 91).

Editing Essentials

To work on a photo, open it in iPhoto's edit view.

Step 1. Select the photo you want to edit.

Step 2. Click the Edit button.

The photo opens in edit view, and new tools and buttons appear (opposite page).

Edit

Step 3. Now what? Here are some the ways iPhoto can help an ailing photo.

Photo First-Aid

Symptom	Cure (and Page)
Red-eye from flash	Red-Eye tool (68)
Poor contrast and "punch"	Enhance button (70); for more control, the Adjust panel (76)
Subject is obscured in shadow or bright areas are washed out	Shadow and highlight recovery (page 78)
Crooked and/or badly framed	Straighten and/or Crop tools (69)
Scratches or blemishes	Retouch tool (71)
Color balance is incorrect	Adjust panel (80)
Photo is "grainy" from low light	Adjust panel (83)

Global Versus Local Editing

When you edit a photo, you change the photo everywhere you've used it—in slide shows, books, and calendars, for example. There's another way to fine-tune an image. When printing a photo or using it in a book, greeting card, or calendar, you can modify the photo's appearance in just that place—without changing its appearance elsewhere.

I'll remind you of these local editing opportunities as we go.

Edit View at a Glance

A row of thumbnails shows adjacent photos. To edit a different photo, click its thumbnail. To hide the thumbnails and get more working room, choose View > Thumbnails > Hide (Option-⌘-T).

To resize the thumbnail browser, drag this bar up or down. Shrink it to get more working room; enlarge it to see the differences between similar shots.

Switch to full-screen edit view (page 84).

Finely control exposure, color balance, sharpness, and more (pages 74–83).

Save any changes and leave edit view.

Save any changes and open the previous or next photo for editing (keyboard shortcut: left or right arrow).

Zoom in and out. **Tip:** When zoomed in, you can quickly scroll by pressing the spacebar and dragging within the photo.

Fix the geometry: rotate a photo (page 29) or crop or straighten it (page 71).

Fix the pixels: use One-Click Enhance (page 70), fix red-eye (page 68), or retouch flaws (page 71).

Apply a variety of effects (page 72).

Three Things to Remember When Editing

Before-and-after view. To see how your photo looked before you made the latest round of changes, hold down the Shift key. By pressing and releasing Shift, you can see a before-and-after view of your latest edits.

Safety nets: undo and revert. Not happy with your very latest change? Choose Edit > Undo. Not happy with the changes you made since you opened the photo? Choose Photos > Revert to Previous, and iPhoto discards your edits and restores the photo to its previous state.

Change your mind? To exit edit view without saving any changes, press the Esc key.

Fixing Composition Problems and Red-Eye

Some photos can benefit from...less. Maybe you weren't able to get close enough to your subject, and you'd like to get rid of some visual clutter. Or maybe a scenic vista is marred by a dumpster that you didn't notice when you took the shot. Or maybe you want to order a print, and you want your photo's proportions to match the size you want.

iPhoto's Crop tool is the answer for jobs like these. By cropping a photo, you can often improve its composition and better highlight its subject matter.

Similarly, some photos need a bit of straightening. It's easy to tilt the camera when you're shooting, making the whole world look just a little crooked.

To put your world on the level, use the Straighten tool. A drag of the mouse is all it takes.

Then there's red-eye. Biologically, it's caused by the bright light of an electronic flash reflecting off a subject's retinas and the blood vessels around them. Aesthetically, it makes people look like demons.

iPhoto can help here, too. The Red-Eye tool gives you a couple of ways to get the red out. Indeed, face recognition even comes into play: if iPhoto '09 detects one or more faces in a photo, one click of the mouse is all it takes to remove red-eye—everywhere it occurs.

Removing Red-Eye

Step 1. Open the photo in edit view.

Step 2. Drag the size slider to zoom in on the subject's eyes.

Step 3. Click the Red-Eye button.

Step 4. If the Auto button is active in the Red-Eye tool panel, iPhoto has detected a face in the photo; click the Auto button.

If the Auto button is inactive, iPhoto didn't detect a face, and you'll need to remove the red-eye yourself.

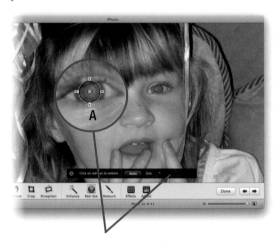

Drag the slider until the tool (A) is slightly larger than the red area of the eye. Then, click the red area of each eye.

Step 5. To turn off the Red-Eye tool, click it again.

Cropping a Photo

Step 1. Open the photo in edit view.

Step 2. Click the Crop button.

Step 3. Adjust the size and position of the crop rectangle to enclose the portion of the image you want to keep, then click Apply.

When you move or resize the crop area, you see a grid that divides the crop area into thirds. You can often improve the composition of a photo by placing its main subject along this grid (see page 165).

To move the crop area, drag inside it.

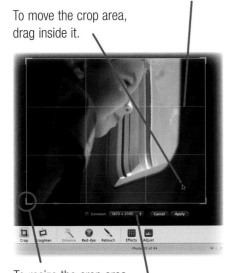

To resize the crop area, drag one of its corners or edges.

You can control the proportions of the crop area so that your photo fits a certain print size or display dimension (see "Constraining the Crop," right).

Notes and Tips

Constraining the crop. You can make the crop area any size you like. But sometimes, you may want to control the proportions of the crop area—to ensure that your photo's proportions match a certain print size, for example.

Click the Constrain box, then choose an option.

For example, if you plan to order an eight- by ten-inch print of the photo, choose 8 x 10.

To switch between a horizontal and vertical crop area, choose Constrain as Landscape or Constrain as Portrait. To override the constrain setting, press Shift while resizing the crop area.

Resetting the crop. To start over, press Option—the Cancel button changes to Reset. Click Reset, and iPhoto restores the original crop rectangle.

Cropping and resolution.

When you crop a photo, you throw away pixels, lowering the photo's resolution. If you print a heavily cropped photo, you may notice ugly digital artifacts. Always shoot at the highest resolution your camera provides; this gives you more flexibility to crop later (see page 162).

The local option. If you're printing a photo on your own printer, or using the photo in a slide show or print project, you might prefer to use iPhoto's zoom tools to crop—that way, you won't change the photo everywhere you've used it. See pages 100 (for slide shows), 122 (for printing), and 139 (for print projects).

Straightening a Photo

Step 1. Open the photo in edit view.

Step 2. Click the Straighten button.

Step 3. Drag the slider left or right, using the on-screen grid as a guide.

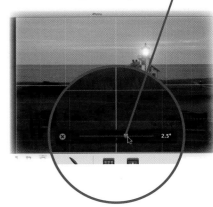

Enhancing and Retouching Photos

Old photos can appear faded, their color washed out by Father Time. They might also have scratches and creases brought on by decades of shoebox imprisonment.

New photos can often benefit from some enhancement, too. That shot you took in a dark room with the flash turned off—its color could use some punching up. That family photo you want to use as a holiday card—the clan might look better with fewer wrinkles and blemishes.

iPhoto's enhance and retouch tools are ideal for tasks like these. With the enhance tool, you can improve a photo's colors and exposure, bring out details hidden in shadows, and rescue a photo you might otherwise delete. With the retouch tool, you can remove minor scratches and blemishes, not to mention that chocolate smudge on your kid's face.

iPhoto's editing features make it easy to fix many common image problems, but iPhoto isn't a full-fledged digital darkroom. You can't, for example, remove power lines that snake across an otherwise scenic vista, nor can you darken only a portion of an image. For tasks like these, you'll want to use Adobe Photoshop or Photoshop Elements—both of which pair up beautifully with iPhoto (see page 92).

Using One-Click Enhance

I've used an old photo in the example below, but don't restrict your use of the Enhance button to your old treasures. Try it out with any photo that needs some punch.

Enhance

To apply one-click enhance, open a photo in edit view, and then click the Enhance button at the bottom of the iPhoto window.

Before

After

Tips

If the Enhance tool isn't doing the job—maybe you feel its results are too harsh—undo your enhancements and turn to the tools in the Adjust panel (see page 74).

And speaking of the Adjust panel, if you happen to have it open when you click the Enhance button, you'll see its sliders jump to different positions, indicating exactly what changes iPhoto is making to improve the image. This can be a good way to learn about image enhancement and improve your own skills with the Adjust panel.

Retouching a Photo

Step 1. Open the photo in edit view.

Step 2. Click the Retouch button.

Retouch

Step 3. Click on or drag across on the flaw you want to remove.

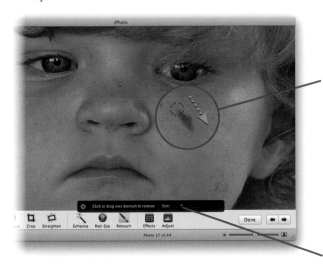

For larger scratches and flaws, try dragging in short strokes. This helps iPhoto blend your retouching into the surrounding area. For small blemishes, a single click is often all you need. Experiment and undo as needed.

You can enlarge or reduce the size of the retouch brush. A larger brush makes short work of large flaws, but you may find it picks up extraneous colors or patterns from surrounding areas. When that happens, undo your work, reduce the size of the brush, and try again.

Notes and Tips

Zoom for precision. To retouch with more precision, use the size slider to zoom in on the area of the image that you're working on. You can also zoom by pressing the 0 (zero), 1, or 2 keys.

Undo and revert. You can undo each mouse click or drag by choosing Edit > Undo Retouch from the Edit menu.

To undo all of your retouching, choose Photos > Revert to Previous. Note that you'll also lose any other edits, such as cropping, that you performed since switching into edit view. Because of this, you might want to retouch first—that way, you won't lose work if you decide to revert. Or take a different approach: Do your cropping and other adjustments, then click Done to exit edit view. Reopen the photo in edit view, and retouch.

Brush keyboard shortcuts. To make the retouch brush smaller, press the left-bracket ([) key. To make the brush larger, press the right-bracket key.

Better around the edges. If you've used earlier iPhoto versions and been disappointed with your retouching results, try again now. In iPhoto '09, the retouch brush does a better job, particularly when retouching a flaw that's located near a sharp edge, such as a stripe in a shirt.

Applying Effects to Photos

With the Effects panel, you can alter a photo to give it a unique look. Evoke the colors of an old, faded tintype. Turn a color photo into a black-and-white one. Blur the edges of a scene to create a gauzy, romantic look. Juice up the colors in a photo or tone them down.

As the tips at right describe, you can apply more than one effect to a photo, and you can apply an effect more than once.

Keep in mind that applying an effect to a photo changes that photo everywhere it appears—in albums, books, slide shows, and so on. If you want to retain the previous version of a photo, be sure to duplicate it before applying an effect: select the photo and choose Duplicate from the Photos menu or use the ⌘-D keyboard shortcut.

And there's a local editing angle, too: You can apply black-and-white, sepia, or antique effects in slide shows and print projects.

Applying Effects

Step 1. Open a photo in edit view.

Step 2. Click the Effects button to display the Effects panel (opposite page).

Step 3. Click the desired effect(s).

Effective Tips

Combining effects. Some effects pair up particularly well. For a dream-like look, try combining Edge Blur with the B&W effect. For an old-fashioned look, pair the Sepia or Antique effects with the Vignette effect. To create an oval border around a photo, combine the Matte and Vignette effects.

Don't be afraid to try offbeat combinations, either. It might seem contradictory to follow the Boost Color effect with the Fade Color effect, but you can get some interesting results when you do.

If you effect yourself into a corner, just click the Original button in the center of the Effects panel to return to safety.

When once isn't enough. You can apply most effects up to nine times: simply click the desired effect's button over and over again. (The two exceptions are the B&W and Sepia effects; clicking their buttons repeatedly will only wear out your mouse.)

iPhoto lets you know how many times you've applied an effect. To backtrack one time, click the left-pointing arrow.

Refining an effect. You can refine the appearance of an effect by using the controls in the Adjust panel (discussed on the following pages). In particular, you can improve the contrast and tonal range of a black-and-white conversion by adjusting the Saturation, Tint, and Temperature sliders. For details, see page 81.

A Gallery of Effects

No single photo is ideally suited to every effect, but that didn't stop me from working my dog into this example.

To remove the effects you've applied, click the Original thumbnail in the center of the Effects panel.

B&W. Convert to black and white.

Sepia. Add a warm brown cast.

Antique. Simulate the faded colors of an old photo.

Fade Color. Decrease a photo's color saturation (for more control, use the Adjust panel; page 80).

Boost Color. Increase a photo's color saturation (for more control, use the Adjust panel; page 80).

Matte. Add a soft-edged white border.

Vignette. Add a soft black border.

Edge Blur. Blur the edges of a photo. **Tip:** Try clicking this one a few times and combining it with the B&W effect.

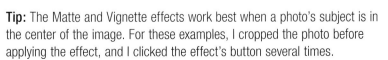

Tip: The Matte and Vignette effects work best when a photo's subject is in the center of the image. For these examples, I cropped the photo before applying the effect, and I clicked the effect's button several times.

Advanced Editing and the Adjust Panel

Some photos need more help than others. That portrait captures the essence of your subject—but it's just a bit dark. That shot of a beautiful white gardenia would be prettier if the flower didn't have a jaundiced yellow color cast. And that shot of the dog playing in the park would be cuter if you could actually see the dog.

To fix problems like these, use the Adjust panel—its controls let you fine-tune exposure, tweak color balance, sharpen details, and more.

The basics of the Adjust panel are a cinch: after opening a photo for editing, summon the Adjust panel by clicking the Adjust button in the edit view toolbar. Then, drag the appropriate sliders left or right until you get the desired results.

That last part—getting the desired results—isn't always a cinch. Adjusting exposure, color balance, and sharpness can be tricky, and knowing a few digital imaging concepts can help you reach your goals. You'll find a detailed look at these concepts in the following pages. Here's the big picture.

A Sampling of Adjustments

Adjust Exposure

Use the Exposure and Levels sliders to brighten or darken photos and improve contrast (page 76).

Fix Color Problems

Use the Saturation, Temperature, and Tint sliders to remove unwanted color casts, increase or decrease color vividness, and more (page 80).

Recover Shadow and Highlight Detail

Use the Shadow and Highlight sliders to bring detail out of dark shadows and overly bright areas (page 78).

The Adjust Panel at a Glance

The histogram is a bar graph that shows a photo's distribution of tonal values—blacks, whites, and everything in between. Knowing how to read the histogram can help you improve brightness and contrast (see the following page).

The Exposure slider adjusts overall brightness; use it and the Levels sliders to fix exposure and contrast problems (page 76).

The Contrast slider increases or decreases the contrast range.

The Saturation slider makes colors less vivid or more vivid (page 80).

Enhance the contrast and sharpness in ways that improve a photo's—you guessed it—definition (page 78).

The Highlights and Shadows sliders restore details hidden in dark shadows and bright areas (page 79).

Low-light or high-ISO shots often have digital noise that the De-Noise slider can help to minimize (page 83).

The white-point tool corrects color casts by adjusting the color of white or gray areas (page 80).

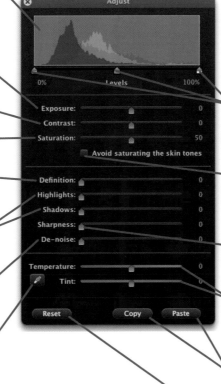

The local angle. You'll find an Adjust panel elsewhere in iPhoto: there's one in the custom print view (page 124) and in the calendar, greeting card, and book views (page 139). These Adjust panels aren't identical to the one in edit view, but they're very similar—and they're great places to adjust a photo without changing it everywhere you may have used it.

The Levels sliders are often the best tools for improving brightness and contrast (page 76).

Adjusting the color of a photo containing faces? This option helps keep skin color accurate (page 80).

The Sharpness slider increases clarity and crispness; sharpening before printing can improve your output (page 82).

The Temperature and Tint sliders adjust color balance; use them to fix unwanted color casts and create special effects (page 80).

Use the Copy and Paste buttons to apply adjustments made in one image to another image (page 87).

Never mind! If you've adjusted yourself into a corner, click Reset to restore all the sliders to their factory settings.

Adjusting Exposure and Levels

The Adjust panel gives you control over many aspects of a photo's appearance, but chances are you'll use its exposure controls most often. For improving a photo's exposure and contrast, use the Levels sliders and the Exposure slider. By adjusting them—while keeping a close eye on the photo's histogram—you can often make dramatic improvements in a photo's appearance.

Which tools should you use? It depends on the photo. Some photos respond better to the Exposure slider, while others benefit from levels adjustments. Still other photos benefit from both approaches: do some initial tweaks with the Exposure slider, then fine-tune the levels.

When you drag these sliders, you tell iPhoto to stretch the photo's existing tonal values to cover a broader tonal range. Oversimplified, when you change the black point, you tell iPhoto, "See this grayish black? I want you to treat it as a darker black and adjust everything else accordingly."

The Levels sliders can often work wonders, but they can't work miracles. If a photo has an extremely narrow contrast range, you may see visible *banding*—jarring color shifts instead of smooth gradations—after adjusting levels. You're telling iPhoto to stretch a molehill into a mountain, and there may not be enough data to allow for smooth gradations in shading and color.

Reading a Histogram

A *histogram* is a bar graph that shows how much black, white, and mid-tone data a photograph has. Pure black is on the left, pure white is on the right, and the mid-tones are in between. iPhoto displays a color histogram that breaks this information down into an image's three primary-color channels: red, green, and blue.

Beneath the histogram is a set of sliders that let you change what iPhoto considers to be pure black, pure white, or mid-tone values.

A Sampling of Histograms

This properly exposed shot has a good distribution of dark, bright, and mid-tone areas.

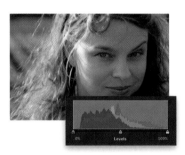

This overexposed shot has very little data in the blacks; everything is bunched up toward the right side—the white side—of the histogram.

Nice cityscape, but it's underexposed; notice the absence of data at the right end of the histogram.

Using the Levels Sliders

Before

Cute kid, flat photo. The histogram tells the tale: there's little data in the brightest whites.

After

The photo's brightness and contrast are improved, and its histogram shows a broader tonal range.

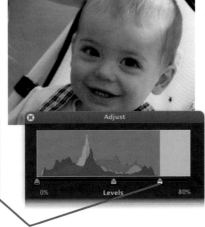

To darken the photo, drag the *black-point* slider to the right.

To adjust the overall brightness of the photo, drag the mid-tone slider.

To brighten the photo, drag the *white-point* slider to the left.

Drag until the sliders almost reach the point where the image data begins. These sloped areas are often called the *shoulders* of the histogram.

Using the Exposure Slider

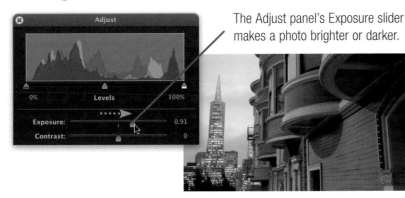

The Adjust panel's Exposure slider makes a photo brighter or darker.

I enhanced this underexposed photo by dragging the Exposure slider to the right. Notice that its histogram is broader than the original (see opposite page).

Note: The Exposure slider works best with raw-format images. For JPEG-format images, the Levels sliders tend to provide more precision. For more details, see page 91.

Adjusting Definition, Shadows, and Highlights

Recovering Shadow and Highlight Details

Cameras don't perceive high-contrast scenes as well as our eyes do. As a result, high-contrast photos are often missing something. Shadows are dark and devoid of detail, or bright areas are washed out to nearly pure white.

Sometimes your camera's exposure meter works against you, too. A bright background may have caused the camera to use an exposure setting that obscures darker foreground details. Conversely, a dark foreground may have led to an exposure setting that blows out details in brighter areas.

The Shadow and Highlight sliders in the Adjust panel can help. (For tips on using both, see the sidebar on the opposite page.)

Out of the shadows. To bring out details hidden in dark areas, use the Shadows slider.

Before

After

Details in the highlights. Bright areas of a photo often contain obscured detail that you can bring out using the Highlights slider.

Before

After

Improving a Photo's Definition

The definition adjustment, new in iPhoto '09, is a great tool for adding punch to a photo. In fact, it's one of the best adjustments you can make to a photo.

Before

To add definition, drag the Definition slider to the right.

After

How it Works

Under the hood, the Definition slider makes localized contrast adjustments throughout the image to subtly improve detail. When you add definition, iPhoto increases the contrast in mid-tone areas of the image—those not-too-bright and not-too-dark areas that lurk in the middle area of the histogram. Adding definition has the effect of making mid-tone areas appear sharper and removing some of the "cloudiness" that digital images can have.

But who cares? The point to remember is this: applying the Definition adjustment to your best shots can often make them even better.

Shadow and Highlight Recovery Tips

Use sparingly. iPhoto '09 does a much better job of shadow and highlight recovery than did earlier versions. Indeed, iPhoto '09 uses some of the identical imaging technology found in Aperture, Apple's professional photo software. (The Definition adjustment is from Aperture, too.)

Still, a little adjustment goes a long way. Drag the sliders too

far, and you may up with an artificial-looking photo that has strange halos where bright and dark areas meet.

Shadows *and* highlights. Scenes with a lot of contrast can often benefit from *both* a shadow and highlight adjustment to bring details out of both. But again, use sparingly: overdo it,

and you'll end up with a flat, artificial-looking photo.

Plays well with others. You can often get the best results by combining adjustments. To recover shadow details, try brightening the photo with the mid-tone or white-point Levels slider, then drag the Shadows slider.

You might even try brightening the photo until highlights appear too bright, then darken them a bit by using the Highlights slider.

And that's a good guideline for all your Adjust panel endeavors: the best results often come from combinations of several adjustments, not just one.

Changing a Photo's Colors

The Adjust panel lets you perform several types of color-related adjustments. With the Saturation slider, you can adjust the vividness of a photo's colors. Turn down the saturation to create a muted, pastel look or to compensate for a camera's overly enthusiastic built-in color settings. Or turn up the saturation to make a photo's colors more intense.

With the Temperature and Tint sliders, you can change a photo's color balance. Fix a color cast introduced by artificial light or caused by fading film. Or create a special effect to make a photo feel warmer or colder.

How can you tell if the colors you see on your screen will accurately translate to an inkjet or photographic print? Advanced Photoshop users rely on display-calibration hardware and other tools to calibrate their systems so that displayed colors match printed colors as closely as possible.

You can apply this strategy to iPhoto. Or you can take a simpler approach. First, calibrate your screen using the Displays system preference. Second, if you'll be creating your own inkjet prints, make test prints as you work on a photo, duplicating the photo as necessary to get different versions.

Finally, as with many aspects of the Adjust panel, there's a local angle to color adjustments. When you're printing a photo or using it in a print project, you can use the Adjust panel in those views to change colors without changing the photo everywhere you've used it.

Adjusting Color Saturation

To make a photo's colors more vivid, drag the Saturation slider to the right. To make colors more muted, drag the slider to the left. If iPhoto detects a face, it activates a feature that prevents your adjustments from altering skin colors. You can also turn the feature on (or off) yourself.

Original

Increased Saturation

Decreased Saturation

Tips

Pale and pastel. To give a pastel-like quality to a photo's colors, decrease the saturation.

Going gray. If you drag the Saturation slider all the way to the left, you create a *grayscale* version of the photo. Generally, the B&W button does a better job, but experiment and see which version you like best.

Note: If the skin-tones box is checked, you can't completely desaturate the photo. To create a grayscale image, uncheck the box.

Watch your gamut. If you significantly increase a photo's saturation, you probably won't be able to print a version that matches what you see on screen. Printers have a much narrower color range, or *gamut*, than does the Mac's screen.

Adjusting Color Balance

To adjust a photo's color balance, use the Temperature slider, the Tint slider, or both.

Temperature. The Temperature slider adjusts a photo's color temperature. To make a photo appear *cooler* (more bluish tones), drag the slider to the left. To make a photo appear warmer (more yellow/ orange tones), drag the slider to the right.

Original

Cooler

Warmer

Tint. The Tint slider adjusts red/green color balance. If you drag the slider to the left, iPhoto adds red, making a photo appear less green. If you drag the slider to the right, you add green and lessen the amount of red. The Tint slider can help remove the greenish color cast that you may find in photos taken under fluorescent lighting.

Colorful Tips

Temperature Tips. Photos taken under incandescent light with your camera's flash turned off tend to have a yellowish cast to them. I like this warm look, but if you don't, try dragging the Temperature slider to the left to cool things off. If the corrected image looks dark, bump up the Exposure or mid-tone Levels slider.

You can often simulate different lighting conditions by shifting a photo's color temperature slightly. Warm up a photo to simulate late afternoon sun, or cool it down to simulate shade or twilight.

Old color photos often take on a reddish-yellow appearance as their color dyes fade. To fix this, drag the Temperature slider to the left a bit.

Gray Balancing. If you have an off-color photo containing an object that you know should be gray or white, click the eye-dropper tool (), then click on part of the photo that should be gray or white. iPhoto adjusts the Temperature and Tint sliders as best it can to make the object a neutral gray.

Better Black and White

iPhoto's B&W effect does a good job of converting a color photo to black and white, but you can often improve on its efforts: after clicking B&W, adjust the Saturation, Temperature, and Tint sliders.

When you drag the color sliders after converting a photo to black and white, iPhoto blends the photo's red, green, and blue color channels in different ways. To make a black-and-white photo appear richer, bump up the saturation after clicking the B&W button. While you're experimenting, drag the Temperature and Tint sliders to see how they alter the photo's tonal values. (For you film fogies, this is the digital equivalent of exposing black-and-white film through color filters.)

After Clicking B&W Button

After Adjustments

Sharpening and Reducing Noise

All digital images—whether captured by a scanner or a camera—have an inherent softness. Some softness is introduced by inexpensive lenses, and some is introduced by imaging sensors and their fixed grid of pixels.

Digital cameras compensate for this inherent softness by applying some sharpening immediately after you take a photo. You can often adjust the amount of sharpness they apply; I like to turn down the sharpness settings on my cameras, preferring to sharpen later, if necessary. (If you shoot in raw mode, your camera applies little or no sharpening to the image; see page 88.)

Inkjet printers and offset printing presses (including the kind used to print iPhoto books, greeting cards, and calendars) also introduce some softness. The bottom line: several factors are working against your image to obscure fine details.

Some sharpening can add crispness to a photo, whether you plan to view it on-screen or print it on paper. But photos that will be printed are particularly good candidates for sharpening.

Sharpening is part of the "balanced diet" that you should consider applying to your best shots. Fine-tune the exposure using the Levels or Exposure sliders. Bring out details hidden in shadows and highlights. Apply the Definition adjustment to add some pop. Fine-tune the color saturation, if you like.

But keep the word *balanced* in mind: apply too much of any adjustment, and you'll get weird, unnatural-looking results.

Sharpening Basics

To sharpen a photo, drag the Adjust panel's Sharpness slider to the right.

After Sharpening

Before Sharpening

Sharpening Tips

Should You Sharpen?

Just because digital images have an inherent softness doesn't mean that you should apply sharpening to every photo you take. First, consider the photo itself. A photo that lacks fine details—say, a close-up of a baby's face—won't gain much from sharpening, and may even be hurt by it. Conversely, a photo containing fine details—such as the one on the opposite page—may benefit greatly from sharpening.

Also consider how you'll be using the photo. A photo destined for an iDVD slide show or iMovie project probably doesn't need sharpening. A photo that you plan to print—either yourself or by ordering prints or a book—is a better candidate for sharpening, especially if the photo contains fine details.

Printing? Sharpen heavily. Don't be afraid to heavily sharpen a photo that you're going to print. Even if the photo looks a bit too sharp on screen, chances are it will print nicely.

Also consider the paper you're using. Premium glossy photo paper shows fine details best, so photos destined for it can benefit from sharpening. On the other hand, matte- and luster-finish photo papers have a fine texture that obscures detail a bit.

The local angle. Just want to sharpen a photo for printing on your inkjet printer? Don't forget the option of sharpening using the Adjust panel in the custom print view—see page 125.

View Right

iPhoto's edit view introduces some softness of its own when it scales a photo to whatever zoom setting you've made. To get the most accurate on-screen view possible, view your photo at 100 or 200 percent when making sharpness adjustments: press the 1 key to view at 100 percent, and the 2 key to view at 200 percent.

How it Works

Regardless of what you see on TV, no digital imaging program can turn a blurry photo into a sharp one. Instead, iPhoto detects boundaries of light and dark, and makes light edges a bit lighter and dark edges a bit darker. When it's done right—that is, not to excess—our eyes perceive this as increased sharpness.

Reducing Noise in Photos

Photos taken in low light—indoors, with the flash turned off, for example—often have a grainy appearance, especially if you've used your camera's menus to turn up the ISO setting (page 162).

With a digital camera, high ISO settings basically amplify the signal from the camera's sensor.

It's a bit like turning up the volume on a radio: it doesn't make the radio more sensitive to weak signals, but it does boost whatever signal is there.

But when you crank up the volume of a weak signal, the static gets louder, too. In a digital photo, this "static" is called *noise*, and it's especially noticeable in

areas of little detail—a blue sky or a smooth-cheeked baby.

At moderate ISO settings, such as 200, noise tends to be subtle and may not even show up in prints. But at high ISO speeds, noise can be deafening, creating a speckled, snowy appearance like that of a weak TV signal.

To quiet down noisy shots, use the Adjust panel's De-Noise slider. The further you drag the slider, the stronger the noise reduction. Applied too heavily, noise reduction can give detailed areas a mottled, plastic look. Experiment with your noisy shots, remembering to zoom in for a closer look.

The Big Picture: Full-Screen Editing

When you're editing and enhancing a photo, it's often helpful to see the big picture—that is, to display your photo at as large a size as possible. When you go big, it's easier to perform color and exposure adjustments and to find flaws that need retouching.

iPhoto's full-screen editing view gives you a picture window into your pictures. Click the Full Screen button, and your Library list and iPhoto's buttons and controls step aside to make room for your photos. Move the mouse pointer to the top or bottom of the screen, and the menu bar or toolbar glide into view.

If you prefer to use full-screen view for all your editing tasks, use iPhoto's Preferences command to always have photos open in full-screen view; see page 86.

Full-screen view teams up nicely with another iPhoto feature: the ability to compare two or more photos in order to find the best shot in a series. You can display two or more photos side-by-side and even edit them.

It's worth noting that you can also compare photos in iPhoto's standard edit view. But, because full-screen view maximizes your screen space, it's the best place for your photo-comparison sessions.

Switching to Full-Screen View

To edit a photo in full-screen view, select the photo and then click the Full Screen button (⬛).

If you're already in the standard edit view, you can switch to full-screen view by clicking the same button.

To display a different photo, click its thumbnail.

You can view and edit photo information in full-screen view; click the Info button to display the Information panel shown here.

If you've zoomed in on a photo, the Navigation panel appears. Drag the rectangle to quickly pan around the zoomed photo.

You can also move to the next or previous photo by clicking the arrow buttons or by using the arrow keys on your keyboard.

To exit full-screen view, click the ⊗ button. **Note:** You can also exit full-screen view by pressing your keyboard's Esc key, although this discards any edits you made.

Comparing Photos

It's always smart to take more than one version of an important shot—to experiment with different exposure settings or to simply increase your chances of capturing that perfect smile.

After you've imported those multiple variations into iPhoto, compare the photos to find the best one. (And if you don't want to see the rest, consider hiding them; see page 36.)

To Compare Photos

Comparing in edit view. If you're already working in full-screen edit view (opposite page), click the Compare button. iPhoto loads the next photo and displays both side-by-side.

To remove a photo from the comparison, click the ⊗.

When you click a different thumbnail, its photo replaces the selected photo (in this example, the one on the left). To compare more than two photos, ⌘-click on their thumbnails. (You can compare up to eight photos.)

From browsing to comparing. You can also set up a comparison *before* entering edit view. Select the photos first, then click the Full Screen button (⬚). For a review of ways to select photos, see page 59.

Tips for Full-Screen View

Show your stuff. Normally, iPhoto hides the thumbnails and toolbar unless you mouse to the top or bottom of the screen. But you can choose to display either or both all the time. To always see the toolbar, choose View > Show Toolbar; for thumbnails, choose View > Thumbnails > Always Show.

Move your thumbs. Thumbnails can appear along the left or right edge of the screen instead of along the top. Choose View > Thumbnails > Position on Left (or Position on Right). Since your screen is wider than it is tall, moving thumbnails to the side uses space more efficiently,

especially when you are working with vertically oriented photos.

Grow more thumbs. You can see more than one row of thumbnails—handy when you want to edit a lot of photos. Choose View > Thumbnails, then choose how many rows or columns you want.

The shortcut menu. In full-screen view, you can still access some editing functions with the shortcut menu: just Control-click within the photo, and choose a command.

Editing Tips

How the Saturation Adjustment Works

I've already mentioned that iPhoto '09 inherits several professional-quality adjustments from its powerhouse sibling, Aperture: shadow and highlight recovery, and the Definition adjustment.

The Saturation adjustment also borrows from Aperture. When the *Avoid saturating the skin tones* option is active in the Adjust panel, iPhoto is actually using an Aperture adjustment called *Vibrancy*. No, the slider's name doesn't change to Vibrancy, but under the hood, iPhoto is applying the same basic approach to adjusting the photo's colors—a selective saturation adjustment that preserves the color of skin tones.

This won't affect how you use the adjustment, but it's a fun piece of iPhoto-geek trivia: when the box is checked, the adjustment is Vibrancy. When the box isn't checked, the adjustment is Saturation.

And speaking of that pesky check box, I mentioned that it's automatically activated when iPhoto detects a face in the photo. If iPhoto misses a face for any of the reasons discussed on page 44, you'll need to click the check box yourself to switch to the skin-friendly Vibrancy adjustment.

And as mentioned on page 81, you can uncheck the box to create a grayscale version of a photo—or to horrifically over-saturate a friend's complexion.

Setting Editing Preferences

Prefer to edit in full-screen view? Choose iPhoto > Preferences, click the General button, then specify that iPhoto will use full-screen view automatically when you open a photo for editing.

To have iPhoto use full-screen view when you click the Edit button, choose this option.

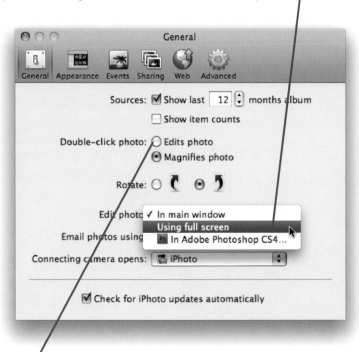

From thumbnail to edit. You can set up iPhoto to jump right into edit view when you double-click a photo thumbnail. This express lane to edit view is handy for those times when you're doing a lot of editing.

Copying and Pasting Adjustments

Sometimes, you might have a series of photos that can benefit from the same adjustments—maybe they're all similarly dark, for example, or all have the same color cast. Or maybe they all come to life when given the same combination of Definition and Sharpness adjustments.

With the Copy and Paste buttons in the Adjust panel, you can apply one photo's adjustments to other photos. After tweaking a photo to perfection, click the Copy button in the Adjust panel. Next, open a different photo in edit view, display the Adjust panel, and click Paste.

The Keys to Editing

You can activate various editing tools by pressing a single key on your keyboard (see the table below).

Keyboard Editing	
For this tool	**Press**
Crop	C
Straighten	S
Red-eye	R
Retouch	T
Adjust panel	A
Effects panel	E
White-point tool	W

While you're pawing your keyboard, remember that you can open a photo for editing by selecting the photo and pressing the Return key—you don't have to click the Edit button. To save changes and return to thumbnail browsing, press Return. To save changes and edit an adjacent photo, press an arrow key. To discard changes and exit edit view, press Esc. To switch to full-screen edit view, press Option-⌘-F.

And don't forget, you can change the size of the retouch brush and manual red-eye–removal tool by pressing the left bracket ([) and right bracket (]) keys.

From Publisher to Editor

Most of the time, you probably enter edit view while browsing your library or an album. But you can also enter edit view while working on a book, calendar, or greeting card: just Control-click on the photo and choose Edit Photo from the shortcut menu.

From Edit Thumbnails to Elsewhere

The thumbnail browser—that row of images at the top of the edit view—is a handy tool for quickly accessing another photo in the same event or album.

But it has another use, too: you can drag a thumbnail from the photo browser directly into an album, book, or slide show. If you're on an editing binge and suddenly realize that a certain photo would go nicely in a specific album, slide show, or book, there's no need to exit edit view. Just drag the photo from the photo browser to the album, slide show, or book.

Shooting in Raw Mode

If you're an advanced photographer, a control freak, or both, there's an image format that may change the way you shoot. The image format is called *raw*, and it's supported by many mid-range and all high-end cameras.

Here's why raw matters. When you shoot in JPEG format, your camera permanently alters the photo: tweaking color balance and saturation, adjusting sharpness, and compressing the image to use less space.

Today's cameras do these jobs well, but you pay a price: you lose some control. You can still adjust the color balance, exposure, and sharpness of a JPEG image, but within a relatively narrow range. Exceed those limits, and you risk visible flaws.

When you shoot in raw mode, your camera saves the exact data recorded by its light sensors. Instead of being locked into the camera's alterations, you get the original, unprocessed image data: the raw data. Transfer this raw image to the Mac, and you can use iPhoto or other imaging software to fine-tune the image to a degree that the JPEG format doesn't permit.

Shooting raw has drawbacks, and many photographers prefer the convenience and efficiency of JPEG. But for pixel perfectionists who want maximum control, raw is the best way to shoot.

Choosing Raw

To shoot in raw mode, venture into your camera's menus and controls—specifically, to those that let you adjust image quality. In some cameras, you'll find these options buried in menus. In others, you can change image quality using buttons on the top of the camera. Check your manual.

Make sure. It's a sad fact of life: each camera company has created its own raw format, and if you have a newly introduced camera, iPhoto may not recognize your camera's raw format images. Before shooting raw, verify that iPhoto supports your camera's raw format. You may find that you need to update to a newer Mac OS X version—Apple often adds support for new cameras when it releases a Mac OS update. For a current list of supported cameras, go to www.macilife.com/iphoto.

Make room. Raw files are often several times larger than their JPEG equivalents. For example, an eight-megapixel JPEG might use 4MB while its raw version uses 16MB. Because you'll get fewer raw images on a memory card, you might want to buy a few extra cards.

Those big files will also take up more space on your hard drive—and on the hard drive that you're using (or should be using) to back up your iPhoto library.

Make time. With some cameras, raw images can take longer to save after you snap the shutter. If you're shooting a fast-changing scene, verify that your camera's raw mode is fast enough to keep up with your subject.

Those large raw files also take longer to transfer to the Mac. Even with the fast USB 2.0 connections built into all current cameras and Macs, you'll wait a bit longer to see your shots.

Learn more about raw-format photography.
www.macilife.com/iphoto

The Basics of Working with Raw Photos

In some ways, working with raw photos in iPhoto is no different than working with JPEG photos. You can import raw photos into your library, edit them using all of the edit-view features I've described previously, and share them using all of iPhoto's sharing features.

Importing raw photos. Aside from making sure you have plenty of free disk space, you don't have to do anything special to import raw photos into iPhoto. If iPhoto supports your camera's raw format, it imports the raw photos and stores them in your photo library.

JPEG companions. When you import raw photos, iPhoto creates JPEG versions of them. You don't see thumbnails for these JPEG companions in your photo library, but they're there.

iPhoto creates these JPEG versions for use by programs that don't understand the raw format. For example, when you access your iPhoto library from a different program, such as iMovie or iDVD, that program uses these JPEG versions.

However, when you open a raw photo in edit view, iPhoto does indeed use the original raw-format image. For details on how iPhoto handles raw images during and after the editing process, see the following pages.

Raw plus JPEG. Some cameras save a JPEG version of a photo at the same time that you shoot a raw version. This is a handy convenience that gives you the best of both worlds: a compact JPEG and a *digital negative*—a phrase often used to describe raw-format images.

When you import photos from such a camera, iPhoto imports both the JPEG and the raw versions of each shot. It also *displays* both versions, and if you're planning to do some editing, you'll want to make sure you open the raw version— you want iPhoto to base your changes on the highest-quality version available.

To see which photo is the JPEG version and which is the raw version, open the Information pane and select one of the photos. iPhoto displays its format in the Kind area of the Information pane.

Max Headroom: The 16-Bit Advantage

I've already mentioned one big benefit of shooting in raw format: you aren't locked into the color, sharpness, and exposure settings made by your camera.

Another advantage deals with something called *latitude* or *headroom*: the ability to make dramatic adjustments without risking visible flaws. Simply put, a raw image is more malleable than a JPEG.

Raw photos have more latitude because they store more image data to begin with. JPEG images are eight-bit images; each of the three primary-color channels— red, green, and blue—are represented by eight bits of data. That means that each channel can have up to 256 different tonal values, from 0 (black) through 255 (white). (Yes, things are getting a bit technical here, but such is life in the raw.)

Most cameras, however, are capable of capturing at least 12 bits of data for each color channel, for a possible 4,096 different levels. When a camera creates a JPEG, it essentially throws away at least one-third of the data it originally captured.

Most of the time, that loss of data isn't a problem. But if you need to make significant changes to an image's exposure

and color balance, the more data you have to start with, the better. Where this extra latitude really pays off is with photos that were poorly exposed or taken under tricky lighting conditions.

Think of the extra data as money in the bank: when times get tough, you'll be glad it's there.

Working with Raw Images

How iPhoto Manages Raw Photos

iPhoto works hard to insulate you from the technicalities of working with raw photos. Here's a summary of how iPhoto works with raw captures.

iPhoto also creates a JPEG "stand-in" for printing and for use by other programs.

When you import a raw photo, iPhoto stores it in your photo library.

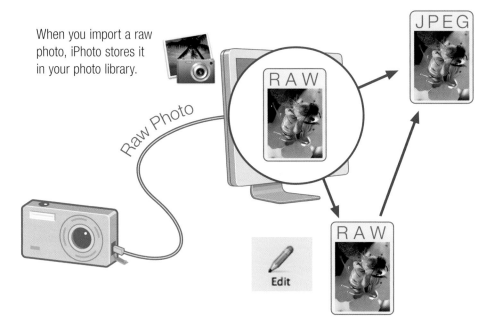

Raw Photo

Edit

When you open a raw photo in edit view, iPhoto uses the original raw data that you imported. The RAW badge shown below appears near the bottom of the iPhoto window. **RAW**

When you leave edit view, iPhoto applies your edits to the raw data, then creates a JPEG photo that reflects the edits. The original raw file always remains unchanged, and you can access it in a couple of ways (see next page).

Editing an Already-Edited Raw Photo

If you edit a raw photo that you've already edited, iPhoto returns to the original raw version of the photo, and applies all the changes you've made—today's as well as yesterday's. This non-destructive editing gives you far more flexibility than earlier iPhoto versions provided. You can edit an image as many times as you like without worrying about introducing quality loss each time.

The exception to the rule. Ah, but there's an exception. If you edited a raw photo using the older iPhoto '06, iPhoto '09 applies your latest edits to the edited JPEG that the older version of iPhoto created. Open that edited raw photo in edit view, and you won't see the RAW badge at the bottom of the iPhoto window—and any new edits you make are applied to the JPEG version.

So what do you do if you've been using iPhoto for years and you want the full power of non-destructive editing? Select the edited version of the raw photo and choose Photos > Revert to Original. iPhoto discards the JPEG version (and any edits you made). Now you can bring the non-destructive editing power of iPhoto '09 to bear.

Get links to the best Photoshop resources.
www.macilife.com/iphoto

Exporting the Original Raw File

There's another way to get to your original raw data after making edits: export the original raw file from iPhoto.

First, select the JPEG version of the photo that iPhoto created after you edited the raw file. Next, choose Export from the File menu. Finally, in the Export Photos dialog box, choose Original from the Kind pop-up menu. Save the file somewhere convenient, such as on your desktop.

When might you use this approach? Here's one scenario. You've edited a raw photo in iPhoto, but then you decide to try editing the original raw file in Adobe Photoshop Elements. You want to keep the version you edited in iPhoto, so instead of reverting the photo or duplicating the edited version, you export a raw version for use in Photoshop.

Raw Photos and Photoshop

As I describe on the following pages, iPhoto pairs up beautifully with the Adobe Photoshop family. This marriage is particularly happy where raw images are concerned: in my experience, Adobe's Camera Raw software does a better job than iPhoto when it comes to decoding and processing raw files. Camera Raw, even the version included with Photoshop Elements, provides more control than iPhoto's edit view—and control is what raw is all about.

I use iPhoto to import and store raw photos, but when I'm after maximum quality, I bring those photos into Photoshop. I fine-tune the photos in Photoshop, export them as JPEGs, then import those JPEGs back into iPhoto for sharing. It's more work, but the results are better.

To ensure that iPhoto supplies Photoshop with the original raw file and not the JPEG stand-in, choose Preferences from the iPhoto menu, click Advanced, and then check the box labeled *Use RAW when using external editor*. If you don't, iPhoto will hand Photoshop a JPEG when you go to edit the raw file—exactly what you *don't* want.

Saving as TIFF

Given that you're obsessed enough with image quality to be shooting in raw mode to begin with, you might lament the fact that iPhoto saves your edited images in the lossy, 8-bit JPEG format. You have a higher-quality alternative: tell iPhoto to use the TIFF format when saving edits to raw images.

To do so, choose Preferences from the iPhoto menu, click Advanced, and check the box labeled *Save edits as 16-bit TIFF files*. The resulting file will be much larger than a JPEG, but it will have that 16-bit headroom described on page 89, and it won't have any lossy compression.

Is it worth the extra storage space? Possibly, particularly for images whose brightness or levels you've altered dramatically. JPEG versions of these images might show that undesirable banding I mentioned on page 76. Consider doing some tests—let your eyes be your guide.

Using iPhoto with Photoshop

The editing features in iPhoto can handle many image-tuning tasks, but at the end of the day, Adobe Photoshop is a better-equipped digital darkroom. Photoshop and Photoshop Elements, its lighter-weight, less-expensive cousin, provide far more sophisticated retouching tools and more ways to improve a photo's lighting and exposure. And as I mention on the previous page, Photoshop can also be a better tool for working with raw-format images.

Photoshop (and Elements—everything on these pages applies to both) has slick features that have no counterparts in iPhoto. A library of exotic visual effects lets you simulate pastels, watercolors, brush strokes, and more. You can cut out the subject of a photo and superimpose it over a different background. You can stitch photos together into dramatic panoramas.

Using Photoshop for retouching doesn't mean abandoning iPhoto. The two programs work well together: you can use iPhoto to import, organize, and share photos, and Photoshop to enhance and retouch them.

Here's an introduction to some ways to turn iPhoto and Photoshop into collaborators.

From iPhoto to Photoshop

A photo in your iPhoto library needs some help. How do you open it in Photoshop? You have a few options.

Drag and drop. If you've already started Photoshop, its icon appears in your dock. To open a photo, simply click on the photo in your iPhoto library and drag it to the Photoshop icon in the dock. When the icon highlights, release the mouse button, and Photoshop opens the photo directly from your iPhoto library. This drag-and-drop technique is handy if you use Photoshop only occasionally.

Important: Don't use this technique to try to open a raw file; you'll end up opening the JPEG stand-in in Photoshop instead. Use the techniques below to send raw images to Photoshop.

Direct connection. If you end up using Photoshop for all your image editing, you can set up iPhoto to directly hand off photos to Photoshop.

Choose Preferences from the iPhoto menu and click the General button. From the Edit Photo pop-up menu, choose In Application. In the dialog box that appears, navigate to your Applications folder, then locate and double-click the icon for your version of Photoshop.

From now on, when you go to edit a photo, iPhoto will hand that photo off to Photoshop.

Note: If you plan to send raw images from iPhoto to Photoshop, be sure to fine-tune iPhoto's preferences, as described on the previous page.

Middle ground. Maybe you use Photoshop frequently, but you also use iPhoto's edit view for cropping and other simple tasks—that's what I do. Head for the middle ground: specify Photoshop as your external image editor as described above, then return to the Preferences dialog box and choose one of the other Edit Photo options, such as In Main Window or Using Full Screen.

This restores iPhoto's factory setting: clicking the Edit button opens a photo in Edit view. But iPhoto doesn't forget that you're also a Photoshop user. To open a photo in Photoshop, Control-click on the photo and choose Edit in External Editor from the pop-up shortcut menu.

A Sampling of Elements Editing Ideas

Recovering Shadow and Highlight Details

iPhoto does shadow and highlight recovery (page 78); Photoshop does it better, providing finer control and better quality—especially if you shoot raw.

The Power of Layers

One of the best reasons to use Photoshop is a feature called *layers*. In Photoshop, an image can have multiple layers, and each layer can contain imagery or image-correction information. By using layers, you can make dramatic modifications to an image without ever altering the original data. This not only gives you more editing flexibility, it helps preserve image quality.

One particularly powerful use of layers involves selective lightening and darkening: changing the brightness of part of a photo without affecting other areas. It's a common technique in darkrooms, it's easy in Photoshop—and impossible in iPhoto.

There is more to layers than I can describe here. To learn about them, open Photoshop's online help and search for *layers* and *adjustment layers*.

Retouch the Flaws Away

iPhoto's Retouch tool does a good job of removing blemishes, dust specks, and other minor flaws. But it's no plastic surgeon.

In this photo, a pair of utility wires slice across a scenic vista. I used two retouching tools to improve the view.

Spot healing brush. Photoshop's *spot healing brush* works much like iPhoto's Retouch tool, only better. Click the spot healing brush tool in the tool palette, then specify a brush size that's slightly larger than the flaw you want to remove.

You can choose a brush size in the Tool Options toolbar, but it's more efficient to use the keyboard: press the right bracket key (]) for a larger brush, and the left bracket key ([) for a smaller one.

Next, simply click on the flaw you want to remove. To remove a larger flaw, such as a scratch or utility wire, click and drag to paint over it.

Clone stamp tool. The spot healing brush works best when the area surrounding the flaw is similar to the area containing the flaw. For this example, the spot healing brush did a great job of removing the wires from the areas surrounded by open sky or water, but it had trouble with areas that were surrounded by fine details, such as the offshore rocks and distant shoreline.

To fix those areas, I used Photoshop's clone stamp tool, which copies pixels from one area of an image to a different area.

After activating the clone stamp tool, point to an area adjacent to the flaw you want to fix. Then, hold down the Option key and click. Option-clicking tells Photoshop what area to use as a guide when healing the flaw, a process Photoshop gurus refer to as "defining the *source point*." After you've done that, paint across the flaw to copy pixels from the source point.

Slide Shows: iPhoto as Projector

With iPhoto's slide show features, you can display on-screen slide shows, complete with background music from your iTunes music library. Choose from several design *themes* that provide flashy transitions between photos. Tell iPhoto how long you want to see each photo, or have iPhoto time your slide show to match the length of the background music.

You can create two different types of slide shows: an *instant* slide show that provides quick results, and a *slide show project* that allows for much more control, including the ability to specify different durations for every photo. When you want to create a slide show and then export it—to burn using iDVD, for example, or to view on your iPod, iPhone, or Apple TV—you'll want to create a slide show project. (For more advice on the best path to take for your slide show needs, see page 103.)

Most of the time, you'll want to add photos to an album before viewing them as a slide show. That way, you can arrange the photos in a sequence that best tells your story. If you're in a hurry, though, just select some photos in your library and then display the slide show as described at right. Or fine-tune an event, hiding photos you don't want to show, then select the event thumbnail.

Somebody get the lights.

Playing an Instant Slide Show

Step 1. Select the photos you want to show.

To show an entire album or event, select it in the Library list. To see a slide show of a favorite face, select that person's tile on the Corkboard. To show scenes from a favorite place, use the map or browser views to focus in on a location.

Step 2. Click the Slideshow button.

The theme chooser appears.

Slideshow

Step 3. Choose a theme.

Optional: Customize your soundtrack and other settings (page 96).

Themes	Music	Settings
Classic	Ken Burns	Scrapbook
Shatter	Sliding Panels	Snapshots

Use settings as default   Cancel   Play

Tip: To preview a theme, point to it. iPhoto displays a sample of the theme's design and transitions.

Step 4. Click the Play button.

Slide Show Themes at a Glance

Here's a brief rundown of the six slide show themes.

Classic. The most basic of the bunch. Photos are separated by a transition whose style you can choose.

Ken Burns. Like Classic, but with the addition of the automatic Ken Burns effect: iPhoto pans and zooms the photos.

Scrapbook. Photos appear inside paper-like frames in a scrapbook whose pages glide into and off of the screen.

Shatter. Sports an edgy transition that separates the color components of a photo, then joins them when the next photo appears. Sweet eye candy.

Sliding panels. Photos glide on and off the screen, usually in groups of two or three.

Snapshots. Photos slide into view from the bottom of the screen, stacking atop each other as playback progresses. When a new photo appears, the photo beneath it becomes black and white—a nice touch.

A Sampling of Style

The animated themes in iPhoto add style to slide shows.

Shatter your audience. The Shatter theme's transitions are great for high-energy subjects: snowboarding, skateboard-ing—or a kid jumping into daddy's arms.

Sweet and sentimental. The Scrapbook theme's rich, organic backgrounds are great for vintage photos, family get-togethers, and other sentimental subjects.

After the Lights Dim

Want to change a slide show during playback? Move the mouse, and a panel appears. Use it to display the themes browser, the music browser, or the settings panel.

(For details on customizing slide show settings and music, see the following pages.)

You can also pause and stop the slide show and move to the previous or next photo.

For another set of controls, point near the bottom of the screen.

A row of thumbnails appears; drag across the row to skim through the slide show, or click a thumbnail to see its photo.

Customizing Instant Slide Shows

Customizing Music Settings

Each slide show theme has its own canned song that plays unless you choose something else—which you can do by clicking Music.

Your iTunes library is a click away, as are your iTunes playlists, your GarageBand compositions, and some sample tunes.

For the sound of silence, uncheck the box.

To search, type a song, artist, or album name.

To preview a song, double-click it or select it and click the ● button.

You can create a song playlist without detouring into iTunes. Check the Custom Playlist box and then drag songs. To reorder, drag songs up and down. To remove a song, select it and press Delete.

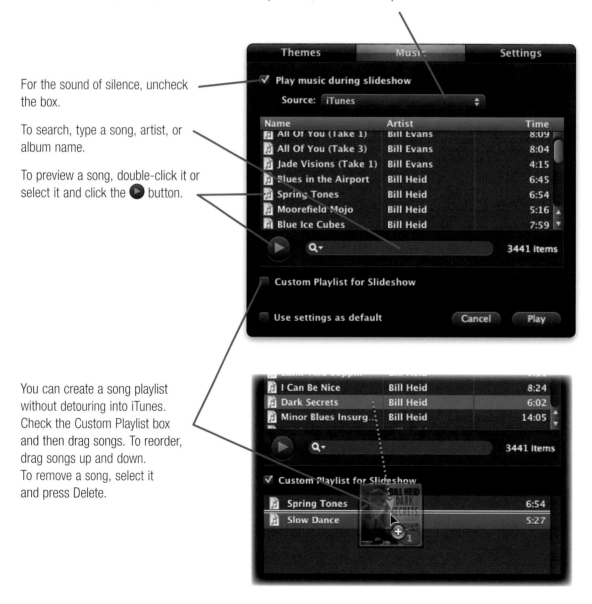

Customizing Slide Show Settings

Specify a duration, or have iPhoto adjust durations to match your soundtrack.

With some themes, you can choose a transition and adjust its speed and direction. To preview the transition, click the thumbnail.

A title slide can appear at the start of the slide show; its text is the name of the event, album, face, or place that you were viewing when you started.

Photos play in random order instead of the order they appear in the iPhoto window.

The slide show repeats until time comes to an end or until you press the Esc key, whichever comes first.

iPhoto zooms images when needed to ensure that the screen is always filled, with no black borders. Vertically oriented photos and photos you've cropped may display strangely.

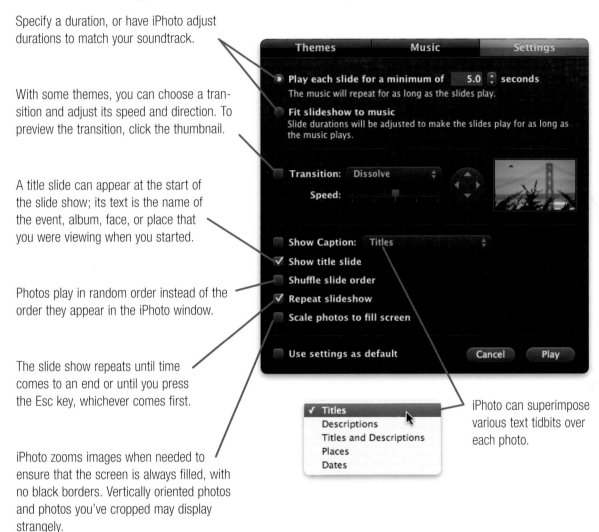

iPhoto can superimpose various text tidbits over each photo.

Creating a Slide Show Project

Instant slide shows provide instant gratification, but with limits. All photos appear for the same amount of time, with the same transition between them. You can't map out your own Ken Burns pan-and-zoom moves. Nor can you export the slide show for burning in iDVD or for viewing on an iPod, iPhone, or Apple TV.

By creating a *slide show project*, you can have all these things and more. Slide show projects appear in the Slideshows area of the Library list. Because they're saved as part of your iPhoto library, you can go back and add to slide show projects any time you want.

Your broader options start with the ability to have different durations for different shots. That view of the skyline? Five seconds. That montage of park scenes? Just a couple of seconds apiece.

The Classic and Ken Burns themes (described on page 95) give you more creative options, too. Mix and match transitions: put a cross dissolve between most vacations shots, for example, but a wipe transition when you change locations. And in both themes, you can tell Ken Burns exactly what to do, setting up moves that best highlight your subjects and tell your story.

When you're done, you can export your work to view on a big-screen TV, iPod, or iPhone—or to bring into iMovie for more editing and YouTube sharing. It all adds up to more creative control than instant slide shows give you.

Starting a Slide Show Project

Step 1. Select some photos; select an album, an event, or a faces tile on the Corkboard; or navigate to a place in Places.

Step 2. Click the [+] button in the lower-left corner of the iPhoto window, or choose File > New Album.

Step 3. In the dialog box, click the Slideshow button, type a name for the slide show, and then click Create.

The slide show editor appears.

To jump to a specific photo, click its thumbnail. To change the order of photos, drag photos left or right. To remove a photo from the slide show, select it and press the Delete key. To select multiple photos for moving or deletion, Shift-click or ⌘-click them.

To change the text of the title slide, point to it and double-click, then type. You can also change fonts and sizes; see page 101.

Move to the previous or next photo in the slide show.

Play or preview the slide show (opposite page).

Choose themes and music, and adjust slide show settings (opposite page).

Drag the size slider to zoom in and show just part of a photo, or to set up the start or end of a Ken Burns move (see page 100).

Customizing a Slide Show Project

If you've tweaked an instant slide show, you'll find the controls in the slide show editor to be familiar—but more powerful.

Themes and music. The theme and music options are identical to those on pages 94–97.

Slide show settings. Many options in the Slideshow Settings panel also resemble their instant slide show counterparts. But several additional options give you more control.

The Transition options appear with the Classic or Ken Burns themes. With the Sliding Panels theme, you have a choice of black or white background.

To jump to the title slide, click the little arrow.

If you'll view the slide show only on your Mac's screen, choose This Screen. If your slide show's destination is a TV (widescreen or otherwise) or an iPhone, choose the appropriate option.

Customize settings for a photo (right).

Adjusting individual photo settings. With the This Slide panel, you can change the duration of whatever photo is displayed in the slide show editor. You can also add a black and white, sepia, or antique effect.

Note: Some themes allow for shorter photo durations than others. For more details, turn the page.

With the Classic or Ken Burns themes, you can also use the This Slide panel to set a transition for a specific photo and to turn the Ken Burns effect on or off. Again, details aplenty lurk on the following pages.

Previewing and Playing a Slide Show

As you create a slide show, you might want to preview your work to get a feel for its pacing. Previewing is also a good way to test some Ken Burns settings.

Previewing. To preview the slide show, click the Preview button. Playback begins with whatever photo appears in the editor. To jump to a different point in the slide show, click a thumbnail image in the photo browser.

Playing back. When you want to see your slide show in its full-screen glory, click the Play button. Your screen goes dark and playback begins.

As with instant slide shows, you can summon some controls during playback. Move the mouse, and the same panel shown on page 95 appears. Use it to pause or stop; skip to the previous or next slide; and change music, themes, and overall settings for the slide show.

Move the mouse pointer to the bottom of the screen, and a row of thumbnails appears. To jump to a photo, click its thumbnail. To scrub through the slide show, drag the small thumbnail preview left or right.

Preview versus playback. In general, when you're in the throes of slide show editing—fine-tuning Ken Burns moves, changing photo durations, adjusting transition timing—previewing is the most convenient way to check your work. And the preview feature lets you start the slide show from any point; by comparison, when you click Play, the slide show always plays from the very beginning.

Creative Options for Slide Show Projects

Using the Ken Burns Effect

The Ken Burns effect adds a dynamic sense of motion to a slide show by panning across photos and zooming in and out.

Two slide show themes allow for Ken Burns moves: Classic and (brace yourself!) Ken Burns. With the Classic theme, no photo has a Ken Burns move, but you can set one up for any photo using the instructions on this page.

Step 1. In the slide show editor, display the photo for which you want to create or customize a Ken Burns move.

Step 2. Click the Settings button to show the Slideshow Settings panel, then click its This Slide tab.

With the Ken Burns theme, *every* photo has an automatic Ken Burns move: iPhoto pans and zooms using settings that it deems appropriate. You can customize those moves, and you can turn Ken Burns off for certain photos if you like.

For some creative advice on zooming and panning photos, see page 203.

Step 3. Be sure the Ken Burns box is checked and set to the Start position, then position the photo as you want it to appear when it's first displayed.

Step 4. Click the End option in the Slideshow Settings panel, then specify the ending setting for the move.

Notes and Tips

Which theme? If you want a Ken Burns move on all or most of the photos in a slide show project, choose Ken Burns. iPhoto adds a move to each photo; you can customize the move or turn it off for those photos that you want to appear static. On the other hand, if you want to add the Ken Burns effect to only *some* photos, choose Classic, then add Ken to those photos that need to move.

No Ken do. To turn off a Ken Burns move for a photo, display that photo in the slide show editor, summon the Settings panel, and then uncheck the Ken Burns box.

Zooming without moving. You want to show just part of a photo in a slide show, but you don't want to crop the photo because that changes its appearance throughout your library. Solution: Make the photo's start and end positions the same.

Panning without zooming. Similarly, you might want to pan across a photo without changing the zoom setting. In this case, make the start and end zoom settings the same (or as close as you can get them).

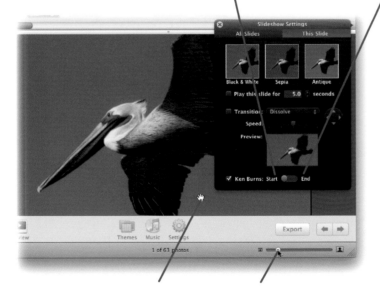

When zoomed in, specify which part of the photo you want to see by dragging within the photo.

To zoom in or out, drag the size slider right or left.

Zooming in Other Themes

The remaining slide show themes don't provide for Ken Burns moves, but you can still zoom and pan a photo to have just part of it appear—it's like cropping the photo without having to actually crop it in edit view.

To do it, display that photo in the slide show editor, then drag the size slider to zoom in. Then, drag within the photo to position it as desired.

If you're working with the Sliding Panels theme—which displays multiple photos at once—be sure to select the photo you want to adjust before hitting that size slider. To select the photo, click it in the thumbnail photos browser.

Formatting Title Text

As mentioned previously, you can begin a slide show with a title slide: in the Slideshow Settings panel, check the Show Title Slide box.

For the title text, iPhoto uses the name of the slide show as it appears in the Library list. But you can change that: just click the text in the slide show editor, then type.

You can also change the font of the text, and even use multiple fonts in a title. Drag across the text to select it, then choose Edit > Fonts > Show Fonts (or just press ⌘-T). Use the Fonts panel to change fonts and type size. To start a new line, press the Return key.

Tip: If you're unhappy with your formatting, jump back to Square One: in the Slideshow Settings panel, uncheck the Show Title Slide box, then check it again. iPhoto restores the theme's original text formatting.

Exporting a Slide Show

You've refined your slide show project to perfection. Now what? Send it somewhere.

To iDVD. To burn a DVD containing the slide show, choose Share > Send to iDVD. iPhoto prepares the slide show and ships it off to iDVD.

To iTunes. Want to view your slide show on an iPod, iPhone, or Apple TV? Send it to iTunes, then sync iTunes with your device.

In the slide show editor, click the Export button. In the Export dialog box, click the check box for each size that you want to export. The blue dots indicate which Apple devices work best at those sizes.

To have the resulting movie added to your iTunes library, be sure to check the box labeled *Automatically send slideshow to iTunes.*

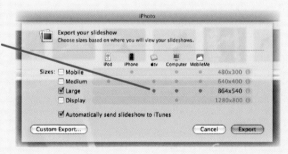

To iMovie. Maybe you'd like to add a voice-over narration to the slide show, or to include it in a larger movie project, or to upload it to YouTube. Export a large version of the movie (click the Large box in the Export dialog box). In iMovie, choose File > Import > Movies, and then bring the movie in. For more iMovie importing details, see page 173.

Slide Show Tips

Video in Slide Shows

If your iPhoto library contains video clips shot with a digital camera, you can use those clips in instant slide shows and slide show projects. iPhoto even lowers the volume of your background music when a movie clip plays so you can hear the movie's audio.

In slide show projects, you can use the Slideshow Settings panel to apply effects to video clips. You can even create Ken Burns moves to pan and zoom across video. It's also fun to use video clips in the Sliding Panels theme, where multiple clips play at once.

Instant Slide Show Tips

iPhoto remembers. When you adjust instant slide show settings—your own music soundtrack, transition settings, and photo durations, for example— iPhoto saves those settings, tying them to whatever you were viewing when you clicked the Play button. For example, if you were viewing an event, your instant slide show settings are saved along with that event. If you were viewing an album, the settings are saved with the album.

The next time you view an instant slide show of that item (event, album, face, and so on), iPhoto uses the settings it saved, and immediately begins playing the slide show. What if you want to change the theme, music, or other settings? Just move your mouse, then use the buttons on the slide show controller to display the themes browser, music panel, or settings panel.

Setting defaults. In a related vein, you can save instant slide show settings as defaults so that iPhoto applies them to subsequent slide shows. After making adjustments with the Slideshow Settings panel, click the check box labeled *Use settings as default.*

Where Exported Slide Shows Live

When you export a slide show, iPhoto creates a movie of its images, transitions, effects, and music. Those movies live in a folder named iPhoto Slideshows, which is contained within the Pictures folder of your home directory.

Slide Shows and Older Macs

To create many of the transitions and slick motion effects in slide show themes, iPhoto relies heavily on the graphics circuitry in your Mac. That circuitry has its own processors and its own memory—it's a computer within your computer, one that specializes in drawing stuff on the screen.

Graphics systems have gotten a lot faster in recent years, and iPhoto slide shows take full advantage of that increased speed. The downside: older Macs lack the punch necessary to run some slide show themes and transitions.

Specifically, a Mac with a G4 processor provides only the Classic and Ken Burns themes. A G5 Mac that has less than 64MB of video memory (vRAM) can run Classic, Ken Burns, Scrapbook, and Sliding Panels. An Intel-based Mac and a G5 Mac with more than 64MB of vRAM can run them all.

To learn how much vRAM your Mac provides, choose About This Mac from the Apple menu, then click the More Info button. When the System Profiler runs, click the Graphics/Displays item in its Contents list. You'll find details on your video circuitry there.

Faces and Slide Shows

iPhoto's ability to recognize faces doesn't stop with the Faces feature. With slide shows, iPhoto tries to position photos containing faces in ways that don't omit part of a face. The automatic Ken Burns move will try to avoid facial damage, for example, as will the Sliding Panels theme. There's no tip here—just a little nod to the Apple engineers who sweated that detail.

Slide Show Strategies

Between iPhoto, iMovie, and iDVD, iLife gives you three ways to present your photos. For quick results that look and sound great, it's hard to beat iPhoto. But other members of the iLife family bring their own advantages to the table (or the screen). The adjacent table summarizes them.

There's one more option: GarageBand. By exporting a slide show and then bringing that movie into GarageBand, you can add music, narration, sound effects, chapter and URL markers, and even make the movie part of a video podcast (see page 352).

Comparing Slide Show Options

Program	Pros and Cons
iPhoto	Provides a nice mix of quick results and broad creative options—plus cool themes, some with Ken Burns options. Limited ability to combine video and stills.
iMovie	Requires more effort, but gives you more editing control and creative options: titles, precise timing to music, fine Ken Burns control. Also provides cool themes, the most versatile features for combining video and stills, direct uploading to YouTube, and features for recording voice narration and creating richer soundtracks.
iDVD	Fewer creative options: all photos have the same duration; no Ken Burns moves, limited mixing of video and stills. But a unique and cool advantage: you can include original images on the DVD-ROM portion of the disc (page 274).

More Slide Show Tips

Use iPhoto to Create Titles

To earn some extra style points, sprinkle some titles into a slide show. For example, create a set of titles—one for each destination—for your vacation slide show.

You already have a great program for making titles. It comes with pre-designed styles that are ready for your own photos and text. The program is called iPhoto.

By combining iPhoto's greeting card features with the Mac's ability to create a PDF file of just about anything, you can create great-looking titles and add them to your slide shows.

Step 1. Select the photo or photos that you want to be part of your title.

Step 2. Click the Card button at the bottom of the iPhoto window.

Step 3. Choose the Postcard style, then choose a theme. (For details on creating greeting cards, see page 146.)

Step 4. Want text? In the greeting card editor, use the Design pop-up menu to choose a design that allows for text. Type your text and perform any other design tweaks.

Step 5. Choose File > Print.

Step 6. In the Print dialog box, click the From button and be sure that the page

range is *1 to 1*. (There's no need to create a PDF of the "back" of your postcard, unless you want to use it in your slide show, too.)

Step 7. Click the PDF pop-up menu and choose Save PDF to iPhoto.

iPhoto and Mac OS X go to work, and a few moments later, your library contains a PDF of your postcard. To see it, click the Last Import item in the Recent list.

Next Stop: London

Your PDF title is ready for its screen debut. If you've already created a slide show, drag the title to the slide show in your Slideshows list. If you haven't created the slide show yet, add the title to the album where you've stashed the slide show's images.

Variations. To animate your title slides, use the Ken Burns effect. Here's a fun trick: Follow your title with the same photo that you used in the title. Apply the Ken Burns effect to the title so that it zooms in slowly, ending at a point where the photo almost fills the viewing area. Use a cross-dissolve effect between the

title and the following photo. When you play your slide show, the title will zoom in, then its background and text will fade away, leaving just the photo.

Here's another way to put Ken to work. Use one of the postcard styles that holds two or more photos, then create a Ken Burns move that slowly pans across the photos.

You can also save a book or calendar page as a PDF and add it to a slide show. Making a slide show of a three-week road trip? Start it with a calendar page whose dates contain photos from the trip. Then, use the Ken Burns effect to pan across the calendar page.

Sharing a Slide Show Using iChat Theater

You have yet another way to share a slide show: iChat Theater. This sublimely cool aspect of Apple's instant-messaging software lets you broadcast a slide show (among other things) to people with whom you're chatting. They'll see Ken Burns moves and transitions, and will even hear your background music.

And your friends don't have to be using the very latest Mac OS X version, either—earlier iChat AV versions can also view iChat Theater broadcasts, as can compatible instant-messaging software for Windows.

Note: iChat Theater can broadcast instant slide shows only; you can't broadcast a slide show project. (Workaround: Export the slide show as a movie, then broadcast the movie using iChat Theater.)

Sharing an Instant Slide Show

Step 1. In iChat, choose File > Share iPhoto With iChat Theater.

A media browser appears.

Step 2. In the media browser, select an album, then click Share.

iChat tells you to invite a buddy to a video chat.

Step 3. Establish a video chat: select a name in iChat's Buddy List window, then click the video camera button (▣) at the bottom of the window.

As soon as your victim accepts the invitation, the slide show begins.

Your Mac switches to iPhoto, where a window lets you control the slide show.

Notes and Tips

Already connected? The instructions at left assume that you haven't yet begun a video chat with someone. If you're already in a video chat, skip Step 3.

Sound options. Your chat buddy will hear whatever music you've assigned to the instant slide show. If your Mac has a microphone, your chat buddy will *also* hear you talk. If you'd rather not broadcast a music soundtrack—maybe you'd prefer to narrate—uncheck the Play Music During Slideshow box in iPhoto. (You'll need to do this before starting the slide show broadcast.)

Conversely, if you don't want your buddy to hear you type or talk during a slide show, click the Mute button (▣) in the Video Chat window.

Sharing other items. The iPhoto/iChat connection goes beyond slide shows. Want to broadcast the photos from an event without creating an album? Start a video chat, then drag the event thumbnail into the Video Chat window.

You can also broadcast just a few photos: select them, then drag them into the Video Chat window.

Sharing Photos via Email

Email takes the immediacy of digital photography to a global scale. You can take a photo of a birthday cake and email it across the world before the candle wax solidifies. It takes just a few mouse clicks—iPhoto takes care of the often tricky chores behind creating email photo attachments.

iPhoto can also make images smaller so they transfer faster. Take advantage of this feature, and you won't bog down your recipients' email sessions with huge image attachments.

Normally, iPhoto uses the Mac OS X Mail program to email photos. Using a different email program, such as Microsoft Entourage? Use the Preferences dialog box to specify your email program.

Step 1. Select the photos.

Select the photos you want to email. Remember that you can select multiple photos by Shift-clicking and ⌘-clicking.

Step 2. Click the Email Button.

iPhoto displays the Mail Photo dialog box.

Step 3. Specify a size, then click Compose Message.

iPhoto can make the images smaller before emailing. (This doesn't change the dimensions or file sizes, of your original images.)

iPhoto estimates the size of the final attachments.

Don't want to share the location information of geotagged photos? Be sure the box is unchecked.

When you click Compose Message, iPhoto adds the photos to a new, blank email, which you can complete and send on its way.

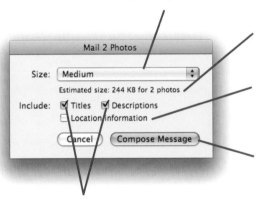

You have the option to include titles and comments along with the images—another good reason to assign this information when organizing your photos.

Exporting Photos By Hand

When you email a photo using iPhoto's Email button, iPhoto uses the name of the original photo's disk file as the name of the attachment. Problem is, most of your photos probably have incomprehensible filenames, such as *200203241958.jpg*, that were assigned to them by your digital camera.

You might want an attachment to have a friendlier file name, such as *holidays.jpg.* For such cases, export the photo "by hand" and then add it to an email as an attachment. Choose Export from iPhoto's File menu, and be sure the File Export tab is active.

Export the photo as described at right. Save the exported photo in a convenient location, such as on your desktop. (You can delete it after you've emailed it.) Finally, switch to your email program, create a new email message, and add the photo to it as an attachment.

The settings below are good starting points for exporting a photo by hand. Here are a few more details and pointers.

The JPEG format is best for emailing, but you might choose the TIFF format if you're exporting a full-resolution version of a photo for use in a page-layout program.

Higher quality settings mean larger image files. Medium is a good compromise.

When you check this box, iPhoto adds the photo title and any keywords to the image's metadata (see page 156). This is useful if you plan to use the photo with other image-management programs, such as Apple's Aperture or Adobe Lightroom.

For emailing, Medium is a good size. You have additional options, though, including the ability to specify exact pixel dimensions.

As with emailing, you can elect to include or omit any geotags the photos might have.

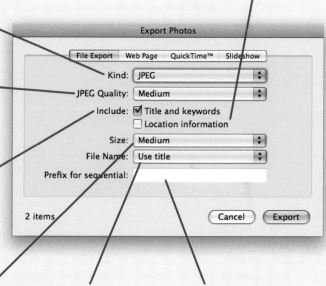

If you titled a photo (page 38), you can have iPhoto use the title as the exported photo's file name. When exporting just one photo, you can choose Filename and then type a name after clicking Export.

Exporting multiple photos? You can choose Sequential from the File Name pop-up menu, and then type a prefix here. iPhoto names the files accordingly. For example, if you type *dog* as the prefix, the files are named *dog1.jpg, dog2.jpg, dog3.jpg,* and so on.

Sharing Photos via MobileMe Galleries

Email is an easy way to share photos over the Internet, but it has its drawbacks. Emailing photos to a large group of friends and family is a chore. And your recipients end up with a collection of photos scattered throughout their email inboxes.

If you have an account with Apple's MobileMe Internet service, you have a much better way to share photos over the Internet: *MobileMe gallery albums.* Publish some photos as a gallery album, and friends and family can view the photos on the Web. Instead of dealing with clumsy email attachments, they can visit a sharp-looking Web page that makes your photos look their best.

That isn't all. You can set up a gallery album with options that no email program can match. Allow visitors to download your photos so they can print them or add them to their own photo collections.

You can even allow visitors to upload their own photos to a gallery album. If the entire family was shooting photos at the reunion, set up a gallery album that lets everyone contribute his or her best shots.

It gets even better. Other iPhoto users can subscribe to your gallery albums—much as they would subscribe to a podcast. Add new shots to a gallery, and they'll automatically appear in someone else's iPhoto. And if you have an iWeb site, you can add your gallery albums to any iWeb page (page 385).

Emailing photos seems kind of old-fashioned, doesn't it?

Creating a Gallery Album

Step 1. Select some photos, or better yet, select an album, an event, a face on the Corkboard, or a place that you've browsed to.

Step 2. Click the MobileMe button or choose Share > MobileMe Gallery

Step 3. Specify your Web gallery options, then click Publish.

To restrict access, choose a different option (see page 110).

Take-out available? To let visitors download your photos, check this box.

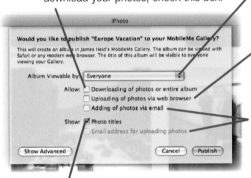

Pitch in? To let visitors upload their own photos, check this box.

Via email? You can add photos to the album by emailing them (see page 110). To let any visitor contribute by email, check the last option, too.

What's in a name? Another good reason to title your best shots (page 38). Didn't add titles? Uncheck the box, lest visitors see names like DSC9843.JPG.

After Publishing

When you click Publish, iPhoto uploads your photos to MobileMe. The gallery album appears in the MobileMe Gallery list.

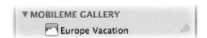

Select this item, and the album's photos appear along with the album's Web address, which you can click (see page 110).

To email someone about your new album, click Tell a Friend.

Working with MobileMe Galleries

Changing a Gallery

You can change a gallery album that you've published—keep it fresh, change settings, and more.

Change the content. To add new photos to the gallery album, drag them to the album in the MobileMe Gallery list. To remove a photo from the gallery, select the photo and press the Delete key. You can also edit photo titles and change the order of photos.

After making changes, click the update icon ( ) next to the published name. iPhoto updates the gallery on the Web.

Change settings. Changed your mind about allowing downloads? Did you decide to make a public gallery private? Select the published gallery in the MobileMe Gallery list, then click the Settings button to access the same options shown on the opposite page.

Collect contributions. If you've allowed others to upload photos, you can update the gallery to grab the latest additions. Click the update icon; if iPhoto finds new photos, it downloads them.

Delete a gallery album. To completely remove a gallery album from your MobileMe account, select the album in the MobileMe Gallery list, and then press the Delete key.

Subscribing to a Gallery

You can subscribe to a gallery album that another iPhoto '08 or iPhoto '09 user has created. When you do, the album appears in your copy of iPhoto. You can enjoy and share the photos without having to visit the Web page, and if the creator of the gallery changes it, iPhoto can update your copy.

Go to the gallery album's Web page, and click the Subscribe button.

A dialog box appears asking whether you want to subscribe via RSS or iPhoto.

Click the In iPhoto button, then click OK. iPhoto displays an "are you sure?" dialog box. Click its Subscribe button, and iPhoto loads the photos from MobileMe and adds the gallery album to the Subscriptions area of the Library list.

▼ SUBSCRIPTIONS
　　Europe Vacation

Now what? You can do almost anything with the photos in a subscribed album: print them, use them in slide shows, create calendars, and so on. You can assign titles and keywords and hide the shots you don't like. But you can't edit a photo—not without some simple trickery (see page 111).

Updating. To update an album to which you've subscribed, click the update icon to the right of its name ( ). iPhoto downloads any new photos.

Auto update. To have iPhoto check your subscriptions automatically, choose iPhoto > Preferences, then click Web. Choose an interval from the pop-up menu.

Unsubscribing. No longer want to subscribe to an album? Select it in the Subscriptions list and press the Delete key. iPhoto gives you the option of moving the photos into your library—if you still want to access the photos but don't care about updating, for example.

What about RSS? As noted at left, when you begin the subscription process, you have a choice of subscribing via RSS. You might take this option if you'd prefer to keep tabs on someone's gallery using your favorite RSS newsreader: Safari, Mac OS X Mail, or a program such as NewsGator's NetNewsWire.

If you have friends who use Windows PCs, they can also subscribe to your albums by using the RSS option. Tell them that—and while you're at it, tell them to get Macs.

MobileMe Gallery Tips

The Gallery Album Page at a Glance

Here's a look at the MobileMe gallery page your online fans will see, along with a tour of its features.

View the gallery index page (below).

Hides (or shows) the toolbar below.

From left to right: Download the album's photos, subscribe to the album, upload photos, email photos to the album, and tell a friend. As shown here, some buttons might be disabled, depending on the album's publishing options.

To view a larger version of a photo, click its thumbnail. When viewing a large version, you have the option to download just that photo (if the publisher has allowed downloads).

View the gallery in different ways.

Change the page background color and adjust thumbnail sizes.

Notes and Tips

The index page. In the upper-left corner of a gallery page is a large button with your MobileMe name; click it, and you see a visual table of contents for all the albums you've published. Each album has its own thumbnail, and you can skim across the thumbnails to see its photos.

When publishing a gallery album, you can prevent it from appearing on the index page. In the Settings dialog box, click the

Show Advanced button, then check the box labeled *Hide album on my Gallery page*.

Why bother? Maybe you've published an album that, for privacy reasons, you don't want to appear on your main index page. Hide the gallery, and folks will have to know its Web address in order to view it.

Other ways to view galleries. You can view Web galleries using the Safari browser

on an iPhone or iPod touch—they appear in a special format for the small screen.

You can also view galleries with an Apple TV. From Apple TV's main menu, choose Photos > MobileMe > Add MobileMe Gallery, then enter the name of the MobileMe subscriber whose gallery you want to view.

Controlling Access to Albums

Who gets to see your albums? You decide when publishing the album, or afterwards. Choose one of these options from the Album Viewable By pop-up menu.

Everyone. Any stranger who finds your gallery pages can see the album.

Only me. Only you—to see the album, you must type your MobileMe account name and password.

Aunt Fern. Okay, it doesn't say that. But you can specify a name and password that visitors must type to see the album. To create a name and password for the album, choose Edit Names and Passwords. In the next dialog box, click the plus sign, and type a name and password. Give that name and password to everyone who needs to see the album.

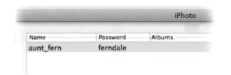

Uploading by Email

When you set up a gallery album to allow uploads via email, MobileMe gives you a "secret" email address for that album. To see the address, select the album in your MobileMe Gallery list—the address appears in the upper-right corner of the iPhoto window. Give this email address to your friends, and they can add photos via email.

jimheid-83pq@gallery.mac.com

To upload a photo via email, send the photo as an attachment to the album's secret email address. The email's Subject field becomes the photo title. You can send multiple photos in one email, if you like.

The iPhone angle. You can use the secret email address to upload photos from an iPhone, but there's an easier way that eliminates pecking out the address.

On your iPhone, display the photo you want to upload. Tap the [icon] button, then tap Send to MobileMe. In the next screen, tap the name of the album where you want the photo to be stored.

Editing a Photo from a Subscription

Normally, iPhoto doesn't let you edit a photo from an album that you've subscribed to. If you open the photo in edit view, all the tools are disabled.

The workaround is easy: Add the photo to an album in your iPhoto library. Then, select the photo in that album and open it in edit view.

A Sampling of Web Gallery Ideas

You might simply use gallery albums to share photos with friends and family without having to use email. But the possibilities go beyond that. Here are a few ideas to get you thinking.

Following along. Hitting the road? Set up a gallery album that allows email uploads from you alone, then email photos as you go—from your iPhone, if

you like. Friends can follow your progress by visiting the gallery page. They can even subscribe to the album to get automatic updates in iPhoto or in an RSS newsreader.

A group effort. Attending a party or any event where cameras are out in force? Set up a gallery album that allows email uploads from anyone, then send

the "secret" email address to the partygoers. (Better yet, create the album *before* the party, and print the email address on the invitation.)

When the partygoers return home, they can email their favorite shots to the gallery or use the gallery's Upload button. The result: a collaborative album.

A kid's world. Want to share photos of the kid? Create a gallery album with restricted access, then give the name and password to folks who deserve to receive them. Set up the album to allow downloads so that grandparents can make their own prints.

Sharing Photos on Facebook

Facebook is one of the most popular social networking sites on the Internet, a place with nearly 200 million members, most of them ex-classmates, ex-girlfriends, or ex-boyfriends of yours.

Okay, I'm joking about that last part, but it is true that millions of people use Facebook to connect with old friends in addition to making new friends and staying in touch with colleagues and family.

You can do a lot of different things on Facebook: post links to interesting Web sites you've seen, join groups and discuss topics you care about, play games, give virtual gifts (I prefer real ones, thank you), and peck out short status messages that let your Facebook friends know what's on your mind.

You can also publish photos, and that's what we're here to talk about. iPhoto lets you publish photos from your iPhoto library directly to your Facebook account. You can control who is able to see the photos, from everyone on Facebook to just your friends.

iPhoto also helps put the *face* in Facebook. For example, if you've named the faces in a photo, iPhoto automatically adds those names to the photo's tags on Facebook. (A *tag* in Facebook is like a keyword in iPhoto: an information tidbit that helps categorize a photo.)

As I describe on these pages, the conduit between iPhoto and Facebook is a two-way street. Here's how to get your photos in front of all those ex-classmates.

Facebook Publishing Essentials

To get the most out of the iPhoto-Facebook connection, it helps to understand a couple of essential concepts.

Getting set up. When you publish from iPhoto to Facebook for the first time, you need to enter the email address and password that you use to log in to Facebook. To avoid having to supply that information each time you publish photos, check the box labeled *Keep me logged in to iPhoto Uploader.*

Important: After typing your login information, be sure to click the blue Login button. If you click the Close button instead, you won't actually log in to Facebook.

Faces information. Facebook can notify people via email when you upload photos containing them. This works nicely with the Faces feature in iPhoto—*if* you set it up to begin with.

The process begins at the Faces corkboard. Select the tile of the person, then click the little *i* button to flip the tile over. Type the person's full name and email address in the fields.

Important: Be sure to type the person's name and email address exactly as they're set up on Facebook. (To verify that information, go to Info tab on the person's profile page.) If you type a variation of the name or a different email address, Facebook won't notify the person when you upload a photo of him or her.

Publishing Photos to Facebook

When you publish to Facebook, iPhoto creates a new album on Facebook for the photos. Even if you publish just one photo, iPhoto creates a new album for it.

Step 1. Select the photos you want to publish.

You can select several photos, an entire event or album, a tile on the Faces corkboard, or just one photo.

Step 2. Click the Facebook button.

Facebook Privacy Options

With this Option	Photos Can Be Viewed by
Everyone	Your friends and people on your networks, as well as friends of anyone who is tagged in the photos.
Friends of Friends	Your friends and their friends, even if they aren't your friends.
Only Friends	Only your friends. This is the most restrictive option, and the one I often prefer to use.

Step 3. Choose publishing options, then click Publish.

iPhoto uses the name or event containing the photo as the name of the new album on Facebook. If you select someone's tile on the Faces corkboard, iPhoto uses that person's name. **Tip:** You can rename the album after you publish it, as described on the following page.

Control who can see the photos (see the table at left).

Have more than one Facebook account? To switch between them, use this button.

A published album appears in the Facebook area of the Library list.

If you select the album, its photos appear, with the Facebook address of the album above them. To open the album in your Web browser, click the address.

Family Reunion
http://www.facebook.com/album.php?aid=10042

Tips for Facebook Publishing

Editing a Published Album

You can add photos to, and remove them from, a published album. And you can do it using iPhoto or your Web browser.

Editing an album in iPhoto. To add more photos, drag them to the album's name in the Facebook area of the Library list.

Click the ⌀ button next to the album's name, and iPhoto connects to Facebook and updates the published album.

To rename an album, edit its name in the Facebook area, then click the ⌀ button.

Similarly, you can edit a photo—crop it or adjust its exposure, for example—that you've published. Select the album in the Facebook list, then open the photo in edit view. When you finish, click the ⌀ button to update the album on Facebook.

To remove a photo from a Facebook album, select the album in the Facebook list. Next, select the photo and press the

Delete key. Click the album's ⌀ button to update the online album.

Editing an album in Facebook. You can also use your Web browser to edit an album directly in Facebook—adding, removing, and changing the order of photos. It's easier to use iPhoto, but maybe you want to work on an album using your Windows PC while at the office. (Hey, that's why I call it *social not-working*.)

When you return to iPhoto and click the album's ⌀ button, iPhoto updates the album in the Facebook list, downloading photos you added and removing photos you deleted.

Changing an album's settings. Having second thoughts about allowing people who might not be your Facebook friends to see photos in an album? Change the settings. Select the published album in the Facebook portion of the Library list, then click the Settings button in the lower-right corner of the iPhoto window. Change the privacy settings as described on page 113.

Deleting an album. To delete an album and its photos from Facebook, select the album's name in the Facebook area of

the Library list, then press the Delete key. When iPhoto displays its "are you sure?" dialog box, click Delete. As is always the case in iPhoto, deleting an album doesn't delete photos from your iPhoto library; it just nixes the album.

If you added more photos to the album using your Web browser (rather than iPhoto), iPhoto asks if you'd like to import those photos into your library before deleting the album. Such a thoughtful program.

Removing Your Account

If you want iPhoto to forget you even have a Facebook account—maybe because you want to sign in using a different Facebook account—click any published album in the Facebook list, then click the Settings button. Finally, click the Remove Account from iPhoto button.

Removing your Facebook account from iPhoto doesn't delete any albums you published on Facebook.

From Facebook to Faces

In Facebook, people who view a photo can use their browsers to add tags that identify the people in the photo.

Click on people's faces in the photo to tag them.

When you sync that photo's album with iPhoto by clicking its 🔄 button, iPhoto reads those tags and passes them on to its Faces feature.

The next time you open that photo in naming view (that is, by selecting the photo and clicking the Name button), you'll see something new: a label for that person's face.

Notice that the label contains the Facebook logo. This is iPhoto's way of saying, "Hey, someone on Facebook added a name tag for this photo. Because the Internet is full of ex-classmates and other crazies, I'm not going to take that at face value. (Get it?) So I'll put the Facebook logo here to let you know this isn't a label that you created. And by the way, until you say this is legit, I'm not going to put a new tile for this person on the corkboard."

What next? To accept the label, click the Facebook logo, fine-tuning the spelling of the name if you like. The Facebook logo disappears, and iPhoto creates a faces tile for that person on the corkboard.

Caleb

Now (or later) you can go through your library and confirm that person in other photos using the maneuvers on pages 40–45.

Another Way to Publish to Facebook

Facebook offers a free plug-in for iPhoto that lets you publish albums. The Facebook Exporter for iPhoto, as it's called, lacks the slick ties with the Faces feature in iPhoto, nor does it provide the two-way conduit that iPhoto provides—the ability to edit an album on Facebook and have your changes reflected in iPhoto.

But Facebook's exporter does have some unique talents, including more control over privacy settings: you can specify that only certain friends may view an album, for example. And if your photos contain captions, the Facebook exporter uploads them, too. iPhoto, by comparison publishes only photo titles.

I've linked to the Facebook exporter's download page at www.macilife.com/iphoto. If you publish photos to Facebook frequently—and you won't miss the integration with iPhoto's Faces feature—give it a try.

Sharing Photos on Flickr

For a serious amateur photographer, there's no better place than Flickr for inspiration and encouragement. Publish your photos, and they become part of your *photostream*—Flickr lingo for your library. Give your photos *tags*—similar to iPhoto keywords—that help you and other Flickr members search. Organize photos into *sets*, which are like albums in iPhoto.

To help people find your shots, submit them to *groups* that deal with subjects relevant to the photos. There are groups for photos of dogs, cats, bridges, food, and, really, anything you can imagine.

Add other Flickr members as *contacts* so you can easily keep an eye on their photos. Comment on each other's images, and add photos you like to your *favorites* so you can go back and enjoy them again. And visit the Explore area to swoon over the most popular of the many thousands of photos that are published on Flickr every single minute.

For a casual photographer, Flickr is a great way to share photos with friends and family. Privacy controls enable you to restrict access to those Flickr contacts whom you've designated as friend or family.

iPhoto lets you publish photos to Flickr with a couple of clicks. A Flickr account is free, but a "Pro" account ($25 per year) gives you much more, including the ability to upload more photos per month. Sign up at flickr.com/upgrade.

Flickr Publishing Essentials

Here are a couple of tidbits you'll want to know before beaming photos from iPhoto to Flickr.

Getting set up. As with Facebook publishing, the first time you go to publish photos on Flickr, you need to take a couple of steps to put Flickr and iPhoto on speaking terms.

Click the Set Up button, and iPhoto switches you to your browser, which opens the Yahoo sign-in page. (Flickr is owned by Yahoo.) After you sign in, a Flickr page appears with a big blue button on it.

OK, I'LL ALLOW IT

Click this button, and another Flickr page notifies you that you successfully authorized "iPhoto Uploader." Now you can return to iPhoto and actually publish something.

How iPhoto publishes to Flickr. I mentioned at left that Flickr lets you organize photos into *sets*, much as iPhoto lets you organize photos into albums.

When you publish something on Flickr, iPhoto creates a new set and adds the photos to it. If you selected just one photo, iPhoto creates a new set for just that photo. And that's a little strange: most of the time, when a Flickr member uploads just one photo, he or she either adds it to an existing set, or doesn't put it in a set at all.

If you think you'll frequently publish only one photo at a time to Flickr—and that you might not always want the photos you publish to be in sets—you might want to investigate some other Flickr publishing options, particularly the one I recommend on page 119.

Check out my Flickr photos.
www.flickr.com/jimheid

Publishing Photos to Flickr

Step 1. Select the photos you want to publish.

You can select several photos, an entire event or album, a tile on the Faces corkboard, or just one photo.

Step 2. Click the Flickr button.

Step 3. Choose publishing options, then click Publish.

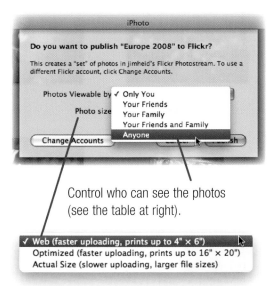

Control who can see the photos (see the table at right).

✓ Web (faster uploading, prints up to 4" × 6")
  Optimized (faster uploading, prints up to 16" × 20")
  Actual Size (slower uploading, larger file sizes)

The Web option is best if you don't anticipate wanting to order large prints. (You've got iPhoto for that anyway.) Another plus: choosing Web lessens the chances that someone will steal your photo and use it for a print project—an occasional problem with photos published for public viewing.

A published album appears in the Flickr area of the Library list.

Flickr Privacy Options

With this Option	Photos Can Be Viewed by
Only You	Guess! Consider this option when you want to use Flickr to back up photos you're shooting on the road: upload full-size versions that only you can access.
Your Friends	Flickr contacts whom you've designated as friends. Your other Flickr contacts won't be able to see the photos, nor will any one else.
Your Family	Flickr contacts whom you've designated as family. Your other Flickr contacts won't be able to see the photos, nor will any one else.
Your Friends and Family	Contacts whom you've designated as friend, family, or both.
Anyone	Guess! When you want to share your photos with the world, not just a select group, use this option.

Europe 2008
http://www.flickr.com/photos/jimheid/sets/72157616446386354/ ◉

If you select the album, its photos appear, with the Flickr address of the album above them. Click the address to open the album—or, in Flickr lingo, its *set*—in your Web browser.

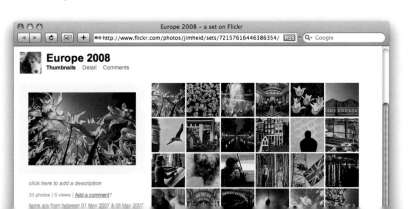

Tips for Flickr Publishing

Notes and Tips

What iPhoto publishes. When you publish a photo, its title becomes the photo's title on Flickr. If you gave the photo a description in iPhoto, the description becomes the photo's caption on Flickr.

iPhoto does not turn your keywords into Flickr tags, however. If you use iPhoto keywords and you'd like them to become Flickr tags when you publish a photo, try the FlickrExport plug-in described on the opposite page.

Editing published photos. When it comes to editing and adding to published albums, the same basic concepts on page 114 also apply to Flickr. If you change a photo in an album you published—edit it to improve its appearance or type a title or description—iPhoto syncs with Flickr and updates the set to which the photo belongs.

Similarly, if you add a photo to a published album, iPhoto uploads it to that album's set. If you delete a photo from a published album, iPhoto removes it from Flickr.

As with Facebook, changes you make using your Web browser are reflected in iPhoto. If you change the title or caption of a photo using your Web browser, iPhoto retrieves the latest text and updates the album. If you add a photo to the set, iPhoto retrieves the photo and adds it to the album. It's all pretty cool.

Locations and Maps

Like geotagging and maps? Flickr was hip to them long before iPhoto was. Flickr taps into the Yahoo maps that its parent company does so well. And as with iPhoto, you can place photos on a map yourself or have Flickr use the geotagging information in photos that have it.

Since you're already taking the time to geotag some photos in iPhoto (right?), you can have iPhoto pass that information on to Flickr, which will, in turn, place your photos on your Flickr map.

But this process doesn't happen automatically. To protect your privacy, both iPhoto and Flickr have some location-related features turned off. To have geotagged photos appear on the map in Flickr, follow these steps.

Step 1. In iPhoto, choose iPhoto > Preferences, then click the Web button and check the box labeled *Include location information for published photos.*

Step 2. In your Web browser, go to flickr.com/account to display your account page.

Step 3. Click the Privacy and Permissions tab, and scroll down to the *Defaults for new uploads* set of options. You'll find two location-related options there.

Who will be able to see your stuff on a map	Anyone
Import EXIF location data [?]	Yes

In the this example, Flickr is set to show location information to anyone who views a photo. But you can also restrict map access to only yourself, to only contacts, or to only those contacts who are family or friends.

Step 4. Tweak the location settings by clicking the Edit link to their right (not shown at lower left). Specify the map privacy option you want, and then change the *Import EXIF location data* option to read *yes.*

From now on, when you publish a geotagged photo, iPhoto will send its location information to Flickr, which will add the photo to your Flickr map.

Flickr to iPhoto: get lost. iPhoto can ferry location information *to* Flickr, but Flickr doesn't have the ability to send location information *to* iPhoto. That means this: If you use Flickr to geotag a photo that you published using iPhoto, don't expect that photo to suddenly show up in your Places list.

The RSS Angle

If you like to use an RSS newsreader to keep up with the world, you'll love Flickr RSS feeds. Subscribe to someone's photostream, and small thumbnails appear in your newsreader when that person uploads new photos. You can also subscribe to specific tags. Subscribe to the *beach* tag, and your newsreader will show everyone's beach photos as they're uploaded.

Subscribing in iPhoto. You can even subscribe to Flickr RSS feeds in iPhoto

itself. Say you'd like to subscribe to my photo feed. (I'm flattered!) Go to my Flickr page (flickr.com/jimheid), scroll to the bottom of the page, and locate the Subscribe links. Control-click on the one that reads *Latest*, then choose Copy Link from the shortcut menu.

Next, switch to iPhoto, and choose File > Subscribe to Photo Feed. Choose Edit > Paste, then press Return.

My photo feed is added to your Subscriptions list, and iPhoto loads thumbnails of my most recent posts.

And remember, Flickr generates feeds for just about everything, including groups. Want to keep an eye on photos added to the Standard Poodle group? Subscribe to its feed. And by the way, you're my kind of person.

Power Publishing with FlickrExport

iPhoto's built-in Flickr support is cool and convenient, but it doesn't do everything serious Flickrites need. For more publishing power, try the FlickrExport plug-in from Connected Flow (www.connectedflow.com).

Unlike iPhoto, FlickrExport supports keywords and tags: when you publish a photo, its iPhoto keywords become Flickr tags. Unlike iPhoto, FlickrExport supports groups: add your photos to the groups you belong to by simply clicking check boxes when you publish them.

FlickrExport also has great geotagging support, and it gives you

more control over the size of the images you upload to Flickr. And unlike iPhoto, FlickrExport doesn't automatically create a new set when you publish: you can choose to add a photo to an existing set, to create a new set, or to simply upload the image to your photostream without adding it to one of your sets.

What do you lose by using FlickrExport? The slick, two-way integration that iPhoto's built-in Flickr support provides. But for serious Flickr addicts like me, that's less important than FlickrExport's great support for keywords and groups, not to mention its more sensible

approach to sets. iPhoto's built-in Flickr support is perfect for occasionally publishing an album of photos, but for daily (if not

hourly) Flickr addicts, FlickrExport is the tool of choice.

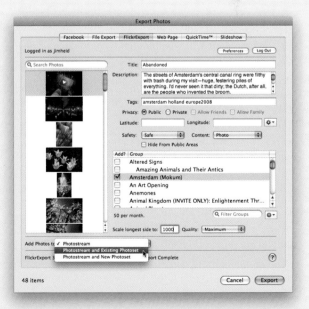

Sharing Photos on a Network

If you have more than one Mac on a network, you can share each Mac's photo library and make it accessible to the other Macs on the network.

Network photo sharing leads to all kinds of possibilities. Keep your "master" photo library on one Mac, and then access it from other Macs when you need to—no need to copy the library from one Mac to another and worry about which library is the most current.

Don't like centralization? Embrace anarchy: let everyone in the family have his or her own photo library, and then use sharing to make the libraries available to others.

Have an AirPort-equipped laptop Mac? Sit on the sofa (or at poolside) and show your photos to friends and family. Or take your laptop to their house and browse their libraries. Network sharing, a laptop Mac, and AirPort form the ultimate portable slide projector.

You can choose to share an entire photo library or only some albums. And you can require a password to keep your kids (or your parents) out of your library.

Activating Sharing

To share your photo library with other Macs on a network, choose Preferences from the iPhoto menu, click the Sharing button, and then click the Share My Photos check box.

To have iPhoto display the names of shared libraries it finds on the network, check this box.

You can share your entire library or only selected albums. To share a specific album, click its check box.

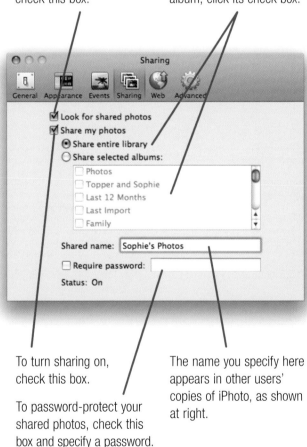

To turn sharing on, check this box.

To password-protect your shared photos, check this box and specify a password.

The name you specify here appears in other users' copies of iPhoto, as shown at right.

Accessing Shared Photos

To access shared photos, choose Preferences from the iPhoto menu, click the Sharing button, and be sure the Look for Shared Photos box is checked. iPhoto scans your network and, if it finds any shared photo libraries, adds their names to the Shares area of the Library list.

To view a shared library, click its name.

To view albums in a shared library, click the little triangle next to the library's name.

To disconnect from a shared library (perhaps to reduce traffic on your network), click the Eject button.

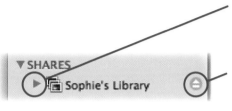

Working with Shared Photos

Searching Limits

You can use the Search box to look for photos in a shared library—within limits. You can search for text in a shared photo's title or description, and you can search by date, but you can't search for keywords.

Slide Show Music

You can view an instant slide show of a shared album, but if the shared album has music assigned to it, you won't hear that music. Instead, iPhoto plays the music for whatever theme you choose.

But here's an interesting twist: you can temporarily assign a song or playlist from *your* local iTunes library to a *shared* album. Just use the techniques described on page 96.

When you assign local music to a shared album, iPhoto doesn't save your assignment. If you disconnect from the shared album and then reconnect, it's back to whatever your chosen theme's song happens to be.

Just Looking

You can view shared photos, and you can email them, order prints, and display a basic slide show. But you can't edit or print shared photos, nor can you send them to iWeb or access them from the photo browsers in the other iLife programs.

To perform these tasks, copy the shared photos you want to your local iPhoto library: select the photos, then drag them to the Library item or to an album.

And what about adding shared photos to slide show projects, calendars, cards, or books? You can do it: if you drag a photo to one of these items in your Library list, iPhoto imports the photo, adds it to your local library, and then adds it to the item.

Note: If you copy shared photos to your library using any of these techniques, iPhoto does not copy the photos' keywords to your local library. If you want to copy some photos to your local library and preserve this information, burn the photos to a CD or DVD (see page 150) and then copy the photos from the CD or DVD to your library.

Folders and Shared Libraries

If you store albums in folders, as I suggest on page 61, you'll be in for an unpleasant surprise when you connect to your library from a different Mac. iPhoto doesn't display the individual albums within a folder. Instead, it simply displays the name of the folder containing the albums. If you select the folder's name, you'll see the photos in *all* of the albums contained in that folder.

The unfortunate moral: when you want to be able to connect to a specific album from a different Mac, don't store that album in a folder.

Printing Photos

Internet photo sharing is great, but hard copy isn't dead. You might want to share photos with people who don't have computers. Or, you might want to tack a photo to a bulletin board or hang it on your wall—you'll never see "suitable for framing" stamped on an email message.

iPhoto makes hard copy easy. If you have a photo-inkjet printer, you can use iPhoto to create beautiful color prints in a variety of sizes. This assumes, of course, that your photos are both beautiful and in color.

When printing your photos, you can choose from several formatting options, called *themes*. You can produce standard prints, but you can also choose themes with elegant borders and mat designs.

Want even more control? A click of the mouse gives it to you. Adjust a photo's appearance, add a text caption, choose different background styles, and more.

So go ahead and beam your photos around the world on the Internet. But when you want something for your wall (or your refrigerator door), think ink.

Printing Standard Prints

A standard print contains just the photo, with no ornamental borders or mats.

Step 1. Select the photo or photos you want to print.

Step 2. Choose File > Print.

Step 3. Choose printing options, then click Print.

For a look at other printing themes, see the opposite page.

Adjust the photo's appearance, add a caption, and more (see page 126).

If you selected multiple photos, you can preview each print by clicking the arrows.

Choose your printer here.

Choose paper and quality settings. For highest quality, choose an option with Fine in its name.

Specify the size of the paper you're using.

Specify the size of the print you want (see below).

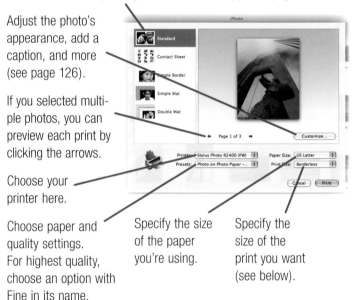

Notes and Tips

Choosing a print size. Most of the time, you'll want a photo to fill the page. But you can also choose a print size that is smaller than the paper size you've chosen. A small image floating within a large expanse is a common framing technique.

Another reason to choose a small print size is to get more than one photo on a sheet of paper—to shoehorn a couple of 4- by 6-inch prints onto a letter-sized sheet, for example (see page 126).

Going borderless. To produce borderless prints, your printer must support borderless printing and you must choose a borderless paper option using the Paper Size pop-up menu.

Beyond Standard Prints

With the print themes in iPhoto, you can produce prints with borders, mats, and more. And by clicking the Customize button in the Print dialog box, you can personalize the themes to match your photos and tastes. For details on customizing print jobs, see the following pages.

Contact Sheet

Prints numerous photos on a page—a handy quick-reference to the photos in an event, album, face, or place. Select multiple photos (or one of the aforementioned items) before choosing Print.

Customizing: Change the background of the page as well as how many images appear across each row. Print titles, captions, dates, and exposure information beneath thumbnails.

Simple Border

Adds a wide border around the image.

Customizing: Change the border style and choose from several layouts, some with text captions and multiple photos on a page.

Single Mat

Simulates the stiff cardboard mat that a framing shop uses to accent a photo and set it off from its frame. The mat has a bevel-cut opening through which the photo appears.

Customizing: Choose from 26 mat colors and styles. Add a white border inside the mat. Choose from several layouts, some with text captions and multiple photos on a page.

Double Mat

Simulates a framing technique that involves using two mats to provide a richer look. A top mat has a large opening that reveals a bottom mat, whose smaller opening reveals the photo.

Customizing: Choose from 26 mat colors and numerous border styles. Choose from several layouts, some with text captions and multiple photos on a page.

Customizing a Print Job

For creating basic prints, the steps on the previous pages are all you need. But you can go beyond the basics to customize many aspects of a print job.

Change the eye candy. Every print theme lets you add a text caption and choose various design layout options. Even the Standard theme provides customizing opportunities, including the ability to print borders and text captions.

Adjust the photo. Here's one of those "local editing" opportunities I discussed back on page 66. You can crop a photo and adjust its exposure, sharpness, and other settings for just a single print—no need to edit the original (and thus change the photo's appearance elsewhere, such as in a slide show).

Print Settings View at Glance

To customize a print job, click the Customize button in the Print dialog box. This opens iPhoto's *print settings view*.

To print multiple photos at once, select them before choosing Print. Use the buttons to the left of the thumbnails to switch between viewing pages (shown here) and the photos used in them.

Reposition a photo within the print area (see opposite page).

Move to the previous or next page in the job.

Apply your settings and print the photos.

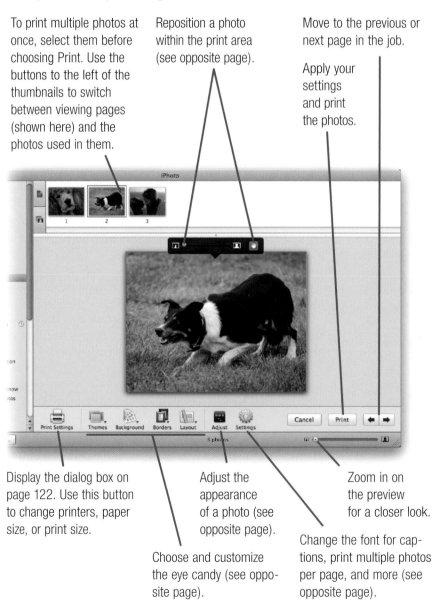

Display the dialog box on page 122. Use this button to change printers, paper size, or print size.

Choose and customize the eye candy (see opposite page).

Adjust the appearance of a photo (see opposite page).

Zoom in on the preview for a closer look.

Change the font for captions, print multiple photos per page, and more (see opposite page).

Perfecting Your Print

Here are the two most common adjustments you can make—ones from which any print job can benefit.

Adjust "cropping." A photo's proportions rarely match the proportions of the paper size you're using. I don't know of any digital camera whose photos perfectly fit an 8.5- by 11-inch sheet.

With some programs, mismatched proportions yield prints with uneven borders. iPhoto eliminates that problem by enlarging an image until it fits the dimensions of the print size you chose. That gives you nice, even borders (or a

fully borderless print), but at a price: parts of the photo's edges are cut off. In this example, iPhoto cut off part of the dog's legs and tail (ouch).

By positioning a photo within the print area, you can control how the photo is cropped. Click the photo, then use the controls above it to zoom and reposition the photo. You can see the results on the opposite page: I dragged the dog (gently!) to fix the unwanted leg surgery.

Adjust appearance. To adjust exposure, contrast, and other image settings, select the photo and click the Adjust button. The Adjust panel, shown on the opposite page, is similar to its counterpart in edit view (pages 74–83), but changes you make here apply only to this print job.

Sharpen up. The single best adjustment you can make is to sharpen. As I said on page 166, ink-jet printers introduce some softness, and sharpening can help. Don't be afraid to crank the sharpness way up—even to 100 percent. Make some before-and-after prints and judge for yourself.

Tip: The one downside of making "local" image adjustments is that iPhoto doesn't save your settings. If you want to make another print a week later using the same settings, you'll have to recreate them by hand. If you anticipate wanting to repeat a print job, jot down the Adjust panel settings you've made.

More Ways to Customize

Use the Background, Borders, and Layout pop-up menus to explore each theme's design options. Here are some tips.

Add a caption. To print a text caption at the bottom of a print, use the Layout pop-up menu to choose a layout with text.

Type the text below the photo. To change the font and size of the entire caption, click Settings. To mix and match fonts within the caption, use the Fonts panel. For details and tips, see page 138.

Multi-photo layouts. Most theme layouts provide options that print two or more photos on a page.

But what if you selected only one photo before choosing Print?

No problem—just add more photos to the print job. When you open print settings view, an item named Printing appears in your Recent list. To add photos to the print job, drag their thumbnails to the Printing item.

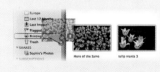

Then, click the Printing item. iPhoto automatically creates additional pages for the new

photos, but you can rearrange the photos as you see fit. To remove a photo from a page, select it and press Delete. To see all the photos in the print job, click the 🖼 button in the thumbnail browser.

Mix and match settings. Normally, when you change a print background or border, iPhoto applies the change to *all* the pages in the print job. But you can also apply changes on a page-by-page basis: just hold down the Option key while choosing a background or border.

Printing Tips and Troubleshooting

Multiple Copies

By tweaking a few print settings, you can print multiple copies of a photo on a single sheet of paper. Have a cute kid photo that you want to send around? Print multiple 4- by 6-inch photos on a letter- or legal-sized sheet, then cut them apart.

Step 1. Select the photo and choose File > Print.

Step 2. Choose the paper size you're using, such as Letter or Legal.

Step 3. From the Print Size pop-up menu, choose a smaller size, such as 3 x 5 or 4 x 6.

Step 4. Click the Customize button.

Step 5. In print settings view, click the Settings button.

Step 6. From the Photos Per Page pop-up menu, choose Multiple of the Same Photo Per Page, then click OK.

Step 7. Click the Print button.

Tips: iPhoto can print guides to help you cut the photos apart. In the Settings dialog box, click the Show Crop Marks box.

You can also use this technique to print multiple photos (but not the same one) on a single sheet of paper. Select several photos, then perform steps 1–5. In Step 6, choose the option labeled Multiple Photos Per Page.

Kill the Cropping

On previous pages, I discussed how iPhoto prevents uneven borders by enlarging a photo until it fills the paper size you've chosen. And I described how you can use print settings view to zoom and pan a photo to crop it as you see fit.

But what if you don't want any cropping at all? Easy. In print settings view, Control-click on a photo and, from the shortcut menu, choose Fit Photo to Frame Size.

Your print will almost certainly have some uneven borders, but it will contain every precious pixel of your original image. You can trim the borders by hand after printing.

Save a PDF

Remember that you can save a print job as a PDF file and use it elsewhere, such as in an iPhoto or iDVD slide show, a print project, or an iMovie project. After customizing the print job, click the Print button. In the final print dialog box (the one you see when you're actually ready to commit ink to paper), use the options in the PDF pop-up menu to create a PDF. To create a PDF and add it to your iPhoto library in one fell swoop, choose Save PDF to iPhoto.

PDF to photographic print. You can combine this PDF technique with Apple's online print-ordering service (page 128). The result: the ability to design a fancy print and then have it printed by Apple.

Design a print, first making sure to choose a paper size that corresponds to the print size you'll order. (For example, if you plan to order an 8 by 10, choose the 8 x 10 paper size.)

Next, use print settings view to choose mats and borders and adjust the photo as desired. Click the Print button, then choose the Save PDF to iPhoto option.

When iPhoto has finished importing the PDF, select it and click the Order Prints button. Complete your print order as described on page 128.

When Prints Disappoint

When your prints aren't charming, read on.

Verify paper choices. In iPhoto's Print dialog box, be sure to choose the preset that matches the type of paper you're using and the quality you're seeking. It's easy to overlook this step and end up specifying plain paper when you're actually using pricey photo paper.

Check ink. Strange colors? Check your printer's ink supply. Many printers include diagnostic software that reports how much ink remains in each cartridge.

Clean up. The nozzles in an inkjet printer can become clogged, especially if you don't print every day. If you're seeing odd colors or a horizontal banding pattern, use your printer's cleaning mode to clean your ink nozzles. Most printers can print a test page designed to show when the nozzles need cleaning. You may have to repeat the cleaning process a few times.

Preserving Your Prints

After all the effort you put into making inkjet prints, it may disappoint you to learn that they may not last long.

Many inkjet prints begin to fade within a year or two—even faster when displayed in direct sunlight. Most printer manufacturers now offer pigment-based inks and archival papers that last for decades, but pigment-based printers are pricier than the more common dye-based printers.

If you have a dye-based printer, consider using a paper rated for longer print life. Epson's ColorLife paper, for example, has a much higher permanence rating than Epson's Premium Glossy Photo Paper.

To prolong the life of any print, don't display it in direct sunlight. Frame it under glass to protect it from humidity and pollutants. (Ozone pollution, common in cities, is poison to an inkjet print.)

Allow prints to dry for at least a few (preferably 24) hours before framing them or stacking them atop each other.

For long-term storage, consider using acid-free sleeves designed for archival photo storage.

Finally, avoid bargain-priced paper or ink from the local office superstore. Print preservation guru Henry Wilhelm (www.wilhelm-research.com) recommends using only premium inks and papers manufactured by the same company that made your printer.

Is all this necessary for a print that will be tacked to a refrigerator for a few months and then thrown away? Of course not. But when you want prints to last, these steps can help.

To learn more about digital printing, read Harald Johnson's *Mastering Digital Printing, Second Edition* (Muska & Lipman, 2005).

Ordering Prints

Inkjet photo printers provide immediate gratification, but not without hassles. Paper and ink are expensive. Getting perfectly even borders is next to impossible, and getting borderless prints can be equally frustrating.

There is another path to hard copy: ordering prints through iPhoto. Choose the Order Prints command, specify the print sizes you want, and iPhoto transmits your photos over the Internet to Kodak's print service. The prints look great, and because they're true photographic prints, they can last longer than inkjet prints.

You can also order prints from other online photofinishers, many of whom also offer free online photo albums and other sharing services. Using these services isn't as straightforward as clicking a button in iPhoto, but it isn't difficult, either. Many services, such as Shutterfly (www.shutterfly.com), offer software that simplifies transferring your shots. The Flickr online photo-sharing site also offers print-ordering services.

And some services offer output options that iPhoto doesn't, such as mouse pads, T-shirts, and even photo cookies. For links to some online photofinishers, see www.macilife.com/iphoto.

To Order Prints

Step 1. Select the photos you want prints of, then choose File > Order Prints.

Step 2. Specify the sizes and quantities you want, then click Buy Now.

The yellow triangle of doom (⚠) indicates that the photo doesn't have enough resolution for good quality at that size; see the sidebar at right for details.

Want a 4 by 6 of every photo you selected? Specify the quantity here.

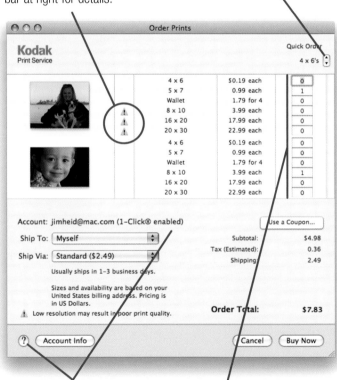

To order prints, you must have an Apple ID account with 1-Click ordering enabled. For help, click the help button.

Specify how many prints you want for each size.

Tip: Order often? Add a button to the iPhoto window. Choose View > Show in Toolbar > Order Prints.

Notes and Tips

Create a Temporary Album

If you're ordering prints from many different events, create an album and use it to hold the photos you want to print. Give the album an obvious name, such as *Pix to Print*. This makes it easier to keep track of which photos you're printing. After you've placed your order, you can delete the album.

As an alternative to creating an album, you can flag photos you want to print. After you've done so, click the Flagged item, then choose Order Prints.

Cropping Concerns

The proportions of most standard print sizes don't match the proportions of a typical digital camera image. As a result, Kodak automatically crops a photo to fill the print size you've ordered.

The problem is, automatic cropping may lop off part of the image that's important to you. If you don't want your photos cropped by a machine, do the cropping yourself, using iPhoto's edit view, before ordering. Use the Constrain pop-up menu to specify the proportions you want.

If you plan to order prints in several sizes, you may have even more work to do. A 5 by 7 print has a different *aspect ratio* than a 4 by 6 or an 8 by 10. If you want to order a 5 by 7 *and* one of these other sizes, you need to create a separate version of each picture—for example, one version cropped for a 5 by 7 and another cropped for an 8 by 10.

To create separate versions of a picture, make a duplicate of the original photo for each size you want (select the photo and press ⌘-D), and then crop each version appropriately.

If you crop a photo to oddball proportions—for example, a narrow rectangle—Kodak's automatic cropping will yield a weird-looking print. If you have an image-editing program, such as Adobe Photoshop Elements, here's a workaround. In the imaging program, create a blank image at the size you plan to print (for example, 5 by 7 inches). Then open your cropped photo in the imaging program and paste it into this blank image. Save the resulting image as a JPEG file (use the Maximum quality setting), add it to iPhoto, and then order your print.

Resolution's Relationship to Print Quality

If you're working with low-resolution images—ones that you've cropped heavily or shot at a low resolution, for example—you may see iPhoto's dreaded low-resolution warning icon (⚠) when ordering prints or a book.

This is iPhoto's way of telling you that an image doesn't have enough pixels—enough digital information—to yield a good-quality print at the size that you've chosen.

Don't feel obligated to cancel a print job or an order if you see this warning. But do note that

you may see some fuzziness in your prints.

The table here lists the minimum resolution an image should have to yield a good print at various sizes.

Print Sizes and Resolution

For This Print Size (Inches)	Image Resolution Should be at Least (Pixels)
Wallet	640 by 480
4 by 6	768 by 512
5 by 7	1075 by 768
8 by 10	1280 by 1024
16 by 20	2272 by 1704

Creating Photo Books

Something special happens to photos when they're pasted into the pages of a book. Arranged in a specific order and accompanied by captions, photos form a narrative: they tell a story.

Put away your paste. With iPhoto's book mode, you can create beautiful, full-color books in several sizes and styles. Arrange your photos in the order you want, adding captions and descriptive text if you like. Choose from a gallery of design *themes* to spice up your pages with layouts that complement your subject. Even add gorgeous travel maps that tap into your Places list to show where your photos were taken.

When you're done, iPhoto connects to the Internet and transfers your book to Apple's printing service, where the book is printed on a four-color digital printing press (a Hewlett-Packard Indigo, if you're curious), and then bound and shipped to you.

iPhoto books are great for commemorating a vacation, wedding, or other special event. They're also open for business: architects, artists, photographers, and designers use iPhoto to create spectacular portfolios, proposals, and brochures.

So don't just print those extra-special shots. Publish them.

Book Publishing at a Glance

The most efficient way to create a book is to first add photos to an album, and then tell iPhoto to create a book based on that album. Here's an overview of the process.

Step 1.

Create a new album containing the photos you want to publish (page 58). Arrange the photos in approximately the same order that you want them to appear in the book. (You can always change their order later.)

Step 2.

Select the album in the Albums list, then click the Book button or the Add button ⊞.

Book

Step 3.

Choose a book type and a theme, then click Choose. For a summary of the types of books you can order, see the sidebar at right.

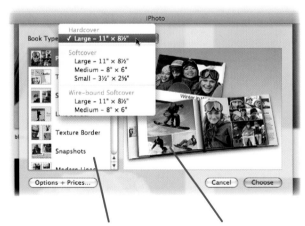

Most book types provide numerous themes. All themes provide coordinated color schemes and several page designs.

Large hardcover books have a dust jacket with a cover and inside flaps that you can customize.

Step 4.

Lay out the book.

You can have iPhoto place the photos for you (the autoflow mode), or you can manually place each photo yourself (see the following pages).

Switch between viewing page thumbnails (shown here) or photos that you haven't yet placed in the book (page 134).

Display your book's pages as a slide show (page 140).

To reposition a photo within its book frame, click the photo and drag the size control and/or the photo itself (page 141).

To jump to a page, click its thumbnail. To rearrange pages, drag them left or right (page 135).

You can view and work with two-page spreads (shown here) or one page at a time (page 135).

Switch themes and page designs and perform other layout and design tasks (pages 134–139).

Step 5.

Click **Buy Book** and pay up using your Apple ID (page 15).

Many page designs allow for text, whose type style you can customize (page 138).

For more layout options, Control-click on a photo (page 141).

Move to the previous or next page.

Zoom in on a page for proofreading and fine tuning.

Book Types and Sizes

You can create several kinds of books with iPhoto. To preview the books, explore the options in the pop-up menu shown in Step 3 on the opposite page. The cost of a book depends on the type of book you order and on its number of pages; see apple.com/iphoto.

Hardcover. The classiest book option, and the priciest. Also called a *keepsake* book, it measures 11 inches wide by 8.5

inches tall. The book's title is foil-stamped on a suede-like hard-cover, and a customizable dust jacket protects the entire affair.

Softcover. Available in three sizes: 11 by 8.5 inches, 8 by 6 inches, and 2.6 by 3.5 inches. The tiniest size is sold in packs of three.

Wire-bound softcover. Available in 11 by 8.5 inch and 8 by 6 inch sizes, this softcover variation has a wire binding that lets the book lay flat.

Planning for Publishing

A book project doesn't begin in a page-layout program. It begins with an author who has something to say, and with photo editors and designers who have ideas about the best ways to say it.

When you create a photo book, you wear all of those hats. iPhoto works hard to make you look as fetching as possible in each of them, but you can help by putting some thought into your book before you click the Book button.

What do you want your book to say? Is it commemorating an event? Or is it celebrating a person, place, or thing? Does the book need a story arc—a beginning, a middle, and an ending? Would the book benefit from distinct sections—one for each place you visited, for example, or one for each member of the family?

And no publishing project occurs without a discussion of production expenses. Is money no object? Or are you pinching pennies?

Your answers to these questions will influence the photos you choose, the book designs you use, and the way you organize and present your photos and any accompanying text. The very best time to address these questions isn't before you start your book—it's before you start shooting. If you have a certain kind of book in mind, you can make sure you get the shots you need.

Here's more food for thought.

Questions to Ask

Here's a look at some of the factors that may influence your choice of book sizes and themes.

What Size Book?

The book size you choose will be dictated by your budget and design goals. On a budget? Use the medium-sized or large softcover formats. Want the largest selection of design options? Go large hardcover. Large book sizes are also best when you want to get as many photos as possible on a page.

Your photos may also influence your choice: for example, if you have low-resolution shots and want to present one photo per page, you may need to choose a medium-sized book to get acceptable quality.

How Much Text?

Most photography books contain more than just photos. Will you want text in your book? If so, how much? Some themes provide for more copy than others.

How Many Photos?

Some themes provide for more photos per page than others. The Travel theme provides up to seven; Picture Book, 16; Folio, only two.

Twilight Walk

What Design Options?

Each book size and type provides its own set of themes. Each theme has its own design options, including different color schemes; different ways to arrange photos on each page; and special photo effects and design elements, such as collages and travel maps.

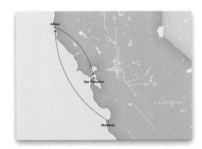

Options to Consider

In this spread, which uses the Travel theme, the left-hand page shows works from the Museé d'Orsay, shown on the right-hand page.

Think about ways to have the left- and right-hand pages comple-ment each other.

The Family Album theme has a warm, sentimental look—perfect for vintage photos.

Don't have high-resolution photos? Consider a medium or small softcover book, or choose page designs with small photo zones or multiple photos per page.

Many themes (including Crayon, shown here) have page designs that allow for text headings and lengthy captions whose formatting you can customize.

In the elegant Folio design, photo titles become headings.

Wire-bound books, available in large and medium softcover sizes, lay flat when opened.

Dust Jacket Decisions

Large hardcover books include a paper dust jacket that can hold text and photos. Besides having front and back covers that you can cus-tomize, dust jackets also have inside flaps that tuck behind the front and back covers.

You can customize these flaps, too. In publishing, it's common for the front flap to describe the book, and for the back flap to describe the author. If there's a lot to say about the book or its subject, the text on the front flap may continue on to the back flap.

Each book theme has several flap layouts: just a photo, text and a photo, just text, and blank. When creating a hardcover book, decide how much you want to talk about your book—and yourself—and choose the appropriate layout.

Book Layout Techniques

Manual or Autoflow?

When you create a book, you can choose to have iPhoto lay out the book automatically by clicking the Autoflow button, or you can take the wheel and drive yourself by dragging photos onto the book's pages. When you create a new book, iPhoto reminds you of these options.

Regardless of the option you choose, iPhoto always creates a book with 20 pages—the minimum a book can contain.

iPhoto also assigns a layout to each page. And that's why I prefer to lay out books manually instead of clicking the Autoflow button. I often want to change the designs that iPhoto has chosen, and if I'm going to do that, I might as well start with a blank slate—why have iPhoto position photos that I'm going to be rearranging anyway?

But that's just me. If you'd rather get immediate results and then fine-tune, click Autoflow. Or mix both approaches. If you want to do something fancy at the beginning of your book—maybe have a full-page photo opposite an introduction text page—lay out those first couple of pages. Then click the Autoflow button to have iPhoto do the rest.

Note that the Autoflow feature adds additional pages to your book if necessary to accommodate the rest of your unplaced photos. Those extra pages will cost you, so if you're watching your production budget, keep an eye on your total page count.

Layout Basics

Each book theme includes numerous *layouts*, each with a different arrangement of text and photos. Some layouts contain just text, some hold just photos, and some hold both.

Choosing a layout. First, navigate to the page you want to change: click the left- or right-arrow buttons or click the page in the thumbnail browser. (If you don't see page thumbnails there, click the ■ button.)

Next, use the Layout pop-up menu to choose a design.

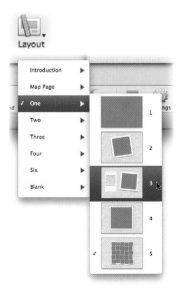

Background options. To change a page's background, use the Background pop-up menu. Background designs vary depending on theme. All themes also let you use a photo as a full-page background; see page 139.

Adding photos. Add photos to the empty frames by dragging them from the thumbnail browser (click the ▣ to see photo thumbnails).

Working with Photos

Adding to a full page. If you drag a photo from the photo browser to a page that already contains photos in each photo frame, iPhoto changes the page type, adding an additional photo frame to accommodate the photo.

With some themes and page designs, iPhoto may add more than one photo frame. For example, in the Picture Book theme, the available page types jump from four photos per page to six. If you add a photo to a fully populated four-photo page, iPhoto switches to the six-photo page type. You can either add a sixth photo or ignore the empty frame. iPhoto will omit it when you order your book.

Incidentally, if a page already has the maximum number of photos supported by that theme, iPhoto won't let you add another one.

Moving to a different page. You can move a photo to a different page. Be sure that your page thumbnails are visible (click the ■ button), then drag the photo to its new page. The same points mentioned previously apply: if the destination page is full, iPhoto may change its page type to accommodate the new photo.

Removing a photo. To remove a photo, select the photo and press the Delete key, or drag the photo up to the photo thumbnails browser. iPhoto moves the photo to the thumbnails area.

You can also remove a photo by Control-clicking on it and choosing Remove Photo from the shortcut menu.

To remove the photo's frame, switch to a page type that provides fewer photos, or simply ignore the empty frame—that's what iPhoto will do when you order your book.

Swapping photos. To swap two photos on a page or spread, simply drag one photo to the other one.

Editing a photo. Need to edit a photo that you've placed on a page? Control-click on the photo and choose Edit Photo from the shortcut menu.

Adding photos from your library. To add additional photos to a book, drag them from your library to the book's name in the Keepsakes list.

Adding and Removing Pages

To add a page, click the Add Pages button. If you're viewing two-page spreads, iPhoto adds a full spread, which is two pages. To add just one page, switch to single-page view (click the ▪ View button).

To insert a new spread or page between two existing pages, use the page thumbnails browser to select the page that you want to precede the new page. For example, to add a new page between pages 4 and 5, select page 4, then click Add Pages.

When you add a page or spread, iPhoto gives the page or pages a layout from the book's current theme, filled with empty photo frames. Customize the layout as desired.

Removing a page. To remove a page, select it in the pages thumbnail browser and press the Delete key. Or, Control-click on a blank area of the doomed page and choose Remove Page from the shortcut menu.

When you delete a page containing photos, iPhoto moves its photos to the photo thumbnail browser so you can use them elsewhere, if you like.

Rearranging Pages

To reorganize your pages, drag their thumbnails left and right in the page thumbnail browser. If you're viewing two-page spreads, you can move spreads back and forth. In the following example, pages 6 and 7 are being moved so they follow pages 8 and 9.

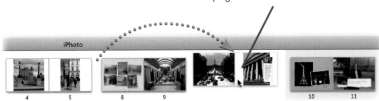

To move individual pages, switch to single-page view. Below, page 4 is being moved so it follows page 5.

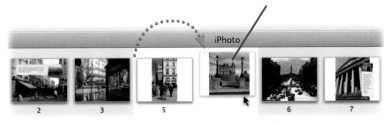

Creating Travel Maps

Many book projects can benefit from a sense of place: the travel book filled with vacation photos, the family reunion book depicting your old stomping grounds, the wedding book with photos from the ski-slope ceremony and the tropical honeymoon. When creating books like these, consider giving your readers some context by adding *travel maps*.

Travel maps are new in iPhoto '09, and they take advantage of the new Places feature. But even if you haven't taken the time to geotag your photos, you can still create travel maps; a handy panel lets you add places to a map even as you create your book.

Every theme in iPhoto provides for a travel map, but the largest variety of map designs is in the Travel Book theme. (Imagine that!) The Travel Book theme provides 20 map designs, ranging from simple, full-page maps to small maps that accompany a full-page photo and some text.

In any theme, you can add gracefully curving arrows or straight lines between destinations: perfect for when your travels took to you more than one place. You can change the font of text on maps, choose between two arrow styles, show and hide the names of countries and other regions, and much more.

Creating a Map

Step 1. Navigate to the page where you want the map.

Step 2. From the Layout pop-up menu, choose Map Page, then choose a map style.

Step 3. Create your map: add places, zoom and pan to highlight locations, and more.

To show more or less of the world in the map, drag the zoom slider.

The title you type appears in a corner of the map.

To have travel lines between places, check this box (opposite page).

Each check-marked place appears on the map (opposite page).

To reposition the map, drag within it.

In the Travel Book theme, many map layouts allow for text and photos. Add them using the techniques described on previous pages.

Managing Places on a Map

You can add places to a map and remove them. You can also change the order in which they appear—important if you're adding travel lines.

Adding a place. To add a place, click the ➕ button at the bottom of the map panel, then type the name of the place. If iPhoto knows about that place, it offers suggestions to complete the name for you.

If iPhoto doesn't know about the place, you can look it up on a map. The process is similar to adding a place in the Places feature; for details, see page 48.

Removing a place. To remove a place from the map, select it and click the ➖ button. Or just uncheck the box next to the place name—that way, you can restore the place if you change your mind.

Rearranging places. iPhoto uses the top-to-bottom order of places to add the arrowheads in travel lines. Thus, your first stop (or your point of origination) should appear first in the list, followed by your second stop, and so on. To rearrange places, drag them up and down.

Notes and Tips

Which style? Using the Travel Book theme? Which of the 20 map styles should you use? That depends in part on your book's topic. For a book about a journey, a full-page map is probably in order. For a book about a family reunion or party that happened in one location, a small map that sits within a full-page photo—maybe also with a column of descriptive text—might be ideal.

More than one. Consider using multiple maps in your book. Start your vacation book with a full-page map that shows all your destinations, complete with arrow lines. Then, for each section that you devote to a particular destination, have a small map showing just that destination.

Font fun. To change the font of map text, click the Settings button. The item named Map Title controls the formatting of the text you type in the Title box. The Map Regions item is the text for countries, and the Place Markers item is for cities and other specific locations.

More customizing. Don't want a title? Omit the text in the Title box. For further customizing, Control-click on a map; a pop-up menu lets you remove the compass, omit the shading and textures (creating a flatter-looking map), omit the names of regions (such as countries), and more.

Using maps elsewhere. You can save a map as a PDF and add it to your iPhoto library. This lets you use the map in a slide show, or even a calendar or greeting card. It also lets you mix and match themes: use one of the flashy map designs from the Travel Book theme in a book that you're creating with a different theme.

Choose File > Print. In the From and To boxes, type the page number containing the map. From the PDF pop-up menu, choose Save PDF to iPhoto. When iPhoto has finished creating the PDF, click the Last Import item in the Library list. There's your "map picture"—ready to use like any other photo.

(For more tips on turning book pages into PDFs, see page 141.)

Tips for Creating Books

Formatting Text

You can format your book's text in several ways.

Globally: the Settings button. When you want to change the font iPhoto uses for every occurrence of an element in your book (such as its captions), use the Settings button. **Tip:** Each book theme provides its own text elements, and some provide more than others. The Settings dialog box is a convenient way to see what elements a theme provides.

Locally: the Fonts panel. Typographic consistency is important for a book like the one you're reading, but for a photo book that contains only a few text elements, a bit of variety can be fun. You can format individual text elements—indeed, individual letters, if you want to—by using the Fonts panel. Select the text you want to format, and choose Edit > Font > Show Fonts (⌘-T).

The triangle of doom. You've typed some text or changed text formatting, and suddenly the yellow triangle of doom appears in the text box. iPhoto is telling you that the text won't fit with its current type specs. Either change formatting or delete some text.

More Tips for Text

Here are more textual tips.

Low-rent formatting control. All themes provide at least one Introduction layout. But don't feel obligated to write an introduction. You can adapt the Introduction page to other uses, such as a title page. You can also move items around on the page by using the spacebar or Tab key to bump a line of text to the right, and by pressing Return to move text down. These tricks don't provide page-layout precision, but they work.

Consider a word processor. Planning a lot of text in your book? Consider using your favorite word processor to write and format the text. Then, move the text into iPhoto as needed: select the text you need for a given page, and copy it to the Clipboard. Next, switch to iPhoto, click in the destination text box, and paste. iPhoto even retains your formatting.

This approach lets you take advantage of a word processor's superior editing features, not to mention its Save command—something iPhoto lacks.

Controlling paragraph formatting. iPhoto doesn't provide controls for adjusting the spacing between lines (leading) or paragraph indents. Solution: Use your word processor. Format your text in a word processor, then copy and paste it into the text box on your book page.

Saving custom text styles. You've
pasted in some custom formatting and would like to save it to apply to future books or to other pages in the same book. Here's how.

First, click within the text box that contains the custom text. Then, Control-click and choose Styles from the shortcut menu's Font submenu. In the dialog box that appears, click the Add to Favorites button. In the *next* dialog box, type a name for your custom style, click both check boxes, then click the Add button.

To use that custom style, select the text you want to format, and Control-click on it to summon the shortcut menu. Choose Styles from the Font submenu, then click the Favorite Styles button. Locate and choose your style in the pop-up menu, and click Apply.

Fun with glyphs. Some of Mac OS X's fonts contain beautiful alternative characters, such as ornamental swashes and flourishes. To explore and use these alternative glyphs, choose Typography from the ✱▾ pop-up menu at the bottom of the Fonts panel. Then, explore the options in the Typography panel.

For a good example, choose the Zapfino font, then check out the Stylistic Variants portion of the Typography panel. The Apple Chancery font also has some interesting alternate characters.

Also, many fonts have old-style numerals that lend a classic look, as shown here with the Didot font.

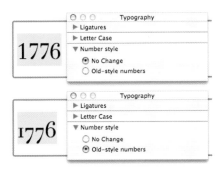

If a font provides old-style numerals, you'll see a Number Style entry in the Typography panel.

Who needs page numbers? Unless you're putting a table of contents or index in your book, you have little reason to print a page number on each page. To remove page numbers, use the Settings dialog box or Control-click on a blank area of a page and make sure that the Show Page Numbers command is unchecked in the shortcut menu.

Adjusting Photos

You can adjust a photo's appearance in the book layout editor. To fine-tune composition, click the photo, then use the controls above the photo to zoom and reposition it.

If you zoom in too far for a given photo's resolution, iPhoto displays the yellow triangle of doom to let you know that you won't get good quality at that zoom setting.

To adjust a photo's exposure or add an effect, click the photo, then click the Adjust button. An adjust panel identical to the one shown on page 124 appears. Add an effect, fine-tune exposure, and make other tweaks without changing the original photo in your library. As with ink-jet prints, adding some sharpening and definition can improve quality.

You can, of course, also open the photo in edit view and do your cropping and exposure adjustments there. But doing so changes the photo everywhere you've used it.

Photo as Background

You can use a photo as the background of a page. Put a photo behind the text that introduces your vacation book. Or use a close-up of a garden as the background for a page of weekend-getaway photos.

Start by clicking the Background pop-up menu and choosing the Photo Background option:

Next, choose a layout and add photos and/or text to the page, as appropriate.

Tip: A busy background photo will overwhelm text or other photos, impairing legibility. Solution: increase the transparency of the background photo. Click the photo, and drag the lower slider to the right until the photo appears faint.

More Tips for Creating Books

Before You Buy

Before you click the Buy Book button to place your order, do one last proofreading pass of any text in your book. And remember, your Mac can help: select the text in a text box, Control-click, and choose Spelling > Spelling and Grammar > Check Document Now.

Placeholder text. Also check to see that you haven't left placeholder text on any pages. (This is the stuff iPhoto inserts for you when you choose a page design that supports text. It usually reads *Insert a description of your book*.) But don't sweat it: if your book contains placeholder text and you click Buy Book, iPhoto warns that the placeholder text won't be printed.

Unused photo frames. Don't worry if any pages have unused (gray) photo frames. iPhoto simply ignores them.

Tip: The fact that iPhoto ignores empty photo frames opens up additional design options. For example, say you're creating a book in the Picture Book theme and you want a page with five photos on it—a page type Picture Book doesn't provide. Solution: choose the six-photo page type, but put only five photos on it.

Preview. To preview your book, Control-click on a blank area of a page and choose Preview Book from the shortcut menu. iPhoto assembles the book and displays its pages in Mac OS X's Preview program.

From Book to Slide Show

iPhoto's book editor view provides a Slideshow button that lets you display the pages of your book as a slide show. This opens up some interesting creative possibilities: you can take advantage of iPhoto's book themes and page designs to create "slides" containing multiple images and text. (In the interest of readability, think twice about using a lot of small text.)

You can also send a "book slide show" to iDVD; while in book-edit view, choose Share > Send to iDVD.

Print It Yourself

iPhoto's Print command is alive and well when you're in book view: you can print some or all of your book for proofreading or to bind it yourself.

Tip: If you know that you'll be printing a book yourself and not ordering it through Apple's print service, create the book in single-sided format. In the book editor, click Settings, then uncheck the Double-sided Pages box.

Printing a specific page. Want to print just one page of a book? Start by expanding the Print dialog box (click the little arrow button to the right of your printer's name). Next, click the left or right arrow under the page thumbnail until you see the page you want to print.

Below the thumbnail, you'll see the current page number and total page count—for example, *5 of 30*. Type the first number in the From and To boxes.

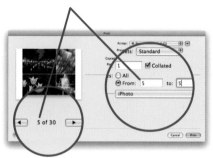

Mirroring a Photo

Want to flip a photo so that it appears "backwards"? Select the photo in its book frame, then Control-click on it and choose Mirror Image from the shortcut menu.

Here's an easy design trick: Add the same photo to the left and right pages of a two-page spread. Then, mirror one of the photos so that the two photos appear to reflect one another.

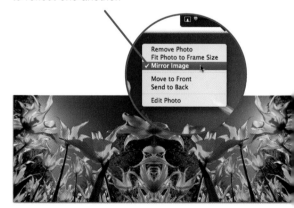

Changing Stacking Order

When you have multiple items on a page, you can change the way they overlap. For example, some themes position photos so they overlap. To change the way two photos overlap, Control-click on a photo and choose Move to Front or Send to Back.

Single-Sided Books

It's worth noting that you can order hardcover books with single-sided pages—just uncheck the Double-Sided Pages box as noted on the opposite page. In a single-sided book, the left-hand page of each spread is blank. That's unlike any coffee-table book I've ever seen, but if it's what you want, iPhoto can accommodate. (Softcover and wire-bound books always have double-sided pages.)

Fun with PDFs

You can perform several PDF-related tricks with your books. For more details on these tricks, see www.macilife.com/iphoto.

Combining book designs. You love one of the page designs from the Family Album theme, but you really want to use the Line Border theme for the bulk of your book. No problem, thanks to Mac OS X's ability to create a PDF file of anything you can print.

Start by creating the page that you'll want to add to a *different* book. For example, if you want to use the Line Border theme for most of your book but the Family Album theme on one page, create the Family Album page.

Next, choose File > Print and navigate to the preview of the page you created, as described on the opposite page. Peck that page number into the From and To boxes of the Print dialog box. Then, from the PDF pop-up menu, choose Save PDF to iPhoto.

After iPhoto creates the PDF, switch over to (or begin) the "main" book, then add the PDF you just created to it. For the page containing the PDF, choose a layout that provides one photo per page. The result: two different themes within one book.

The spread at lower left presents some old photos using the Family Album theme opposite some new photos and the Line Border theme.

Other ways to use book-page PDFs. You can also order a print of a book-page-turned-PDF. When you use the Save PDF to iPhoto option in the Print dialog box, the resulting image has enough resolution to produce a 16 by 20-inch print. So create a fancy page, complete with a travel map if you like, and turn it into a poster.

And because iPhoto considers that book page to be just an ordinary image, you can also use the page image in a slide show, in an iMovie project, or add it to a calendar. Want to create a greeting card containing a travel map? Create the page, save it as a PDF, then add it to a greeting card.

A PDF of the entire book. To create a PDF of your entire book, Control-click on the area outside the book's pages, then choose Save Book as PDF from the shortcut menu. Then what? You decide. Post the PDF on your iWeb site. Include it in the DVD-ROM portion of an iDVD project (page 274). Email it to friends who use Microsoft Windows—just to mess with them.

Creating a Photo Calendar

Store-bought calendars can be gorgeous, but they lack a certain something: *your* photos. Why build your year around someone else's photos when you can build it around your own?

With the calendar-publishing features in iPhoto, you can create calendars containing as few as 12 months and as many as 24. Choose from numerous design themes, each of which formats your photos and the dates of the month in a different way. Then drag photos into your calendar, fine-tuning their cropping and appearance along the way, if you like.

Commercial calendars usually have national holidays printed on them. Yours can, too—and then some. You can add your own milestones to your calendar: birthdays, anniversaries, dentist-appointment reminders. If you use Apple's iCal software, you can even import events from iCal and have them appear in your calendar.

When you're finished, click the Buy Calendar button. iPhoto transfers your photos and design to Apple's printing service, which prints your calendar and ships it to you. A 12-month calendar costs $19.99. Each additional month is $1.49.

And you don't have to postpone your foray into calendar publishing until next year. You can have your calendar begin with any month you like.

The Big Picture

Step 1. The most efficient way to create a calendar is to first add the photos you want to publish to an album.

Tip: To further streamline your layout work, sequence the photos in the album in the same general order in which you want them to appear in the calendar.

Step 2. Click the Calendar button. The Themes panel appears.

Step 3. Choose a theme (click its name to see a preview of its design), then click Choose or press Return.

Have a big year.
Calendars measure 13 inches wide by 10.4 inches high—perfect for hanging on a wall.

Step 4. Specify calendar details, then click OK. Here's your first big opportunity to customize the calendar so it contains dates that are important to you.

How many months? Type a number between 12 and 24 or click the arrow buttons.

When? Choose a starting month and a year.

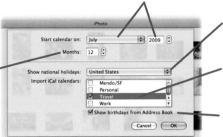

Veterans Day? Deepavali? Queen's Day? Specify your preferred national holiday list, or choose None.

Use iCal? To include iCal dates in your calendar, check the box next to the calendar.

Store birthdays in Mac OS X's Address Book program? You can automatically include them in your calendar.

Step 5. Drag photos into your calendar's pages, or click the Autoflow button.

Switch between viewing calendar thumbnails (shown here) or photos you're using in the calendar (page 144).

Switch views and perform various design tasks (page 144).

Layout for the lazy: click Autoflow, and iPhoto adds photos for you (page 144).

To replace this placeholder text with your own, select the text and type.

View the next or previous month.

Zoom in on a page for proofreading and fine tuning.

Step 6. Step through each month of the calendar, fine-tuning designs and adding custom date items as desired (see the following pages for details and tips).

You can adjust a photo's position within its frame.

Each calendar design offers a variety of photo layouts, some providing space for captions.

Step 7. Click [Buy Calendar] and pay using your Apple ID (page 15).

To add text to a date, click its name and type the text in the box that appears. As page 145 shows, you can also add photos and captions to specific dates.

You can adjust a photo's appearance without affecting the original photo.

Tips for Creating Calendars

Choosing Photos

When creating a calendar, try to choose photos that relate to a given month. Use photos of a family member for the month of his or her birthday. If you have some particularly fine holiday shots, use them for the month of December. This sounds obvious, I know, but you'd be surprised how many times I see iPhoto calendars with photos that bear no relationship to the months in which they appear.

Think vivid. I've ordered several calendars, and in my experience, photos with soft, muted colors often print poorly. You're likely to see faint vertical stripes, sometimes called *banding*, in the photos. I get the best results when I use photos that have bright, vivid colors. Black-and-white photos work beautifully, too, provided they have strong contrast.

Layout Techniques

Laying out a calendar involves many of the same techniques behind book creation (pages 130–141). You can add photos by hand, dragging them from the thumbnails area into specific months, or you can click the Autoflow button and have iPhoto sling the photos into your year as it sees fit. As with books, I prefer the manual layout technique for calendars.

How many photos in a month? iPhoto's calendar themes, like its book themes, provide multiple page designs. Some designs provide for just one photo for a given month, while others allow for a half dozen or more.

I like to minimize the number of photos I use each month. Bigger photos have a more dramatic look, and they're easier to see and appreciate when the calendar is hanging on a wall at the opposite end of a room. For most of my calendars, I put just one photo on each month.

That's a rule that begs to be broken, and I do break it now and then. If I have relatively low-resolution photos and iPhoto displays its yellow warning triangle, I'll switch to a page design that has smaller photo frames. Or if I have a series of photos that tells a story about a particular month, I'll choose a page design that lets me use all of those photos.

Top, bottom, or both? Normally, iPhoto's calendar view displays both halves of a given month—that is, the upper portion, where your photos appear, and the lower portion, where the days and weeks are displayed. Between those two halves is the spiral binding that holds the calendar together.

But when you're fine-tuning a calendar's design, you may find it useful to display only the upper or lower portions. The answer? Tear out the spiral binding. Click the single-pages View button (▪), and iPhoto displays only the upper or lower portion of a month.

To switch between viewing the upper or lower portion of a month, display the calendar's page thumbnails (click the ▪ button at the top of the thumbnails area), then click the thumbnail of the page you want to view.

Adding Photos to Dates

When creating a calendar, your photo options aren't limited to just the page above each month. You can also add photos to individual dates. To commemorate a birthday, add a photo to the birthday girl's date. To never forget your anniversary, put a wedding photo on the date. (Another good way to never forget an anniversary is to forget it just once, but this method is not recommended.)

To add a photo to a date, drag it from the thumbnails area of the calendar.

To remove a photo from a date, select the date and press the Delete key.

Don't Forget About the iCal Angle

When creating a new calendar, you can choose to have iPhoto include event information from iCal. You can also add iCal data to an existing calendar by clicking the Settings button and checking the appropriate Import iCal Calendars box.

Don't use iCal to manage your life? You can download thousands of calendars from iCalShare (www.icalshare.com). Because I like my calendars to include the phases of the moon, I subscribed to a lunar calendar at iCalShare. When I'm creating a new calendar, I simply check the moon-phases calendar and iPhoto does the rest.

Improving Your Calendar Typography

Many of the typographic tips that apply to books (pages 138–139) also apply to calendars.

Global formatting. You can change the fonts that iPhoto uses for various elements of the calendar—its dates and captions, for example—by clicking the Settings button, then clicking Styles. Most of the items in the Settings dialog

box are self-explanatory. The two that are less than obvious are Page Text and Comments. The Page Text item controls the font in which dates, days of the week, and the month appear. The Comments item controls the formatting of custom text that you add.

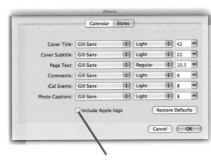

While you're visiting the Styles portion of the Settings dialog box, uncheck the box labeled *Include Apple logo*. I love the

Mac, but I also like my calendars to be free of advertising.

Local formatting. As with books, you can also override iPhoto's font settings and apply formatting to individual text items, but within limits: you can't apply local formatting to a specific date. (For example, you can't have February 14 appear in a bold red font.) You can apply local formatting only to comments and photo captions. To do so, display the item's text box (click on the date, and the text box zooms into view), then select the text and use the Fonts panel as described on pages 138–139.

Customizing Photos on Dates

You can customize the way a photo appears on a date.

iPhoto displays the date to which the photo belongs.

To display a text caption adjacent to the photo, check the Caption box. iPhoto uses the photo's title as the caption text, but you can replace that text by selecting it and typing your own. (For details on assigning titles to photos, see page 38.)

As with slide shows and books, you can fine-tune a photo's composition without having to use the Crop tool. Drag the size slider to zoom in, then drag the photo within its frame until it's positioned as desired.

Photo captions appear on an adjacent date, with an arrow pointing to the photo. To choose where the caption appears, click an arrow. In this example, I've clicked the left arrow, telling iPhoto to display the caption on the date to the left of the photo.

Creating Greeting Cards and Postcards

Let us hereby resolve to never buy a greeting card from a store rack again. Okay, maybe that's a bit strong. But with the greeting card and postcard features in iPhoto, you can definitely curtail your contributions to Hallmark's balance sheet.

An iPhoto greeting card measures 5 by 7 inches, and is of the "tent" variety—folded on its top. (Assuming you use a horizontally oriented photo, that is: if you use a vertically oriented photo, the card's fold is on the left side.) In quantities of 1 to 24, cards cost $1.99 each. Order 25 to 49 cards for $1.79 each; 50 or more cards are $1.59 each.

As for postcards, they measure 4 by 6 inches and cost $1.49 each (1–24), $1.29 each (25–49), or $.99 each (50 or more). The back of a postcard can contain a full block of text or you can use a standard postcard-mailing format, complete with a "place postage here" box.

Greeting cards and postcards are printed on a heavy card stock and include matching envelopes. Even if you order a postcard with a "place postage here" box, you still get an envelope—complete with an embossed Apple logo on its flap.

So forget this era of email and instant messaging, and use iPhoto to create some old-fashioned correspondence. Your recipients will thank you.

Creating a Greeting Card

Step 1. Select the photo that you want on the greeting card.

Step 2. Click the Card button.

Card

Step 3. Choose Greeting Card from the pop-up menu, choose a theme, then click Choose or press Return.

I'm partial to the Picture Card theme, which prints a borderless photo.

Step 4. Replace the card's placeholder text with your own and then fine-tune the design, if desired (opposite page).

Tip: To have the inside of the card appear blank, just leave the placeholder text as is—or, if you're nervous about getting a card that contains the heartwarming message *Insert Title*, delete the placeholder text.

Step 5. Proofread any text you added, then proofread it again. Then, click Buy Card and pay using your Apple ID (page 14).

Creating a Postcard

Step 1. Select the photo you want to include on the postcard.

Step 2. Click the Card button.

Step 3. Choose Postcard from the pop-up menu, choose a theme, then click Choose or press Return.

The themes are similar to their greeting-card counterparts.

Step 4. Replace the card's placeholder text and then fine-tune the design, if desired.

Step 5. Do that proofreading thing you do so well, then click Buy Card and pay using your Apple ID.

Tip: Want to use a book layout as a card? Follow the instructions on page 141, then add the resulting "page image" to a card that uses the Picture Card theme.

Card Design Tips

Switching postcard styles. To switch between a self-mailing postcard and one that tucks into an envelope, select the back of the postcard, then use the Design pop-up menu.

Switching designs and backgrounds. All card themes provide more than one design option for the front of the card. Many themes, for example, provide an option that lets you type some text on the front of the card. To access different designs, select the front of the card, then use the Design pop-up menu.

Many theme designs also offer a selection of background colors or textures. You can access

them by using the Background pop-up menu.

Fine-tuning photos. As with books, slide shows, and calendars, you can adjust the appearance and positioning of a photo without having to edit the original. Simply click on the photo, then use the slider to zoom in as desired. To position the photo within its frame, drag it.

Why is this kid smiling?

To fine-tune the photo's exposure, click the Adjust button.

Fun with fonts. As with books and calendars, you can customize the font formatting of your card in two ways: by using the Settings button, or by bringing up the Fonts panel (⌘-T). The latter option lets you format text on an individual word (or character, if you want to taunt the design police) basis.

And while you're having fun with fonts, note that the text-formatting tips outlined on pages 138–141 also apply to cards.

Print it yourself. As with books, you can print greeting cards and postcards on your own color inkjet printer. Just choose the Print command while the card editor is visible. Note that if you plan to use both sides of the card, you'll need to use inkjet paper designed for double-sided printing.

Kill the apple. Ever conscious of brand recognition, Apple prints its logo on the back of a greeting card. If you'd rather not provide the free advertising, click the Settings button and uncheck the box labeled *Include Apple logo on back of card.*

More Ways to Share Photos

Now it's time to talk about some of the more obscure sharing options in iPhoto. Most people who use iPhoto share photos using the avenues I've already described: email for zapping some shots to a few friends; MobileMe, Flickr, and Facebook for putting photos on the Web; slide shows and iDVD for presenting photos with glitz and glamour; and print products for creating keepsakes.

But there's more. You can also export photos in a kind of bare-bones slide show format: a simple cross dissolve between each shot, some background music, but no glitzy themes, no title slide, and no Ken Burns. Why would you want to? You can have a background color or image appear behind photos, and you can type specific pixel dimensions for the resulting movie.

Big deal, right? The fact is, slide show projects and the Export button give you far more control. But when you want to create a simple QuickTime slide show, iPhoto can accommodate.

In a similar vein, you can export photos as a set of plain-looking Web pages. And again, MobileMe galleries and iWeb photo pages are usually better options, providing a flashier presentation and more controls. But exported Web pages can have a few advantages, as I describe at right.

Looking for still more ways to share? Redecorate your Macintosh desktop with your favorite photo. Or, use a set of photos as a screen saver.

It's obvious: if your digital photos aren't getting seen, it isn't iPhoto's fault.

Exporting Web Pages

You can export photos and albums as Web pages. iPhoto creates small thumbnail versions of your images, as well as the HTML pages that display them. (HTML stands for *HyperText Markup Language*—it's the set of codes used to design Web pages.)

To export a Web page, select some photos or an album, choose File > Export, then click the Web Page tab. Specify the page appearance and dimensions of the thumbnails and the images. You can also have additional information appear with each photo, such as its title, caption, location, and metadata (page 157).

After clicking the Export button, click the New Folder button to create a new folder. (The export process will create several folders, so it's a good idea to stash everything in one folder.)

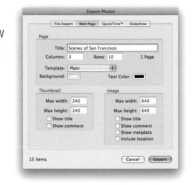

Notes and Tips

Viewing the site. To view the Web pages, open the folder you created to house them, then double-click the file named *index.html*. You'll see a set of thumbnails on a page that resembles the bland Web sites of the mid 1990s. iWeb it isn't—but the page will load quickly.

Using the site. What next? If you have a Web server, you can stash these files there. If you use a Web editor, such as Adobe Dreamweaver, you can customize the pages and clean up their 1990s-vintage code.

Burning the site. You can also burn the Web pages on a CD and mail them to others. They can use a Web browser to view the pages on their Macs or PCs.

No renaming. Don't rename the index.html file or any other files or folders that you exported. If you do, the links won't work.

Better HTML. To get nicer-looking HTML pages out of iPhoto, try an add-on called BetterHTMLExport (www.geeksrus.com). It has several design templates and lets you create your own.

Exporting a Basic QuickTime Movie

Step 1. Select some images or select an event, an album, a Faces tile, or a place in Places, then choose File > Export.

Step 2. To access movie-export options, click QuickTime.

Specify the duration for each image to display.

You can specify that iPhoto add a background color or background image to the movie. The color or image appears whenever the dimensions of the currently displayed photo don't match that of the movie itself. (For example, in a 640 by 480 movie, the background will be visible in photos shot in vertical orientation.) The background will also be visible at the beginning and end of the movie—before the first image fades in and after the last image fades out.

This tab summons the standard Export dialog box shown on page 101.

Specify the desired dimensions for the movie, in pixels. The preset values shown here work well, but if you specify smaller dimensions, such as 320 by 240, you'll get a smaller movie file—useful if you plan to distribute the movie over the Internet.

If you've assigned music to the album or slide show, iPhoto adds it to the movie. To create a silent movie, uncheck this box. **Note:** If you plan to distribute your slide-show movie, don't use songs from the iTunes Store; see page 156.

Step 3.
To create the movie, click Export and type a name for the movie.

Using Photos as Desktop Images and Screen Savers

iPhoto lets you share photos with yourself. Select a photo and choose Share > Set Desktop, and iPhoto replaces the Mac's desktop with the photo you selected.

If you select multiple photos or an event or album, your desktop image will change as you work,

complete with a cross-dissolve effect between images. It's an iPhoto slide show applied to your desktop.

Another way to turn an iPhoto album or event into a desktop screen saver is to use the Desktop & Screen Saver system preference—choose the album

in the Screen Savers list (right).

Warning: Using vacation photos as desktop images has been proven to cause wanderlust.

Burning Photos to CDs and DVDs

The phrase "burning photos" can strike terror into any photographer's heart, but fear not: I'm not talking about open flames here. Fire up your Mac's burner, and you can save, or burn, photos onto CDs or DVDs. You can burn your entire photo library, an album or two, some favorite events, a slide show, or even just one photo.

iPhoto's burning features make possible all manner of photo-transportation tasks. Back up some photos: burn some particularly important events and then stash the disc in a safe place. Move photos and albums from one Mac to another: burn a selection, then insert the disc in another Mac to work with them there.

iPhoto doesn't just copy photos to a disc. It creates a full-fledged iPhoto library on the disc. That library contains the images' titles and keywords, any albums that you burned, and even original versions of images you've retouched or cropped. Think of an iPhoto-burned disc as a portable iPhoto library.

That's all grand, but your burning desires may be different. Maybe you want to burn photos for a friend who uses Windows, or for printing by a photofinisher. That's easy, too.

So back away from that fire extinguisher—we've got some burning to do.

Burning Basics

Burning photos involves selecting what you want to burn, then telling iPhoto to light a match.

Step 1. Select items to burn.

Remember that you can also select multiple items by Shift-clicking or ⌘-clicking on each one (page 59).

You can also select multiple books and other keepsake items, folders, and slide shows—iPhoto can burn them, too. Indeed, burning a disc is the only way to move a keepsake item or slide show project from one Mac to another.

Step 2. Choose Burn from the Share menu.

iPhoto asks you to insert a blank disc.

Tip: If you burn discs frequently, you can have iPhoto display a Burn button in its toolbar. Choose View > Show in Toolbar > Burn.

Step 3. Insert a blank disc and click OK.

iPhoto displays information about the pending burn. You can add photos to or remove them from the selection, and iPhoto will update its information area accordingly.

Tip: Give your disc a descriptive name by typing in the Name box.

Step 4. Click the Burn button.

iPhoto displays another dialog box. To cancel the burn, click Cancel. To proceed, click Burn.

iPhoto prepares the images, then burns and verifies the contents of the disc.

Working with Burned Discs

When you insert a disc burned in iPhoto, the disc appears in the Shares list. To see its photos, select the disc's name.
Note that the disc's photos aren't in the iPhoto library

on your hard drive—they're in the iPhoto library on the disc.

A small triangle appears next to the disc's name. To view the disc's items, click the triangle.

You can display photos on a disc using the same techniques that you use to display photos stored in your iPhoto library. You can also display instant slide shows, email photos, and order prints.

However, you can't edit photos stored on a burned disc, nor can you create an iWeb photo album, a MobileMe gallery album, a slide show project, a book, a calendar, or a greeting card. To perform these tasks, add the photos to your photo library as described at right.

Copying Items from a Burned Disc

To modify an item that's stored on a burned disc, you must copy it to your iPhoto library.

To copy an item, select it and drag it to the Events or Photos item in the Library area.

Note: When copying a keepsake item (such as a book) or a slide show project to a different Mac, be sure that the destination Mac contains the same fonts or music used in the book or slide show.

Burning for Windows or Photofinishers

Here's how to burn photos for a friend who uses Windows, or for printing by a photofinisher. You can also use these steps to burn a disc for a fellow Mac user who doesn't use iPhoto.

Step 1. Prepare a disc.
Insert a blank CD or DVD in your Mac's optical drive. The dialog box below appears.

Type a name for the CD and click OK. The blank disc's icon appears on your desktop.

Step 2. Copy the photos.
Position the iPhoto window so that you can see it and the blank disc's icon. Drag the photos that you want to burn to the icon of the blank disc.

As an alternative to dragging photos, you can also select them and use the File menu's Export command to export copies to the blank disc. This approach gives you the option of resizing the photos and changing their file names.

Step 3. Burn. To burn the disc, drag its icon to the Burn Disc icon in your dock. (The Burn Disc icon replaces the Trash icon when you've selected a blank disc.) In the dialog box that appears next, click the Burn button.

Creating and Managing Photo Libraries

iPhoto is designed to manage thousands of photos without bogging down. And its photo-management features are aimed at helping you find that photo of a needle in your photo of a haystack.

I mention this as a way of saying that you may be completely happy having just one master iPhoto library, even if it becomes huge. Just remember to back it up often.

Still, a lot of people like to keep multiple libraries and switch among them. Some people do it for backup convenience: it's easier to sling a smaller library over to a DVD-R or an external hard drive.

For some people, multiple libraries are a way of further categorizing photos. Vintage scanned photos in one library, newer digital shots in another. Or a separate library for each year. Or each vacation.

But what about when you want to make a slide show or some other project? Because all the photos for a project must be in the same library, you might have to do a lot of work to gather the photos you need into one library.

Also, having multiple libraries defeats some of iPhoto's filing features. You can't tell iPhoto, "Show me all my photos of Toby" if some of those photos are in other libraries.

For these reasons, I keep all my photos in one library. It weighs in at about 180GB (I just checked), and iPhoto still purrs.

But if you prefer to maintain separate libraries, here's what you need to know.

Creating a New Library

Before creating a new library, you may want to back up your existing library by dragging your iPhoto Library to another hard drive or, if it will fit, by burning it to a DVD. For some backup strategies, see the sidebar on the opposite page.

Step 1. Quit iPhoto.

Step 2. Locate your iPhoto Library and rename it.

To quickly locate the library, choose Home from the Finder's Go menu, then double-click the Pictures folder, where you'll find the iPhoto Library.

Step 3. Start iPhoto.

iPhoto asks if you want to locate an existing library or create a new one.

Step 4. Click Create New.

iPhoto proposes the name iPhoto Library, but you can type a different name if you like.

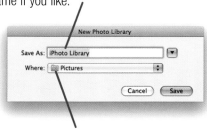

You don't need to store your library in the Pictures folder; see the sidebar below.

Step 5. Click Save, and iPhoto creates the new, empty library.

Switching Between Libraries

There may be times when you want to switch to a different iPhoto library—for example, to access the photos in an older library. It's easy: at the Finder, locate the library you want to use, and double-click it. If iPhoto is running, a dialog box appears that asks if you're sure you want to switch libraries.

Click the Relaunch button, and iPhoto quits, then restarts with the other library.

Managing and Backing Up Your Library

Storing Photos Elsewhere

Normally, iPhoto stores your photo library in the Pictures folder. You might prefer to store your library elsewhere, such as on an external hard drive.

To store your photo library elsewhere, quit iPhoto, then simply move the iPhoto Library wherever you like. If you're copying the library to a different disk, delete the original library after the copy is complete. To open the library after you've copied it, just double-click its icon.

Backing Up

In the film days, you had to fall victim to a fire or other disaster in order to lose all your photos. In the digital age, it's much easier to lose photos; all it takes is a hardware failure or software glitch.

Please don't let photo loss happen to you.

Back up your photos. An easy way to back up is to buy an external hard drive and drag your iPhoto Library over to it now and then.

For a more sophisticated approach, use the Time Machine feature in Mac OS X Leopard. It backs up your entire hard drive every day and lets you, as Apple says, "revisit your Mac as it appeared in the past." (In iPhoto, you can browse your Time Machine backups by choosing File > Browse Backups.)

You can also burn your most important photos to DVDs, although these optical discs aren't as permanent as you might think. They can develop problems after just a few years, especially if stored in a warm environment.

As you can see, you have backup options aplenty. For the sake of your photos, use at least one of them.

Getting Old Photos into iPhoto

You love your digital camera and the convenience of iPhoto, and it would take an act of Congress to force you to use film again.

And yet the past haunts you. You have boxes of negatives and slides that you haven't seen in years. If you could get them into iPhoto, you could organize them into albums and share them through Web albums, slide shows, prints and books, and even movies and DVDs.

Many services will scan slides, negatives, and prints for you, with retouching and color restoration available as options. One of the most popular is ScanCafe (www.scancafe.com), which charges as little as $.25 per scan.

If you'd rather do the job yourself, you need a scanner. Here's an overview of what to look for, and some strategies for getting those old photos into iPhoto.

Scanning the Options

Before you buy a scanner, take stock of what types of media you'll need to digitize. Do you have negatives, prints, slides, or all three? Not all scanners are ideal for every task.

Flatbed scanners. If you'll be scanning printed photos, a *flatbed scanner* is your best bet. Place a photo face down on the scanner's glass, and a sensor glides beneath it and captures the image.

Repeating this process for hundreds of photos can be tedious. If you have a closet full of photos, you may want to look for a scanner that supports an automatic document feeder so you can scan a stack of photos without having to hand-feed the scanner. Some flatbeds include photo feeders that can handle up to 24 prints in sizes up to 4 by 6 inches. Other scanners accept optional document feeders. Just be sure to verify that the document feeder can handle photos—many can't.

Film scanners. A print is one generation away from the original image, and may have faded with time or been poorly printed to begin with. Worse, many photos are printed on linen-finish paper, whose rough texture blurs image detail when scanned. Bottom line: you'll get better results by scanning the original film.

Many flatbed scanners include a film adaptor for scanning negatives or slides. A flatbed scanner with a film adaptor is a versatile scanning system, but a *film scanner* provides much sharper scans of negatives and slides. Unfortunately, this quality will cost you: film scanners cost more than flatbeds.

Many film scanners provide a dust- and scratch-removal option called Digital ICE (short for *image correction/enhancement*). Developed by Kodak's Austin Development Center (www.asf.com) and

licensed to numerous scanner manufacturers, Digital ICE does an astonishingly good job of cleaning up color film. However, it doesn't work with black-and-white negatives.

Scanning Right

Whether you use a flatbed or film scanner, you'll encounter enough jargon to intimidate an astronaut: histograms, tone curves, black points, white points. Don't fret: all scanners include software that provides presets for common scanning scenarios, such as scanning for color inkjet output. Start with these presets. As you learn about scanning, you can customize settings to optimize your exposures.

The right resolution. A critical scanning setting deals with how many dots per inch (dpi) the scanner uses to represent an image. Volumes have been written about scanning resolution, but it boils down to a simple rule of thumb: If you're using a flatbed scanner and you plan to print your scans on a photo inkjet printer, you can get fine results with a resolution of 180 to 240 dpi. If you plan to order photographic prints from your scans, scan at 300 dpi. Scanning at more than 300 dpi will usually not improve quality—but it will definitely use more disk space.

Film scanners are different. A film scanner scans a much smaller original—for example, a 35mm negative instead of a 4 by 6 inch print. To produce enough data for high-quality prints, a film scanner must scan at a much higher resolution than a flatbed. The film scanner I use, Minolta's Scan Elite 5400, scans at up to 5400 dpi.

This difference in approach can make for even more head scratching when it comes time to decide what resolution to use. Just do what I do: use the presets in the scanning software. I typically choose my film scanner's "PhotoCD 2048 by 3072" option, which yields a file roughly equivalent to a six-megapixel image.

Special circumstances. If you plan to apply iPhoto's or iMovie's Ken Burns effect to an image, you'll want a high-resolution scan so you can zoom in without encountering jagged pixels. Experiment to find the best resolution for a specific image and zoom setting.

In a related vein, if you plan to crop out unwanted portions of an image, scan at a higher resolution than you might normally use. Cropping discards pixels, so the more data you have to begin with, the more cropping flexibility you have.

Format strategies. Which file format should you use for saving images? As I've mentioned before, the JPEG format is *lossy:* it sacrifices quality slightly in order to save disk space. If this is the last time you plan to scan those old photos, you may not want to save them in a

lossy format. When scanning my old slides and negatives, I save the images as TIFF files.

Photos, Meet iPhoto

Once you've scanned and saved your photos, you can import them into iPhoto.

Filing photos. To take advantage of iPhoto's filing features, you may want to have a separate iPhoto event for each set of related photos. In the Finder, move each set of related photos into its own folder, giving each folder a descriptive name, such as *Vacation 1972*. Next, drag each folder into the iPhoto window. iPhoto gives each event the same name as its corresponding folder.

You can delete the folders after you've imported their shots, since iPhoto will have created duplicates in iPhoto Library. (If you prefer to retain your existing filing system, you can set up iPhoto to not copy the photos to the iPhoto Library; see page 33.)

Turn back the clock. To make your iPhoto library chronologically accurate, change the date of the photos and events to reflect when the photos were taken, not when they were imported (see page 39).

While you're sweating the details, consider geotagging photos whose locations are particularly significant. And jump over

to the Faces item to see if iPhoto recognizes someone from Back Then.

Time for retouching. You can use iPhoto's Retouch tool to fix scratches and dust specks, and its Enhance button and Adjust panel to fix color and exposure problems. For serious retouching, though, use Photoshop Elements or Photoshop. To learn more about digital retouching, I recommend Katrin Eisman's *Photoshop Restoration and Retouching, Third Edition* (New Riders, 2005).

Plug in to photo enhancement. Old photos do fade away, typically acquiring a blue or red tint as their dyes, well, die. If you have patience and a good eye for color, you can improve an old photo's color using iPhoto's Adjust panel or Photoshop.

If you have $99, you can buy a Photoshop plug-in that does the job for you. Digital ROC Pro, from Kodak, does an amazing job of improving faded photos. Digital ROC also works in Photoshop Elements. You can download a trial version of it, and more, at www.asf.com.

iPhoto Tips

Purchased Songs and Slide Shows

You can use songs from the iTunes Store for slide show soundtracks. But if you plan to export the slide shows as QuickTime movies, using the technique described on page 149, note that the songs will play only on computers authorized for your iTunes account. The workaround: burn the songs to an audio CD, then re-rip them into iTunes, and use those unprotected versions for your soundtracks.

Note that this limitation applies only to iTunes purchases that are shackled by digital rights management (DRM) copy protection. At this writing, virtually all iTunes songs are not DRM-protected, so you can use them in your slide shows without worrying about whether they'll play on other computers.

But if you have tunes purchased back in the day, you'll need to resort to this workaround to get them to play. (To determine whether a song is copy-protected, go to iTunes, select the song, and choose File > Get Info. In the information dialog box, click the Summary tab, and look for the Kind item. If the file is protected, its kind reads *Protected AAC Audio File.*)

Note that all this nonsense applies only to a slide show that you export as a bare-bones QuickTime movie. If you use the Export button to save a slide show as a movie, even shackled songs will play back fine on other computers.

Controlling the Camera Connection

Normally, when you connect a camera or an iPhone, your Mac plops you into iPhoto. You might prefer that it didn't—it can be annoying when you're simply syncing your iPhone, for example.

To control what happens when you connect a camera to your Mac, choose iPhoto > Preferences. Click the General button, and in the Connecting Camera Opens pop-up menu, choose No Application.

Keywords for Movies and Raw Photos

Normally, assigning keywords to photos is your job (page 54). But iPhoto automatically assigns keywords to two types of items that you import: movie clips and raw-format images.

Movies get the keyword *Movie*, and raw images get the keyword *Raw*. Remember, you can use smart albums to quickly display items with one or more keywords. For example, to see all the movies in your iPhoto library, create a smart album whose criterion is Keyword is *Movie*.

Entering Custom Crop Proportions

With the Constrain pop-up menu in edit view, you can tell iPhoto to restrict cropping rectangles to standard proportions (page 69). If you want non-standard proportions, choose Custom from the Constrain pop-up menu and enter the

proportions in the boxes that appear. Note that you can't enter fractional values: 8.5, for example, is rounded up to 9.

Hiding Event Titles

If you're browsing your photo library in Photos view, you can have iPhoto hide event titles and show your entire library as one massive set of thumbnails. In Photos view, choose View > Event Titles. It's a cumbersome way to view your library, but you might find it useful when assigning keywords or renaming photos.

To restore some sanity to Photos view, choose View > Event Titles again.

Rebuilding Your iPhoto Library

If iPhoto is acting up—for example, taking forever to launch, running unusually slowly, or not displaying photo thumbnails—try rebuilding your iPhoto library. Quit iPhoto, then hold down the ⌘ and Option keys while starting iPhoto. A dialog box appears asking if you're sure you want to rebuild your library and giving you several options for doing so.

If your image thumbnails appear gray or blank, try selecting the first two options. If iPhoto crashes or refuses to load photos when you first launch it, try the third

Get links to iPhoto add-ons and
additional online photo services.
www.macilife.com/iphoto

option. If some of your photos seem to have disappeared, try the "recover orphaned photos" option. And if iPhoto is misbehaving in several ways, check all five options.

Important: To avoid the risk of making a bad situation worse, consider backing up your iPhoto Library before trying to rebuild your library.

Non-Destructive Editing and Older Libraries

On page 66, I discussed how iPhoto has non-destructive editing that maximizes quality by always applying your edits to the original version of an image.

There's an exception to this rule, and it concerns iPhoto libraries created in iPhoto '06 or earlier versions. Specifically, if you edit a photo that you previously edited using an older iPhoto version, iPhoto '09 applies your latest changes to the *edited* photo, not to the original. Thus, you don't have the full advantage of non-destructive editing.

The solution? If you want to edit a photo that you've already edited using iPhoto '06 or an earlier version, revert to the original version of the photo. Choose Photos > Revert to Original (or, for raw images, Reprocess Raw). This discards edits you made in the past, and new edits will be applied to the original version of the photo.

Inside the iPhoto Library

The iPhoto Library item is a *package*—a special kind of Mac OS X folder. If you double-click the iPhoto Library item, your Mac simply starts or switches to iPhoto.

But there *is* a way to get inside if you must. Control-click on the iPhoto Library item and choose Show Package Contents from the shortcut menu. Inside, you'll find a bevy of folders and files that constitute your library.

Leave them be. Always use iPhoto to add or remove photos to or from your library: drag photos into and out of the iPhoto window.

EXIF Exposed: Getting Information About Photos

Digital cameras store information along with each photo—the date and time when the photo was taken, its exposure, the kind of camera used, and more. This is called the *EXIF* data. It's also often called *metadata*.

iPhoto saves this EXIF data when you import photos. To view it, select a photo and choose Photos > Show Extended Photo Info (⌘-Option-I).

Not all of this information will be useful to you, but some of it might. If you have more than one digital camera, for example, you can use the window's Photo tab to see which camera you used for a given shot. If you've geotagged a photo, its location information appears here, too. And as I mentioned on page 62, you can use smart albums to search for various metadata items. At the very least, you can see what kind of exposure settings your camera is using.

More iPhoto Tips

Including Photos in Documents

You may want to include photos in documents that you're creating in Microsoft Word or other programs. It's easy: just drag the image from iPhoto into your document.

If you use Apple's iWork software—Keynote, Pages, and Numbers—your job is even easier. All three programs provide media browsers much like those in the iLife programs: access your photo library directly, search for a photo, and then add it to a document by dragging it from the media browser.

If you drag an image to the Finder desktop or to a folder window, iPhoto makes a duplicate copy of the image file. Use this technique when you want to copy a photo out of your library.

Caution: Merging Faces

You can move Corkboard tiles around to rearrange faces in whatever order you like: just click and drag them. But take care: if you drag one tile *atop* another, iPhoto merges those two faces: the face you dragged takes on the name of the face you dragged it to. (And there's a sentence I never thought I'd type.)

If you accidentally drag one face tile atop another, sprint right up to the Edit menu and choose Undo Merge Faces.

Scroll-Wheel Map Zooming

Apple's Mighty Mouse—and most third-party mice—have scroll wheels that let you scroll documents by rolling a little wheel. With this tip, you can customize iPhoto so that moving a scroll wheel zooms in and out of the map display in the Places feature.

Quit iPhoto, then, at the Finder, go to the Utilities folder inside your Applications folder, and start the Terminal program. Finally, carefully type the following and then press the Return key.

Now fire up iPhoto, click your way to the Places map, and zoom. By the way, if you have an Apple laptop that provides a multitouch trackpad, you'll find that this tip also lets you zoom in and out using the pinch gestures.

If you don't like scroll-wheel zooming, you can disable the feature by using the same Terminal line printed here, replacing YES with NO.

Emailing Movies

iPhoto can store movie clips that your digital camera takes, but it can't email them. When you select a movie, the Email button is disabled.

The workaround is easy. Start a new, blank email message, then position the iPhoto window so you can see the movie thumbnail and your message. Finally, drag the movie thumbnail from the iPhoto window into the blank email message.

```
defaults write com.apple.iphoto MapScrollWheel -bool YES
```

Fun with Mosaics

What's better than a great photo? Dozens or hundreds or even thousands of great photos combined into a photo mosaic.

Here are a few ways to make mosaic magic.

Use Leopard's screen saver. The screen saver in Mac OS X has a dazzlingly cool mosaic option. A full-screen version of a photo appears, then grows gradually smaller as other photos appear around it. As the photos get ever tinier, you see what's going on: they're forming a mosaic of yet another photo. The process then repeats with a different photo—it's mesmerizing.

Open the Desktop & Screen Saver system preference, click the Screen Saver button, then choose the Mosaic display style.

Make a life poster. With Zykloid Software's Posterino, you can turn a collection of photos into a full-page poster. Choose from a variety of layout options and templates, then add the poster to iPhoto and order a print or make your own. Or use the poster in an iMovie project, and pan across a year's worth of photos with the Ken Burns effect.

Make a photo mosaic. With a free program called MacOSaiX, you can create a stunning photo mosaic—a single photo made up of thousands of separate photos, each chosen by the software to match the color and tonal qualities of part of the original photo.

This mosaic, created by the free MacOSaiX software, is made up of over 1200 photos. To see and download the original, visit my Flickr photos (www.flickr.com/photos/jimheid) and search for *mosaic*.

159

Photos and Your iPod or iPhone

Except for the tiny shuffle, all current iPods can store and display photos. (Some older models can, too.) Stash some favorite shots on your iPod, then show them to friends, family, or the person sitting next to you on the plane. Or connect your iPod to a TV set and view your shots on its screen.

Scroll through photos one at a time at your own pace, or have your iPod display a slide show, complete with music from your iTunes library. You can even play the game of chance and view a slide show in shuffle mode—which photo will appear next?

Just as iTunes is the conduit between your music library and your iPod, it's also the bridge between your iPhoto library and your iPod. Using iTunes, you can copy all photos and albums, or only the ones you want to carry with you.

Because large photos devour space, iTunes creates a small, iPod-friendly version of each shot before transferring it to the iPod. You can also choose to transfer the full-resolution photos. This can be a handy way to back up photos or take them to a friend's house for sharing.

Here's how to turn your iPod into a pocket slide projector. Unless otherwise noted, everything on these pages also applies to the iPhone and iPod touch.

Step 1. Create Albums

There are several ways to transfer photos to an iPod. For example, you can transfer your entire photo library or just the albums you want to carry along with you.

For the latter approach, use iPhoto to create an album containing the photos you want to show. If you want to create iPod slide shows for several different events—your summer vacation, the Halloween party, your family reunion—create a separate album for each event. (For tips on creating albums, see pages 58–65.)

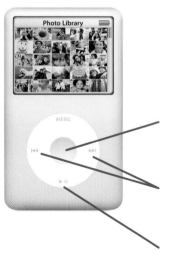

Viewing Photos on an iPod

When you use the iPod's menus to select an album or folder, the iPod displays thumbnail versions of your photos. To scroll the thumbnails, use the click wheel.

To see a full-screen version of the highlighted photo, press the Center button.

To display the next and previous screen of thumbnails, press Next or Previous.

To begin a slide show, press the Play/Pause button.

Step 2. Sync Your iPod

Connect your iPod to your Mac. In the Devices list at the left side of the iTunes window, select the iPod.

To access photo-updating options, click Photos.

To transfer photos stored in a folder that isn't part of your iPhoto library, use the pop-up menu.

To transfer only some albums, choose this option and then check the albums you want to transfer.

Check this box to include full-resolution photos, which are stored on the iPod in a folder named Photos. To access the originals, activate the iPod's disk mode. (Note: this option isn't available for the iPhone or iPod touch.)

Click Apply to have iTunes prepare and transfer the photos.

Step 3. Start the Show

Navigate to the album that holds the photos you want to display, and press (or tap) the Play/Pause button. If your iPod is connected to a TV, you have the option of viewing the slide show on the big screen.

To jump to the previous or next photo, during the slide show press the Previous or Next buttons. To pause the slide show, press Play/Pause. To end the show, press Menu (clickwheel iPods) or the Home button (iPhone and iPod touch).

Tip: Use the iPod's menus to adjust slide show settings, such as the duration for each photo and whether a transition appears between each one.

Touching Your Photos

To view photos on an iPhone or iPod touch, tap the Photos button on the home screen, then tap the album you want to view. A screen of photo thumbnails appears. To view a photo, tap it.

Return to the album thumbnails.

To hide photo controls, tap the photo. To restore the controls, tap again. To view the previous or next photo, flick across the screen. To zoom in, double-tap the photo. You can also use the standard pinch and drag maneuvers to zoom and pan.

Don't forget to rotate your hand-held projector 90 degrees to view horizontally oriented photos.

Left to right: display photo options, such as emailing; view previous photo; start slide show; view next photo.

Mastering Your Digital Camera

Resolution Matters

Always shoot at your camera's highest resolution. This gives you maximum flexibility for cropping, for making big prints, and for the Ken Burns effect in iPhoto and iMovie. You can always use iPhoto to make photos smaller (for example, for emailing or Web publishing).

Shutter Lag

Many digital cameras suffer from a curse called *shutter lag*—a delay between the time you press the shutter button and the moment when the shutter actually fires.

Shutter lag occurs because the camera's built-in computer must calculate exposure and focus. If you're shooting fast-moving subjects, it's easy to miss the shot you wanted.

The solution: give your camera a head start. Press and hold the shutter button partway, and the camera calculates focus

and exposure. Now wait until the right moment arrives, then press the button the rest of the way.

ISO Speeds

In the film world, if you want to take low-light shots, you can buy high-speed film—ISO 400 or 800, for example. Fast film allows you to take nighttime or indoor shots without the harsh glare of electronic flash.

Digital cameras allow you to adjust light sensitivity on a shot-by-shot basis. Switch the camera into one of its manual-exposure modes (a common mode is labeled *P*, for *program*), and then use the camera's menus to adjust its ISO speed.

Note that shots photographed at higher ISO speeds—particularly 800 and higher—are likely to have digital *noise*, a slightly grainy appearance. For me, it's a happy trade-off: I'd rather have a sharp, naturally lit photo with some noise than a noise-free but blurry (or flash-lit) photo.

Higher ISO speeds can also help you capture fast-moving action by day. The higher speed forces the camera to use a faster shutter speed, thereby minimizing blur. That shot on this page of Mimi leaping into the air? Shot at ISO 400.

White Balance

Few light sources are pure white; they have a color cast of some kind. Incandescent lamps (light bulbs) cast a yellowish light, while fluorescent light is greenish. Even outdoors, there can be light-source variations—bluish in the morning, reddish in the evening. Each of these light sources has a different *color temperature*.

Our eyes and brains compensate for these variances. Digital cameras try to do so with a feature called *automatic white balance*, but they aren't always as good at it. That's why many cameras have manual white balance adjustments that essentially let you tell the camera, "Hey, I'm shooting under incandescent (or fluorescent) lights now, so make some adjustments in how you record color."

White balance adjustments are usually labeled WB, often with icons representing cloudy skies ☁, incandescent lamps ☼, and fluorescent lighting ⊟. You'll probably have to switch to your camera's manual-exposure mode to access its white balance settings.

Sharpness and Color Settings

Digital cameras do more than simply capture a scene. They also manipulate the image they capture by applying sharpening and color correction (including white balance adjustments).

Some photographers don't like the idea of their cameras making manipulations like these. If you're in this group, consider exploring your camera's menus and tweaking any color and sharpness settings you find.

For example, many cameras have two color modes: "standard" and "real." The "standard" mode punches up the color saturation—something you can do yourself with iPhoto. I'd prefer to capture accurate colors and make adjustments later. A "real" mode—or its equivalent on your camera—gives you more-natural color. You can always punch it up in iPhoto if you must.

The same applies to sharpness. Most cameras offer a variety of sharpening settings, and when I'm shooting JPEG images, I like to reduce the camera's built-in sharpening. If I feel an image needs some sharpening later, I'll do the job in iPhoto or Photoshop.

And of course, remember that for maximum control, you should shoot in raw mode, in which the camera doesn't apply any color or sharpness adjustments.

Custom White Balance

Most cameras also let you create a custom white-balance setting. Generally, the process works like this: put a white sheet of paper in the scene, get up close so the paper fills the viewfinder, and then press a button sequence on the camera. The camera measures the light reflected from the paper, compares it to the camera's built-in definition of *white*, and then adjusts to compensate for the lighting.

If you're a stickler for color and you're shooting under strange lighting conditions, creating a custom white balance setting is a good idea.

Better still, shoot in raw mode if your camera allows it. Then you'll have complete control over color balance.

Stay Sharp

A camera's built-in LCD screen is great for reviewing a shot you just took. But the screen is so tiny that it's often hard to tell whether the photo is in sharp focus.

Most cameras allow you to zoom in on a photo while displaying it. I like to zoom in and verify that my photo isn't blurred—especially if the subject is still in front of me and I have another chance.

If your camera has an electronic viewfinder, it can be a superior alternative to the LCD screen for reviewing your shots, especially in bright light.

Your Camera's Histogram

If you read through pages 76 and 77, you've seen the value that a histogram display can offer for making exposure adjustments.

Many mid-range and all high-end cameras can display a histogram, too, which you can use to adjust exposure settings *before* you take a photo.

With your camera in one of its manual-exposure modes, activate the histogram display. Then adjust your exposure settings—shutter speed, ISO speed, and aperture—so that the histogram's data is as far to the right-hand side of the graph as possible without introducing white clipping. (Remember, white clipping means lost highlight detail.)

Photography gurus call this technique *exposing to the right*, and it ensures that you're getting as much image data as your camera is capable of capturing.

Photographer Michael Reichmann, publisher of the magnificent Luminous Landscape site, has written an excellent tutorial on using histograms when shooting. I've linked to it on www.macilife.com/iphoto.

Learning More

To learn more about digital photography and Photoshop, I heartily recommend *Real World Digital Photography* by Katrin Eisman, Seán Duggan, and Tim Grey (Peachpit Press, 2004).

Tips for Better Digital Photography

Get Up Close

Too many photographers shy away from their subjects. Get close to show detail. If you can't get physically closer, use your camera's zoom feature, if it has one. If your camera has a macro feature, use it to take extreme close-ups of flowers, rocks, seashells, tattoos—you name it. Don't limit yourself to wide shots.

Vary Your Angle

Don't just shoot from a standing position. Get down into a crouch and shoot low—or get up on a chair and shoot down. Vary your angles. The LCD screen on a digital camera makes it easy—you don't press your eye to the camera to compose a shot.

Changing your angle can be a great way to remove a cluttered background. When photographing flowers, for example, I like to position the camera low and aim it upwards, so that the flowers are shot against the sky.

Avoid Digital Zooming

Many digital cameras supplement their optical zoom lenses with digital zoom functions that bring your subject even closer. Think twice about using digital zoom—it usually adds undesirable artifacts to an image.

Position the Horizon

In landscape shots, the position of the horizon influences the mood of the photo. To imply a vast, wide open space, put the horizon along the lower third of the frame and show lots of sky. (This obviously works best when the sky is cooperating.) To imply a sense of closeness—or if the sky is a bland shade of gray—put the horizon along the upper third, showing little sky.

This rule, like others, is meant to be broken. For example, if you're shooting a forlorn-looking desert landscape, you might want to have the horizon bisect the image to imply a sense of bleak monotony.

Crop Carefully

You can often use iPhoto's cropping tool to fix composition problems. But note that cropping results in lost pixels, and that can affect your ability to produce high-quality prints. Try to do your cropping in the camera's viewfinder, not iPhoto.

Kill Your Flash

I turn off my camera's built-in flash and rarely turn it on. Existing light provides a much more flattering, natural-looking image, with none of the harshness of electronic flash.

Dimly lit indoor shots may have a slight blur to them, but I'll take blur over the radioactive look of flash any day.

Beware of the Background

More accurately, *be aware* of the background. Is a tree growing out of Mary's head? If so, move yourself or Mary. Are there distracting details in the background? Find a simpler setting or get up close. Is your shadow visible in the shot? Change your position. When looking at a scene, our brains tend to ignore irrelevant things. But the camera sees all. As you compose, look at the entire frame, not just your subject.

Embrace Blur

A blurred photo is a ruined photo, right? Not necessarily. Blur conveys motion, something still images don't usually do. A photo with a sharp background but a car that is blurred tells you the car was in motion. To take this kind of shot, keep the camera steady and snap the shutter at the moment the car crosses the frame.

You can also convey motion by turning this formula around: If you pan along with the moving car as you snap, the car will be sharp but the background will be blurred. A canine-oriented example is above.

Compose Carefully

Following a couple of rules of thumb can help you compose photos that are more visually pleasing.

First, there's the age-old *rule of thirds*, in which you divide the image rectangle into thirds and place your photo's subject at or near one of the intersections of the resulting grid.

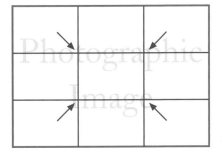

Place your photo's subject at or near these intersections.

This composition technique yields images that are more visually dynamic. The Crop tool in iPhoto's edit view makes it easy to crop according to the rule of thirds (page 69).

A second technique is to draw the viewer's eyes to your subject and add a sense of dynamism by using diagonal lines, such as a receding fence.

No Tripod?

If you want to take sharp photos in low light, mount your camera on a tripod. If you don't have a tripod handy, here's a workaround: turn on your camera's self-timer mode—the mode you'd usually use when you want to get yourself in the picture—then set the camera on a rigid surface and press the shutter button. Because you won't be holding the camera when the shutter goes off, you won't risk getting a blurred shot.

iMovie:
Making Movies

The Macintosh
iLife '09

iMovie at a Glance

Video editing is the process of assembling video clips, still images, and audio into a finished package that tells a story, conveys a message, and keeps your audience from falling asleep.

iMovie lets you edit video, but it also lets you *manage* it. Just as iPhoto helps you store and organize photos, iMovie helps you keep track of the video you shoot.

That's important, because we're shooting more video than ever. New, tiny video cameras make it easy to capture memories wherever we go. Many new camcorders don't even use tape, instead recording movies on built-in hard drives or on memory cards like those used by your digital camera. And speaking of digital cameras, many of them can shoot video clips, too.

iMovie keeps track of your video in a central place called the *Event Library.* You can browse your Event Library and relive memories with just a couple of mouse clicks. Don't have time to edit a finished movie? That's fine. Just browse your events and watch your life flash before your eyes.

When you want to assemble some clips into a finished project, iMovie is ready—and indeed, it lets you edit video quickly and efficiently. Create as many projects as you like, and switch between them with a click. Add titles, scene transitions, and even beautiful, animated travel maps and visual montages. Then share your final product on the Web, on a DVD, or on your iPod, iPhone, or Apple TV.

Quiet on the set.

Movie Making: The Big Picture

Making a movie is a multi-step process that iMovie makes easier than ever. If you're new to video editing, start small. Create a short movie—a minute or so. Try your hand at a simple music video: some video, a few still photos from iPhoto, a soundtrack from iTunes, a couple of titles. This is a great way learn the art and science of editing, and to appreciate its magic.

Here's a look at the steps involved in a typical movie-making project—and the topics the rest of this chapter explores.

Import assets. Bring in video from a camcorder, then review your shots. If you like, mark your favorites and add keywords for convenient searching. Consider analyzing the footage for image stabilization.

Sequence clips. Select your best footage in the Event browser and add it into your project. Trim clips as needed to fine-tune their length.

Sound good. Add music, sound effects, narration, or any combination of the three. Fine-tune audio levels for each.

Add eye candy. Create transitions between clips, create titles, and, if you like, add special elements, such as theme graphics, video effects, and picture-in-picture effects.

Refine. Review your work, refining edits, clip durations, and audio levels. If your movie is destined for DVD, add chapter markers. View your project in full-screen view.

Share. Publish your epic on MobileMe or YouTube, or export it for use in iDVD or for viewing on an iPhone, iPod, or Apple TV.

Get links to iMovie resources aplenty.
www.macilife.com/imovie

Your edited movies appear in the Project Library (page 184).

Add text titles to your movies (page 228).

The *playhead* indicates the current playback location. You can *skim* video clips by moving the mouse pointer over them (page 176).

Add background music from your iTunes library (page 216).

Add sound effects and narration (pages 216–223).

Your video plays in the *Viewer*, which is also a work area for some adjustments.

From left to right: Add music (page 216); add photos (page 200); create a title (page 228); create a transition (page 224); add a map or background (page 236).

Play an event's video.

Play your project within iMovie's window, or full-screen.

Import video from a camcorder (pages 170–173).

The Event Library gives you fast access to the video you've imported. Select an event, and its video appears in the Event browser to the right.

Work with audio, video, and photos.

Mark snippets of video for later use or deletion (page 178).

View each clip as a single thumbnail image, or "unroll" it into a *filmstrip* (page 176).

Importing DV and HDV Video

The first step in an iMovie editing project usually involves importing video that you've shot. If you're using a miniDV or HDV camera, you can connect the camera to your Mac's FireWire jack and use iMovie's camera mode to bring in your video. (If you're using a camera that connects using USB, your import procedure will be a bit different; see page 172).

With camera mode, you can control your camera using the transport buttons in iMovie's Import window. There's no need to grope for the tiny buttons on your camera when you need to rewind, fast-forward, stop, or play. Click the on-screen transport buttons, and iMovie sends the appropriate signals to your camera through the FireWire cable. Video professionals call this *device control*.

When you import video, the footage is organized into events—much as iPhoto organizes photos. You can create a new event or have iMovie store footage in an existing event. As in iPhoto, you can browse events by skimming across them, and you can assign keywords to help you locate footage later.

Importing video may be the start of your editing journey, but one step should come before you embark: making sure you have enough free disk space. Digital video eats disk space like I eat Oreos: for miniDV video, you'll need about 200MB of free space for each minute of video. For HDV video, you'll need a few times that amount. Bottom line: think about buying an external hard drive and using it for your video endeavors.

Importing from a FireWire Camera

Step 1. Connect your DV or HDV camera to your Mac's FireWire jack.

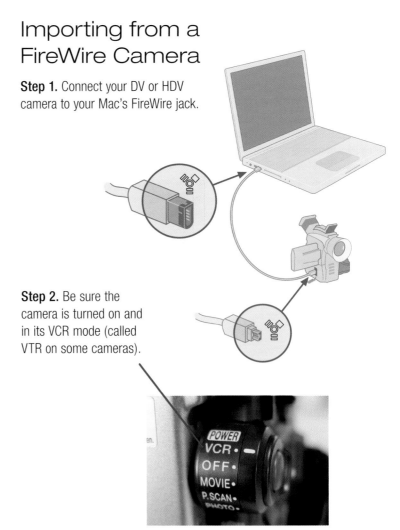

Step 2. Be sure the camera is turned on and in its VCR mode (called VTR on some cameras).

Tip: To store imported video on an external hard drive, simply create the video's event on the external drive. If you've already started the project and it's on your internal drive, see page 180 to learn how to move events and projects between drives.

Note: If you own a FireWire camcorder and either an aluminum MacBook or MacBook Air, you can't import video from a FireWire camera. These Macs lack FireWire, and there's currently no easy way (short of using another Mac) to get video into them.

Step 3. To start importing, click Import or press the spacebar while the tape is playing back.

The playback buttons control your camera.

Automatic mode rewinds the tape and imports all footage. Manual mode lets you choose which clips to import.

If more than one camera is attached, choose your camera from the Camera pop-up list.

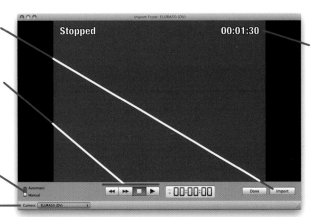

iMovie displays the time code that your camera recorded on the tape. This can help you keep track of where you are on a tape as you fast-forward or rewind.

Step 4. Type a name for the new event. To add video to an existing event, choose the event; see page 176.

It's convenient to use this feature now, but it costs you in time (page 212).

iMovie displays each clip you import in the Event browser.

Note: As your camera plays back, you'll see its video in the Import window.

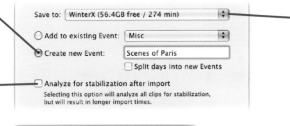

If you have more than one hard drive, you can use the Save To pop-up menu to specify where you want the footage to be stored.

HD Differences

HD Importing from an HDV camera? Under some circumstances, you may experience an odd delay as the video comes in: the tape may finish playing, but you'll still see video being displayed in iMovie's Import window. The video's motion may also appear jerky.

This occurs because your Mac must transcode (convert) the HD video into a format that allows for fast editing. This process occurs more or less in real time, depending on whether you're running other programs that may be fighting for their share of processor power.

To minimize the delay, close other applications. Also consider turning off Mac OS X's Time Machine backup feature while importing.

One ramification: it's a bit harder to tell when to stop importing, since your Mac may be displaying footage that the

camera actually played back seconds or minutes earlier.

For more precise control when selectively importing HD footage, view the footage on your camera's LCD screen during the import, and use your camera's buttons to stop and start playback.

Importing Video from Other Sources

Camcorders have come a long way in a short time. All camcorders used to capture footage to tape—many sizes and formats of tape, but always to cassettes of magnetic tape.

Thanks to the onward march of technology, a growing number of cameras record footage directly to solid-state memory cards, internal hard disks, or DVDs. Indeed, many people shoot video exclusively using digital "still" cameras—the kind you usually use with iPhoto.

The benefits? No more rewinding or fast-forwarding to find a scene—and no more stacks of tapes sitting on the shelf and waiting to be digitized.

The shift isn't just a matter of media. The new tapeless formats compress video in various ways to save significant amounts of storage space.

iMovie can import clips from most tapeless cameras. (Apple has published a list on its Web site; I've linked to it at www.macilife.com/imovie.) The import process is a bit different—and more convenient—than the steps outlined on the previous pages.

iMovie can also import movies stored in your iPhoto library or elsewhere on your hard disk. And if you're an iMovie veteran with older iMovie HD projects, iMovie '09 can import them, too—to a degree.

Note: To import AVCHD footage, you need a Mac with an Intel processor. However, a utility called VoltaicHD (www.shedworx.com/voltaichd) can convert the raw AVCHD video files on PowerPC-based (or Intel-based) Macs.

Importing from a Tapeless Camera

Step 1. Connect your camera to the Mac's USB port. (Even if your camera includes a FireWire port, iMovie recognizes tapeless formats only via USB.)

Step 2. Be sure that the camera is turned on and set to its PC Connect mode.

Step 3. In the Import window, choose an import mode. Automatic grabs all clips in the camera's memory. Want to be selective? Choose Manual, then click the checkboxes beneath each clip that you want to import. (You may want to click Uncheck All and then select the clips.)

Step 4. Click Import All or Import Checked, as appropriate.

Step 5. Name the new event. To store the footage in an existing event, choose the event's name (see page 176).

Think you might use the cool image stabilization feature with this footage? Check this box, then practice patience (page 212).

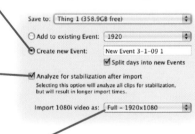

If you're importing high-definition 1080i video, choose a size. The full size retains the camera's highest dimensions (typically 1920 by 1080 pixels, but some cameras capture only 1440 by 1080); the Large option reduces the dimensions to 960 by 540 pixels. For advice on which size to choose, see the sidebar on the opposite page.

Step 6. Click OK and take a break while iMovie copies the footage and transcodes it into the editable AIC (Apple Intermediate Codec) format. When it's finished, click Done.

Importing Footage from Your Hard Disk

Step 1. Choose File > Import Movies.

Step 2. Locate the movie file and choose an event (or create a new event). For HD video, specify the Large or Full size option.

To have iMovie move the video file to your movie library, choose the Move Files option; to have iMovie make a duplicate of the video file, choose Copy Files.

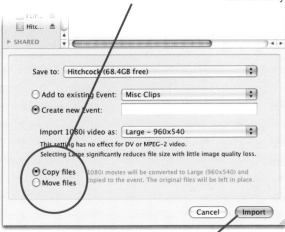

Step 3. Click Import or press Return.

Drag from the Finder. You can also drag video files directly from the Finder to an event's name in the Event Library. Doing so moves the video files to iMovie's library storehouse; to duplicate the file instead, keeping the original in place, press and hold the Option key as you drag.

Tip: If your movie is made up entirely of video already on your hard disk (in other words, no camera importing is involved), consider creating a new, empty event to hold its footage: choose File > New Event (page 177).

Recording Using an iSight

If you own a Mac with a built-in iSight camera, or you own an old external iSight, you can record directly in iMovie. Open the Import window and choose the iSight from the Camera menu. Click Capture to specify an event and start recording. (smile!). To end recording, click Stop.

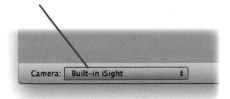

Large versus Full HD

HD You paid good money for the extra pixels that HD video gives you, so why reduce the size by importing footage at the Large size? The answer depends on what you're shooting. For most home uses, reducing the size to 960 by 540 won't produce a noticeable difference in the video quality—but it does ease the processor strain on iMovie when throwing around full-resolution HD video, not to mention reducing the amount of disk space consumed (13 GB for one hour of footage compared to 40 GB for the full quality, according to Apple).

In fact, the term *full quality* is a bit misleading. To make the footage easier to handle, iMovie tosses out some of the image information (specifically, one field of interlaced video); progressive video remains intact. If you're concerned about getting the absolute highest quality possible, a program such as Final Cut Express or Final Cut Pro is a better choice.

A Short Lesson in Video Formats

If you have a standard, miniDV camcorder and you're anxious to start making movies, feel free to skip this little lesson and move on to page 176. But if you want to use video from a different kind of device—or you're curious about one of iMovie's most intriguing capabilities—read on.

Just as music and photos can be stored in a variety of digital formats, video also comes in several flavors. And, as with music and photos, each video format takes its own approach to organizing the bits and bytes that make up your media.

In early iMovie versions, projects were based on one video format: DV. You could import other formats into iMovie, but iMovie would convert that footage into DV format. DV was iMovie's native tongue, and using other formats meant a translation step that took time, used up disk space, and often compromised video quality.

Times change. New types of video devices have appeared, and iMovie has evolved to keep pace: iMovie '09 provides native support for several video formats. iMovie '09 is multilingual, and as a result, you have the flexibility to edit video from a wider variety of video devices, ranging from Apple's iSight (which is built into many Mac models) to many digital camera models to the new breeds of high-definition cameras from companies such as Sony, Canon, and JVC.

iMovie's basic operation is identical regardless of which video format you use. There are some subtleties to some formats, and I'll share them as we go. But first, let's look at the video languages iMovie understands.

How Square Are Your Movies?

Many of the differences among video formats aren't visible at first glance, but one of the differences definitely is: the *aspect ratio* of the video frame.

We encountered the concept of aspect ratio when looking at iPhoto cropping techniques (page 68). The phrase simply describes how square or rectangular an image frame is.

Early iMovie versions were limited to one aspect ratio: the standard 4:3 ratio used by most TV sets, DV camcorders, and digital cameras.

Four units of width... ...for every three units of height.

Going wide. iMovie also features the ability to work with and create widescreen video in the 16:9 aspect ratio—the format common in high-definition TV sets.

Sixteen units of width... ...for every nine units of height.

The widescreen format provides a more cinematic experience.

Pronunciation guide. Making video small talk at the local coffee shop? The expressions *4:3* and *16:9* are usually pronounced "four by three" and "sixteen by nine." Technically, "four *to* three" and "sixteen *to* nine" are more accurate, since these expressions are ratios. After all, when was the last time you heard a bookie describe "2 by 1" odds on a horse?

Video Formats: A Scorecard

One of the quiet, yet revolutionary, features of iMovie is that it doesn't care much about which video format you throw at it. You can stick with one format throughout a project, mix formats within the same project, or apply an aspect ratio that's different from the original footage.

That said, iMovie can't read *everything*: uncompressed HD, for example, remains in the realm of professional tools, such as Final Cut Pro. Here's a look at the formats you can use with iMovie '09.

AVCHD. High definition (HD, for short) TV is gaining momentum, and the new breed of HD camcorders is helping. HD formats such as AVCHD and HDV bring high-definition videography to advanced amateurs and budget-minded professionals (and, as prices come down, to the rest of us). AVCHD is based on MPEG-4; it's used by camcorders that record 1080i or 1080p footage directly to a built-in hard disk, removable memory cards, or DVDs.

HDV 1080i and HDV 720p. HDV records to MiniDV tape and always uses a 16:9 aspect ratio. The images below illustrate the difference between DV and 1080i resolution.

MPEG-2 and MPEG-4. Many digital cameras shoot their movie clips in these formats, as do a growing number of compact video cameras (even HD models) that connect via USB.

DV. Still the most common format used by digital camcorders. Now that the era of high-definition TV is upon us, the DV format is often described as a *standard definition* format.

DV Widescreen. Most DV camcorders can shoot in widescreen mode, often by simply cropping the top and bottom of the video frame. (To shoot in this mode, use your camcorder's menus to activate 16:9 mode.) You don't get the picture quality of high-definition TV, but you do get that cinematically wide image.

iSight. Apple's iSight camera is built into some current Mac models and used to be available as a separate camera. (You'll still find them on eBay.) The iSight is designed for video chatting using iChat, but makes a great low-budget TV camera, too.

1080i (HDV and AVCHD): 1920 by 1080 pixels

DV: 720 by 480 pixels

Browsing Your Video Library

iMovie isn't just about editing video; it's also about managing it. Indeed, one of the great strengths of iMovie '09 is that it lets you organize and keep track of the video you import. You might say that iPhoto has taught iMovie a thing or two about organization.

And as with a photo library, the more accessible and organized your video library is, the more likely you'll spend time exploring and enjoying it.

Here's a look at the basic explorer's tools iMovie '09 provides. We'll explore more video-management tools on the following pages.

Browsing Events

iMovie stores video you import as a series of events, which appear in the Event Library area. To browse the footage in an event, select the event.

Skimming and playing. It's easy to browse your iPhoto library: all the photos are there for you to see. Video, however, involves time—what you see at the beginning of a clip is just a hint of what happens later, requiring you to watch the entire thing (or keep it all in your head).

iMovie's skimming feature lets you conquer time.

Move the mouse pointer over a clip to quickly scan the footage. As you skim, the frame beneath the playhead appears in the Viewer.

Don't want to hear audio as you skim? To quiet things down, click the Audio Skimming button (or press ⌘-K).
Tip: To temporarily turn off audio skimming, press the Control key as you skim.

Play time. To play video at actual speed, point to the spot on a clip where you want playback to begin, then press the space bar.

To watch all the footage in an event, select the event in the Event Library, then click the Play or Play Full Screen button.

Using the Event Browser

The Event browser shows the clips in an event. You can customize how those clips appear.

The big picture. When you want to see as many clips as possible in the Event browser, drag the clip size slider all the way to the right, until the word All appears next to it. In this view, you see just one frame per clip. When you're assessing some newly imported footage or just reliving some memories, this is an efficient way to view clips.

A closer look. When you're editing, you'll want to see more of each clip in the Event browser. It's essential for selecting which portions of clips you want to use in your project.

And seeing more of the clips is easy: just "unroll" your clips into *filmstrips* by dragging the clip size slider to the left. The further to the left you drag, the more frames you see. At the leftmost setting, iMovie displays a thumbnail for every half-second of video—great for precision work.

Thumbnail sizes. To control the size of the clip thumbnails, drag the thumbnail size slider above the Event Library. Want to see as many clips as possible on the screen? Make the thumbnails small. Need to see the differences between similar-looking clips? Make the thumbnails big.

The thumbnail setting applies to clips in both the Event browser and the Project browser.

Working with Events

Renaming an event. To change the name of an event, double-click its name, type a new name, and press Return.

Splitting an event. For organization's sake, you may sometimes want to split one event into two. Maybe you have an event containing footage from a morning hike with the kids and a nighttime poker game with friends. Those are very different events, and you might like your movie library to reflect that.

To split an event, click the clip that you want to be the first clip of the new event. (In this example, that would be the first poker game clip—the clip where you tuck the ace up your sleeve.) Then, choose File > Split Event Before Selected Clip.

Merging Events. At other times, you might decide that two or more events really constitute just one. Maybe you have several events containing footage from your Paris vacation, and you'd like to see them stored as just one.

Select the events you want to combine, choose File > Merge Events, and give the new event a name.

Creating a new event. You don't have to wait until you import video to create a new event. With an existing event selected, choose File > New Event, and iMovie creates an empty event named with today's date.

Tip: You can also Control-click on selected events and use the shortcut menu to merge them.

More Ways to View the Event Library

You can customize the way events appear in the Event Library.

iMovie organizes events into years. If you shoot a lot of video, you might want more viewing precision: choose View > Group Events by Month.

Moving footage between events. Sometimes, you might want to move a clip from one event to another. Maybe your latest import revealed some new-puppy footage that you forgot was in your camera, and you'd like to move those clips into the New Puppy event that contains the rest.

Begin by selecting the event that contains the clips you want to move. Next, select the clips you want to move (use the Shift-click and ⌘-click maneuvers to select multiple clips). Finally, drag the selected clips to the event where you want them.

To see your library displayed according to the hard drives that contain it, click the Group Events by Disk button (or choose View > Group Events by Disk). When a disk is disconnected or otherwise offline, it doesn't appear in the list.

Want to see each day of an event displayed separately? Choose View > Show Separate Days in Events. To see the clips organized from newest to oldest, choose View > Most Recent Days at Top.

Managing Video

Just as iPhoto provides features for organizing and keeping track of photos, iMovie provides features for managing the video in your Event Library.

And just as with iPhoto, you don't have to use any of these features. But as your video library grows, you may find that locating specific clips becomes cumbersome. You may also find yourself running low on hard drive space.

iMovie's video-management tools can help on both counts.

Keep or Trash? Marking Video

Your first job after importing some video will probably be to sit back and enjoy it —to watch the footage, smile at the good stuff, and cringe at the bad. As you watch, you may get ideas for ways to edit the video into a finished project.

As you audition your footage, you can *mark* sections of it to reflect your smiles and grimaces. The best stuff? Mark it as a favorite. The stuff your enemies may use against you someday? Mark it for deletion.

Playing favorites. To mark a clip, start by selecting part or all of the clip. (See page 183 for details on selecting clips.) Then, turn to the toolbar.

Thumbs up: mark the selection as a favorite (keyboard shortcut: press the F key).

Not sure: unmark the selection (press U).

Thumbs down: reject the selection (press R).

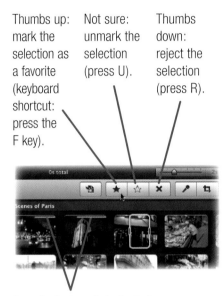

Favorite footage is indicated by a green line.

By skimming, selecting, and tapping the keyboard shortcuts for each of these buttons, you can very quickly group your footage into these best, worst, and "I'll decide later" categories.

Controlling what you see. Using the Show pop-up menu below the Event Library, you can control what iMovie displays in the Event browser.

Normally, iMovie shows your favorite footage and anything that you haven't marked. To see only your favorite footage, choose Favorites Only. iMovie hides unmarked and rejected footage.

To see everything, choose All Clips. And to see only the awful stuff, choose Rejected Only. iMovie indicates rejected footage with a red bar.

Advanced Marking

As you become accustomed to marking footage, you might want to take advantage of a more powerful marking mode. Choose iMovie > Preferences, and check the Show Advanced Tools box.

The marking tools now work differently. Click the Mark as Favorite button, for example, and then drag across the range of frames to be marked. When you're done, the tool is still active, so you can drag across another clip and mark it— saving you a couple of clicks.

Deleting Footage

Frames that you've marked as rejected remain in the Event Library, even if they're not visible. If you *know* you'll never use those clips and want to free up some disk space, choose Rejected Only from the Show pop-menu, then click the Move Rejected to Trash button.

iMovie moves rejected footage to the Finder's Trash, which you can then empty.

Organizing Footage with Keywords

Like iPhoto, iMovie lets you assign descriptive *keywords* to video: Dog, Beach, Vacation, Paris, and so on. You can then organize and search based on keywords.

Note: To access iMovie's keywording features, you must turn on the Show Advanced Tools option in the Preferences dialog box.

Creating Keywords

iMovie has a small set of keywords already defined. They're a good start, but you'll want to create your own keywords to reflect the subjects in your footage.

Begin by displaying the Keywords window: click the toolbar's Keywords button.

To create a keyword, click in the New Keyword box, type the keyword, then press Return or click Add. The new keyword appears in the Keywords window.

The first nine keywords get a single-key short-cut—a numeral 1 through 9. If you want a keyboard shortcut for a particular keyword, drag it so that it's one of the first nine in the Keywords window.

To delete a keyword, select it and click Remove.

Assigning Keywords

To assign keywords to some footage, again summon the Keywords window. Next, check the boxes next to the keywords you want to assign. (You can also tap the single-key number shortcuts for keywords that have them.)

Finally, select the footage that you want to mark with those keywords. Below, I'm assigning a few keywords to some footage of a famous dog.

Tip: You can also select a range of footage, click the Keywords button on the toolbar, and *then* choose the keywords in the Keywords window.

Sorting by Keywords

Here's where your organizational fortitude pays off. You can view your footage by keyword.

First, click the Keyword Filtering button (). This displays the Keyword Filtering pane.

Next, click each keyword you want to search for; a green Include button lights up to the left of the keyword. Use the buttons at the bottom of the pane to specify how you want to search. To search for all the keywords you've checked, click All. (Example: "Show me all the footage with the keywords Paris, Outdoor, and Close-up.") To search for any of them, click Any. ("Show me anything that has Paris or Outdoor or Close-up.")

You can also hide footage and narrow your search by clicking the red Exclude button to the left of the keyword. ("I don't want to see any close-ups from Paris right now.")

The results of all this clicking appear in the Event browser. Here, I'm searching for any footage that has the Paris keyword but not the Closeup keyword.

Tips for Managing Video

Relocate Projects and Events

Even with today's huge hard drives, you'll eventually be pinched for space as you add more video—especially HD video—to your iMovie library. (For a refresher on video file sizes, see page 170.)

But hard disks are relatively cheap and growing in capacity every year; a *1 terabyte* (TB) drive now goes for less than $150. When your Mac's internal hard disk becomes clogged with video and you want to migrate older projects and events to another disk, let iMovie be the burly mover who hauls them to their new home.

Relocating a project. To relocate a project, click the Project Library button to view your projects, then drag the one you want to move to the icon of the destination hard disk. Here, it's moving day for the project named Shilshole Marina.

When you release the mouse button, iMovie asks what you'd like to copy: only the project file or the file *and* the events containing its video files.

It's generally smartest to choose the *Copy project and events* option, since it puts everything in one place. A project and its events *can* reside on different drives, but if a drive becomes unavailable, you won't be able to edit the footage. (If that happens, hover over the yellow warning icon, and iMovie displays the missing clip's location.)

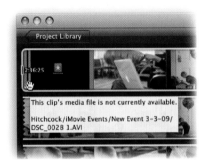

Relocating events. Relocating events is just as easy: In the Event Library, drag an event to a different hard disk.

(If you can't see other disks in the Event Library, choose View > Group Events by Disk, or click the disk button in the upper-right corner of the Event Library area.)

Tip: Dragging a project or event to a new disk creates a new copy at the destination. If you'd rather move the files instead of copy them, press ⌘ as you drag.

Archiving Video from Tapeless Cameras

When MiniDV tape camcorders were the only game in town, you could rely on having the original tape as a backup of your footage. But what about footage stored on a tapeless camcorder's internal hard disk or removable memory card? Cards have never been cheaper, but it's still impractical to buy new ones for each video shoot.

The answer: archive. iMovie's archive feature copies video from your tapeless camcorder to your hard disk—but without transcoding the files. For example, AVCHD files stay in their native compressed format, taking up less space than if you imported them. You can also use this feature to quickly offload video so that you can erase the card for more shooting.

In the Import window, click Archive All.

Choose a destination for the files, and supply a name for the folder that iMovie will create. iMovie copies the contents of the camcorder's memory card or hard disk to your hard drive.

When you want to use the footage, import the archived video files into iMovie. Choose File > Import > Camera Archive and locate the archive folder. iMovie transcodes the footage as if it were coming directly from the camcorder.

Tip: You can archive video files from the Flip MinoHD and other cameras that store video in MPEG-4 format, but importing the files using the Camera Archive import method doesn't work. Instead, bring the video in by choosing File > Import > Movies.

Adjust Clip Date and Time

During import, iMovie notes the date and time your video was shot. To see the date and time, choose View > Show Playhead Info and skim across a clip.

But what if your camcorder's clock was set wrong? Or maybe the footage you're importing doesn't have time information—perhaps it's from a digital still camera stored in iPhoto or imported from a movie file.

No problem: select one or more clips in the Event browser, then choose File > Adjust Clip Date and Time. In the dialog that appears, change the date, time, or both.

Video for the Ages

One problem with hard drives is that they're less reliable than tape: one hard drive crash, and hours of video can be lost forever. Play it safe: have multiple backups. If you store archived video on an external drive, buy another drive of similar capacity and duplicate it using a program such as SuperDuper (shirt-pocket.com) or Carbon Copy Cloner (www.bombich.com).

As the drives fill, replace them with higher-capacity drives and move their contents using the same software. And now and then, check that the video is intact by opening some files. (My friend Adam Engst of TidBITS has proposed every Friday the 13th as International Verify Your Backups day. So far, the United Nations hasn't bought in.)

Another archive option is to burn footage to DVDs, but they're likely to last only a few years before their data is unreadable. And yes, all this archiving is a hassle—but it's a party compared to losing video.

External Hard Drive Options

Contemplating more hard drive storage? Here are some things to keep in mind.

Look for a drive with a FireWire or FireWire 800 interface. You'll spend a bit more, but FireWire is faster than USB. Also get a drive with a speed of at least 7200 RPM.

For Macs lacking FireWire, such as the MacBook Air or newest MacBook, USB is your only option. On these Macs, it's better to use the external drive as an archive rather than for live editing work.

Some newer drives include an eSATA (external serial ATA) port, which is much faster than FireWire. To use eSATA, you'll need an eSATA expansion card (for a tower Mac) or ExpressCard (for a MacBook Pro) and cable. iMacs need not apply.

It may be more economical to buy a "bare" internal hard drive and a separate, empty hard drive enclosure (OWC, at mac-sales.com, sells many enclosure models). When it's time to move up to a higher-capacity drive, you can re-use the enclosure for the new drive.

For still more storage, consider the Data Robotics Drobo (www.drobo.com), an enclosure that accepts up to four bare Serial ATA drives. The Mac sees the drives as one volume, and the Drobo automatically maintains a backup of your data spread across the drives, which form what's called a *RAID*, or *redundant array of inexpensive disks*.

Creating a Video Slide Show

You've imported some video from your camera and maybe you also imported some movies that were already on your hard drive. Now what?

This chapter is filled with all sorts of details about how to manage, categorize, and finesse your video. But if you're like me, you want to jump right into editing and then tackle the finer points as you progress.

Here's a little lesson that introduces the basic techniques and tools for editing in iMovie. We're going to make a "video slide show"—a series of video clips, each four-seconds long, accompanied by some background music. In the interest of immediate gratification, I'll skip over the details and just give you the big picture.

Making a Movie

Step 1. Choose File > New Project, type a name for your project, and choose the aspect ratio that matches that of the video you imported.

Step 2. Choose a theme, such as Photo Album (this enables the option to automatically create transitions and titles), then click Create.

You certainly don't have to use a theme for every project you create, but this is a nice opportunity to see the visual spice that themes can bring to your projects.

Step 3. In the Event Library, select the event containing your video. The event's video footage appears in the Event browser.

Step 4. In the Event browser, skim the mouse pointer over a clip. When you see a scene you'd like to add to the slide show, click on the clip.

When you click a clip, iMovie automatically selects four seconds' worth of video, starting at the spot where you were pointing. The yellow border marks the selected footage.

Step 5. Click the Add Selection to Project button, or simply press the E key, its keyboard shortcut.

iMovie adds the selected four seconds to your project.

Step 6. Repeat Steps 3 and 4 a few times.

After clicking a clip, try dragging it from the Event browser to the project—that's a very common way of working in iMovie.

Because the option to create transitions and titles was active in Step 2, iMovie adds those elements based on the theme you selected. (You can edit them later.)

Tip: Want to see more of each clip in your event? Drag the slider at the lower-right corner of the Event browser.

Step 7. Add a background music soundtrack.

Display the Music and Sound Effects browser by clicking its button. Find a tune, then drag it to the background of your project; the entire background turns green.

Step 8. Play your movie.

Click one of the two play buttons below the

Project browser. The button on the left plays the movie full-screen.

Step 9 (optional). Change transitions.

Want to see how easy it is to make changes? Double-click one of the transitions between two clips. In the Inspector, click the Transition button, then choose another style and click Done.

Tip: If no theme is applied to your project, you can change the style of all transitions at once. Choose File > Project Properties. Check the box labeled

Automatically Add, then choose a transition from the pop-up menu and click OK.

The Project Properties dialog box controls overall project settings: its aspect ratio, durations of transitions and photos, and more.

Step 10. Play your movie again.

It's that easy to assemble a quick movie: Click a clip, add it to the project, and repeat. There's much, much more you can do, of course, and the rest of this chapter tells all.

Essential Notes and Tips

Never destructive. When you assemble a project in iMovie, you're never altering your original source video (the footage you imported). This isn't old Hollywood, where editors cut and spliced film and unwanted footage fell to the floor. iMovie simply keeps track of which parts of each clip you want to use, and in what order. You're always able to change edits and use footage that you didn't use the first time around.

At the same time, the house-keeping features covered on pages 178–179, let you delete unwanted footage and free up disk space.

Full-screen controls. When playing a movie full-screen, try moving the mouse—controls appear that let you jump to a specific spot in the movie or play a different project.

How many seconds? If you like iMovie's click-and-add editing technique, you may want to customize how much video iMovie selects when you click a clip. Choose iMovie > Preferences, click Browser, and drag the slider labeled Clicking in Events Browser Selects. Want to create a fast-paced video? Choose a short duration, such as two seconds. Creating a leisurely montage of scenic shots? Think longer.

Selection tips. Clicking a clip is just one way to select some of its footage. You will also frequently select video by dragging across a clip. This lets you select a *specific* amount of footage: as you drag, the thumbnail and the Viewer display the frame currently under the playhead. A little time readout also appears next to the clip; it shows how many seconds you've selected.

To select an entire clip in the Event browser, press Option while clicking the clip.

To select more than one clip at a time, ⌘-click on each clip, or Shift-click to select a range of

clips—standard Mac selection maneuvers.

Clip details. As you work, you might want to display information about a clip. Choose View > Playhead Info. A little banner appears above the playhead containing information about the current clip.

Keyboard shortcuts abound. As you get familiar with iMovie, start exploring its keyboard shortcuts—there are lots of them, and they can help you edit efficiently. (For a list, choose Help > Keyboard Shortcuts.)

Creating a Movie Project

One of the many beauties of iMovie is that you don't actually have to do any editing in order to enjoy your video. You can relive those memorable events by simply browsing footage that you've imported into your Event Library—just as you can enjoy your photos in iPhoto without having to publish a book.

But as we saw with iPhoto, something special happens when you turn raw material into a finished, polished product. An iPhoto book (or any other iPhoto project) shows your photos at their best and lets you tell a story.

The same applies when you create a project in iMovie. Select just the best parts of an event, and then sequence them in a way that tells a story, brings a laugh, or simply recalls good times. Then share your project in a variety of ways.

iMovie lets you create as many projects as you like. Your projects appear in the Project Library, and you can switch from one project to another with the click of a mouse. iMovie even automatically saves your work as you go along.

Here's how to get started.

Creating a New Project

Step 1. Click the New Project button (or choose File > New Project or press ⌘-N).

The New Project dialog box appears.

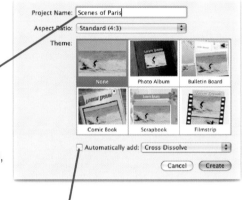

Step 2. Type a name for your project, and choose its aspect ratio (see page 174). Choose a theme if you want to use one. (You can apply, change, or remove a theme later, too.)

To have iMovie create transitions between clips as you add them, check this box and choose a style from the pop-up menu.

Step 3. Click Create or press Return.

iMovie displays placeholder rectangles in a new, empty project.

Accessing your projects. To work on a different project, click the Project Library button in the upper-left corner of the iMovie window.

To open a project, select it and click Edit Project or double-click the project.

Skim through the entire movie without opening it.

Notes and Tips

Renaming. To change a project's name, double-click the title in the Project Library, then type a new name and press Return.

Deleting. To delete a project, select it and press ⌘-Delete. Change your mind? Choose Edit > Undo Delete Project—and do this before you do anything else.

Duplicating. To make a duplicate of a project, Control-click on the project's name and choose Duplicate Project from the shortcut menu. This is a great way to experiment with different editing approaches.

Share without opening. You can share a selected project in the Project Library without opening it. (For sharing specifics, see pages 238–241).

Format flexibility. You can change the aspect ratio of a project at any time: choose File > Project Properties (⌘-J).

You can combine this flexibility with the Duplicate Project command to create, for example, one version of a movie for your 16:9 widescreen TV, and another version for your 3:2 iPhone: duplicate a completed project, then select the duplicate, and change its aspect ratio.

Browse projects full screen. When playing a project in full-screen view, you can also browse and play back your other projects. Move the mouse to reveal a Cover Flow view of your projects.

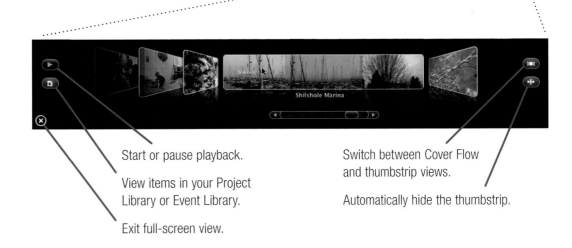

Start or pause playback.

View items in your Project Library or Event Library.

Exit full-screen view.

Switch between Cover Flow and thumbstrip views.

Automatically hide the thumbstrip.

Adding Clips to a Movie

A clip in the Event Library is like a baseball player on the bench. To put the clip on the playing field, you must add it to a project.

Select part or all of a clip using the techniques described in the sidebar on page 183, then drag it into the Project area.

Tip: Want to insert a clip between two clips that are already on the timeline? Just drag the clip between them—a green vertical line appears between the clips to indicate the insertion.

Other Ways to Add Clips

Usually, you work with one clip at a time, dragging it to the project as you sequence your movie. But there's more than one way to work with clips.

Drag several at once. You can add multiple clips to a project at once. Select each clip by ⌘-clicking on it, then drag the clips to the project as a group.

Add to Project button. With a clip or range of frames selected in the Event browser, click the [⊞] button or simply press E. iMovie adds the selected footage to the end of your movie. This can be a fast and efficient way to build a movie: select some footage, press E, select more footage, press E, and so on.

Paste from the Clipboard. You can also add a clip to a project using the Paste command. Select a clip in the Event browser—or a clip that's already in your movie—and cut or copy, then paste. You can even paste clips from a different iMovie project.

Using the Add to Project tool. Here's another great rapid-fire editing technique. In iMovie's preferences dialog box, check the Show Advanced Tools box; this changes the workings of the Add to Project button. Click it and select some footage in the Event browser—the footage is immediately added to the end of your project.

Here's the best part: the tool is still active and ready for action. Drag across some more footage in the Event browser, and iMovie adds it to the project. Try it. You'll be impressed with how fast it lets you sling footage into your project.

Swipe into place. If you're using iMovie on a MacBook, MacBook Pro, or MacBook Air made after October 2008, swipe three fingers on the Multi-Touch trackpad from bottom to top to add a selected clip to the project.

More Room to Work

When you're in the throes of editing, there are a few things you can do to free up space in iMovie's window. To see more event footage, click the hide button below the Event Library. To show them, click the buttons again.

To gain more work space for your project's timeline, swap the position of the event and project panes: click the Swap Events and Projects button.

iMovie also provides a few preset window arrangements: to explore them, choose Window > Viewer. You might prefer the Large setting when cropping footage or photos, or when using the Ken Burns

effect (page 200). When you're working mostly in the timeline and Event browser, the Small setting gives you more room.

You can change how iMovie divides its window by clicking and dragging any blank area of the toolbar. And finally, if you have a second monitor attached to your Mac, choose Window >

Viewer on Secondary Display to pull the viewer out of the iMovie interface altogether and onto the other monitor (make sure Show Advanced Tools is enabled in iMovie's preferences). Take advantage of these interface-customizing features. You'll spend less time scrolling and more time editing.

Editing Basics

In a well-edited video, the cuts between scenes occur at exactly the right moments. In movies, the action cuts between two actors as they converse, reinforcing both the dialog and the drama. Every moviegoer has experienced this, probably without even thinking about it.

iMovie provides several features that let you edit your video. You can trim the start or end point of a clip within the project timeline or by using a separate window called the *Clip Trimmer*.

You'll find yourself using these essential tools a lot as you work video into a manageable rough cut. From there, you may turn to more advanced tools, including the Precision Editor, to refine the edits. Stay tuned to the following pages, as well as to pages 244–247. (And check out page 207 to learn how beat markers can perform a lot of these edits for you.)

Action! It's a common word in the movie business, and it's a common menu in iMovie: every clip has an Action menu. Choose it to display commands for working on that clip.

Skimming tip. Annoyed that skimming to the end of a line in the filmstrip forces you to mouse back to the beginning to start at the next line? Save your wrists: when you reach the end of a line, hold the Shift key and keep moving your mouse to the right—iMovie automatically moves you to the start of the next line.

Trimming Techniques

Trimming is the process of changing where a clip starts and ends. You might need to trim clips when editing dialog or when timing clips to match a musical background or narration.

Trimming directly. To trim a clip directly in the project, drag across a clip to specify the range of frames you want to keep. Then, choose Edit > Trim to Selection (⌘-B).

Alternatively, you can drag to select frames you want to remove, then press the Delete key.

In either case, iMovie doesn't delete the footage you've trimmed; it simply hides it. You can restore the footage by using the trimmer.

Using the Clip Trimmer. For more trimming precision, use the Clip Trimmer. Select the clip you want to trim, then choose Window > Clip Trimmer, or press ⌘-R. (You can also click the Action menu icon on the clip and choose Clip Trimmer.)

The Event browser is temporarily replaced by the Clip Trimmer.

To change the clip's start point or end point, drag the left or right handle. As you drag, the Viewer displays the current frame. To preview the trim, click the Clip Trimmer's Play button. When you're finished, click Done.

Editing Tips

Single-frame trimming. To trim in single-frame increments, point to the handle you want to trim, then press Option along with the left- or right-arrow key.

Splitting a clip. There are times when you might want to split one clip into two—to relocate a portion elsewhere in the movie, for example. To split a clip, drag to select some frames, then choose Edit > Split Clip. Alternatively, position the playhead, Control-click, and choose Split Clip from the shortcut menu (or just press ⌘-Shift-S).

Note: If you want to cut the clip into two pieces, be sure that your selection extends all the way to the beginning or end of the clip; if you select a range of frames in the middle of the clip, iMovie cuts at both ends, leaving you with three pieces.

More precision in the Project browser. To edit with single-frame precision in the Project browser, point to the left or right edge of a clip, then hold down the ⌘ and Option keys. An orange outline appears that lets you drag the edge in one-frame increments, up to one second.

Tip: Like this option? Choose iMovie > Preferences, click Browser, and check the Show Fine Tuning Controls box. Now when you select a clip, tiny fine-tuning buttons appear at the left and right side of the clip. Click the appropriate button to change the start or end point of the clip.

Reordering Clips

You may often decide that a certain clip would be more effective elsewhere in your project. To move a clip, select it in the Project browser and drag it to a new location in the filmstrip. iMovie lets you move only entire clips, so if you want to move just a portion of a clip elsewhere in your movie, split the clip first.

Tip: If you own a Mac laptop introduced after October 2008, swipe three fingers left or right on the Multi-Touch trackpad to quickly reorder a clip before or after an adjoining clip.

Changing Clip Speed and Direction

That video of Junior's winning soccer game could use some slow-motion instant replays; iMovie provides them. Double-click a clip in the Project browser to bring up the Inspector, then click the Clip button. (Or simply choose Clip Adjustments from the clip's Action menu.)

Want to see that winning goal in reverse? Click the Reverse box.

To slow down the clip, drag the slider to the left. To speed up the clip, drag the slider to the right. The slider gives you a range of 12.5 to 800 percent.

You can also type a specific percentage or duration. **Tip:** These boxes give you a much wider range than the Speed slider: you can type any percentage value from 5 to 2000 percent.

To apply the change, click Done.

Notes and Tips

Depending on the format of your source video, you may see a Convert Entire Clip button instead of the speed controls. Click the button to convert the clip to AIC (Apple Intermediate Codec), then the controls appear.

Changing clip speed also affects the clip's audio. Unless you're after a weird effect, mute the clip's volume: choose Edit > Mute Clip.

Advanced Editing Techniques

Performing Slip Edits

You may sometimes want to use a different part of a clip that you've added to a project, but to maintain the clip's duration. Maybe you have a five-second shot of a beach, and you realize that a different part of the original source clip looks better.

Open the clip in the Clip Trimmer, then drag the entire yellow selection border left or right (the mouse pointer looks like a hand with an arrow on it: 🖑). This tells iMovie to use a different part of the source clip, but to not change the clip's duration in your project; this is called a *slip edit*.

Tip: Slipping also works in the Project browser when you're cutting down footage, and it works in the Event browser when you're selecting portions of clips to add to your movie.

Performing Insert Edits

When you drop a clip from an event onto existing footage in the Project browser (as opposed to dropping it onto the space *between* clips), iMovie presents a pop-up menu asking what you'd like to do.

Choosing Insert splits the existing clip and places the new clip into the gap. All of the first clip's footage is still part of your project, but is now interrupted by the new clip: the action cuts from the first part of the original clip to the clip you inserted, and then jumps back to the second half of the original clip. And accordingly, the total duration of your project increases by the length of the new clip. This is called an *insert edit*.

Tip: If you later reposition the two halves of the original clip side-by-side, iMovie recognizes them as two halves of a split clip. To join those halves back into one clip, choose Edit > Join Clip.

Performing Replace Edits

One of the beauties of editing digital video is that you can change your mind. You may find a scene that works better than one you've already placed in a project, or you might decide to use footage of the same scene shot from a different angle. For situations like these, a *replace edit* is the answer.

A basic replace edit. Drag some video from an event and drop it onto a clip in your project. From the pop-up menu that appears, choose Replace. The existing clip in your movie disappears and the new clip takes its place. If the new clip is shorter or longer than the one that it replaced, the total length of your project becomes shorter or longer, too.

This basic replace edit is the one to use when you simply want to replace one clip with another ("You know, that other shot of the Eiffel Tower is better than the one I used originally."), and you don't care whether the project becomes longer or shorter as a result.

Advanced replace edits. But what if you want to insert a clip into your movie without changing the project's duration? Maybe you've made edits that match up with music or sound effects, but then you decide to add or change a clip. If the standard replace edit was the only option available to you, you'd have to try to make an identically timed selection in the Event browser before moving it to your movie—and that's the definition of the phrase *trial and error*.

Fortunately, iMovie provides some advanced flavors of replace edit that let you replace clips without changing the total length of a project. **Note:** To use these options, you must activate the Show Advanced Tools option in iMovie's General preferences.

Step 1. In the Event browser, select some footage that you want to use as the replacement footage.

Step 2. Drag the footage you've selected from the Event browser, and drop it onto an existing clip in the project.

Step 3. In the menu that pops up, choose the Replace option you want.

The first frame of your selection becomes the first frame of the replaced footage. Use this one when you have the perfect starting point for your clip and you want iMovie to figure out where it should end in order to perfectly replace the clip in your project.

The last frame of your selection becomes the last frame of the replaced footage. Use this one when you have the perfect ending point for your clip and you want iMovie to figure out where it should start.

With each option, iMovie uses as much video from the source clip as is needed to match the original clip's duration, even if that doesn't match your selection. For example, if you select 10 seconds of video and chose Replace from Start when dropping onto a 20 second clip, the result is 20 seconds of new video that starts with the beginning of your selection.

Note: If the video you're dragging from the Event browser is shorter than the clip in your project, iMovie warns that the duration of the project will be reduced. To cancel the edit, click Cancel. To complete the edit, click Continue.

What's the point? In the video world, these kinds of advanced replace edits are called *three-point edits*. In traditional editing systems, such as Final Cut Pro, you'd set an In point and Out point on a source clip to define the start and end of a selection (those are two of the three points). Then, in your project's timeline, you'd set one In point *or* Out point (the third point) defining where to align the incoming footage. The duration of the source clip determines the length of the edit in the timeline.

But who cares about all that? The point is, iMovie's advanced replace edit options give you plenty of control.

This is a great edit to use when you want to line up the action that's in the middle of a clip with a sound effect in your project. Select the clip in the Event browser, skim to find the point of interest within it, then click and drag it into your project. When you hover over the clip you want to replace, you can skim to find the exact point with which you want your clip to line up (maybe it's a sound, such as a door slam). iMovie will determine where the clip needs to start and end in order to perfectly replace the clip in your project. iMovie is essentially lining up the point you clicked on in your clip with where you drop it in your project.

Creating Cutaways

A *cutaway* is a common video-production technique. Think of Barbara Walters nodding solemnly while Fabio describes what kind of tree he'd like to be. Or maybe the video changes to show a close-up of Grandma's garden as she talks about it.

Try it yourself. Want to experiment with cutaways? Go to www.macilife. com/imovie and download the Cutaway Example Footage archive. Double-click the archive after downloading it, then open the folder named Cutaway Footage and read the instructions inside.

Note: Cutaway edits are available only when iMovie's advanced editing tools option is active. To verify that it is, choose iMovie > Preferences, and make sure that the Show Advanced Tools box is checked.

Step 1. Get Your Shots

Begin planning cutaway shots when shooting your video. After Grandma talks about her garden, shoot some close-ups of the plants she talked about. While you're shooting the school play, grab a couple of shots of the audience laughing or clapping. Or after you've shot an interview, move the camera to shoot a few seconds of the interviewer nodding. (In TV news, this kind of shot is called a *noddie*.)

Tip: Have a digital still camera that takes high-quality video? Pop it on a tripod, and use it to shoot short cutaway shots. Import the footage into iPhoto, then access it through iMovie's media browser. The video quality won't match exactly, but your viewers may never notice. And your cutaways will be authentic rather than staged.

Step 2. Insert the Cutaway

With your footage imported, you're ready to add the cutaway clip.

In the Event browser, select the video that represents the cutaway shot. Next, drag the selection to the spot in your project where you want the cutaway to appear. (Don't worry about being precise—you just want to get the cutaway in place for now.) Release the mouse button, and from the pop-up menu that appears, choose Cutaway.

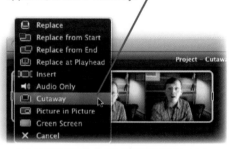

The cutaway appears on a new track above the filmstrip.

Step 3. Fine Tune

Play the cutaway portion of the project to see how your edit looks. If you want to fine-tune the cutaway's position, click the middle of the cutaway clip, then drag left or right to position it. The shadowed area below the clip indicates the filmstrip video hidden by the cutaway.

Make sure your primary and cutaway footage exist as separate clips.

Notes and Tips

Editing a cutaway. For the most part, you can edit a cutaway using the same techniques you use for other clips. Drag its handles to change the clip's duration, or click the Action menu and choose Clip Trimmer to edit it there. If you want to slip the clip (see page 190), do so in the Clip Trimmer. You can also apply audio edits to the cutaway (see page 220).

You can also have multiple cutaway shots right next to each other. You can't, however, perform insert or replace edits on a cutaway.

Creating a cutaway transition. You can have a cross-dissolve transition before and after the cutaway instead of just a straight cut. Double-click the cutaway clip to display the Clip Inspector. In the Cutaway Fade area of the Inspector, click Manual. To adjust the speed of the transition, drag the slider.

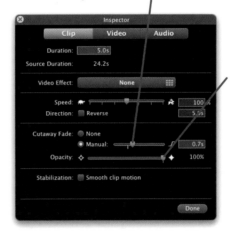

Adjusting opacity. Normally, a cutaway clip is completely opaque: it covers up the clip below it. But you can also have it appear semi-transparent. Try out some creative options: superimpose a gauzy close-up of champagne glasses over the dancing wedding couple, and use the transition option to have it fade in and fade out at its beginning and end.

To adjust opacity, double-click the cutaway, and in the Inspector, drag the Opacity slider.

Displaying timecode. For very precise cutaway adjustments—and, indeed, for any precise editing work—you prefer to view clip durations as timecode instead of as seconds. Choose iMovie > Preferences and check the Display Time as HH:MM:SS:Frames box.

Watermarking video. Looking for an easy way to watermark your video? Create an image file with a transparent background, save it as a PNG image, and add that as a cutaway (see page 201).

The Precision Editor at a Glance

When you're just slinging together some favorite pieces of footage, you probably won't need advanced editing techniques. But when you need to cut with precision, iMovie can be a surprisingly sharp scalpel, thanks to the new Precision Editor.

Don't get me wrong: the Clip Trimmer is a fine tool for refining footage. But the Precision Editor gives you more control over the edits between clips. Just as film editors line up strips of film, and then cut and splice them together, the Precision Editor aligns two clips for manipulation. The way the Precision Editor displays the two clips makes it easy to adjust how the clips work with each other. You can make more precise edits to transitions. And you can move a video clip's audio portion without detaching it from the video.

The Precision Editor resembles a traditional *timeline*, that thing Apple did away with in iMovie '08 in favor of the filmstrip. The Precision Editor provides many of the same editing conveniences of the "traditional" timeline that long-time iMovie users were accustomed to—and adds some unique strengths. One big advantage the Precision Editor provides over a timeline is that you can see not only the footage you're using in the movie, but also the footage you *aren't* using—the stuff you've trimmed. On the other hand, you can't perform a slip edit (page 190) in the Precision Editor as you can in most timelines and in iMovie's Clip Trimmer.

Here's the big picture behind iMovie's sharpest editing tool.

Precision Editor Essentials

When you summon the Precision Editor, it replaces the Event browser in the iMovie window (opposite page). There are several ways to access the Precision Editor.

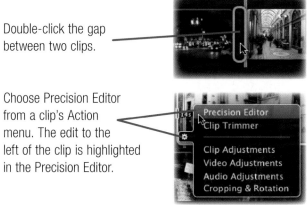

Double-click the gap between two clips.

Choose Precision Editor from a clip's Action menu. The edit to the left of the clip is highlighted in the Precision Editor.

Choose Window > Precision Editor. If a clip is selected, the edit to its left is highlighted. If nothing is selected, the very first edit in the project appears.

Press ⌘-/. Using the keyboard shortcut highlights whichever edit is closest to the mouse pointer, regardless of whether a clip is selected.

Notes and Tips

Maximize the size. For the best view of the Precision Editor, expand iMovie's window to fill your screen (choose Window > Zoom), and then choose Window > Viewer > Small (or press ⌘-8). These maneuvers reduce the size of the Viewer and increase the size of the Precision Editor.

Another way to use the Precision Editor. Don't let its name lead you to think that the Precision Editor is useful only when you're making razor-sharp edits. You can also use it as your primary editing tool: throw a bunch of clips into a new project, then use the Precision Editor to refine the clips' durations, clicking the Show Next Edit and Show Previous Edit buttons to jump from one clip to the next. Try it.

Video clip's audio track.

The cut point between two clips.

Show or hide extras, such as titles and voiceovers.

Show or hide audio tracks.

Play the current edit: click to preview three seconds around the currently selected cut point (see related tip, below).

Tip: Clicking the Play Current Edit button is the same as pressing the right-bracket (]) key to play three seconds around the playhead in the Project browser, except that in the Precision Editor, it plays around the cut point. To quickly review an edit you've made in the Precision Editor, press] instead of mousing up to the button.

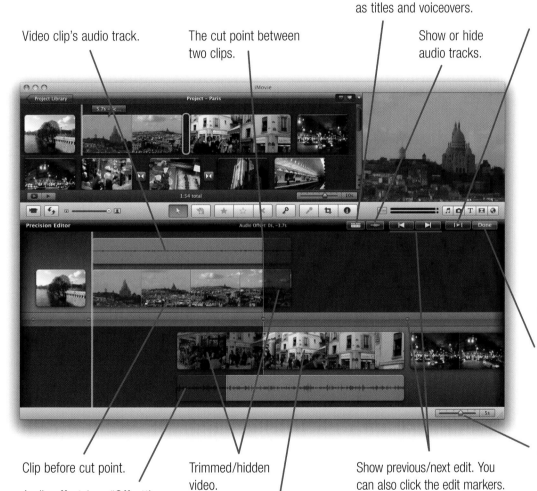

Exit the Precision Editor. **Keyboard shortcut:** Return or Esc.

Zoom out for a bigger picture of your edits; zoom in for maximum precision.

Clip before cut point.

Audio offset (see "Offsetting Audio," on page 199).

Trimmed/hidden video.

Clip after cut point.

Show previous/next edit. You can also click the edit markers.

Editing with the Precision Editor

Many edits are completely straightforward: one clip follows another. But sometimes you run into exceptions. How can I change the start and end points of two clips without changing the movie's overall duration? How can I keep the end frame of one clip, change the starting frame of the next clip, but make the first clip's audio extend into the next clip's video?

Thanks to the close-up view the Precision Editor provides—the way it lets you clearly see how clips relate to each other—you can tackle these and many more editing challenges. You may use all of these tools on a regular basis, or you might use one or two now and then. The precision is there when you need it.

Tips. As you use the Precision Editor, you can quickly check your work by skimming across the shaded gray area above or below the video and audio tracks.

And since your aim is to edit with precision, you might prefer that iMovie display time in timecode, which includes frames in its notation instead of tenths of a second. Choose iMovie > Preferences, click General, then check the Display Time as HH:MM:SS:Frames box.

Setting the Cut Point

The most basic use of the Precision Editor is to change the cut point between two clips—the point where one clip is replaced by another. There are a couple of ways to do it.

By repositioning clips. Skim over a clip, keeping an eye on the Viewer to locate the frame where you want the edit to take place. Click once on a clip to position the cut point at that location.

You can also drag a clip left or right instead of clicking on a specific point. When you do, the Viewer displays that clip's frame at the cut point. When you see the frame where you want the cut to take place, release the mouse button.

By repositioning the cut point. You may find it easier or more intuitive to move the cut point itself. When you position the mouse pointer over the cut point, it appears light blue and slightly wider. However, the point behaves differently depending on which part you drag.

If you drag the cut point in the upper clip, the edit point in that clip changes, but the edit point in the bottom clip doesn't change. This lengthens or shortens the project's duration, depending on the direction you drag.

If you drag the cut point in the bottom clip, the edit point in the bottom clip changes but the frame in the top clip doesn't. This, too, will change your project's total duration.

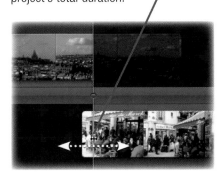

If you drag the cut point in the row between the two clips, the cut points in each clip move in tandem. For example, dragging to the right extends the top clip while cutting frames from the bottom clip. This method keeps the duration of your project unchanged. (Video pros call this a *roll edit*.)

Editing Transitions

When you want to make fine adjustments to a transition, the Precision Editor is the place to go.

To adjust the duration of a transition, drag its left or right edge. As you drag, the Viewer shows which frame starts or ends the transition. (For more on transitions, see page 224.)

Trimming in the Precision Editor

Typically, you can't use the Precision Editor for trimming a clip; after all, that's what the Clip Trimmer is for. But it turns out you *can* use the Precision Editor to do a little bit of clip snipping.

In the Precision Editor, position the mouse pointer within the gray horizontal boundary that separates the clips; the playhead appears in the corresponding section of the Project browser. Next, hold down the

Shift key and press the left- or right-arrow keys to start a selection. You can then adjust the selection's length by dragging its edges, or you can reposition it in the Project browser.

To make an edit, Control-click (or right-click) the selection and choose an edit, such as Trim to Selection or Split Clip.

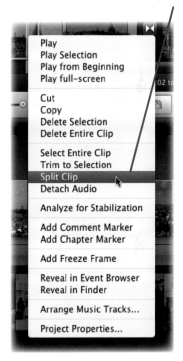

Once you make the edit, iMovie kicks you out of the Precision Editor. To quickly return to it, press the ⌘-/ keyboard shortcut.

Tips for the Precision Editor

Viewing All the Little Extras

The Precision Editor normally shows only the two clips you're editing and their transitions, but you can work with other elements there, too. As the previous page showed, you can display the audio waveforms associated with each video clip by clicking the 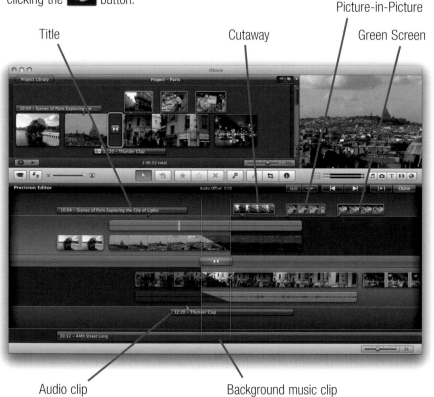 button.

To see even more elements, click the button. With this option active, the Precision Editor shows audio clips, background music, cutaways, picture-in-picture effects, and green-screen footage. (And if you don't know what some of those items are, fear not: I'll cover them soon.)

Editing Them, Too

Just as when you're working in the Project browser or the Clip Trimmer, you can use the Precision Editor to shorten or lengthen extras. For example, to increase or decrease the duration of a title, drag its left or right edge.

To reposition an item, drag it left or right.

For more precision (and isn't that why you're here?), use the size slider in the lower-right corner of the iMovie window to zoom in. Conversely, when you want to see a lot of your project at once—maybe to move a clip a large distance—zoom out.

What you can't do. You can't use the Precision Editor to pin a background music clip, access any of the clips' Inspector windows, add new content (such as audio clips), or change title or transition styles. For these jobs, use the Project browser.

Moving Extras with the Keyboard

To adjust the position of an audio clip or title using the keyboard, click on it in the Precision Editor, then press the left-arrow or right-arrow keys.

Title   Cutaway   Picture-in-Picture   Green Screen

Audio clip   Background music clip

Offsetting Audio

One of the cooler ways to use the Precision Editor is to offset a video clip's audio without having to detach the audio and edit it as a separate clip. When you offset audio, one clip's audio plays while another clip's video appears.

When might you use this technique? Say you have a shot of the Paris skyline followed by a shot of a street café scene, complete with accordion music. To set the mood, you want the café scene audio to begin playing before you actually cut to that scene. That's a job for audio offsetting.

In the Precision Editor, click the ▬◆▬ button to reveal the audio waveform. The shaded areas indicate audio that doesn't play in the project.

Next, drag the cut point within the audio waveform that you want to offset. In this example, I want the sound from the bottom clip to start playing while the top clip is still visible, so I've dragged the bottom clip's audio waveform cut point to the left.

It's that easy. When you play back the edit, you'll hear the café audio play while the skyline shot is still visible.

Here's another example of audio offsetting. Say you shot a couple of scenes of your kid jumping into a pond. For added visual punch, you want to cut between the two scenes at the moment that he splashes into the water—but you want to use the audio of the first shot.

If this example sounds familiar, it's because Apple has created a nice video tutorial that shows how to make it work. I've linked to it at macilife.com/imovie.

Tip: To reposition the audio cut points in both audio waveforms simultaneously, hold the Shift key while dragging. This technique makes the audio switch from one clip to another without any overlap.

In my Paris café scene example, you might use this technique if you don't want any of the Paris skyline shot's audio to play when the café scene audio begins. Maybe the skyline shot has a lot of wind noise and you'd rather it didn't intrude on the accordion music.

Adding Photos to Movies

Photographs are mainstays of many types of movies, especially montages and documentaries. With the Photos browser in iMovie, you can add photos from your iPhoto library to your movies. You can also add photos that aren't stored in your iPhoto library by dragging them into iMovie.

When adding photos to movies, consider taking advantage of iMovie's *Ken Burns* effect to add a sense of dynamism to your stills. Why name a feature after a filmmaker? Think about Ken Burns' documentaries and how his camera appears to move across still images. For example, a shot might begin with a close-up of a weary face and then zoom out to reveal a Civil War battlefield scene.

That's the Ken Burns effect. Now, Ken Burns himself would probably call it by its traditional filmmaking terms: *pan and scan* or *pan and zoom*. These terms reflect the fact that you can have two different kinds of motion: panning (moving across an image) and zooming (moving in or out).

Whatever the effect's name, its result is the same: it adds motion and life to otherwise static images. If the slide show projects in iPhoto don't give you the precise editing control you crave, try making a photo montage in iMovie. Indeed, its ability to create beautiful photo montages makes iMovie worth trying even if you don't have a video camera.

Adding a Photo from Your iPhoto Library

Step 1. Click the Photos button, or press ⌘-2.

To view a specific album, choose its name from the list.

Step 2. Select the photo. You can select multiple photos by Shift-clicking or ⌘-clicking on them.

Step 3. Drag the photo to the project. To insert the photo between clips, drag to the space between clips, as shown here.

Step 4. To customize the Ken Burns move, double-click the Crop button in the photo's thumbnail, or click the Crop tool in the Toolbar and select the photo in the project. Adjust the move as described below, then click Done.

To pan-zoom a photo, specify the start and finish settings for the move: that is, how you want the photo to look when it first appears, and how you want it to look at the end of its duration.

iMovie automatically applies the Ken Burns effect. To switch modes, click Fit or Crop (see below).

Tip: You can change the default mode using the Initial Photo Placement pop-up menu in the Project Properties dialog (choose File > Project Properties or press ⌘-J).

Specify the desired starting setting by resizing (drag the corners or sides) and moving the green Start box.

Reverses your settings—for example, turns a zoom in into a zoom out.

Specify the last frame of the move by resizing and moving the red End box.

The yellow arrow indicates the direction of the pan.

Preview the Ken Burns effect.

Cropping and Fitting

Don't want Ken Burns? You can choose to fit the entire static photo in the frame (you may see black bars at the edges, depending on the aspect ratio of the photo) or to fill the screen with the photo (cropping some of the image).

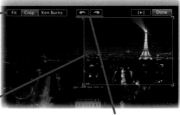

Cropping also lets you focus on part of an image to improve its composition—or remove the unwanted tourist spoiling the shot.

Rotate the photo 90 degrees.

Photo Tips

Photos from elsewhere. You can also use photos that aren't stored in your iPhoto library. To access a folder of photos, drag the folder to the top of the Photos browser; it appears in a folder named Folders (what folderol!). You can also drag an image file from the Finder directly to the project. The Photos browser also shows pictures from Photo Booth and from Apple's Aperture software, if you have them.

Change photo duration. Double-click a clip, or choose Clip Adjustments from its Action menu. Enter a new Duration value, and specify whether the new duration applies to the selected photo or to all photos in the project.

Adding a photo cutaway. Instead of dropping a photo in the space between clips, drop it directly onto a clip. From the pop-up menu that appears, choose Cutaway. (Activate Show Advanced Tools in iMovie's preferences for this to work.) This approach lets you keep the video's audio while a photo appears, without having to trim the video clip.

For even more fun, create an image with transparency, save it as a PNG file, and add it to a movie using this technique. The underlying video shows through the transparency, while the opaque pixels of your image appear overlaid on top. (For example, you could make a logo appear in a corner without obscuring the entire screen.)

Tips for the Ken Burns Effect

Video Formats and Photo Proportions

iMovie's support for multiple video formats introduces some special considerations for importing photos.

4:3 formats. Working in a standard (4:3) format, such as DV? If you plan to show a photo at actual size, be sure your photos' proportions match the 4:3 aspect ratio of these formats. Otherwise, the photos won't completely fill the video frame: they will have black borders.

Most digital camera photos have a 4:3 aspect ratio. If the photos you want to use don't have these proportions, you have two options. The easiest option is to simply crop in iMovie: in the Viewer, click the Crop button. A green crop area appears; its aspect ratio matches that of your project. To change which part of the photo appears, resize the crop area.

The more drastic option is to crop your photos in iPhoto. From the Constrain pop-up menu in iPhoto's edit view, choose 4 x 3 (DVD). Remember, cropping alters the photo in your library and anywhere else it appears. If you want an uncropped (or differently cropped) version of a photo, duplicate the photo before cropping it.

HD **HD format.** Photos can look beautiful in high-definition format, but in their original form, they will definitely not fill the video frame. Instead, they'll appear *pillarboxed*, with fat black borders on their left and right edges.

Simply use iMovie's Crop tool to crop the photo to match your project's 16:9 aspect ratio. If you'd prefer to give iMovie cropped photos to begin with, use iPhoto's Constrain pop-up menu to specify a custom crop proportion of 16 x 9 (HD).

Note: You won't see black borders when you apply the Ken Burns effect to photos, because iMovie restrains

the Before and After states to the photos' dimensions. That means, for example, you can't start zoomed-in on a vertical photo and pull out to reveal the entire picture: the After state is only as wide as the image.

Changing Settings

You've applied the Ken Burns effect and now decide that you want to change the clip's pan or zoom settings. Select the clip in the project timeline, then double-click the Crop button on the clip or click the toolbar's Crop button. Now make the desired adjustments in the Viewer and click Done.

Starting over. If you don't like the way you've set up a Ken Burns move or a crop, it's easy to restore the photo to its original state. First, double-click the photo's Crop button or select the Crop tool and then click the photo in the project timeline. Next, click the Fit button in the Viewer.

Image Resolution and Zooming

iMovie imports photos at their full resolution. This lets you zoom in on part of a photo and still retain image sharpness.

However, if you zoom in on a low-resolution image or one that you've cropped heavily in iPhoto, you will probably notice some chunky-looking pixelation. So think twice about zooming in on low-resolution images unless you want that pixelated look.

HD If you're working in a high-definition format, you may find that you can't zoom in very far on photos that have relatively low resolution (for example, two megapixels), at least not without seeing ugly visual artifacts.

Searching for Photos

The Photos browser in iMovie contains a search box; use it to search for text present in a photo's title, description, or keywords. You can also focus your search on only keywords or star ratings; use the pop-up menu in the search box.

You can also have iMovie display photos taken around the same time that you shot an event's video—handy for those of us who schlep both still and video cameras on trips. Check the Show Photos box below the Photos browser, then choose a date range.

Zoom to Tell a Story

Creative use of zooming can help tell your story. When you zoom in, you gradually focus the viewer's attention on one portion of the scene. You tell the viewer, "Now that you have the big picture, this is what you should pay attention to."

When you zoom out, you reveal additional details about the scene, increasing the viewer's sense of context. You tell the viewer, "Now that you've seen that, look at these other things to learn how they relate to each other."

Go Slow

Unless you're after a special effect, avoid very fast pans and zooms. It's better to pan and zoom slowly to allow your viewers to absorb the changes in the scene.

One way to control the speed of the zoom is to extend the duration of the clip. A 10-second Ken Burns move is smoother than a two-second one.

Another way to control the speed of the zoom is to simply zoom less. A gentle zoom is less visually jarring anyway.

Vary Your Zoom Direction

Variety is the spice of zooming. If you're creating a photo montage and zooming each image, consider alternating between zooming in and zooming out. For example, zoom in on one image, then zoom out on the next. If you add several photos at once, iMovie automatically sets up their Ken Burns moves this way.

A fine example of this technique lives elsewhere within iLife: iPhoto's automatic Ken Burns effect alternates between zooming in and zooming out. So does the screen saver in Mac OS X.

Cropping for Composition

Cropping is a good way to make a photo fit the aspect ratio of a project, but that isn't its only application, of course. You can also crop to simply improve a photo's composition.

Advanced Ken Burns Techniques

Ken Burns has some limitations. One is that you can't "hold" on a certain frame. You might want to have a 10-second clip in which the photo zooms for the first eight seconds and then remains static for the last two. Or maybe you want to zoom in part way, freeze for a couple of seconds, and then continue zooming.

Ken can't do that.

Another limitation is that you can't combine multiple moves in a single clip. For example, you might want to pan across a photo and then zoom in on part of it.

Ken can't do that, either.

At least not without a little finessing. It's actually possible to accomplish both of these tasks in iMovie. Here's how.

Holding on a Frame

To hold on a frame, start by adding a photo to the project timeline.

Step 1. Set up the Ken Burns effect as desired and then apply it, as described on page 200.

Step 2. Copy the clip (press ⌘-C). Then, point to a blank area of the Project browser (that is, not to any clips), and paste the clip (⌘-V) to create a duplicate right after the original.

Step 3. Double-click the clip's Crop button to edit the Ken Burns settings, and then select the End state (the red box). Click the Reverse button to set the End state as the start state.

Step 4. Click the Crop button to remove the Ken Burns effect but retain the same cropping as the last frame of the original clip. Click Done.

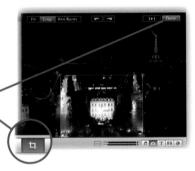

Step 5. Copy and paste the second—cropped—clip, double-click the Crop button on the clip, and click the Ken Burns button. The cropped area becomes the Start box.

Step 6. Configure the Ken Burns settings for the clip, then click Done. If you like, adjust each clip's duration settings to set the timing you want.

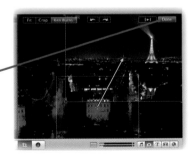

Tip: You can also start by holding on a frame, and then panning and zooming. First, apply the Ken Burns effect, then copy and paste the clip. Set the second photo's state to Crop, and position it before the Ken Burns clip.

Combining Moves

A variation on the opposite page involves combining two kinds of moves: for example, zooming in on part of a photo, and then panning from left to right.

Set up the first Ken Burns move you want, then copy that clip. Move the playhead away from any clip, then paste. Open the second clip's Ken Burns editor, click its Reverse button, then set up the second Ken Burns move.

Beyond Ken Burns: Other Pan-Zoom Tools

Ken Burns isn't the only game in town. Other pan-zoom tools are available that work with iMovie.

Photo to Movie. Photo to Movie by LQ Graphics (www.lqgraphics. com) makes it very easy to create pan-zoom effects. Create your effect in Photo to Movie, export it as a QuickTime movie, and then bring it into iMovie and add it to your project.

Photo to Movie's results are superior to those created by the Ken Burns effect. Photo to Movie does a better job of what animators call *ease in* and *ease out*: rather than motion abruptly starting and ending, the motion starts and ends gradually. The results have a more professional appearance.

PhotoMagico. This cool program from Boinx (www.boinx. com) makes gorgeous slide shows and montages, and like Photo to Movie, also provides ease-in and ease-out features. It's available in a couple of flavors, and is also included with some versions of Roxio's Toast burning software.

Working with Markers

Bookmarks, Post-It notes, bread crumbs: we rely on various technologies to keep us from getting lost. iMovie provides several kinds of *markers* that you can use for a variety of chores. Markers don't appear in your finished video—they work behind the scenes to help you make it better.

Comment markers are simply virtual bookmarks that you can tuck into a project's filmstrip. Want to go back and refine a section later? Set a comment marker to mark your place.

Chapter markers work together with iDVD to let you create convenient access points for your viewers. You've probably used chapter features when watching Hollywood DVDs: accessing scenes of interest using on-screen menus, or pressing buttons on your remote control to jump to next and previous scenes. With chapter markers in iMovie, you can give your own blockbusters these same navigational goodies. Chapter markers also work in GarageBand, where you can do additional audio tweaking or create a video podcast.

And then there are *beat markers*, which are huge labor savers when you want your edits to synchronize with music or narration. Tap out beat markers as your movie plays, then tell iMovie to position edits based on the marker locations.

Here's how to make your mark in the video world.

Note: To create comment and chapter markers, you must enable the Show Advanced Tools option in iMovie's General preferences.

Using Comment and Chapter Markers

Setting a marker. Drag a new marker from the comment icon or chapter marker icon in the Project browser to any location in your movie, then type a name for the marker and press Return.

In this example, I've added a chapter marker to the beginning of a scene.

The name of the marker will become the name of a chapter button in iDVD.

Editing a marker. To adjust a marker's position, drag it in the Project browser or Precision Editor. To rename a marker, double-click it and type. To delete a marker, select it and press Delete.

Navigating with markers. To jump to a specific marker, use the pop-up menu to the right of the marker icons. (It looks like a down-pointing triangle: ▼ .)

Ways to Use Chapter Markers

How might you use chapter markers? That depends on your video.

Weddings. Create chapters for each of the day's main events: the bridesmaids beautifying the bride, the groom arriving, the ceremony, the reception.

Kids' birthday parties. Create chapters for each phase of the party: the guests' arrival, the games, the presents, the fighting, the crying.

Vacations. Create chapters for each day or for each destination you visited.

Documentaries. Create chapters for each of the main subjects or periods of time that you're documenting.

Training. Create chapters for each subject or set of instructions.

Video podcasts. Create chapters for each new subject, or when you want a clickable image that leads to a Web page.

(For details on sending a completed project to iDVD, see page 240.)

Editing to Music with Beat Markers

One great use of beat markers is to create a sequence of scenes whose cuts occur in rhythm with a song. Here's how to make your own music video.

Phase 1: Set the Markers

Step 1. Create a new, empty project, then drag a song into it.

(For details on adding music to a project, see page 216.)

Step 2. Choose Clip Trimmer from the song's Action menu, or press ⌘-R.

Step 3. In the Clip Trimmer, set beat markers using any of the following techniques.

By dragging them. Drag a beat marker from the beat marker icon to a spot on the waveform where you'll want an edit.

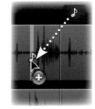

By positioning the playhead. Place the playhead where you want a marker, then Control-click and choose Add Beat Marker from the shortcut menu.

On the fly. This is how I like to set beat markers for music: start playback, and tap the M key each time you want a marker.

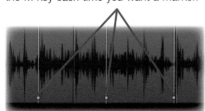

By tapping M in rhythm with the song, you can pound stakes into the ground, then build your video around them.

Changing markers. To reposition markers in the Clip Trimmer, drag them. To delete a marker, drag it off of audio waveform; the marker disappears in an animated puff of smoke. To delete all beat markers, Control-click the waveform and choose Remove All Beat Markers from the shortcut menu.

Phase 2: Edit to the Markers

With beat markers in place, you're ready to add clips.

Step 1. Choose View > Snap to Beats, and make sure the command is check-marked.

Step 2. Drag clips and/or photos into the project.

Add them one at a time or drag a bunch at once. Either way, iMovie makes cuts at the beat markers.

Making Changes

When editing a beat-matched video, keep a few things in mind to keep things on the beat.

Adding a beat marker. If you add a beat marker and it's within a clip you've already added, iMovie splits the clip at that spot. This makes it easy to replace one of those clips with another using the replace-edit techniques from page 191. (Alternately, if you extend the duration of a clip past the next beat marker, iMovie ignores that marker.)

Editing. It's easy to throw things out of sync when editing a beat-marked video. Indeed, iMovie warns you of this if you try to delete a clip.

The safest way to keep your cuts in sync with the markers is to *replace* clips rather than delete or insert them. Again, the replace-edit techniques on page 191 make it easy to replace clips.

Applying Effects

Special effects are the spices of the movie world. When used sparingly, they enhance a movie and add appeal. When overused, they can make your audience gag.

iMovie includes a full spice rack of special effects. The Aged Film effect makes a clip look like old movie film, complete with scratches and jitter. Vignette darkens the edges to add emphasis to your subject. Bleach Bypass desaturates colors to mimic a chemical alteration used in film.

Not all of the effects are dramatic. Black & White strips color completely, while the Flipped effect simply flips the video horizontally, as though you were viewing it in a mirror.

You can apply effects to multiple clips at once: Shift-click to select a range of clips, or ⌘-click to select clips that aren't next to each other in the timeline.

In addition to its spice rack of effects, iMovie also provides video-adjustment features that work much like their counterparts in iPhoto, giving you control over color levels, exposure, white balance, and more.

Effects and adjustments aren't limited to video, either. You can also apply them to photos that you've imported. So have fun, but remember: too much spice is worse than none at all.

Adjusting Color, Exposure, and More

In addition to changing a clip's duration and dimensions, you can adjust its color to fix lighting problems or to create special effects.

Step 1. Select a clip or a photo, then choose Video Adjustments from its Action menu to display the Video Inspector.

Tip: You can also display the Video Inspector by selecting a clip and tapping the V key.

Step 2. Make the adjustments in the Video Inspector, then click Done.

The histogram, Levels adjustments, and sliders work like the ones in iPhoto (page 76).

If a clip's color is off, try clicking something in the scene that's supposed to be white or gray. Or drag the circle inside the White Point color wheel. For example, if the clip has a blueish color cast, drag the circle into the yellow region to counteract it.

To have iMovie optimize the clip's levels, click Auto.

Notes and Tips

More color controls. With Show Advanced Tools enabled in iMovie's General preferences, you get additional gain sliders to adjust red, green, and blue colors separately.

Applying adjustments elsewhere. Want to copy the adjustments you made and apply them to other clips? Use the Paste Adjustments command; see page 244.

Applying Effects

Step 1. Select a clip in the Project browser, and then display the Clip Inspector.

To display the Clip Inspector, double-click the clip, choose Clip Adjustments from the Action menu, or (my favorite), just press the I key.

Step 2. In the Inspector, click the Video Effect button.

The Inspector flips over to reveal that spice rack of effects.

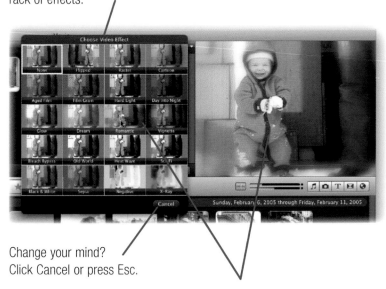

Change your mind?
Click Cancel or press Esc.

The thumbnails show how your clip will look with the effect. To see a larger preview in the Viewer, point to an effect. To see how the effect will look across the entire clip, skim across the effect's thumbnail.

Step 3. Click the effect you want, then click Done to close the Clip Inspector.

Notes and Tips

More than just video. You can also add effects to still photos, cutaways, picture-in-picture clips, and maps.

Some things never change. Applying an effect doesn't change the clip's appearance in the film-strip; instead, a tiny *i* appears in the clip's upper-right corner. To edit the effect, double-click the i.

Combining effects.
Unfortunately, iMovie lets you apply only one video effect at a time to a clip. If you long for the look of black-and-white aged film, you can't achieve that look directly. But there are workarounds.

To make any clip with an effect appear black and white, first apply the effect, and then bring up the Video Inspector by clicking the Video button or pressing V. Drag the Saturation slider all the way to the left, then click Done.

Another work-around is to export the clip (page 240) after you've applied one effect, then re-import it and apply another effect. For the black-and-white aged film look, desaturation is an easier approach. But for combining other effects, such as Hard Light and Raster, the export-and-import routine is your best bet.

Creating Green-Screen Effects

One of iMovie's flashiest effects is Green Screen, which automatically makes green areas of a clip transparent so you can overlay the footage onto a different background. Think of a TV meteorologist getting the forecast wrong while standing in front of an animated map, or of a video podcast host reporting from her basement—but appearing to be on a beach.

iMovie's Green Screen feature doesn't deliver the same results as professional editing or compositing software, but it does a pretty good job, especially if you sweat a few simple details when shooting your original footage.

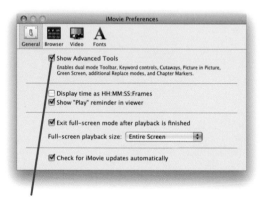

Note: To use green screening, you must enable the Show Advanced Tools option in iMovie's General preferences.

Superimposing Video

Step 1. Record your subject in front a green screen, observing the lighting and color tips on the opposite page, then import the video into iMovie.

Step 2. Add the background clip—the one in front of which you want your subject to appear—to your project.

The clip can be a video clip, a photo, a solid color, or an animated background clip. You can't use a travel map as a background, however (page 236).

Step 3. Drag your green-screen footage from the Event browser onto a clip in your project that you want to use as a background.

When you release the mouse button, a pop-up menu appears.

Step 4. From the pop-up menu, choose Green Screen.

The clip appears above the filmstrip with a green border. iMovie automatically renders the green areas transparent.

Notes and Tips

Editing green-screen clips. As with cutaways (page 192), you can move green-screen clips by dragging them; you can also lengthen or shorten them by dragging the clip's handles.

Creating a garbage matte. If an area of the image is not fully transparent—due to uneven lighting, a shadow on the green screen, or an edge beyond the screen being visible—you can apply what video editors call a *garbage matte* to excise that area from the clip.

With the clip selected, click the Cropped button in the Viewer. A box with corner handles appears. Drag the handles so the box is more focused on your subject; anything outside the box is made transparent regardless of what it contains.

If your subject moves around a lot, cropping the image to create a matte can be difficult, since the crop area applies to the entire clip. You can alter the crop area throughout the video by adding the green-screen clip in several pieces, applying a separate crop to each piece. Unfortunately, you can't just split a green-screen clip; you must add the pieces separately.

Subtract Last Frame. If you shot some empty green-screen footage at the end of the clip (as recommended at right), head for the Clip Adjustments window and click the Subtract Last Frame box; this helps iMovie determine what should be left out when the video is superimposed.

No transitions, please. You can't apply a transition to a green-screen clip.

Wacky effects. Don't restrict your green-screen endeavors to weather forecasts—

throw a couple of random clips together and apply green screening to them. You can get some interesting effects for music videos and similarly psychedelic endeavors.

Tips for Shooting Green-Screen Footage

You don't need to get fancy to create a screen. Ten dollars worth of green felt from a fabric store, or even a piece of green poster board, will work.

But for the best possible results, use paper or fabric that is *chroma green:* the broadcast industry's official color for green-screen work. This shade of green is also available as paint, in case you're thinking of redoing the living room. One source for chroma-green supplies is eefx.com.

Make sure you have plenty of even light to avoid casting shadows on your green screen. Position your subject a couple of feet away from the screen, too.

Avoiding green. Don't wear green clothing or include green objects in the shot—those areas will appear transparent in your final composite.

When you're done shooting, have your subject step out of the shot so you can shoot a moment or two of just the green screen. This lets you take advantage of iMovie's Subtract Last Frame option.

Watch out for reflective surfaces that could pick up a touch of the surrounding green color. Having a shiny tea kettle in the shot is asking for trouble.

Fixing spillover. If you do have some green reflective spillover on your subject, try this: Select the green-screen clip, open the Video Adjustments window (press V), and then reduce the Green Gain amount. You may also find that increasing the Blue Gain will help offset the increase in red hue that occurs when reducing the Green Gain. The results depend on the nature of your clip, but it's worth a try.

Cropping and Rotating Video

iMovie lets you crop and rotate not only stills (page 200), but also video clips. Rotating is handy for those times when you shoot a clip with your camera held in vertical orientation, as though it were still camera, forgetting that people aren't likely to want to lay on their sides to

watch. (Don't laugh—it's a common mistake.)

Select a clip, then click the toolbar's Crop button, or choose Cropping & Rotation from the clip's Action menu.

To rotate a clip, click one of the rotation arrows: [←] [→].

To crop the clip and improve its composition, click the Crop button in the Viewer, then resize the crop rectangle.

To preview your work, click the Viewer's Play button. When you're finished, click Done.

211

Stabilizing Shaky Video

Today's camcorders take care of most of the details that used to bedevil casual shooters. Auto-focus, exposure compensation, automatic white balance adjustment—features like these let you focus on the action instead of the settings.

As cameras have become smaller and lighter, though, another problem has become prominent: camera shake. A lot of video looks as if it was shot from a roller coaster during an earthquake.

Many new camcorders now include built-in image stabilization, which does indeed help, especially when you're zoomed in and every little camera nudge is exaggerated. But even footage shot with a stabilized camera can often use some smoothing out.

The image stabilization feature in iMovie can help. Tell it to go to work, and iMovie analyzes every frame of video and determines how to zoom and reposition each frame to smooth out excessive shake.

You can have iMovie analyze video when you import it (convenient, but time consuming), or you can analyze clips only when you use them (less work for your Mac, but your creative flow is interrupted). When you add an analyzed clip to a movie, you can specify not only whether to apply stabilization, but also how much to apply.

Image stabilization can't take the place of shooting on a tripod, but it can make your video look like it was shot with an expensive Steadicam. But most important, it can cut down on motion sickness in your audience.

Stabilization Essentials

You can apply stabilization as you edit, or you can analyze entire clips or the entire event first. The former approach is less work for your Mac, but it disrupts your editing. Twiddling your thumbs while iMovie analyzes isn't the best way to keep your creative juices flowing.

Analyzing an entire event means going out to lunch (or to bed) while iMovie works, but your editing process isn't interrupted. And there's no big cost in disk space—the analysis files are small.

I recommend analyzing an entire event. Build it into your production schedule. Import video, and let iMovie analyze it while you live your life.

Analyzing takes four to eight times the duration of a clip, depending on the movement in the video and on your Mac's speed. So analyzing an hour of footage could take four to eight hours—my kind of lunch break.

Analysis Options

When you import. At import time (pages 170–173), click the Analyze for Stabilization After Import option. iMovie scans the footage immediately after adding clips to the Event Library.

In the project filmstrip. If you'd rather analyze footage on the fly, click a clip's Action menu and choose Clip Adjustments. Then click the Smooth Clip Motion box.

iMovie analyzes only the footage you've used in the project. If you extend the clip's duration—using the Clip Trimmer, for example—the newly added frames are analyzed when you make the edit, and while you thumb-twiddle.

In the Event browser. To analyze an entire clip in the Event browser, Control-click on it and choose Analyze for Stabilization from the shortcut menu. Or bring up the Clip Inspector and click the Analyze Entire Clip button.

Learn more about stabilization
and download an example.
www.macilife.com/imovie

Using Stabilized Footage

If a clip in the Event browser has already been analyzed, simply add it to the project. Stabilization is automatically enabled—a little badge appears on the clip.

Notes and Tips

Adjusting settings. To be able to smooth a clip's jerkiness by moving it around as it plays, iMovie needs to zoom in on the clip a bit. With some video formats, such as standard-definition DV, this can create a fuzzy look. You can restore some sharpness—and, alas, some jerkiness—by backing off: drag the Maximum Zoom slider to the left a bit. Play the clip, and let your eyes judge.

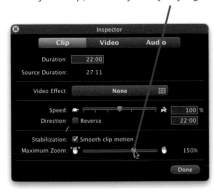

To turn a clip's stabilization off, open the Clip Inspector and uncheck the Smooth Clip Motion box.

Trim the dreck. If the beginning or end of a clip is *very* shaky, trim it out for better results.

Can't settle down. Some clips contain too much motion for iMovie to smooth. iMovie indicates unsalvageable frames with a wavy red line.

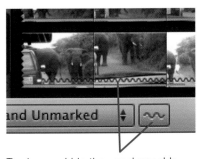

To show or hide the unsalvageable frames, click the wavy-lined button. **Tip:** In addition to using the wavy red line, iMovie creates a keyword named *Excessive Shake*, which you can filter (page 179).

Problem clips. Some clips just don't stabilize correctly. Say you have a scene where a person rides a bicycle through the frame in a clip that was shot from a moving car. You might see iMovie suddenly try to pan along with the bicyclist as the program tries to figure out what it should use as a reference point. If this happens, zoom out to decrease the amount of stabilization, or turn off the feature for that clip.

Higher shutter speeds are better. If your camera allows you to choose a higher shutter speed, do so before shooting. You'll lessen unsightly motion blur after stabilization.

The CMOS problem. *CMOS* is an acronym that refers to a kind of light sensor used in many cameras. CMOS-based cameras use a *rolling shutter* that exposes different portions of the frame at different points in time, taking about a fiftieth of a second to grab a complete frame.

And that can cause big problems with stabilization. The problem is that you can move the camera faster than it can capture a complete frame. Thus, you may see ugly jittering after stabilization. This jitter can be especially apparent with very jerky footage: stuff you shot while walking, for example. AVCHD camcorders are typically CMOS-based, and this is a problem not likely to go away any time soon. The tip? If you have an AVCHD cam, at least *try* to shoot steady.

Creating Picture-in-Picture Effects

Picture-in-picture is more than just a TV-set feature for watching two ballgames at the same time. In iMovie, this effect gives you a new set of creative options for combining two video clips, two photos, or any combination of the two.

Show two different scenes at once to give viewers more context: while Susie waits for a train, Bill waits for her at an outdoor café. Or show two different views of the same scene: a wide shot of a café, and an inset view showing a close up of Bill nervously stirring his coffee.

Combine stills and video: as a full-screen photo displays, inset some video footage of the same scene. Or give your video podcast that TV-news look: as the main shot shows you at the anchor desk, pop in a small picture of whatever you're talking about. Or just combine any two clips in ways that produce creative effects.

In high-end video programs, such as Final Cut Pro, creating picture-in-picture effects is fairly labor intensive. In iMovie, it takes a few clicks.

Note: To create picture-in-picture effects, you must enable Advanced Editing Tools in iMovie's General preferences.

Adding a Picture-in-Picture Clip

Step 1. In the Event browser, select the footage you want to use as a picture-in-picture (PIP) clip.

You can also select a photo in the Photos and Movies browser.

Step 2. Drag the clip or photo on top of an existing clip in your project.

A pop-up menu appears.

Step 3. From the pop-up menu, choose Picture in Picture.

The clip appears above the filmstrip, a turquoise border around it.

To change the clip's duration, drag its handles or use the Clip Trimmer. To fine-tune the clip's position, drag it left or right on the filmstrip. You can also apply audio and video adjustments as well as effects.

Notes and Tips

Twice the sound. When you combine two video clips, both clips' audio plays back. Use the Audio Adjustments Inspector (press A) to adjust the volume or duck the filmstrip clip's sound (page 220).

Adjusting size and position. A new PIP clip appears as a small rectangle near the upper-right corner of the Viewer. But that doesn't have to be its permanent home—or size. Select the picture-in-picture clip, and some controls appear in the Viewer.

To resize the clip, drag one of its corners; the aspect ratio remains the same.

To position the clip within the viewer, drag the center of the clip. iMovie displays yellow guides to help you center the clip, or line it up against the edges (with some room to spare). Here, a guide shows that the clip is vertically centered.

Get more PIP tips and download examples.
www.macilife.com/imovie

Adding PIP Effects

A newly created PIP clip simply appears and then disappears, but you can add one of three effects that appear when the clip starts and ends.

Begin by summoning the Clip Inspector: double-click the clip or choose Clip Adjustments from its Action menu. (Or my favorite: select the clip and press the I key.)

From the PIP Effect pop-up menu, choose an effect.

The clip begins as a pinpoint and expands to its full size. When the clip ends, it shrinks back to a pinpoint and disappears. The origin of the pinpoint depends on the clip's location: it zooms in from the closest edge or corner, except when the clip is centered within the viewer, when it comes from the middle.

The clip fades in and fades out.

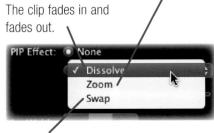

The primary clip shrinks to become the picture-in-picture clip, then returns to full screen.

To adjust the effect's duration, use the slider below the pop-up menu.

Tip: Double-clicking the picture-in-picture box in the Viewer also brings up the Inspector.

Changing the Clip's Appearance

A freshly added picture-in-picture clip is just a borderless block of video on your screen, but you can customize its appearance to make it more visible against the background clip.

Choose from none, thin, or thick.

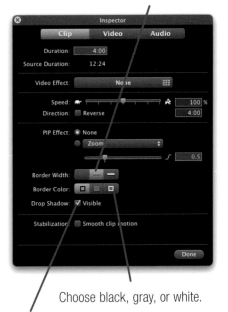

Choose black, gray, or white.

Display a tasteful drop shadow.

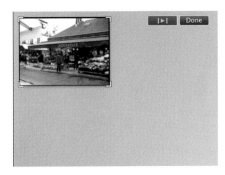

The Slide Show Angle

While procrastinating—er, I mean, *researching*—one day, I came up with a way to use PIP to spice up an iPhoto slide show project. Export a slide show project from iPhoto in Large quality, then bring that into iMovie. Add it to a project, then add it *again* as a PIP clip. Resize the PIP clip until it almost fills the screen. Then, add an effect or change the contrast and background of the main clip beneath it, adding a border and drop shadow to the PIP clip while you're at it.

The effect is beautiful: as the slide show plays, a ghostly version of it forms a border around it. Check it out at www.macilife.com/imovie.

Tip: If you're using several picture-in-picture clips in a project, here's a way to keep their positions and appearance consistent. Refine one clip to perfection, then select it and choose Edit > Copy. Next, select another PIP clip and choose Edit > Paste Adjustments > Picture in Picture (or press ⌘-Option-U).

Adding Audio to Movies

In movie making, sound is at least as important as the picture. An audience will forgive hand-held camera shots and poor lighting—*The Blair Witch Project* proved that. But give them a noisy, inaudible soundtrack, and they'll run for the aspirin.

Poor quality audio is a common flaw of home video and amateur movies. One problem is that most camcorders don't have very good microphones—their built-in mikes are often located on the top of the camera where they pick up sound from the camera's motors. What's more, the microphone is usually far from the subject, resulting in too much background noise. And if you're shooting outdoors on a windy day, your scenes end up sounding like an outtake from *Twister*.

If your camcorder provides a jack for an external microphone, you can get much better sound by using one. On the following pages, you'll find some advice on choosing and using microphones.

If you've already shot your video or you can't use an external mike, there is another solution: don't use the audio you recorded. Instead, create an audio *bed* consisting of music and, if appropriate, narration or sound effects (see page 219).

iMovie provides several features that you can use to sweeten your soundtracks. Take advantage of them. And if they don't do the job, consider bringing your movie into GarageBand for additional sonic seasoning (page 354).

Importing Music from Your iTunes Library or GarageBand

Use the Music and Sound Effects browser to bring in music from your iTunes library or GarageBand.

Step 1.

Click the Music and Sound Effects button in the toolbar, or press ⌘-1.

Step 2.

Select iTunes or GarageBand in the list of audio sources.

Note: In order to be able to preview a GarageBand project in the media pane, or add the song to your movie, the project needs to be saved with an iLife preview.

The project "GuitarStuff" cannot be used because it was not prepared with an iLife preview.

Would you like to open "GuitarStuff" in GarageBand so you can save it with an iLife preview?

    No   Yes

For details, see page 333.

Step 3.

Locate the song you want to import.

You can choose a specific playlist from the list of sources.

Use the Search box to quickly locate a song based on its name or its artist's name.

To play a song, select it and click this button, or simply double-click the song's name.

Step 4.

Drag a song to your project. Where you drop the song determines how iMovie treats it.

Background music. Drag the song to the edge of the background area of your project (the background turns green). The song becomes a background music track that plays behind the audio of the video footage.

Audio clip. To tie the audio to a specific video clip, drop the audio onto the clip, positioning it at the frame where you want playback to begin. The audio is locked to that video clip: move the video, and the audio moves with it.

Tip: You can stack as many audio clips as your ears can bear. For details on managing audio, see page 220.

Recording an Audio Narration

You can record narration directly within iMovie.

To begin recording, click the Voiceover button in the toolbar (or press O) and then click the point in your movie where you want to begin recording. iMovie gives you a three-second countdown and then starts recording. To stop recording, click again in the browser. (To cancel recording, press Esc.) When you're done, close the Voiceover window.

As you record, iMovie adds your narration to the filmstrip (as a purple audio clip), positioning it at the playhead's location.

Setting levels. For the best sound, you want to record loud, but not too loud. At its loudest, your voice should illuminate iMovie's volume meter as mostly green. If you push the levels into the red, your sound will be distorted.

Good

Bad

Tips. The Voiceover window has some controls that can improve recording quality. To reduce background noise, such as room echo, use the Noise Reduction slider. To add aural "punch" to your recording, click the Voice Enhancement check box.

Tips for Recording Better Sound

Upgrade Your Microphone

To get better sound, get a high-quality external microphone and place it close to your subject.

Before you buy an external mike, determine whether your camcorder can accept one. Some inexpensive camcorders don't provide a jack for an external mike; others may require an adapter that connects to the bottom of the camera. Most mid-range and all high-end camcorders have external mike jacks. On most cameras, it's a ⅛-inch stereo minijack.

Clip-on. Microphones come in all sizes and designs. Some are specialized—for example, a *lavaliere* mike, which clips to a lapel or shirt, is great for recording a single voice, such as that of a teacher (or TV host). But a lav mike is unsuitable for recording a musical performance.

Shotgun approach. When you can't get the mike close to your subject but still want to reduce extraneous noise, consider a *shotgun* mike. In a shotgun mike, the microphone capsule is mounted within a long barrel designed to reject sound coming from the side of the mike. Shotgun mikes are popular in TV news and movie making. They're sensitive enough to be located out of the video frame, and their highly directional sensitivity means they won't pick up noise from cameras and crew members.

A shotgun mike works best when mounted on a *boom*, a long pole (often hand-held) that allows the mike to point down at the subject. When you see a video crew with one person who appears to be holding a fishing pole with a long tube on the end of it, you're seeing a shotgun mike (and a sound technician) in action.

Two in one. The most versatile mike you can buy is a *single-point stereo* mike. A stereo mike crams two microphone capsules into a single package. Each capsule is precisely positioned relative to its companion, thus eliminating one of the biggest challenges of stereo recording: getting accurate balance and separation between the left and right channels. I use the AT822 from Audio-Technica (www.audio-technica.com).

With high-quality extension cables, the mike and camera can be up to about 25 feet apart. At greater distances, you risk losing some high frequencies and picking up hum and other electrical noise.

A balanced alternative. When you need to run cables longer than 25 feet or so—or when you want the best possible quality and are prepared to pay for it—consider a *balanced* mike. All of the aforementioned mikes are available in balanced and unbalanced versions. A balanced mike is wired in a way that reduces electrical noise and allows for cable runs of up to 100 feet or so. Balanced mikes cost more than unbalanced ones, but professionals and serious amateurs prefer balanced mikes due to their resistance to electrical noise and their support for longer cable runs.

A balanced mike typically uses an *XLR* connector, and only high-end camcorders have XLR jacks. But there is a way to connect a balanced mike to an unbalanced miniplug jack: the DXA-2 adaptor from BeachTek (www.beachtek.com). A compact metal box that attaches to your camera's tripod mount, the DXA-2 requires no external power supply and has built-in knobs for adjusting volume levels.

Placement is Everything

To do justice to any mike, position it properly. For that school play or recital, use a mike stand and position the mike high, pointing down toward the stage at about a 45-degree angle. If you can't set up your own mike stand, just try to get the mike at least a few feet off the stage and as close to center stage as possible.

How close should the mike be? That depends on what you're recording (see the table at right). The closer the mike is to a sound source, the less room noise and reverberation it picks up.

But if the mike is too close, stereo separation is exaggerated—some sounds come only from the left speaker, others only from the right, and sounds in the center are louder than they should be. Move the mike too far away, and you get a muddy-sounding recording with too much room reverb.

When recording a live performance, try to show up for rehearsals so that you have time to experiment with different mike distances. If your camera has a headphone jack, connect a good pair of headphones—ones whose cups surround your ears and thus block out external sounds. Record a test, play it back, and listen.

For recording narrations, consider assembling a makeshift sound booth that will absorb room echo and block computer and hard drive noise. Glue some sound-absorbing acoustical foam onto two sheets of plywood or foamcore. (See www.soundsuckers.com for a wide selection.) Position the two sheets in front of you in a V shape, with the mike at the narrow end. If you're on a tight budget, use blankets, pillows, carpet remnants, or even a coat closet. The idea is to surround yourself, and the mike, with sound-absorbing material.

Another major microphone manufacturer, Shure, has published some excellent mike-placement tutorials. Download them at www.shure.com.

A Field Guide to Mike Placement

Scenario	Ideal Mike Position
Solo piano	About a foot from the center of the piano's harp, pointed at the strings (open the piano's recital lid).
Wedding ceremony	As close to the lovebirds as possible. Many wedding videographers attach a wireless lavaliere mike to the groom or the officiator. (Bridal gowns tend to rustle too much.) A mike hidden in a flower arrangement may also work.
Narrator	6 to 9 inches from the speaker's mouth, angled downward. To avoid plosive problems, use a windscreen and position the mike just off to the side, pointing at the mouth. Alternative: a lavaliere mike.
Choral group	1 to 3 feet above and 2 to 4 feet in front of the first row of the choir.
Birthday party around a table	On an extended floor stand, angled downward. Alternative: on a tabletop desk stand, pointing at the birthday kid.

Creating an Audio Bed

If you weren't able to get good audio when you originally shot your video, consider muting your video's audio track and just putting a music bed behind your shots. Create a montage of shots, using beat markers (page 207) to help you time your edits to the music.

And finally, a related tip: If you're shooting scenes where the audio is mostly ambient sound—the waves at the beach, the din of a party—shoot a few minutes of uninterrupted video, keeping the camera stationary. After importing the video, you can use only the clip's audio. In iMovie, drag the clip on top of another clip in your project, and then choose Audio Only from the pop-up menu that appears. The clip's sound appears as an audio clip below the filmstrip. Now mute the audio of the other clips (see page 220). This technique eliminates jarring sound changes between shots.

Working with Audio

Adjusting the volume of an audio track is a common task. And when you combine audio in any way—mixing music, sound effects, dialog, and background sounds—you almost always need to adjust the relative levels of each sound to create a pleasing mix.

iMovie provides several ways to work with sound levels. You can reduce the volume of an entire sound clip. You might do this if you're mixing music with the sound of the surf, and don't want the waves to drown out the music.

You can also vary a track's volume level over time. When combining music and narration, you might want the music to start at full volume, fade when the narrator talks, then return to full volume when she stops—a feature called *ducking*.

Just as with video, you can change the duration of audio clips. You can trim directly in the project timeline or, for more precision, summon the Clip Trimmer or Precision Editor, both of which have the added benefit of displaying audio *waveforms*. A waveform looks a bit like the penmanship of an earthquake seismograph. Back-and-forth lines indicate the intensity of the shaking—in this case, of the sound wave. Being able to see your sound is a big help when trimming audio tracks.

Making Audio Adjustments

To control audio levels, use the Audio Adjustments Inspector. Select the clip whose audio you want to tweak, then choose Audio Adjustments from its Action pop-up menu, or just press A.

Quiet down (or speak up):
Change the volume of the selected clip.

Pipe down for a moment: to have iMovie reduce the volume of concurrently playing audio (such as background music), check Ducking. The selected clip's volume is unchanged, but other audio gets quieter. The higher the setting, the quieter the other audio gets.

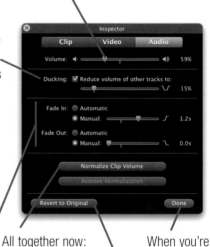

Fades: To have a clip's audio fade in or fade out, click Manual, then drag the slider to specify the fade duration, in seconds. For no fade at all, drag all the way to the left.

All together now: iMovie can make volumes consistent across multiple clips. Click Normalize, then select another clip and click Normalize again. Repeat for each clip.

When you're finished, click Done.

Change your mind? Click to restore the clip's original levels.

Managing Background Music

Adding background music to a project is easy, but there's more to the story. You can have multiple songs in a project—just drag them to the project's background, as shown on page 217. When you add multiple songs to the background, they play one after the other, separated by a one-second crossfade.

Rearranging background music. To change the playback order of your project's songs, choose Edit > Arrange Music Tracks.

Drag the songs to change their playback order, then click OK.

Pinning audio. You can *pin* a background song to a specific clip so that it begins playing when that clip appears—and so that it moves along with the clip as you edit and change your project.

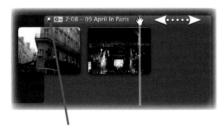

To pin a background song, drag the song until the little pin is above the video frame where you want playback to begin. The green background icon turns purple.

To make the song float again, select it and choose Edit > Unpin Music Track.

Tips: For projects with several pinned tracks, it's often easier to use the Edit menu's Arrange Music Tracks command to unpin tracks.

If you pin a music clip and then add another background song, the new song fills in any gap between the last floating song and the pinned clip.

Trimming Audio

To change the duration of an audio clip, trim it—either directly in the project or in the trimmer.

In the project. To trim audio in the browser, point to the beginning or end of the clip and then drag left or right.

Tip: You can also trim clips in the Precision Editor, but in a different way; see page 195.

In the Clip Trimmer. For more control, use the trimmer: select the song and choose Clip Trimmer from the song's Action menu (⌘-R).

Preview your work.

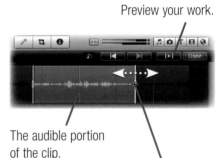

The audible portion of the clip.

To change the clip's duration, drag the yellow handle at the beginning or end of the clip.

Slipping audio edits. Sometimes, you may want to keep the duration of a clip the same, but change which part of it plays—maybe you need 50 seconds of a song behind some footage, but you want a *different* 50 seconds.

Easy: in the Clip Trimmer, drag within the middle of the audible portion to perform a *slip edit*.

More Sound Advice

Waveform Tip

To work with more precision when viewing waveforms in the Clip Trimmer, zoom in: drag the thumbnail slider to the right, and drag the clip size slider to its leftmost position (the half-second setting).

Trimming Audio

You can trim the start and end of an audio clip using the same techniques described on page 188. As with video clips, you can reclaim audio that's outside of a clip's boundaries by resizing the clip.

Scrubbing Audio

Here's a handy way to locate the exact spot to trim or split an audio clip. First, be sure that audio skimming is on: choose View > Audio Skimming (⌘-K). Next, open the clip in the trimmer, and slowly skim across its waveform. Your audio plays back, but is slowed down. The sound even plays backwards when you skim to the left. (Beatles fans: import some *White Album* songs from your iTunes library and have fun.)

Extracting Audio

At times, you may want to use only the audio portion of a clip. For example, you're making a documentary about your grandmother's childhood and you'd like to show old photographs as she talks.

To do this, Control-click the clip and choose Detach Audio from the shortcut menu, or choose Edit > Detach Audio.

iMovie creates an audio track containing just the audio portion of the clip and mutes the video clip.

You can now position still images and other clips in the space above the audio in the filmstrip. You can also drag the audio elsewhere in the timeline.

Repeating Sound Effects

You might want some sound effects to play for a long period of time. For example, iMovie's Hard Rain sound effect is less than 10 seconds long, but maybe you need 30 seconds of rain sounds for a particular movie.

For cases like these, simply repeat the sound effect by dragging it from the Music and Sound Effects browser to the project as many times as needed. You can also duplicate a sound by Option-dragging it in the project. If the sound effect fades out (as Hard Rain does), overlap each copy to hide the fade.

You can build magnificently rich sound effect tracks by overlapping sounds. To create a thunderstorm with a bit more punch, for example, drag the Thunder and Rain sound effect so that it overlaps Hard Rain. And don't forget to use iMovie's audio controls to fine-tune the relative levels of each effect.

Camcorder Sound Settings

Most miniDV camcorders provide two sound-recording settings: 12-bit and 16-bit. Always record using the 16-bit setting. If your sound and picture synchronization drift over the course of a long movie, it's probably because you recorded using 12-bit audio.

Copying Audio

Get links to sources of sound effects and music.
www.macilife.com/imovie

Copying Audio Adjustments

You've adjusted an audio clip and would like to apply the same adjustments to other audio clips. Select the adjusted clip and choose Edit > Copy. Then select other clips and choose Edit > Paste Adjustments > Audio (⌘-Option-A).

When you don't want to use the audio from a series of video clips, this is the easiest way to mute the clips. Mute one, choose Copy, select the others (⌘-click on each one), then paste the adjustment.

Sources for Sound Effects and Music

Sound Effects

iMovie's library of built-in sound effects, accessed through the audio section of the Media browser, covers a lot of aural ground.

But there's always room for more sound, and the Internet is a rich repository of it. One of your first stops should be FindSounds (www.findsounds. com), a Web search engine that lets you locate and download free sound effects by typing keywords, such as *chickadee*. SoundHunter (www.soundhunter. com) is another impressive source of free sound effects and provides links to even more audio-related sites.

Most online sound effects are stored as WAV or AIFF files, two common sound formats. To import a WAV or AIFF file, use the File menu's Import command or simply drag the file directly to the desired location in the time-line viewer.

Managing Sound Effects

If you assemble a large library of sound effects, you might find yourself needing a program to help you keep track of them. You already have such a program: it's called iTunes. Simply drag your sound effects files into the iTunes window. Use the Get Info command to assign descriptive tags to them, and you can use

iTunes' Search box to locate effects in a flash. You might even want to create a separate iTunes library to store your sound effects.

Music Sources

You'll find a symphony's worth of music on the Internet. For private, non-commercial projects, try Freeplay Music (www.freeplaymusic.com). You can download and use its music clips for, yes, free. For commercial projects, however, be sure to carefully read the company's rate card and licensing requirements.

Plenty of music is also available from sites such as SoundDogs, KillerSound, and Award Winning

Music. These sites have powerful search features that let you locate music based on keywords, such as *acoustic* or *jazz*.

Loopasonic (loopasonic.com) is another cool music site. It offers hundreds of music loops—repeating riffs—that you can assemble into unique music tracks and use in GarageBand (which, of course, you can use to compose your own movie music).

And for building custom-length music tracks, you can't beat SmartSound's Sonicfire Pro software (www.smartsound. com). Sonicfire Pro provides an expandable library of songs, each of which is divided into blocks that the software can assemble to an exact length.

Adding Transitions

Visual transitions add a professional touch to your project. Transitions also help tell a story. For example, a cross-dissolve—one clip fading out while another fades in—can imply the passage of time. Imagine slowly dissolving from a night-time campfire scene to a campsite scene shot the following morning.

Similarly, iMovie's wipe transitions, where one clip pushes another out of the frame, are each a visual way of saying "meanwhile..." Imagine using a wipe transition between a scene of an expectant mother in the delivery room and a shot of her husband pacing in the waiting room, chain-smoking nervously. (Okay, so this is an old-fashioned maternity movie.)

The Fade to Black and Cross Dissolve transitions are "desert-island" transitions—the ones you'd want when stranded on an island (perhaps while editing an episode of *Survivor*). But unless you are stranded on an island, don't limit yourself—experiment with other types of transitions.

Like effects, transitions are visual spice. Season your video with them, but don't let them overpower the main course: your subject.

Creating a Transition

To add a transition between two clips, first display the Transitions browser: click the Transitions button, choose Window > Transitions, or press ⌘-4.

To add the transition, drag it between two clips in the timeline or clip viewer.

To see a preview of a transition, point to it (don't click) in the Transitions browser.

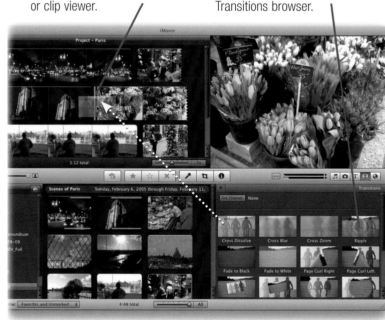

In the project, each transition style has its own icon so you can identify it at a glance.

Changing a Transition's Duration

After adding a transition, you can change its duration: select it and choose Transition Adjustments from the Action menu or the Window menu (or press I). Enter a new duration in seconds, and specify whether the new duration applies to just that one transition or to all transitions in the project. Finally, click Done.

The precision alternative. For much greater control over a transition's length and option, open the Precision Editor. It's the best place to refine a transition's length, because you see the footage it affects as you edit it. (See page 194 for more on the Precision Editor.)

Double-click the space above the transition (not the transition icon itself), or choose Window > Precision Editor (⌘-/).

To change the transition's duration, drag its left or right edge.

To retain its duration but reposition it relative to the surrounding clips, drag the middle of the transition.

Testing the Transition

To see the finished transition, select it and choose View > Play Selection (or press the forward-slash key).

If you aren't happy with the transition, you can delete it (press the Delete key) or choose Undo.

Inserting a Clip at a Transition

When you create a transition between two clips, you establish a connection between those clips.

If you need to insert a new clip between those two clips, simply drag it to either side of the transition, and iMovie drops it into place.

Changing a Transition

Change your mind about using a particular transition style? To change an existing transition, grab a new transition from the browser and drop it directly onto the old one. This works in the Precision Editor as well as the Project browser.

Tip: You can also switch styles without opening the Transitions window. With the transition selected, press I to bring up the Transition Adjustments window, then click the Transition button.

Next, click the transition you want, skimming over the thumbnails to preview ones you're considering.

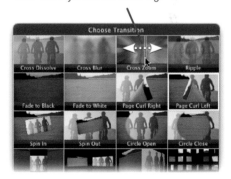

And here's a technique that requires even less work: if your project already contains one of the transitions you want, Option-drag it to an existing transition to change that transition.

More Transition Techniques

Adding a Transition Between All Clips

You can have iMovie automatically add a transition between every clip in your project. This can be a nice way of adding visual polish to a "video slide show"-style project.

To begin, choose File > Project Properties (⌘-J).

In the Transitions area, check the Automatically Add box, choose a style from the pop-up menu, and click OK.

Next, iMovie asks how you'd like to apply the transitions—and it asks using two very verbose and not entirely clear options.

The first option works well when you want to guarantee that the footage you selected before the transition is the footage that's seen, regardless of what it does to the project's overall duration.

Choose the second option if you've already edited the video to synchronize with an audio clip (such as background music) and don't want the project's overall duration to change. The risk with the latter choice is that frames you deliberately edited out could become visible during the transition—your awesome rollerblade jump becomes less awesome when the viewer sees that you polished the pavement half a second after your initial edit.

After you've activated auto transitions, iMovie continues to add transitions when you add new clips to the project.

Tip: Did you go a little crazy with mixing transition styles throughout your project, and now want to switch them all to one style? You might be tempted to turn to the Transitions Adjustment window and its Applies to All Transitions checkbox, but that affects only durations, not styles.

Instead, enable the Automatically Add option and choose a transition type from the pop-up menu. iMovie will change all existing transitions to the style you chose.

Removing auto transitions. If that's too much lockstep conformity, return to Project Properties and uncheck Add Automatically. After you click OK, you have

another choice to make: whether to keep the footage that was used by the transitions; to maintain the clips' durations; or to leave all the transitions in place so you can remove or edit them individually.

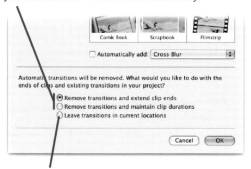

The last option is handy if you want to customize some of the transitions (something iMovie doesn't let you do with automatically added transitions). Turn off auto transitions, but tell iMovie to leave the transitions in place. Then, customize the transitions you want to change, and manually delete the ones you don't want.

If you attempt to change a transition style when automatic transitions are enabled, iMovie displays a message giving you the option of turning off the automatic transitions feature.

Note: If you change a transition style in the Precision Editor or in the Transition Adjustments Inspector, you can get away with the change and keep automatic transitions enabled. (This may well be a bug, so don't count on always having this capability.)

Theme-Specific Transitions

If you applied a theme to your project, either when you created it or in the Project Properties dialog, you'll see theme-specific options in the Transitions browser.

Add a theme transition to your project just as you would a regular transition. If the transition includes more than two drop zones (areas that include clips from your project—displayed as pictures on a bulletin board, for example), you can select the transition and choose which clips appear. To learn how, see page 234.

When Durations Go Wrong

It happens now and then: you go to increase the duration of a transition, and the result is a transition with a duration *shorter* than what you asked for—and the transition is marked with orange numbers.

This happens when not enough footage remains in a clip to accommodate the duration you want. In the above example, 3 seconds became 2.3 seconds because that's how much footage remained in the clip.

To fix the problem, open the edit in the Precision Editor and adjust the clips so there's plenty of footage on each side of the transition. Then, extend the transition's edges to the duration you want.

This workaround isn't always possible—your source clip may just not contain enough frames. Taking a peek in the Precision Editor will tell you for sure.

Creating Titles

What's a movie without titles? Incomplete. Almost any movie can benefit from text of some kind: opening and closing credits, the superimposed names of people and places, or simply the words "The End" at, well, the end.

iMovie's Titles browser is your ticket to text. There are more than 30 title styles, and you can customize their text in a variety of ways.

Regardless of the style you choose, you'll get the best results with sturdy fonts that remain legible despite the limited resolution of television. For example, at small text sizes, Arial Black often works better than Times, which has ornamental serifs that can break up when viewed on a TV set.

You'll also get the best-looking titles if you choose colors conservatively. Avoid highly saturated hues, especially bright red, which can "bloom" when viewed on a standard-definition TV set. High-definition formats are less prone to these problems, but since your video may still end up being viewed on standard-definition TVs, a conservative approach is smart. iMovie helps you in this regard: its title styles and their color options work great on TV.

Roll the credits.

To Create a Title

Creating a title involves choosing the title style, dragging the title to the project, and then editing the text and its formatting.

Step 1. Click the Titles button to display the Titles browser.

Step 2. Choose the title style you want and drag its icon into your project. You can superimpose title text over a video or photo clip or have it appear against a black or custom background.

Superimposing. To superimpose text over a clip, drop the title onto the clip. As you drag the title near the clip, a blue highlight indicates where the title will appear: over the first half of the clip, the last half, or the entire clip. (You can change this later.)

Tip: To create a title that's four seconds long, press the Shift key when dragging the title to the project. (Unless you're the verbose type, four seconds is plenty of time for a typical title.) The blue highlight indicates the title's start and end.

Over a custom background. To have the title text appear on a background, drop the title between two clips. From the Choose Background window that appears, click a decorative backdrop; the first four are even animated.

Step 3. In the Viewer, type the text of the title, then specify the title text and font settings.

To preview the title, click the ▐▶▌ button in the Viewer. **Tip:** In title styles that provide multiple text boxes, you can jump from one box to the next by pressing the Tab key.

See the opposite page for an overview of title settings.

Step 4. Click the Done button in the Viewer.

Formatting Title Text

Each title style has its own font style. But many title styles also allow you to customize font formatting. You have options aplenty.

iMovie's font panel. iMovie has its own font panel. To display it, select a title that you've added to your project, then click the Show Fonts button in the Viewer.

Show Fonts

The Choose Font panel gives you a choice of nine fonts, nine colors, and nine text sizes. Choose a font, size, and text color, then click Done.

To preview in the Viewer how a font, color, or size will look, skim across it. (This is ridiculously cool.) To choose an option, click it.

Larger sizes tend to be more legible on TV sets.

Control text alignment and style. The outline style tends to tacky.

For even more font fun, use the system Fonts panel (below).

Using the System Fonts Panel

You can also summon the standard Mac OS X Fonts panel for your text endeavors. Generally, I recommend sticking with iMovie's Choose Fonts panel—its selection of fonts, colors, and sizes look good on TV. But if you want access to fonts that the Choose Fonts panel doesn't display, turn to the system Fonts panel.

The big advantage the system Fonts panel provides is the ability to mix and match fonts and sizes within a single panel. Other niceties: you can loosen or tighten the spacing between characters, and you can choose just about any size and color you want.

(With this great power comes great responsibility: don't torment your viewers with a mish-mash of fonts and sizes. And note that very vibrant colors will often display strangely on a TV set.)

To format just part of a title's text, drag across the text in the viewer, then use the system Fonts panel.

Tip: In the iMovie Choose Font panel, any changes you make apply to the entire title. For example, if you have a title in the Centered style, with its large headline and smaller subhead, clicking a new size makes both lines the same size. To restore the second line's smaller size, head for the system Font panel, select the second line, and change its size.

Changing a Title

Need to change an existing title? In the project, select the title. Next, make your changes in the Viewer. Finally, click the Done button.

To move a title, drag it within your project. To change its duration, drag either of its edges.

To change a title's style, drag a new style from the Titles browser onto the clip where the current title rests.

To change a title's custom background, double-click the background clip to summon the Inspector, and then click the

Background button and choose a new background.

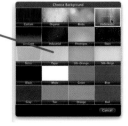

Tips for Titling

Choosing More Colors

To choose a color for title text, click the Color button in the system Fonts panel. Click on the color palette to choose your hue. To match a color that appears in a clip, click the magnifying glass icon, position the pointer over the color you want to pick up, and then click.

Photoshop Titles

You can use Adobe Photoshop or Photoshop Elements to make gorgeous, full-screen titles. You can add photos, create color gradients, shadow effects, and more.

To create a title in Photoshop, specify an image size appropriate to your project's video format. For widescreen projects, use pixel dimensions of 1920 by 1080. For iPhone projects, use 808 by 540. For standard projects, use 720 by 540.

Next, create your title, and avoid putting any text in the outer 10 percent of the screen. (It might get cut off when the title appears on a TV set.) And to avoid flicker, make the thickness of any horizontal lines an even number of pixels (for example, 2, 4, 6). Save the file as a JPEG or PNG. If the title will be superimposed over existing video, make sure it has a transparent background and save the file as a PNG.

To add the title to your movie, simply drag the file's icon directly to the project filmstrip. To superimpose the title over a clip, add the image as a cutaway (see page 192).

Because you added the title as a photo, you can apply the Ken Burns effect to it. Indeed, you can combine a Photoshop graphic with iMovie's built-in title styles to create titles with text superimposed over a moving background. Create a background graphic, then import it and apply a slow pan. Superimpose a title over the graphic.

You could also extract a page from an iPhoto book using the technique on page 141 and use it as a title background.

Stay Title-Safe

TV sets generally cut off the outer edges of a video frame, and that can cause problems with some of iMovie's title styles. If you plan to send your project to iDVD, avoid using the subtitle lines of any of the title styles except for Centered—they're likely to be cut off when you view your video on a TV set. And if you use any of the left-aligned title styles, bump the text to the right a bit by pressing the spacebar a few times.

Theme Titles

When you apply a theme, the Titles browser gains eight additional title styles that match the theme. Indeed, the Titles and Transitions browsers are the only ones that let you change the project's theme outside the Project Preferences dialog box.

Besides being stylish, theme titles are also clever. The Credits styles, for example, picks up your name from the Mac's Address Book program, automatically adding, for example, *Directed by Jim Heid* to movies. (If you want to change the default name—paging Alan Smithee!—choose a different card in Address Book and choose Card > Make This My Card.)

Note: You can't change the font styles in theme titles.

Four-Way Intersection

A secret lurks within the Four Corners title style. When you add it, the two lines of text each appear from two screen edges (such as the left and bottom) and exit from the opposite two (the right and top). When you add another Four Corners title after the first, the effect is the same, but the text has a different color and appears from different screen edges. Adding four successive Four Corners titles gives you a slightly different effect each time: left/bottom, top/right, right/bottom, and top/left.

Fonts Preferences

The iMovie Choose Font panel brings preset styles to iMovie. Want to have the same typographic style in each episode of your online science fiction romantic dramedy? Simply click the same typeface in the Choose Font panel for each opening title sequence.

You can change the list of typefaces and the choice of colors that appear in the Choose Font panel. Choose iMovie > Preferences, then click Fonts. To replace one of the preset fonts with a different one, click the arrows to the right of the font name, then choose a new font and style. For colors, click a swatch to display the Colors palette, then select a new hue.

Translucent Titles

When you're specifying colors in iMovie's Fonts preferences, notice the Opacity slider at the bottom of the Colors palette. Dragging the slider to the left increases the color's transparency. When you apply that transparency to a title, the letters become partially see-through. (An Opacity slider is available on the system Fonts panel, too.)

Titles Stay Put

A title is attached to the clip to which it's assigned, just as you'd expect. However, if you use the Clip Trimmer to slip a clip (see page 190), the title remains fastened to its original frame. Thus, a title that initially appeared at the beginning of a clip could appear in the middle of the clip after the edit. To reposition the title, drag it.

Adding Style with Themes

Watch any TV show, and you'll see that video producers rely on a standard vocabulary of visual building blocks—elements that identify major portions of the show and serve to tie scenes together.

A show opens with a flashy graphic containing text and imagery. The first segment is introduced with another graphic. A city scene appears, and a superimposed lower-third graphic identifies the scene. One scene completes, then a short bumper appears as a visual separator before the next scene begins.

These visual seasonings are sprinkled throughout the rest of the show, and then the credits roll. These elements of imagery are often called *motion graphics*, and for good reason. Instead of being static text and graphics, they employ slick animation that adds visual appeal. Words don't just fade in and fade out; they glide into view, superimposed over elegant, moving backgrounds.

It's the kind of eye candy we're used to seeing on TV, and you can serve it up in your productions with the video themes built into iMovie. Apply a theme to your project to add titles and transitions that unite the movie around a common visual style.

The Elements of a Theme

Each of iMovie's five themes provides several transitions and titles, many of which also provide an area where you can type some text.

Here's a look at the pieces that make up a theme.

Opener. The first theme title displays a montage of photos or movies, culminating with a title. The opener appears at the beginning of your epic.

Credits. You know what they are. Each theme includes three credits designs.

Lower third and upper third. True to its name, a lower third occupies the lower portion of the screen; an upper third is anchored to the top. They're ideal for identifying the people or places in a shot.

Simple. The Simple title is like the standard Centered title style, but in the typeface and style used by the theme.

Transitions. Each theme provides four companion transitions, each of which zooms out of one clip, pans across the theme's background to another, and zooms back in to the next clip.

Applying a Theme

You have the option to choose a theme for a project when you first create a project (see page 184). But you don't have to choose the theme then. To apply or change a theme at any time, choose File > Project Properties (⌘-J), or click the Set Theme button that appears in the Titles browser and Transitions browser.

To get a taste of a theme's design, skim over a thumbnail. To choose a theme, click it.

By itself, applying a theme doesn't affect a single frame of your project—the theme visuals occur in titles and transitions. If you click the Automatically Add Transitions and Titles checkbox, iMovie adds an opening title to the beginning of your movie and a credit title to the end,

you would other titles (page 228) and transitions (page 224).

Tip: If you want to use just a few elements of a theme without going all out, go right ahead. Choose a theme in the Project Properties dialog box, but uncheck Automatically Add Transitions and Titles. The theme elements are available in the Titles and Transitions browsers for you to use *a la carte*.

Switching Themes

Switching to a different theme is easy, even if you've set up a lot of titles and transitions. Bring up the Project Properties dialog box or click Set Theme in either the Titles or Transitions browser. Choose a new theme, and then click OK.

Removing a Theme

Change your mind about using a theme in a project? Remove it. Go back to the Project Properties dialog box and set the theme to None. iMovie removes any themed titles or transitions, and asks you how you want to deal with existing transitions.

iMovie restores clips to the durations they had before any transitions were added, and deletes all transitions, themed or otherwise.

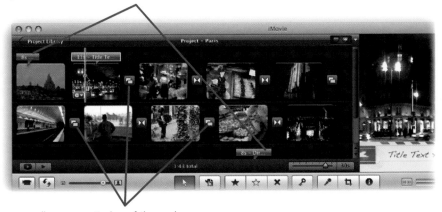

as well as a smattering of themed transitions and some dissolves. Theme elements appear gold colored.

In the Titles and Transitions browsers, theme-specific items appear at the top of the list. Drag them to your project just as

All clips keep their current durations; all transitions are deleted.

Themed transitions go away, but non-themed transitions remain.

Tips for Working with Themes

Specifying Clips in a Theme Transition

Some theme transitions zoom out to reveal several still images: photos on a bulletin board, for example, or panels in a comic book. iMovie automatically fills those drop zones with footage you've used in your project, but you can take the reins yourself and specify what appears in the drop zones.

Step 1. Click to select a theme transition that you've already added to the project. If it contains more than two still frames, the Viewer shows the entire transition image with numbers for each drop zone. In the Project browser, numbered pins indicate which frames are being used.

Step 2. To set a specific frame in your project as the still image for a drop zone, drag a pin to that frame.

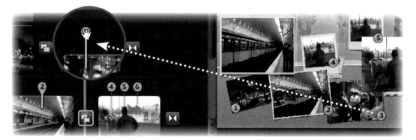

Change your mind? Position the mouse pointer along the middle of the pin until the pointer looks like scissors, then snip—er, click. The pin returns to its original location.

Editing Theme Transitions

Setting durations. You can edit theme transitions using many of the same techniques you use to edit ordinary, non-theme transitions.

To change a theme transition's duration, double-click it or choose Transition Adjustments from its Action menu. Or open the transition in the Precision Editor and edit it there.

You can also change the duration of all transitions in the project to the same amount, or specify a duration for new transitions. Choose File > Project Properties (⌘-J), click Timing, then adjust the Theme Transition Duration slider.

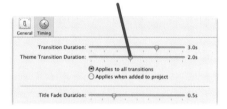

Tips: For non-theme transitions, a half-second duration is usually fine. But for theme transitions that display a lot of different images in drop zones, consider a longer duration: a second or more. Give your viewers a chance to see the images in the transition. If the transition is very short, it'll just look like you dropped the camera while shooting.

And note that because themes are so timing intensive, they don't mix particularly well with the beat markers described on page 207.

Changing a style. To change the style of a themed transition in your project, drag a new one (whether themed or not) from the Transitions browser and drop it onto the existing transition in your project's filmstrip. Similarly, to change a themed title, drag a new one from the Titles browser.

If you change the style of a theme transition, iMovie resets the still-image pins for the transition.

Maps and themes. Here's a little piece of cinematic-cartographic minutia that you might not even care about. If you've applied the Bulletin Board theme to your project, you'll notice a map tacked up on the bulletin board in transitions.

Normally, that map uses the Educational Globe style. But if your project already contains a globe or map of a different style, such as Old World Map, iMovie uses *that* style in the transition to maintain consistency.

If, on the other hand, your project contains several different map styles, the transition image uses the Educational Globe style: the default style for the Bulletin Board theme.

Creative Tips for Themes

Who needs credit? Although the Credits title styles are designed for credits, the Apple Police won't break down your door if you use them for something else. Need a stylish transition between footage shot on a morning hike and shots of a barbeque that same day? Use one of the Credits styles and edit its text to read *Later that day...*

For that matter, who needs text? The backgrounds and animations for iMovie's themes are gorgeous—why restrict them to just titles? I'll sometimes use one of the Credits styles from the Bulletin Board theme to present a segment of video: for example, a 10-second shot of a train pulling into a stop at the Paris Metro.

To set up something like this, add a clip to a project, then drag one of the Credits title themes to the clip. Extend the length of the title to match the duration of the clip, then—here's the simple trick—use the Viewer to delete the text of the title. You've just turned a title into a slick motion graphic.

This trick works best with the credits in the Bulletin Board theme and the Scrapbook theme, and with the main title of the Filmstrip theme. In the other themes, when you delete the title text, you end up with a blank item, such as a scrap of paper that would normally hold the title's text, obscuring part of the image; it looks a little weird.

Creating Travel Maps

Pack a bag and grab your fedora—it's time to travel.

Travel maps in iMovie are a lot like travel maps in iPhoto books—except they move. iMovie travel maps are beautiful animations that depict your journeys in a visual style made popular in movies featuring a certain hardscrabble, whip-toting adventurer. An animated red line starts in one city and then extends to another, indicating the passage of distance and time.

Adding a map to a movie takes just a few clicks. Pick a map style; there are several. Drag the map to your project. Use an Inspector to specify your starting and ending locations. It's that easy.

You can choose from two basic types of maps: a rotating globe that spins cities into view, and a flat world map that pans like a Ken Burns move. Within each type are several styles, giving you plenty of creative options for your cinematic cartography.

Let's go.

Adding a Map

Here's how to add a map to a project.

Step 1. Click the Maps and Backgrounds button (or press ⌘-5).

The maps browser appears.

These map styles are animated: the top four use globes, while the bottom four use flat maps.

These are still images; you can add them and then create Ken Burns moves to pan and zoom. You can't add locations to these maps, however.

Step 2. Drag a map style from the Maps and Backgrounds browser into your project, dropping it at the spot where you want the map to appear.

The Map Inspector appears.

Step 3. Specify map locations and other settings. To preview your work, tap the spacebar. When you're finished, click Done.

Type a duration. You can also change the map's duration later by dragging its edges in the project filmstrip.

Maps can have video effects, too (opposite page).

To specify start and end locations, click the appropriate button, then choose a location (opposite page).

Specifying Map Locations

When you click one of the location buttons in the Map Inspector, the Inspector flips over to reveal the Choose Location panel. Specify the location you want and click OK.

iMovie knows about 4,000 cities, airports, and places (such as the Eiffel Tower).

Scroll through them if you're a glutton for punishment, or simply type a city, airport code, or place name in the box.

You may want the location to appear as something other than the place or city name—for example, *Our Parisian Hideaway* instead of just *Paris*. If so, type the text you want.

Notes and Tips

Swapping locations. When you've specified both a start and end location, the Inspector displays a swap button (⊞). Click it, and iMovie swaps the two locations.

As I describe in the sidebar below, this is handy when you want to create a second map that depicts your route home.

How far is it? When you've specified two locations, the Inspector displays the distance between them. That's a cute little detail, but it's also useful. Create a title: *5575 miles to Paris*. Or use the distance in a voiceover narration: *We flew 5575 miles and all I got was this lousy T-shirt*.

Off the map. What if your start or end location isn't in iMovie's database? Go to Get Lat Lon (www.getlatlon.com) to retrieve latitude and longitude coordinates for any place on earth, then type the numbers in the search field.

Tips for Maps

Changing a map style. To change to a different map style, drag the new animated map style on top of an existing map in the Project browser. Your destinations, duration, and any video effect remain intact.

Spotlighting one location. You don't have to specify an end location. Choosing just a start location makes the map center on that city; it's a nice way to

visually introduce where your movie takes place.

Apply a video effect. You can add video effects to a map (see page 208). For a great retro look, use the Aged Film effect with an Old World Globe map. In the Map Inspector, click the Video Effect button, choose an effect, then click Done.

Maps and titles. You can superimpose titles over maps: *Our Hawaiian Vacation* or

Road Trip! Use the same techniques described on pages 228–231.

Easy location selection. When you're globetrotting to multiple destinations, iMovie is the flight attendant who wants to make your travel less stressful. When you add another map, its Start Location is automatically set as the previous map's End Location.

Round tripping. When it's time to show the path home, copy

your map by pressing Option and dragging the map elsewhere in your project. Next, double-click the copy or choose Clip Adjustments from its Action menu. In the Map Inspector, click the swap button to switch the two locations.

Maps and transitions. If you add a transition before or after a map, iMovie completes the map animation before starting the transition.

Sharing to MobileMe, YouTube, and iTunes

First things first: the Internet isn't the best medium for sharing digital video. Internet video involves transferring a lot of data, and that can mean lengthy downloads, quality compromises, or both.

But if you've made a short movie and you're willing to make some compromises, you can use iMovie to prepare your work for cyberspace.

From the Share menu, you can publish a movie to your MobileMe Gallery (if you're a MobileMe subscriber), upload it to YouTube, or prepare it for a video-capable iPod, iPhone, or Apple TV. For Internet movies, iMovie compresses the movie heavily to make its file size smaller. In the process, you get an introduction to The Three Musketeers of Internet Video: jerky, grainy, and chunky.

A movie compressed for the Internet contains fewer frames per second, so motion may appear jerky. The movie's dimensions are also much smaller—as small as 176 by 144 pixels, or roughly the size of a matchbook. And depending on the options you choose, the sound quality may not be as good as the original.

The best way to watch a movie is on a big screen. (That's where Apple TV shines: share your movie to iTunes, and you can sync it to Apple TV and watch it on your widescreen TV set.) But if you're willing to trade some quality for the portability of an iPod or the worldwide reach of the World Wide Web, iMovie is ready.

Publishing to a MobileMe Gallery

Choose Share > MobileMe Gallery. Specify the settings shown below, then click Publish.

iMovie compresses the movie and uploads it to your MobileMe Gallery. When that's done, a dialog box lets you view the page or tell a friend.

Name your shared movie.

Tell us about it: the description you write appears on the Gallery page.

Click the checkbox for each size you want to publish. Offering more than one size lets you accommodate various Internet speeds. The blue dots indicate which Apple devices and services work best at those sizes—but note that the Large size yields huge downloads with lengthy movies.

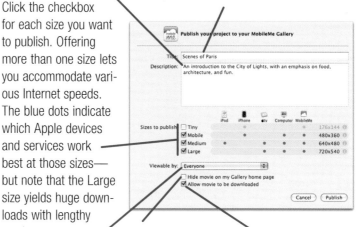

Share your production with the world, with a select few, or with just you. Choose Edit Names and Passwords to allow selective access to your movies (below).

To hide the movie on your Gallery index page (page 376), check this box.

For keeps? To allow viewers to download the movie to their hard drives, check this option.

Tip: Point to the ⓘ icon at the right end of each setting, and iMovie shows some details about how the movie will be encoded—and estimates its file size. Here, we see that a two-minute movie will yield a 57.6MB file in the Large setting—on the big side.

Sharing to YouTube

iMovie can upload movies directly to the popular and addictive YouTube video sharing site. (You'll need a free account; sign up at www.youtube.com.)

Step 1. Choose Share > YouTube.

Step 2. Type a title and description, but don't stop there. Choose a category and enter keywords in the Tags field—make your video easier to find in searches.

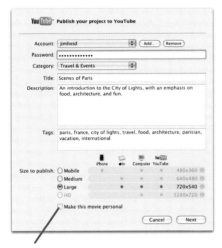

Click this option to restrict who views the movie.

Step 3. Click Next to review the YouTube Terms of Service (welcome to the entertainment business!), then click Publish to upload the movie.

Sharing to iTunes

Sharing your movie to iTunes is the key to getting your movie to an iPod, iPhone, or Apple TV.

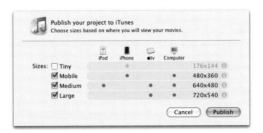

Step 1. Choose Share > iTunes.

Step 2. Choose the sizes you want to share.

After iMovie compresses the movie, it copies the movie to your iTunes library. Use iTunes to sync the movie to your iPod, iPhone, and Apple TV.

Note: 16:9 movies don't cleanly fit the proportions of the iPod's screen; the movie will be letterboxed with borders above and below the image. This applies to the iPhone and iPod touch, too.

After the Sharing

After you've shared a movie, an icon to the right of its name in the Project Library shows which sizes are published, and a bar at the top of the Project browser indicates where it's been shared.

If you change a shared movie, iMovie warns you that the shared version is out of date.

Don't want to share anymore? Choose the appropriate Remove command in the Share menu.

More Ways to Share Movies

Most of iMovie's sharing features are directed to specific outlets, such as YouTube or iTunes. But your movies can play in other venues, too. Want to add a movie to an iDVD or iWeb project? Share it to the Media browser, and it becomes available to any program that offers a Media browser—not only iDVD, iWeb, and GarageBand, but Apple's iWork applications, too.

You can also export a movie in a way that gives you access to the full range of QuickTime compression settings. Normally, iMovie's sharing features insulate you from compression technicalities, but when you want to get your hands dirty, iMovie provides the gardening tools.

And for you professional movie makers, iMovie can also export a Final Cut XML file, which is a plain text file containing instructions for Final Cut Pro or Final Cut Express to build a project based on your edits. It's the easiest way to move from a rough cut in iMovie to finer finishing work in Final Cut.

Sharing to the Media Browser

When you share a project to the Media browser, the movie becomes available in the Media browsers of other iLife programs, such as iDVD and iWeb, not to mention other software that supports Apple's Media browsers.

Step 1. Choose Share > Media Browser.

Step 2. Click the checkboxes for the sizes you want to create. The table indicates which sizes are appropriate for which devices and services.

Step 3. Click Publish.

iMovie encodes the movie and makes it available to other applications. You can then import the movie into iWeb (page 391); GarageBand (page 354); or iDVD (page 258).

Exporting a Movie File

You can export a movie using iMovie's friendly presets without having to send the movie to iTunes. Choose Share > Export Movie, then choose a size.

Why bother? Here's one way you might use this feature. Say you're creating a DVD containing some video. How about also including a standalone version of the video, encoded for viewing on an iPod or iPhone? Export the movie to your hard drive, then add it to your DVD's DVD-ROM folder (page 274). Instruct your DVD's recipients that they can insert the DVD in their computers, copy the exported version of your movie to their iTunes library, and then carry it with them.

You might also use the Export Movie command to create a movie file that you'll upload to a Web server. Use the Tiny preset, and you can even create a movie file small enough (more or less) to email to someone.

Exporting a QuickTime Movie

To export your project as a QuickTime movie, choose Export Using QuickTime from the Share menu.

Choose a preset from the pop-up menu.

Now what? iMovie's Tiny, Mobile, Medium, and Large sharing presets deliver great results for most uses. The additional presets in the Export dialog box give you even more options. But to really plumb the depths of QuickTime's exporting options, choose Movie to QuickTime movie from the Export pop-up menu, and then click the Options button.

This leads to an increasingly technical maze of dialog boxes that let you adjust everything from the video frame size to the sound sampling rate. Unless you know your compression, you're best off leaving the settings to iMovie.

To learn about compression, see *iMovie '09 & iDVD for Mac OS X Visual Quickstart Guide*, by Jeff Carlson (Peachpit Press, 2009). For more QuickTime resources, see www.macilife. com/imovie.

Sharing On Flickr

Although Flickr is best known for online photo sharing, you can also post videos of up to 90 seconds in length.

To prepare a project for Flickr, choose Share > Export, and choose the Medium option. Save the movie somewhere convenient, such as on your desktop.

To publish the video on Flickr, use the Flickr Uploadr (a free download from flickr. com), or point your browser to www.flickr. com/upload.

Exporting as Final Cut XML

If you're accustomed to working in Apple's intermediate and advanced video editing applications, but want to take advantage of iMovie's Event Library and fast cutting capabilities, there's an easy bridge between iMovie and Final Cut Pro or Final Cut Express.

But first, a few caveats. This feature transfers only the basic cut information (start and end points); any transitions you've added are converted to cross dissolves; and only the audio levels of video clips are retained. Titles, audio clips, video adjustments, cropping, and Ken Burns

effects are ignored. So, use iMovie to whip up a rough assembly and then hand it off to Final Cut for finessing. The file references the iMovie Event's source files, so you're not creating new versions and duplicating content on your hard disk.

To export for Final Cut, choose Share > Export Final Cut XML, and then specify a name and location for the file. Finally, import that file from within Final Cut.

Fun with Freeze Frames

You see it all the time in movies and TV shows: a scene begins with the action frozen, and suddenly the still image springs to life. The frozen image often has a special effect, too—maybe it's been altered to look like a faded photograph. When what appears to be an old photo suddenly turns Technicolor and starts moving, the effect can be magical.

In Hollywood, they use expensive equipment and expensive artists for cinematic tricks like this. You can do it for free using iMovie, and it's a cinch. Simply save a still image from the very beginning of a particular clip, then apply one or more video adjustments to it. Once you've altered the freeze frame, it just takes a few clicks to complete the effect.

This effect can be a fun way to introduce an event that just screams nostalgia—a kid opening presents, a family sitting down to a Thanksgiving feast, or some kids hitting a slope for some sloppy sledding. Start your scene with this effect, superimposing some title text if you like, and you've instantly gone beyond a run-of-the-mill home movie.

Note: At this writing, iMovie '09 contains a bug dealing with freeze frames and clips that you've stabilized. A frame created from a stabilized clip will contain the entire original frame, not just the area that iMovie zoomed in on for stabilization. If you want the frames to match (and usually, you do), use the Crop tool to zoom in slightly on the freeze frame. Or check to see if Apple has released an iMovie update that fixes this bug.

Step 1. Trim as needed.

Once you've chosen a video clip for this project, trim its start point so the clip begins at the most appropriate spot. For example, if there are a few seconds of jerky camera movement before Junior starts opening presents, trim the clip to remove the bad footage.

Step 2. Create a freeze frame.

Next, point to the very first frame of the trimmed clip, Control-click, and choose Add Freeze Frame from the shortcut menu.

iMovie adds a still frame just before the video clip.

Note: If you create a still frame from the middle of a clip, iMovie splits the clip, with the freeze frame positioned in the middle.

A still frame always has a duration of four seconds. To change its duration, choose Clip Adjustments from the Action menu and specify a new value in the Duration dialog box.

Play it back if you like: select it and press the forward-slash key (the shortcut for the Play Selection command).

Step 3. Add the effect.

Now you're ready to alter the appearance of the freeze frame. If you're after a nostalgic look, try giving the clip an aged-film look.

First, if it's not already open from Step 2, bring up the Clip Adjustments window.

Next, click the Video Effect button. If you like, skim over each effect to see a preview in the Viewer. For this example, choose the Aged Film effect.

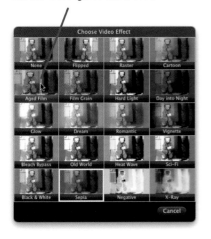

To apply the effect, click Done.

Step 4. Adjust the transition.

For this project, you want the effect to fade away shortly before the end of the clip; this enables the freeze frame to blend cleanly with the live-action clip that will follow it.

To accomplish this, add a Cross Dissolve transition between the two clips. To change the transition's duration, double-click the transition or choose Transition Adjustments from the Action menu, then specify a duration and click Done.

Because the transition overlaps the still image and moving footage, you may see a subtle shift at the end of the transition where the two images no longer line up.

To fix this, copy the still image, move the playhead to the end of your video, and choose Edit > Paste to make a duplicate. Position the dupe after the transition and reduce its duration so it appears only briefly after the transition finishes. Finally, go back to the Transition Adjustments window (press I) and change Video Effect to None.

Now sit back and admire your work. Click the Play Project from Beginning button (normally or using the Full Screen button).

Optional steps. Want to jazz up your effect even more? Apply the Ken Burns effect so that the freeze frame first appears zoomed in a bit, then zooms out to its actual size just before the dissolve.

To add a title to the freeze-frame clip, use the Titles browser as described on page 228.

Variations on a frozen theme. You can also turn this trick around: have a scene suddenly freeze and then turn into an old movie frame. This can be a fun way to end a scene.

To do it, save a frame from the last frame of a clip. Then, put the modified freeze frame after the clip from which it came and add the transition between the two.

iMovie Tips

Copying and Pasting Clips

You can make additional copies of a clip by copying it to the Clipboard and pasting it into the Project browser (you can't paste into the Event browser). If you want to experiment with different effects or cropping schemes, select the clip and choose Edit > Copy, then choose Edit > Paste. Another way to duplicate a clip is to press the Option key while dragging the clip.

You can even move clips from one project to another by copying and pasting them. You aren't using additional disk space when you do—you're simply making additional references to the source footage in your Event Library.

Copying and Pasting Adjustments

Just as you can copy and paste clips, you can also copy and paste the *adjustments* that you apply to clips. For example, if you've used the Video Adjustments window to brighten a murky clip, you can apply the same settings to other clips shot at the same time.

First, select an adjusted clip and choose Edit > Copy. Next, select the clip or clips to which you want to apply the adjustment. Finally, sprint up to the Edit menu and choose the appropriate command from the Paste Adjustments submenu: All (⌘-Shift-V), Video (⌘-Option-I), Audio (⌘-Option-A), Crop (⌘-Shift-R), Cutaway (⌘-Option-U), Video Effect (⌘-Option-L), Stabilization (⌘-Option-Z), Speed (⌘-Option-S), or Map Style (⌘-Option-M).

Pasting replaces any previous adjustments you may have made to the clips.

Customizing the Media Browsers

When you open the Music and Sound Effects browser, iMovie presents the contents of your iTunes library in a list. To customize the columns that appear, Control-click on the list, then use the Show Columns submenu to change which information appears.

And if you're a visual-memory person? Check out the Display as Icons option—it displays each track as an icon with its album art.

Customizing the Photos browser.
Want to see larger (or smaller) photo thumbnails? Drag the size slider to the right (or left). To see photos displayed as a list, Control-click in the photo thumbnails area and choose Display as List from the shortcut menu.

And if you don't need to see the list of albums and events all the time, drag the divider between the albums and the photos toward the top of the browser; the source list becomes a pop-up menu.

This tip applies to the Music and Sound Effects browser, too.

Print Your Movie

No, that isn't a mistake. iMovie can print your video (on paper) as a handy visual reference. Select either a project name or an event (or multiple events) and choose Print Project or Print Event from the File menu. Choose a number from the Preferred Number of Pages pop-up menu and choose whether to include the colored bars for event metadata, such as favorites or keywords (but not, alas, the keywords themselves).

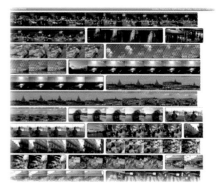

Click Print, and iMovie runs off a copy for you. The Clips Size slider determines how many thumbnails appear on the page.

Movies from Your Digital Camera

You can add movie clips taken by a digital camera to your iMovie projects. If a movie you want is in your iPhoto library, you can locate it by clicking the iPhoto Videos item in the Event Library. If the movie isn't in your library, simply locate its icon on your hard drive and drag it into the Event Library.

But let's step back and look at the greater question: why bother? Compared to the quality you get from a real video camera, the movies from most digital cameras look genuinely awful.

And yet there are some good reasons to consider using a digital camera movie in an iMovie project.

It's all you have. If you don't have a camcorder but want to include some video in a movie project (as opposed to still photos and Ken Burns clips), use your digital camera. Adjust its menu settings to get the largest frame size and highest quality your camera is capable of. iMovie enlarges the video frames to fill the screen, so you'll get better results from larger movies.

For a special effect. Video producers often spend big bucks to get video that looks pixilated and has jerky motion. With digital-camera movies, those "effects" are standard equipment. Have a video camera? Shoot some footage using it and your digital camera's movie mode. Then cut between the two for a cool effect.

For the sound. When I was in Paris, I wanted to capture the sound of the many street musicians who play in Metro stations. I shot digital camera movies and imported them into my iPhoto library. In iMovie, I added still photos of the street musicians to the timeline and applied the Ken Burns effect to the photos. Then, I added the audio portions of the digital camera movies by dragging the movie to the Project browser and choosing Audio Only from the pop-up menu. The result: a montage of still photos with an authentic soundtrack.

Importing iMovie HD Projects

iMovie '09 can import projects created in the old iMovie HD, but the results aren't pretty. Effects, titles, and music tracks are discarded, and all transitions are converted to Cross Dissolve transitions. Clips in the Clip viewer are put into a new event, and any clips in the timeline go into a new project. If all those trade-offs sound acceptable, choose File > Import > iMovie HD Project, locate the project, and click Import. Otherwise, finish your old projects in iMovie HD and use iMovie '09 for new movies.

Navigation Tips

Play Around Playhead

When you make an edit, you'll often find yourself moving the playhead a few seconds before the edit to replay that section and see how it turned out.

Rather than back up and play by hand, press the bracket keys to play *around* the playhead. Pressing [plays one second before and after the playhead's location; pressing] plays three seconds on each side.

Control-Click

Remember that you can Control-click on just about anything to bring up a shortcut menu that lets you perform relevant tasks. Try Control-clicking on a clip in the Event browser, and on audio and video clips in the Project browser.

Keyboard Shortcuts

I've mentioned iMovie's keyboard shortcuts throughout this chapter, but it's worth repeating: they're huge wrist savers. Get a complete list by choosing Help > Keyboard Shortcuts.

More iMovie Tips

Saving Disk Space

Hard disk filling up? Get another one. Or, in the meantime, consider using iMovie's Space Saver command. Space Saver can mark clips as rejected if they aren't added to any project, not marked as a favorite, or both. You won't be able to dig into your archives for unused footage later, but you will free up space.

Choose File > Space Saver, choose which type of footage to reject, and then click Reject and Review.

The Rejected Clips view appears in the Event browser, where you can verify that you do want to get rid of the nixed footage. To delete the clips from the Event Library, click the Move Rejected to Trash button. Finally, switch to the Finder and empty the Trash.

Consolidating a Project's Media

As I've mentioned, I recommend storing all of a project's assets—its video footage, audio files, and so on—on the same hard drive that holds the project itself. This lets you move the drive to a different Mac and still have access to everything in the project.

If you didn't do that before but now you've seen the error of your ways, iMovie can help. Choose File > Consolidate Media, then choose an option.

If you have plenty of hard drive space, consider using either the Copy the Events or the Move the Events option. That way, you'll have access to footage you didn't use. (Copying leaves the media behind on the original drive; moving deletes the media from the drive after it's been copied.)

To consolidate but save disk space, choose Copy the Clips. iMovie copies only the video you actually used in the project.

Regardless of the option you choose, iMovie also copies to the project's hard drive any iTunes songs that you might have used.

If the Consolidate Media command is disabled, then all of the project's media are already on the same disk as the project itself.

Accessing Your Project's Media

iMovie '09's files are freely accessible in the Finder—making it easy to find source files, but also increasing the risk of damaging a project by removing or altering files you shouldn't.

Project files are located in a folder called iMovie Projects; it's located in the Movies folder of your Home directory. The file names end in the extension .rcproject. (Those files, incidentally, are packages that contain the editing data as well as the thumbnails iMovie generates.)

Your imported source footage is stored in the iMovie Events folder in your Movies folder, with each event in its own folder. When working in iMovie, you can Control-click a clip and choose Reveal in Finder to locate the media file directly.

If you specified an external hard disk as the location for an event while importing (see page 170), you'll also find an iMovie Events folder at that disk's top-level directory. Even if you use footage from an external hard disk, the project files remain saved in your Home directory.

Normally, you shouldn't have to delve into any of these folders—let iMovie manage their contents for you. But should you have the need or urge to go spelunking, now you have a map.

Get more iMovie tips.
www.macilife.com/imovie

Exporting Sound

There may be occasions when you want to export part or all of the audio track of your project. Maybe you want to bring it into an audio-editing program, such as SoundStudio or Amadeus, for fine-tuning. Or maybe you recorded a music recital and you'd like to bring the performance into iTunes or GarageBand.

To export your project's soundtrack, choose Export Using QuickTime from the Share menu. In the Save dialog box that appears, choose Sound to AIFF from the Export pop-up menu. Click Options, then choose the desired audio settings.

If you'll be bringing your audio back into iMovie, use the default options. If you'll be importing the audio into iTunes or GarageBand, choose 44.1 kHz from the Rate pop-up menu.

Burning Movies to CD and Video CD

The best way to share a finished movie on a shiny platter is to burn it to a DVD. But you can also burn a movie to a CD that will play on any Mac or Windows computer that has QuickTime. You might take this route if you want to send a movie to a friend who has a computer, but no DVD player. (While you're at it, make a note to buy a cheap DVD player for your friend.)

To start, choose Share > Export Movie, choose the Mobile option, and click Export. Next, insert a blank CD into your Mac's optical drive and copy the movie to the CD.

If you have Roxio's Toast software, you can also create a Video CD. This video format is very popular in Asia, and somewhat obscure everywhere else. But most stand-alone DVD players can play Video CDs, as can all current personal computers. (To play Video CDs on a Mac, use Mireth Technology's MacVCD X software, available at www.mireth.com. And if you don't have Toast Titanium, you can also make Video CDs using Mireth Technology's iVCD.)

Video on a Video CD is compressed in MPEG-1 format. The image quality is a far cry from that of the MPEG-2 format used on DVDs; Video CD image quality is more akin to that of VHS videotape. One reason is because the video frame size is smaller—352 by 240 pixels, instead of DVD's 720 by 480. Another reason is that the video itself is compressed more heavily—about 90:1, compared to roughly 30:1 for MPEG-2. But on the plus side, a Video CD can shoehorn about an hour of video onto a CD-R disc.

A variation of the Video CD format is called *Super Video CD*, or *SuperVCD*. On a SuperVCD, video is stored in MPEG-2 format, yielding better quality than a Video CD. The SuperVCD format also allows for many DVD-like features, such as alternate language tracks. Its video quality still falls short of a DVD's, however.

Video CD and SuperVCD are second-best alternatives to DVDs, but any alternative is better than none. For background on the Video CD and SuperVCD formats, see www.vcdhelp.com.

What's in a Double-Click?

In iMovie '09, double-clicking a clip brings up the Inspector, which is a jarring change if you're accustomed to iMovie '08, where double-clicking a clip caused it to play back.

If you prefer the old way, choose iMovie > Preferences, click Browser, and change the Double-click To option from Edit to Play.

Improving Graphics Performance

For many tasks—displaying transitions and titles, superimposing video, and much more—iMovie relies on the processor on your Mac's graphics card, just as iPhoto does when playing slide shows.

If you use iMovie a lot and you're buying a new Mac, you might want to investigate some of the extra-cost graphics cards that are available through the online Apple store and elsewhere. Similarly, a card containing more memory (for example, 512MB) will deliver better performance than a card containing less (for example, 256MB).

Along the same lines, if you have an older Mac Pro tower or even a 2GHz dual-processor Power Mac G5—the oldest Power Mac on which iMovie will run—you could see a boost in iMovie's performance by upgrading to a new graphics card.

Ultimately, you know what this means: becoming an iMovie user is a great excuse to buy that new Mac you've been wanting.

Tips for Making Better Movies

Editing takes more than software. You also need the right raw material. Advance planning will help ensure that you have the shots you need, and following some basic videography techniques will make for better results.

Plan Ahead

Planning a movie involves developing an outline—in Hollywood parlance, a *storyboard*—that lists the shots you'll need to tell your tale. Professional movie makers storyboard every scene and camera angle. You don't have to go that far, but you will tell a better story if you plan at least some shots.

Consider starting with an *establishing shot* that clues viewers in on where your story takes place—for example, the backyard swimming pool. To show the big picture, zoom out to your camcorder's wide-angle setting.

From there, you might cut to a *medium shot* that introduces your movie's subject: little Bobby preparing to belly flop off the diving board. Next, you might cut away to Mary tossing a beach ball. Cut back to Bobby struggling to stay afloat, and then finish with a long shot of the entire scene.

Keep in mind that you don't have to shoot scenes in chronological order—sequencing your shots is what iMovie is for. For example, get the shot of Mary's throw any time you like and edit it into the proper sequence using iMovie.

Steady Your Camera

Nausea-inducing camera work is a common flaw of amateur videos. Too many people mistake a video camera for a fire hose: they sweep across a scene, panning left and right and then back again. Or they ceaselessly zoom in and out, making viewers wonder whether they're coming or going.

A better practice is to stop recording, move to a different location or change your zoom setting, and then resume. Varying camera angles and zoom settings makes for a more interesting video. If you must pan—perhaps to capture a dramatic vista—do so slowly and steadily.

And, unless you're making an earthquake epic, hold the camera as steady as you can. If your camera has an image-stabilizing feature, use it. Better still, use a tripod or a monopod, or brace the camera against a rigid surface. iMovie's image stabilization feature can help, but you'll get higher quality video (and won't have to wait as long) by shooting steady video up front.

Compose Carefully

The photographic composition tips on page 164 apply to movie making, too. Compose your shots carefully, paying close attention to the background. Get up close now and then—don't just shoot wide shots.

Record Some Ambient Sound

Try to shoot a couple of minutes of uninterrupted background sound: the waves on a beach, the birds in the forest, the revelers at a party. As I've mentioned previously, you can extract the sound from this footage and use it as an audio bed behind a series of shots. It doesn't matter what the camera is pointing at while you're shooting—you won't use the video anyway.

Add just the video's audio to any clip, as described on page 222.

Shooting with Compression in Mind

If you know that you'll be distributing your movie via the Internet—either through a Web site or email—there are some steps you can take during the shooting phase to optimize quality. These steps also yield better results when you're compressing a movie for playback on a mobile device, and they even help deliver better quality with iDVD.

First, minimize motion. The more motion you have in your movie, the worse it will look after being heavily compressed. That means using a tripod instead of hand-holding your camera, and minimizing panning and zooming. Also consider your background: a static, unchanging background is better than a busy traffic scene or rustling tree leaves.

Learn more about digitizing old tapes and movies.
www.macilife.com/imovie

Second, light well. If you're shooting indoors, consider investing in a set of video lights. A brighter picture compresses better than a poorly lit scene. To learn about lighting, read Ross Lowell's excellent book, *Matters of Light and Depth* (Lower Light Management, 1999).

Vary Shot Lengths

Your movie will be more visually engaging if you vary the length of your shots. Use longer shots for complex scenes, such as a wide shot of a city street, and shorter shots for close-ups or reaction shots.

Be Prepared, Be Careful

Be sure your camcorder's batteries are charged; consider buying a second battery so you'll have a backup, and take along your charger and power adapter, too. Bring plenty of blank tape or media cards, and label them immediately after ejecting them. To protect a tape against accidental reuse, slide the little locking tab on its spine.

Don't Skimp on Footage

Don't just get one version of a shot, get several. If you just shot a left-to-right pan across a scene, for example, shoot a right-to-left pan next. The more raw material you have to work with, the better.

Converting Analog Video and Movies

Somewhere in your closet is a full-sized VHS camcorder—the kind that rested on your shoulder like a rocket launcher. You want to get that old VHS video into your Mac.

If you have a DV camera, chances are it has a *pass-through* mode that enables you to use it as an analog-to-digital converter. Connect the video and audio output jacks on the VHS deck to your DV camera's video and audio input jacks. If your VHS deck and camcorder each provide S-video jacks, use them to get the best picture.

Next, put your camera in VCR or VTR mode, and read its manual to see if you have to perform any special steps to use its pass-through mode. With some cameras, you must make a menu adjustment. With others, you simply need to remove the tape.

After you've made the appropriate connections and adjustments, you can play your VHS tape and click iMovie's Import button to record the converted footage coming from your camera.

Analog-DV Converter

A faster way to get analog video into your Mac is through a converter, such as those sold by Formac Electronics, DataVideo, Sony, and others. These devices eliminate the time-consuming process of dubbing VHS tapes to DV format. Connect a converter to your Mac's FireWire jack, then connect your old VHS rocket launcher to the converter's video and audio inputs. Then, launch iMovie and use its import features to bring in VHS video.

When importing VHS video, you may notice a thin band of flickering pixels at the bottom of the image. Don't worry: these artifacts won't appear when you view your finished video on a TV screen.

Converting Films

As for those old Super 8 film-based flicks, you'll need to send them to a lab that does film-to-video transfers. Many camera stores can handle this for you. The lab will clean your films, fix bad splices, and return them along with videotapes whose contents you can bring into the Mac. If you have a DV camcorder, be sure to use a lab that will supply your converted movies on DV cassettes—you'll get much better image quality than VHS or DVD provides. Some labs also offer optional background music and titles, but you can add these yourself once you've brought the converted video into the Mac.

I wrote a feature article on digitizing old tapes and movies for *Macworld* magazine's June 2004 issue. The article is available online; I've linked to it at www.macilife.com/imovie.

iDVD:
Putting it All Together

iDVD at a Glance

iDVD lets you burn movies and photos to DVDs, complete with menus you can fully customize.

Designers and photographers can use iDVD to assemble digital portfolios that they can hand out like brochures. Filmmakers and advertising professionals can distribute rough cuts of movie scenes and commercials to clients and colleagues. Businesspeople can create in-house training discs and video archives of corporate meetings. Videographers can offer DVDs of weddings and other events. And home-movie buffs can preserve and share family videos and photographs.

Creating a DVD involves choosing and customizing a menu design and adding the movies and photos you want to include on the DVD. You can perform these steps in any order and preview your work along the way. When you've finished, you can commit the final product to a shiny platter.

Starting a New iDVD Project

Creating a DVD with iDVD involves creating a new project document, choosing and customizing a menu design theme, and adding content. Here's how to get started.

Step 1. Choose File > New or click the Create a New Project button.

Step 2. Name your iDVD project, choose an aspect ratio, then click Create.

Standard is the best choice if your DVD will contain 4:3 video (page 174) or will be shown mostly on 4:3 televisions.

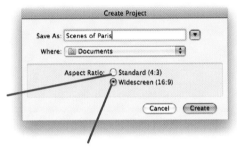

Go wide if the DVD contains 16:9 video and you'll be viewing the DVD on widescreen TVs. Widescreen is also great for photos.

Note: You can change the aspect ratio later if you like.

Step 3. Now what?

Choose a theme and fine-tune it if you like (pages 254–257). Add movies to your DVD (page 258). Create slide shows containing your photos (pages 260–263). Explore the authoring and menu-customizing features described later in this chapter. Preview your work as you go (page 255), then burn the final product (page 276).

A Short Glossary of DVD Terms

authoring The process of creating menus and adding movies and images to a DVD.

button A clickable area that plays a movie or slide show, or takes the user to another menu.

chapter A video bookmark that you can access from a menu or with a remote control. Creating chapters in a movie lets viewers jump to specific sections.

DVD-R The blank media that you'll use most often when burning DVDs. A DVD-R blank can be burned just once.

DVD-RW A type of DVD media that you can erase and reuse.

menu A screen containing clickable buttons that enable users to access a DVD's contents.

motion menu A menu whose background image is an anima-

tion or movie, a menu that plays background audio, or both.

MPEG-2 The compression format used for video on a DVD. MPEG stands for *Moving Picture Experts Group*.

Many themes have *drop zones*, special areas into which you can drag photos or a movie (pages 255–257).

To add a movie to your DVD, drag it into iDVD's window (page 258). iDVD creates a button, whose appearance you can customize (page 269).

To create a custom menu background, drag an image from iPhoto or another program to the iDVD window (page 269).

Each menu on your DVD has a title, whose position and formatting you can customize (page 268).

Many themes have several menu designs, ideal for a DVD containing multiple menus (page 266).

Add a new menu (page 267), movie (page 258), or slide show (page 260).

View your DVD's menu structure and modify its content in Map view (page 272).

Display the Menu Info window (left), a floating window for setting options.

Change the contents of drop zones (page 256).

Preview menus containing motion or background audio.

Preview your DVD before burning it (page 254).

To burn your finished DVD, click Burn (page 276).

Choosing and Customizing Themes

A big part of creating a DVD involves choosing which menu theme you want. iDVD includes menu themes for many types of occasions and subjects: weddings, parties, vacations, kids, and more. Many of these themes have motion menus containing beautiful animations and background music.

In iDVD, all themes are designed for widescreen presentation. Although iDVD can't yet burn high-definition discs, you can take advantage of the more cinematic 16:9 aspect ratio if you shot widescreen video. You can also create your project in the older 4:3 aspect ratio, if that better suits your movie formats and TV set.

Your design options don't end once you've chosen a theme. Many of iDVD's themes provide *drop zones*, special areas of the menu background into which you can drag photos or movies. Drop zones make it easy to customize a theme with your own imagery.

Most drop zones have special effects that iDVD applies to the photos or movies that you add to them. For example, the Reflection White theme puts your imagery in a set of 3D panels that glide like a moving art gallery. The Road Trip theme puts your imagery in a scrapbook—and if you look closely, you'll see that the pages cast shadows on each other.

Most themes provide "dynamic" drop zones that move around the screen. And as the following pages describe, you have more options for managing the contents of drop zones.

Choosing a Theme

Step 1.

If the list of themes isn't visible, click the Themes button.

Step 2.

Choose the theme you want by clicking it.

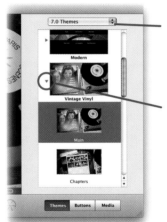

Use the pop-up menu to access themes from older versions of iDVD.

Click the disclosure triangle next to a theme family to reveal specific menu themes.

Tip: When you select a new theme, iDVD may ask if you want to switch between a widescreen or standard-definition aspect ratio. If you get tired of this nagging, click Do Not Ask Me Again before clicking Keep or Change.

Note: In order to see a theme's motion, you must have motion turned on. To turn motion on or off, click the Motion button. As you work on your DVD, you'll probably want to turn motion off since iDVD performs better this way.

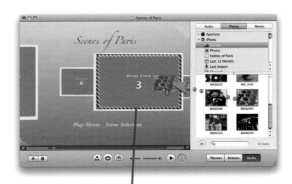

Adding Items to a Drop Zone

iDVD provides several ways to add items to drop zones. Here's the technique you're likely to use most often. For details on more drop zone techniques, see the following pages.

Step 1.

Click the Media button. Then, to access photos in your iPhoto library, click the Photos button. To access movies, click Movies.

Step 2.

In the photo or movie media browser, select the item or items you want to add. You can select multiple photos or an entire album. If you add multiple photos to a drop zone, iDVD displays them successively as the menu is displayed. You can add up to 99 items to a drop zone.

Step 3.

Drag the selected items into the drop zone.

As you drag into a drop zone, a dotted line indicates the drop zone's boundaries.

Step 4.

To fine-tune an item's position within the drop zone, hold the ⌘ key and drag it using the hand pointer 🖐.

Previewing and Testing Your Work

As you work on a DVD, you'll be anxious to see how the final product will look. To find out, use iDVD's preview mode. Click the Preview button, and iDVD turns itself into a DVD player and starts playing your DVD.

In preview mode, an on-screen remote control lets you navigate—choose menu buttons, jump to chapters, and watch the movies and slide shows you've added to your DVD.

Displays a movie's menu.

Displays the top-most menu on DVDs that contain multiple menus.

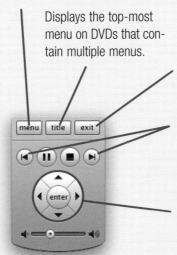

Exits preview mode.

Jumps to the previous or next chapter in a movie, or to the previous or next photo in a slide show.

Click the arrows to navigate. Click Enter to choose the highlighted menu button.

Preview mode plays back whatever is displayed in iDVD's window. If your main menu is visible, that's what plays back. If you're working on a slide show, the slide show begins playing.

Using iDVD's preview mode is a great way to check your work, but you shouldn't rely on it as your only testing tool. As you near the end of your project, create a disc *image* and use Mac OS X's DVD Player program to test it (see page 278). Then burn a disc and test it in your DVD player.

Working with Drop Zones

Here are some tips for working with drop zones.

Drop Zones Versus Menu Buttons

It's important to understand the difference between drop zones and buttons. A drop zone is merely an area of imagery within a DVD menu—it isn't a clickable button that your viewers can use to watch your DVD. A drop zone is a piece of eye candy; a button is a navigation control that plays a movie or slide show, or jumps to another menu.

How to tell the difference. As you drag items into the menu area, how can you tell whether you're dragging into a drop zone or creating a button? Easy: When you're dragging into a drop zone, a dotted-line pattern appears around the edges of the drop zone, as shown on the previous page.

If you don't see this pattern, you aren't in the drop zone, and you'll end up creating a button or changing your DVD's background image. If that happens, head for the Edit menu and choose the Undo command.

Navigating Dynamic Drop Zones

In most themes, drop zones are *dynamic*—they move around on the screen or they appear and disappear as a motion menu plays.

How do you add items to a drop zone that's behind another drop zone or not even visible?

Use the motion playhead. At the bottom of iDVD's menu area is a horizontal motion playhead that lets you scrub through a menu: drag the playhead left and right, and iDVD plays the motion menu, displaying its drop zones. Simply drag the playhead until the drop zone you want is visible.

(If you don't see the motion playhead, choose Show Motion Playhead from the View menu.)

Use the drop zone editor. Double-click on any drop zone, and iDVD displays the drop zone editor. You can add photos and

movies to drop zones by dragging them into the editor.

You can also display the drop zone editor by choosing Edit Drop Zones from the Project menu.

Autofill. Want quick results? Let iDVD do the work. Choose Project > Autofill Drop Zones, and iDVD fills all drop zones with images from the media in your DVD. You can fine-tune the results if you like.

Older themes. Both the motion playhead and drop zone editor also work with iDVD's older themes.

Introductory Animations

Many iDVD themes provide introductory animations. For example, in the Vintage Vinyl theme, the stack of album sleeves slides into position before the menu buttons become visible.

These animations are cute, but you might not always want to use them. They're fine on a DVD's main menu, but on a submenu (such as a scene selection menu for a movie), they slow down your DVD's users, who must wait for the animation to finish before they can access the menu's buttons.

Solution: Turn off the introductory animations when you don't want them. Just click the little check box at the left edge of the motion playhead. Or, display the Menu Info window and uncheck the Intro or Outro boxes.

Other Ways to Add Items

You can also add items to a drop zone by dragging them from the Finder: simply drag the items' icons into the drop zone or drop zone editor. And you can drag photos from iPhoto and other programs directly into a drop zone.

Another way to add items is from the shortcut menu: Control-click within a drop zone, and choose the Import command; or, choose Fill with Content to grab media used elsewhere in the project.

Removing and Rearranging Items

To remove the contents of a drop zone, drag the item out of the drop zone. When you release the mouse button, the item disappears in a puff of smoke. As an alternative to dragging, you can also Control-click within the drop zone and choose Clear Drop Zone Contents from the shortcut menu.

What if you have a drop zone containing multiple items and you want to remove a few of the items—or even just one? Here's how. Double-click the drop zone to display the drop zone editor, then double-click the entry for the drop zone that you want to edit. iDVD displays the drop zone photos editor, where you can delete individual items.

You can also use the drop zone photos editor to rearrange the order in which items in a drop zone are displayed: just drag the items around. And you can add items to a drop zone by dragging them into its editor.

Adding Movie Clips from iMovie

In the Media pane, click the Movies tab and select an iMovie project that's been shared to the media browser. Drag the shared movie into a drop zone.

What if you want to use just part of a video clip in a drop zone? You can't use iMovie's cropping or trimming features to indicate which portion you want to keep. That's because these features don't actually delete any video; they simply tell iMovie which parts you want to use. If you drag a cropped clip into an iDVD drop zone, the entire clip plays in the drop zone.

To control how much of the movie plays in the drop zone, click on the drop zone that contains the movie. iDVD displays a set of crop markers above the movie; drag the markers left and right to specify which portion of the movie should play.

Browsing a Drop Zone

If you have a drop zone that contains multiple items, you can quickly scan through the drop zone's contents without having to open up the drop zone editor. Click on a drop zone, and a small slider pops up; to scan through the drop zone's items, drag the slider back and forth. If, while browsing, you decide to rearrange the drop zone's contents, click the Edit Order button below the slider.

Preview Glitches?

When you've added movies or high-resolution photos to a menu's drop zones, you may see and hear some problems when you preview the menu: the drop zones' motion may appear jerky, and the menu's background audio may break up as it plays.

Not to worry—these problems won't occur on your final DVD. Indeed, the problems often go away once the menu has had a chance to play through once.

Adding Movies to Your DVD

iDVD's job is to integrate and present assets from other programs. The assets you're most likely to add to your DVDs are movies you've created in iMovie or another video-editing program, such as Apple's Final Cut Express or Final Cut Pro.

You can add movies to your DVDs using a couple of techniques. iDVD can accept movies in just about any QuickTime-compatible format (for some examples of movies you can't use, see page 280). You can also use 16:9 movies in either HDV or DV Widescreen format. If you use high-definition movies, however, note that iDVD will convert them to standard-definition for display—not because it wants to, but because it has to. Today, the high-definition DVD landscape is still in flux, with a couple of standards vying for acceptance.

In the meantime, your high-definition movies will still play in all their widescreen glory if you play your DVD on a wide-screen TV set. On a conventional TV, they'll play in letterboxed format.

Video on a DVD is compressed, or encoded, into a format called MPEG-2. As the sidebar on the opposite page describes, iDVD performs this encoding either as you work or after you click the Burn button.

Adding a Movie Using the Movie Browser

Step 1.

Click the Media button, then click the Movies button.

iDVD lists movies contained in iMovie as well as your Movies folder, iPhoto, and iTunes. To have iDVD list movies located elsewhere on your hard drive, choose Preferences from the iDVD menu, click the Movies button, and add additional folders to the list.

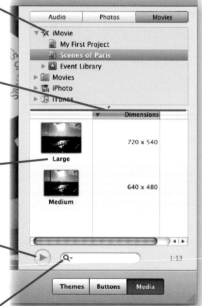

Available movies appear here.

For best quality, use the Large version of iMovie projects that you've shared to the media browser (see page 240)

To preview a movie in the movie browser, select the movie and click this play button, or simply double-click the movie.

Use the Search box to locate a movie in the browser.

Step 2.

Drag the desired movie into your DVD's menu area.

iDVD adds the movie to your DVD and creates a menu button for it.

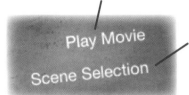

If the movie contains DVD chapter markers, iDVD creates two buttons: one named Play Movie and another named Scene Selection. If the movie lacks DVD chapters, iDVD simply creates one button, giving it the same name as the movie itself. To rename any button, select it and edit the name.

Tip: If you don't want iDVD to create a chapter submenu— or if you'd like iDVD to ask if you want one—use the options in the Movies portion of the Preferences dialog box.

Other Ways to Add a Movie

You can also add a movie by dragging its icon from the Finder into the iDVD window, or by choosing File > Import > Video. These techniques are convenient if you store your movies on an external hard drive and you don't feel like adding the drive to the movie browser using the Preferences command.

You can also use the media browser to add video clips from your iTunes or iPhoto libraries (although you can't burn your video purchases from the iTunes store). For more details on using digital camera movies in iDVD projects, see page 280.

Tips for DVD Movies

Encoder Settings

You can have up to two hours of video on a disc—four hours, if you have a dual-layer DVD burner (see page 276). By adjusting iDVD's encoder settings, you can control how much video will fit as well as the quality of the video itself. Choose iDVD > Preferences, click Projects, and cast your eyes on the Encoding pop-up menu. (You can also change encoding settings for an individual project as described on page 281.)

The Very Best

If you have more than one hour of video—or you want the best quality iDVD is capable of— choose Professional Quality. In this mode, iDVD puts on its thinking cap and analyzes your video twice, with the goal of compressing it as little as possible.

You get great quality and two (or four) hours on a disc, but be patient. Encoding upwards of two hours of video may take several hours, even on speedy modern Macs.

The Next Best

For high quality in less time, choose High Quality. iDVD analyzes your video like the Professional Quality setting does, but it performs just one pass instead of two.

The Very Fastest

If you have under an hour of video, consider the Best Performance option. The video still looks great and encoding is much faster. When you choose Best Performance, iDVD encodes while you work.

For more encoding insights, see page 279.

Using Movies from Final Cut

iDVD can also encode Final Cut Pro or Final Cut Express movies. Export the movie by choosing QuickTime Movie from the File menu's Export submenu. (In older Final Cut versions, this command is Final Cut Movie or Final Cut Pro Movie.) If the movie has chapter markers, be sure to choose the Chapter Markers option in the Markers pop-up menu of the Save dialog box.

Creating DVD Slide Shows

iDVD slide shows are a great way to share photos. Even low-resolution photos look spectacular on a television screen, and they can't easily be copied and redistributed— a plus for photographers creating portfolio discs. (You can, however, opt to include the originals on the disc, as described in "The DVD-ROM Zone" on page 274.)

iDVD provides a few ways to create a slide show. You can use iDVD's photo browser to drag a few photos or an entire album or event into the iDVD window. You can also use the Send to iDVD command in iPhoto to send an album, an event, a selection of photos, or a saved slide show to iDVD. And you can manually drag photos from iPhoto (or anywhere else) into iDVD's slide show editor.

As the following pages describe, you can give your slide shows background music from your iTunes library and fine-tune other aspects of their appearance. You can also choose to have transitions between images; iDVD gives you twelve transition styles from which to choose (see page 262).

Each image in a slide show can be any size and orientation; however, vertically oriented images will have a black band on their left and right edges.

Slide shows aren't even limited to still images. As with iPhoto, you can sprinkle movies into them, too. Make a slide show containing just movies if you like. Try *that* with your slide projector.

Creating a Slide Show Using the Media Browser

Step 1.

In iPhoto, create an album that contains the photos you want in the slide show, sequenced in the order you want them to appear (see page 58). You can also create a slide show from an entire event's worth of photos.

Step 2.

In iDVD, click the Media button, then click the Photos button.

Your iPhoto library and its events and albums appear here. To display more photos or albums, drag the horizontal separator below the album list up or down.

The photos in your library or a selected album appear here.

To search for a photo based on its title, type part or all of its title here.

Step 3.

Locate the desired album or event and drag it into the iDVD menu area.

Tip: Be sure you don't drag the album or event into a drop zone; see "Working with Drop Zones" on page 256.

iDVD creates the slide show and a menu button for displaying it. iDVD gives the button the same name as the album or event, but you can rename the button to anything you like.

Creating a Slide Show Within iPhoto

You can send photos to iDVD from within iPhoto, and with a couple of different options.

Slide show project. If you've created a slide show project, you can add it to iDVD and retain its custom Ken Burns moves, theme settings, and other goodies. In iPhoto, select the slide show in your Slideshows list. Then, choose Send to iDVD from the Share menu. iPhoto creates a video version of the slide show and ships it off to iDVD.

If you need to revise the slide show, first delete it from your iDVD project. (Select its button and press Delete.) Then, return to iPhoto, make your changes, and choose Send to iDVD again.

If you create a 16:9 (widescreen) slide show in iPhoto, iDVD displays it in widescreen format.

Basic slide show. Here's the technique to use if you don't need Ken Burns moves and you'd prefer the advantages of a DVD slide show (for example, more efficient use of disc space and the ability to easily include original images on your disc). In iPhoto, select an album, an event, a Faces tile, a place, or a series of photos. Then, choose Send to iDVD from the Share menu.

You can revise this type of slide show directly within iDVD using the techniques on the following pages.

Creating a Slide Show from Scratch

You can also create a blank slide show and then manually add photos to it.
You might use this technique to add photos that aren't stored in your iPhoto library.

Step 1.

Choose Add Slideshow from the pop-up menu or choose Project > Add Slideshow (⌘-L).

iDVD adds a button named My Slideshow to the currently displayed menu. Rename this button as desired.

Step 2.

Double-click on the button that iDVD just created. The slide show editor appears.

Step 3.

Drag photos (or a folder containing photos) into the slide show editor. Or, display the photo browser and drag photos from your iPhoto library.

Tip: You can add a movie to a slide show, too—just drag it into the editor from the movies browser or elsewhere.

Refining a Slide Show

When you create a DVD slide show, you can fine-tune it using the slide show editor. To display the editor, double-click the slide show's menu button or icon in Map view.

When checked, this box superimposes arrows over the images as a hint to viewers that they can move back and forth in the slide show using their DVD remote controls.

Check this box, and the slide show will repeat until the cows come home— or at least until your DVD's viewer presses the Menu or Title button on his or her remote control.

Switch between list view and thumbnail view.

To display these options, click the Settings button.

To have iDVD store the original images on the DVD, check this box. (For details, see page 274.)

To edit a photo's title or comment, click its text. If Show Titles and Comments is checked, the text appears during the slide show.

If you've added movies to the slide show, check this box to quiet the background music while a movie plays.

To change playback order, drag images. You can select multiple images by Shift-clicking and ⌘-clicking.

You can specify a duration for the images, or have the slide show timed to match its soundtrack. If the slide show has a soundtrack, the Manual option isn't available.

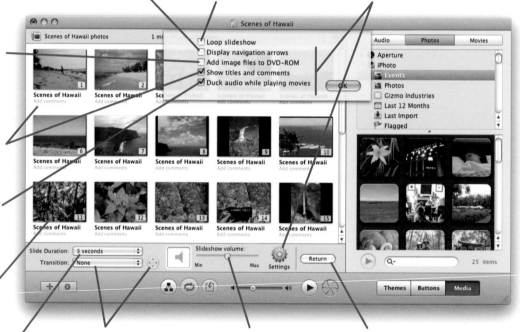

You can have transitions between photos. For some transition styles, you can also specify a direction, such as a left-to-right wipe.

Adjust the volume of the slide show's soundtrack.

Return to the menu that leads to this slide show.

Tip: To delete a photo from the slide show, select it and press the Delete key. This doesn't delete the photo from your hard drive, it just removes it from the slide show.

Adding Music to Slide Shows

You can add a music track to a slide show. One way to add music is by using the iTunes browser in iDVD. Click the Media button, then click the Audio button. Locate the song you want (use the search box if need be), then drag it to the Audio well. To add an entire playlist, drag it to the Audio well.

You can also drag a song directly from the iTunes window or, for that matter, from any folder on your hard drive. And you don't even have to drag an *audio* file: if you drag a QuickTime movie to the Audio well, iDVD will assign its audio to your slide show.

Music and timing. How iDVD matches your soundtrack to your slides depends on the option you choose from the Slide Duration pop-up menu. If you choose a specific duration, such as five seconds per slide, iDVD repeats your soundtrack if its duration is shorter than the slide show's total length. If the soundtrack is longer than the slide show, iDVD simply stops playing the soundtrack after the last slide displays. (To have the music fade at the end of the slide show, use the Slideshow portion of the Preferences dialog box.) And if you choose the Fit to Audio option, iDVD times the interval between image changes to match the soundtrack's duration.

To remove a slide show's background music, drag the icon out of the Audio well. When you release the mouse button, the icon vanishes in a puff of smoke.

Slide Show Tips

TV-Safe Slide Shows

Normally, when you view a slide show on a TV screen, you don't see the outer edges of each photo. This is because TV screens typically crop off the outer edges of an image. If you want to see your images in their full, uncropped glory, choose iDVD's Preferences command, click the Slideshow button, and check the box labeled Always Scale Slides to TV Safe Area. When this option is active, iDVD sizes images so they don't completely fill the frame—thus eliminating cropping.

Beyond 99 Slides

The DVD specification limits the number of images in a slide show to 99. Fortunately, iDVD lets you work around this limitation. You can drag more than 99 photos into the slide show editor, and, thanks to some clever technical trickery, iDVD is able to present them as one slide show.

What iDVD can't do is make your viewers patient enough to sit through all those shots.

Making a Magic iDVD

When you want to create a DVD in a hurry, use the Magic iDVD feature.

Magic iDVD presents you with a single window containing a list of menu themes, a set of drop boxes for holding movies and photos, and a media browser for accessing your audio, photos, and movies.

Choose a theme, then drag movies into the drop boxes. To create DVD slide shows, drag photos to the drop boxes. Drag an entire event or album from iPhoto or build a slide show one photo at a time by dragging individual photos into the same box. Want a music soundtrack for a slide show? Drag an audio track into the slide show's drop box.

When you're done, preview your work by clicking the Preview button and using iDVD's standard preview features (page 255). Then click the Burn or Create Project buttons, and iDVD builds your project for you, even creating chapter submenus for movies containing DVD chapters (page 259).

Magic iDVD may be all you need for many projects. And if you need to customize or enhance the DVD it creates, you can bring the rest of iDVD's authoring features to bear. Indeed, Magic iDVD is a great way to rough out a project that you plan to refine later.

Here's how to make DVD magic.

Magic iDVD versus OneStep DVD

iDVD provides two ways to go from zero to DVD with very few steps. Which method should you use, and when?

When to go OneStep. Use OneStep DVD when you want to burn just one movie to a DVD and you don't need navigation menus. When you use OneStep DVD, you don't have the opportunity to customize menu designs—there aren't any. As page 267 describes, OneStep DVD creates an *autoplay*, or *kiosk-mode*, DVD: the disc begins playback as soon as you insert it into a computer or DVD player.

When to go Magic iDVD. Use Magic iDVD when you want navigation menus and more than one piece of content on your DVD—for example, a couple of movies and some slide shows.

To Make a Magic iDVD

Step 1. Choose File > Magic iDVD.

Step 2 (optional). Edit the DVD title.

Step 3. Choose a theme for the DVD by clicking one of the theme thumbnails. (To access additional themes, use the pop-up menu above the row of thumbnails.)

Step 4. To add video to the DVD, click the Movies button in the Media pane, then drag one or more movies into the drop boxes.

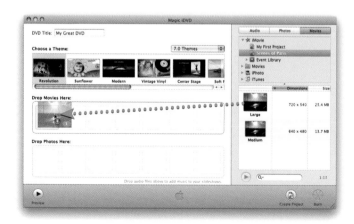

Tips: You can also drag movies directly from folders on your Mac's hard drive. (To have iDVD list movies from other folders in its media browser, use the Preferences command as described on page 258.)

Need to add multiple movies? Simply Shift-click or ⌘-click on each one to select the movies, then drag them as a group, as shown on the opposite page. When you release the mouse button, each movie appears in its own drop box.

Step 5. To add a slide show to the DVD, drag photos into the photos drop boxes. Each box represents a different slide show.

Tips: You can drag albums or events from iPhoto, or folders of photos from your hard drive or a CD. If you like to

overwork, you can drag individual photos to a drop box, one at a time. You can also combine approaches. For example, you can drag an entire album or event to create a slide show, then drag individual photos to that slide show's drop box to add them to the show.

And just as you can add multiple movies at once, you can create multiple slide shows at once. Shift-click or ⌘-click on each event or album in the Photos media browser, then drag the items as a group. Each item becomes its own slide show.

Step 6 (optional). To add music to a slide show, drag an audio file from the Audio media browser (or elsewhere on your hard drive) to the slide show.

A speaker icon appears on the slide show's thumbnail to indicate that it has a soundtrack.

Step 7. Preview or finish up.

Check your work. To preview the DVD, click the Preview button. When you exit preview mode, you return to the Magic iDVD window.

Ready to bake. If you're happy with the job Magic iDVD has done, click the Burn button. iDVD creates a project containing your content, then immediately switches into burn mode. (For burning details, see pages 276–279.)

Further refinement. If you want to refine the project—for example, to customize some menus or refine your slide shows—click the Create Project button. iDVD creates a project that you can customize using the techniques described throughout this chapter.

Behind the Magic

Here's a look at how Magic iDVD does its design. And remember, you aren't locked into its magical decisions. You can customize anything in the projects that Magic iDVD creates.

Main title. The name you type into the DVD Title box becomes the title of your main menu.

Submenus. Your DVD's main menu will contain buttons that link to submenus for playing the DVD's movies and slide shows.

Chapter menus. Similarly, if you add a movie containing DVD chapter markers, you get a submenu for accessing those chapters. For themes that have separate chapter menu designs (as do all of the new iDVD themes), iDVD uses the chapter menu design for the chapter menu.

Drop zones. iDVD automatically adds movies to the drop zones of whatever menu theme you choose. If your DVD contains only slide shows, iDVD uses photos from the slide shows for the drop zones.

Planning and Creating Menus

When creating a DVD, you're also design-ing a user interface. If your DVD contains a couple of movies and a slide show, the interface will be simple: just one menu containing a few buttons.

But if your DVD will contain a dozen movies and another half-dozen slide shows, it will need multiple menus. And that means that you'll need to think about how to structure a menu scheme that is logical and easy to navigate.

As you plan a complex DVD, consider how many buttons each menu should have. In iDVD, a menu can have up to 12 but-tons. That's a lot—too many choices for a main menu. If you have several movies and slide shows to present, it's better to create a set of *submenus* that logically categorize your content.

It's a balancing act: create too few menus, and you present your viewers with a daunting number of choices. Create too many, and you make them spend time nav-igating instead of viewing.

All of the 7.0 themes in iDVD are designed with submenus in mind, as are the 6.0 themes. (To switch between these themes, which are numbered to correspond with the version of iDVD that first included them, use the pop-up menu in the Themes browser.)

You don't have to use these themes for projects containing submenus, but at least note their underlying philosophy: it's a good idea for a submenu to share some common design traits with the menus that lead to it.

Planning Your DVD

If your DVD will be presenting a large number of movies or slide shows, you need to plan how you will make that content available to the DVD's user. How many menus will you need? How will you categorize the content in each menu? This process is often called *information design*, and it involves mapping out the way you want to catego-rize and present your content.

A good way to map out a DVD's flow is to create a tree diagram depicting the organization of menus— much as a company's organizational chart depicts the pecking order of its management.

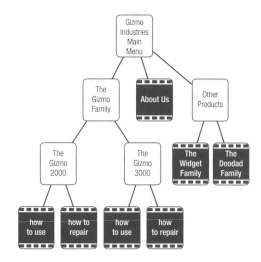

The chart shown here depicts the flow of a DVD a company might create to promote its new Gizmo product line. A main menu contains three buttons: two lead to other submenus, while the third plays a promotional movie about the company.

The submenu "The Gizmo Family" leads to two additional submenus, one for each Gizmo model. The "Other Products" submenu leads to two mov-ies that promote other fine products.

Creating Additional Menus

To create a submenu, choose Add Submenu from the  pop-up menu or choose Project > Add Submenu.

To design the new menu and add content to it, double-click its button. You can customize the look of each submenu independently of other menus.

Each submenu has a return button that, when clicked, returns the user to the menu that led to the submenu.

A DVD in OneStep

If you just want to slap some video onto a DVD and you don't want menus, chapters, or slide shows, check out the OneStep DVD feature.

Insert a blank DVD in your Mac's optical drive, connect your DV camera via FireWire, and choose OneStep DVD from the File menu. iDVD rewinds your tape, captures video until it reaches the end of the tape, and then encodes the video into MPEG-2 format and burns it to disc. When you insert the burned disc in a DVD player, the video begins

playing back immediately. You can also create a disc from a movie file instead of an attached camcorder; choose File > OneStep DVD from Movie.

OneStep DVD is a fast way to create a DVD, but it isn't a perfect method of backing up a tape—you don't have as much flexibility to edit the video in the future. You can't extract the video from a DVD without some effort (see page 280), and even then, the quality won't be as good as the original, since the video will have been compressed.

OneStep Tips

Controlling the capture.
Normally, OneStep DVD rewinds a tape to the beginning and then begins capturing video. If you begin capturing from the middle of the tape, press your camera's Stop button during the rewind process, then immediately press its Play button. iDVD will begin capturing at that point.

Similarly, to stop the capture before the tape reaches the end, press your camera's Stop button, and iDVD burns what you captured up to that point.

Beware of breaks. If your tape contains a lengthy gap between scenes—a segment of blank tape with no timecode—OneStep DVD will probably stop importing video when it encounters that gap.

Reclaiming disk space.
OneStep DVD stores your captured video in a hidden folder on your hard drive (to see where, choose iDVD > Preferences, then click Advanced). These files are deleted the next time you restart your Mac.

Customizing Menus

The design themes built into iDVD look great and, in some cases, sound great, too. But you might prefer to not use off-the-rack designs for your DVDs.

Maybe you'd like to have a custom background screen containing your company logo or a favorite vacation photo. You might like the background image of a particular iDVD theme, but not its music or its buttons' shape or typeface. Or maybe you'd just like to have the title of the menu at the left of the screen instead of centered.

You can customize nearly every aspect of your DVD's menus and navigation buttons. With the Buttons pane and the Menu Info window, you can modify buttons, add and remove background audio, change a menu's background image, and more.

You can also create text labels—for example, some instructions for DVD newbies or a few lines of commentary about the DVD's subject.

iDVD almost provides too many customizing capabilities. You can even have a different shape and style for *each* button on a menu. As with all design tasks, restraint is a virtue. Have fun with your menu designs, but don't lose sight of the menu's main purpose: to provide convenient access to your DVD's contents.

Moving Items Around

Normally, iDVD positions buttons on a fixed grid. This keeps them lined up nicely, but you can also manually specify a button's location—perhaps to line it up with a custom background image.

Simply drag buttons (or other objects) wherever you like.

When you drag a button or other object, iDVD displays positioning guides to help you align items. (You're free to ignore these guides.) If you want to return to the fixed grid, click the Inspector button, then, in the Menu Info window, click Snap to Grid.

Changing Menu Durations

You like a particular motion menu but you don't want to use all of it. Maybe you don't need all eight drop zones in the Reflections themes. Just shorten the menu's duration. Go to the Menu Info window, then drag the Loop Duration slider until the menu is the desired length.

This technique works best with themes that don't have background music, so either choose a theme that lacks music or delete the music (see page 270).

Adding Text

To add descriptive text, captions, or instructions to a menu, choose Add Text from the Project menu (⌘-K). A text area appears; drag it to the desired location, then click within that text area, and type. To start another line, press Return.

To format the text, choose a font and size from the pop-up menus that appear below it, or use the Inspector window; see the opposite page.

Kill the Watermark

iDVD displays the Apple logo watermark on each menu screen. To get rid of it, choose Preferences from the iDVD menu, click the General button, and then uncheck the Show Apple Logo Watermark box.

Staying TV Safe

TV sets omit the outer edges of a video frame—a phenomenon called *overscan*. To make sure buttons and other menu elements will be visible on TV sets, choose the Show TV Safe Area command in the View menu, and avoid putting buttons or other elements in the shaded area.

Get links to more iDVD menu themes.
www.macilife.com/idvd

Changing the Background Image

To change the background image of an iDVD menu, simply drag an image into the menu area. For the best results, be sure to use a photo with proportions that match your project's aspect ratio: 4:3 for standard television or 16:9 for wide-screen or HD television. You can ensure these proportions when cropping in iPhoto: from the Constrain pop-up menu, choose 4 x 3 (DVD) or 16 x 9 (HD).

Tips: Some photos make better back-grounds if you reduce their brightness and contrast so the image doesn't over-whelm the buttons. In iPhoto, duplicate the image and then adjust the bright-ness and contrast of the duplicate.

If you replace the background on a theme that has a drop zone, the drop zone remains. To remove drop zones after replacing a background, go to the Menu Info window and uncheck the Show Drop Zones and Related Graphics box.

Want a plain white background? You can download one from www.macilife. com/idvd. You can also make your own patterned or solid-colored backgrounds in a program like Photoshop Elements. Create a graphic with dimensions that are 640 by 480 pixels (854 by 480 pix-els for widescreen), save it as a JPEG image, and then drag it into iDVD.

If your project contains several menus, you can apply one menu's custom

design to other menus in the project; see page 271.

And, if you decide you'd rather just have the theme's original background, simply drag the custom background's image thumbnail out of the Background well (above the Loop Duration slider) in the Menu Info window.

Customizing Button Shapes

To change a button's shape, select it and display the Buttons pane.

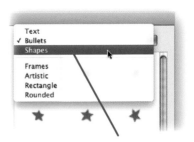

The first three options in the pop-up menu control formatting of text-only labels; the categories below them offer buttons with video or photo previews. Click a shape to choose it.

You can also control the size of the buttons by dragging the Size slider.

Changing Button Text Labels

When you choose a button shape, your buttons consist of text labels and little thumbnail images or movies. In the Button Info window, you can change where a button's text labels appear in relation to the button's thumbnail image.

To customize button labels, choose an option from the pop-up menu.

To add a soft shadow to some text, select the button or label and click the Shadow box.

Each button style has its own style of highlight, which appears when a user selects the button. To change the high-light color, click the Highlight Color well.

You can also change the font, font color, and type size for button text and for the menu's title and any text you've added. If you don't like the results, choose the Undo command as many times as needed to get back to where you started.

Tip: To format all of a menu's buttons at once, select them all first. Click on one button, then press ⌘-A. Similarly, to select every text item you've added, click one item and then press ⌘-A.

To return the buttons to the theme's style, select them and choose Advanced > Reset Object to Theme Settings.

More Design Tips

Adding Transitions

You can have a transition between menus. For example, when your DVD's viewers choose a button to go to a movie, you can have the menu appear to peel away to reveal the movie.

You can choose from a dozen different transition styles. For menu transitions, I'm partial to cube, page flip, or wipe—each conveys the notion of moving from one area to another.

You create menu transitions by assigning them to buttons. You can assign a different transition to every button in a menu, but in the interest of good taste, it's better to stick with just one or two different transition styles. For example, you might choose the cube transition for buttons that go from one menu to another, and the fade through black transition for buttons that lead directly to movies and slide shows.

To assign a transition to a button, select the button and then choose the desired transition from the Transition pop-up menu in the Button Info window. Some transitions, such as cube, also allow you to specify a direction—set this by choosing from the second Transition pop-up menu.

Varying the direction of transitions can be a nice way to add variety without resorting to using a lot of different transition styles. For example, when a viewer chooses a button to go to a slide show, you might have a cube that rotates to the left. For a different button that leads to another menu, you might have a cube transition that rotates downward.

Tip: If you've mixed and matched transitions and decide you'd prefer to use just one transition style, you don't have to change the transitions one button at a time. Just use iDVD's map view to change the transitions in one fell swoop; see page 273.

Note: A menu transition is, unfortunately, a one-way street. That is, a transition appears only as you drill *down* into a DVD's menu structure. If you navigate from a submenu back to a main menu, you don't see a transition.

Moving Buttons Between Menus

To move a button from one menu to another, select the button and choose Cut. Next, move to a different menu (use map view to get there in a hurry), then paste.

You can also *copy* a button instead of pasting it. You might do this to provide access to a piece of content from several different menus.

For example, say you've created a series of online help screens in the form of a slide show. To make the online help available from every menu in your DVD, copy its button and then paste it into each menu.

New Menu from Selection

After adding numerous items to a DVD, you realize that a particular menu has too many buttons. The solution: move some of those buttons to a new menu. But don't wear out your wrists cutting and pasting. Just select the buttons you want to move (Shift-click on them), then sprint up to the Project menu and choose New Menu from Selection. iDVD removes the selected buttons and stashes them in a new menu.

Silencing Motion Menus

You might like the look of a motion menu, but maybe you don't want any music or sound effects to play. To silence a motion menu, go to the Menu Info window and drag the Menu Volume slider to its leftmost position. If you change your mind, raise the volume level. To silence the menu for good, drag the icon out of the Audio well, and it disappears in an animated puff of smoke.

Audio-Only Menus

Conversely, maybe you would like some background audio to play, but you don't want motion in your menus. First, choose a theme that lacks motion, or replace an existing motion theme's background with a static image. Next, drag an audio file, iTunes playlist, or QuickTime movie into the Menu pane's Audio well. To hear the audio, click the Motion button. A menu can play for up to 15 minutes before it loops.

Motion Buttons

In many themes and button styles, iDVD also applies motion to your movie buttons: small, thumbnail versions of the movies play back when the menu is displayed.

You can even specify which portion of the movie plays: just drag the slider that appears above the movie or in the Button Info window.

To specify how much of a movie plays in a motion button, drag the Loop Duration slider in the Menu Info window.

There are times when you might not want a movie's button to be a thumbnail movie. Maybe the movie thumbnail distracts from the motion menu's background. In any case, simply enable the Still Image checkbox. Now use the slider to choose a static thumbnail image for the movie.

If you're using a theme that has text-only buttons, you can add motion or thumbnail buttons by choosing a different button style in the Buttons pane.

Copying Custom Menus

Your project contains several menus and you've customized one of them. Now you decide you'd like to apply your design to all the menus in your project. Easy: choose Apply Theme to Submenus from the Advanced menu.

Conversely, if you've customized a submenu and want to apply that design to the project's other menus, choose Apply Theme to Project.

Copying Button Styles

You've changed a button's text and color, and would like to apply that formatting to other buttons. Easy: select the formatted button and choose Edit > Copy Style. Then select one or more other buttons and choose Edit > Paste Style.

Saving a Theme Design

Happy with the results of a menu-design session? Save your customized theme as a "favorite," and you can apply it to future projects with one mouse click.

Choose Save Theme as Favorite from the File menu. If you have multiple user accounts on your computer, you can make the custom theme available to all users: check the Shared For All Users box.

The new theme appears in the Themes pane. To see it, choose Favorites or All from the themes pop-up menu. On your hard drive, saved themes are stored in your home directory in the following path: Library > Application Support > iDVD > Favorites. Shared themes are stored in the same path at the root level of the drive.

Fading Menu Audio

To have a menu's audio fade out at the end of the menu loop, enable that feature in the General portion of the Preferences dialog box.

More Themes

Want to go beyond the themes that are built into iDVD? Try out some of the themes from DVDThemePak (www.DVDthemepak.com). The company offers more than a dozen theme and button collections. They look great and are inexpensive.

Navigating and Authoring with Map View

iDVD's map view lets you see the organization of your DVD project using a display that looks a lot like the organizational chart depicted on page 266.

In map view, you can see at a glance how your project is organized. More to the point, you can get around quickly. By double-clicking the icons in map view, you can jump to a specific menu or preview a slide show or movie. Need to drill down into a deeply nested submenu to do some design work? Display the map, then double-click the submenu's icon.

Map view is about more than just seeing the big picture. You can use it to rearrange submenus, change menu themes, create menu transitions, and add content to your DVD. You can also use map view to loop a slide show or movie so that it plays over and over again. And you can use map view to have a movie or slide show start automatically when your DVD is played.

To switch to map view, click the Map button. To exit map view, click the Map button again, double-click an icon in the map, or click the Return button in the lower-right corner of the map.

Customizing Your View

When you're on the road, sometimes you need the big picture and sometimes you need street-by-street details. Map view provides this flexibility, and then some.

Switch between left-to-right (shown here) and top-to-bottom views.

To scroll quickly, press the Option key and drag within the map.

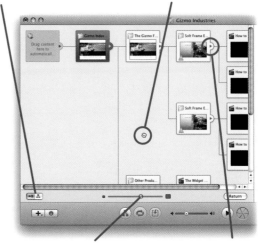

To zoom in and out on the map, drag the size slider. When zoomed out, you see only icons representing folders, slide shows, and movies.

If you don't need to see a particular set of icons, click the right-pointing triangle to hide them and free up viewing space.

When you zoom in, iDVD displays small thumbnail images as well as names of menus and other content.

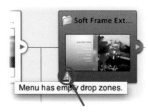

Menu has empty drop zones.

See a warning triangle? Point to it, and iDVD displays details about the problem.

Authoring in Map View

Customizing Menus

To customize a menu in map view, select the menu by clicking it once. To change the menu's theme, use the Themes panel. To change the menu's background, audio, drop zones, or text formatting, use the Menu Info window. To change the appearance of all buttons on a menu, use the Buttons pane; to set a transition, use the Button Info window.

Here's the best part: you can customize multiple menus at once. Just Shift-click on each menu you want to change, and then use the panes to make your changes.

Note: When you use map view to specify a transition for a menu, every button on that menu will use the same transition. If you want a different transition for some of the menu's buttons, assign a transition to each button individually as described on page 270.

Rearranging Your Project

Want to move a slide show or other item to a different menu? Simply drag the item's icon to another menu.

Checking Transitions

To see which transitions a menu uses, point to the menu's icon, and a description of the transition appears.

Adding Content to a Menu

To add content to an existing menu, drag it from the media browser or the Finder to the menu's icon.

If you drag a movie or iPhoto album to an existing menu, iDVD creates a button for that item.

You can also change a menu's background image using the map: just drag a single image to the menu's icon. (For more details on customizing menu backgrounds, see page 269.)

Looping a Movie or Slide Show

To have a movie or slide show *loop* (play over and over), select its icon and choose Loop Slideshow from the Advanced menu.

(When you aren't in map view, you can specify looping by selecting a movie's or slide show's menu button and choosing Loop.)

Adding AutoPlay Content

On many DVDs, a movie appears when the DVD begins playing—an FBI warning, for example, or a movie-studio logo.

You can use map view to add this *AutoPlay* content to your DVD. Simply drag a movie, a photo, a set of photos, or an entire iPhoto album to the project icon.

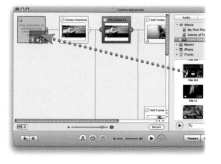

If you drag photos to the project icon, you can double-click the project icon to open the slide show editor where you can specify transitions and add background music (page 262).

Don't want an AutoPlay item after all? Just drag it out of the project icon, and it disappears in a puff of pixel smoke.

Creating a Kiosk DVD

Want a movie or slide show to play automatically and continuously? Drag it to the project icon and then, with the project icon still selected, choose Loop from the Advanced menu.

Adding DVD-ROM Content

One of the reasons why the DVD format is so versatile is that it can accommodate not only video, sound, and pictures, but also any disk files that you may want to distribute.

Here's the scoop on this aspect of DVD authoring, along with a peek under the hood to see how MPEG-2 compression manages to squeeze up to two hours of video onto a 4.7GB DVD.

The DVD-ROM Zone

A DVD can hold more than video and slide shows; it can also hold "computer files"—Microsoft Word documents, PDF files, JPEG images, and so on. You might take advantage of this to distribute files that are related to your DVD's content.

If you've created an in-house training DVD for new employees, you might want to include a PDF of the employee handbook. If you've created a DVD containing a couple of rough edits of a TV commercial, you might also include some PDFs that show the print versions of your ad campaign. If you've created a DVD promoting your band, you might include some audio files of your tunes.

When a DVD-Video disc also contains files intended to be used by a computer, it's said to have a *DVD-ROM* portion. If users play the DVD in a living-room DVD player, those files are invisible. However, if they use that same DVD with a personal computer, they can access the files.

Including Photos

As described on page 262, when creating DVDs containing slide shows, you can have iDVD copy the original images to the DVD-ROM portion. In the slide show editor, click Settings, then check the box labeled Add Image Files to DVD-ROM.

This option is ideal for photographers who want to distribute high-resolution versions of their images along with slide shows. You might also find it a useful way to back up a set of digital photos. The slide shows serve as a handy way of viewing the images, while the original, high-resolution files are archived in the DVD-ROM portion of the disc.

Note: If your slide show includes raw-format photos from iPhoto, iDVD includes both the raw-format originals and the JPEG stand-ins that iPhoto created. If you'd rather not include the raw originals (or the JPEGs), save your DVD as a disc image and edit the contents of the disc image as described on page 279.

Tip: If you *always* want to include a slide show's original images on your DVD, choose Preferences from the iDVD menu, click the Slideshow button, then check the box labeled Always Add Original Photos to DVD-ROM Contents.

Including Other Content

To add other types of files to your DVD, choose Edit DVD-ROM Contents from the Advanced menu. Use the DVD-ROM Contents window to manage and organize the contents of the DVD-ROM folder.

Your DVD will contain a folder with the name of your project plus *DVD-ROM Contents*.

To add files to the DVD-ROM area, drag them into the DVD-ROM Contents window, or use the Add Files button. To delete a file from the DVD-ROM area, select it and press the Delete key.

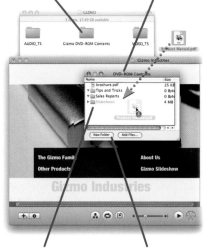

If you've added photos from one or more slide shows to the DVD-ROM area, they appear in a folder named Slideshows. You can't rename this folder or move it to another folder. To delete it, return to the slide show editor and uncheck its DVD-ROM box.

You can create additional folders within the DVD-ROM folder, and you can drag files or other folders into it.

MPEG: Compressing Space and Time

One of the jobs iDVD performs is to compress your movies into MPEG format, the standard method of storing video on DVD-Video discs. Like image and audio compression,

MPEG is a *lossy* format: the final product lacks some of the quality of the original. But as with image and audio compression, the amount of quality loss depends on the degree to

which the original material is compressed.

Like JPEG, MPEG performs spatial compression that reduces the storage requirements of

individual images. But video adds the dimension of time, and MPEG takes this into account by also performing *temporal compression*.

The key to temporal compression is to describe only those details that have changed since the previous video frame. In an MPEG video stream, some video frames contain the entire image; these are called *I-frames*. There are usually two I-frames per second.

An I-frame describes an entire scene: "There's a basketball on a concrete driveway."

Sandwiched between those I-frames are much smaller frames that don't contain the entire image, but rather only those pixels that have changed since the previous frame.

"It's rolling toward the street."

To perform temporal compression, the video frame is divided into a grid of blocks, and each square is examined to see if anything has changed. Areas that haven't changed—such as the stationary background in this example—are simply repeated in the next frame.

This is why video with relatively little motion often tends to look better than video that contains a great deal of motion. When little changes from one frame to the next, the quality of each frame can be higher.

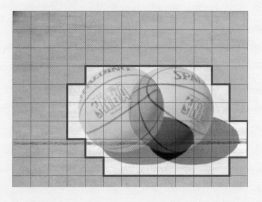

Burning Your DVD

You've massaged your media and made your menus. What's next? Burning the final product onto a blank DVD. Simply click iDVD's Burn button and insert a blank disc. But before you burn, read the following tips.

Preview First

Before you insert that pricey blank DVD, preview your work by clicking iDVD's Preview button. Use the iDVD remote control to step through your menus and spot-check your video, slide shows, and any menu transitions you've added. And don't forget to proofread your menu titles and button text.

Consider a Disc Image

Before you burn, consider creating a *disc image*, a kind of virtual disk that can be extremely useful for testing and burning. You'll find full details on working with disc images on page 278.

If your DVD has a lot of menus, transitions, and content, consider creating a disc image and using Mac OS X's DVD Player program to test it. And if you have a slower Mac—or just seem to have trouble burning reliably—creating and burning a disc image can be a great way to increase your success rate.

Note: If you will be burning a dual-layer DVD, do not try to burn it from a disc image. For details, see page 278.

Run Lean

When burning a DVD, avoid running complex programs that put a lot of demands on your system. Recording a track in GarageBand while also burning a DVD is not a good idea, for example. Also, consider turning off file sharing and quitting any disk-intensive programs.

What Kind of Media?

Several types of writable DVD media exist: DVD-R, DVD-RW, DVD+R, and DVD+RW. Previous versions of iDVD could handle the DVD-R format only, but iDVD is now much more versatile. It can burn any of the aforementioned formats, assuming your DVD burner supports them. All of the SuperDrives in today's Macs can; older SuperDrives support the DVD-R and DVD-RW formats only.

The differences between the "minus" and "plus" camps are technical ones and don't have much bearing on your burning endeavors. The more important difference deals with R and RW: an RW disc can be erased and reused roughly 1,000 times. If you insert an RW disc that already contains data, iDVD even offers to erase it for you.

RW discs are great for testing, although as the following page describes, you're more likely to encounter playback problems on some DVD players. Also,

RW discs are more sensitive to damage and aging than write-once discs.

If you're interested in the technical details between the minus and plus formats, read Jim Taylor's superb DVD FAQ at www.DVDdemystified.com.

Dual-Layer Differences

All of today's Macs include SuperDrives capable of burning on dual-layer DVD+R media. With a dual-layer drive, you can burn nearly 8GB, or about four hours' worth of video.

To verify that your Mac is capable of dual-layer burning, choose Project > Project Info, and click on the DVD Type pop-up menu. If you have a dual-layer drive, you'll have the option of specifying dual-layer media.

Incidentally, if you have a single-layer SuperDrive but would like to double your pleasure, you can buy external dual-layer burners that work just fine with iDVD. But note that more is not always better. Dual-layer burned discs often do not play in standalone DVD players, and may lack the longevity of single-layer discs.

Will It Play?

You've burned a disc and are ready to show it off to your boss. You pop the disc into the conference room DVD player and proudly press the play button—and nothing happens.

Welcome to The Incompatibility Zone. The sad fact is, some DVD players and personal computer DVD drives are unable to read burned DVD media. Generally, older DVD players and drives are most likely to have this problem, but you may encounter it in newer players, too.

Roughly 85 percent of DVD players can read DVD-R and DVD+R discs, and about 80 percent can read DVD-RW and DVD+RW discs. Those are good num-

bers, although they won't be of much solace if your player—or your boss's—is in the minority.

The picture is much more bleak when it comes to dual-layer DVD burning: a large percentage of DVD players have trouble playing dual-layer burned DVDs. If you're shopping for a new DVD player, be sure to verify compatibility with the type of media you plan to burn. And diplomatically inform your friends, family, and colleagues that if they have problems playing your DVD, the fault probably lies with their players.

Making More

You can burn multiple copies of a DVD using iDVD, but you might find the job

easier with Roxio's Toast or Popcorn software, both of which provide copying features. Or, make a disc image and use Mac OS X's Disk Utility program to burn multiple copies (see page 278).

If you need to have more than a few copies of a disc—for example, 2,000 training DVDs for a large company—you'll want to work with a replicator. Most replicators will accept a burned DVD as a master.

One excellent source for low-volume replication is CreateSpace (www.createspace.com), which also provides e-commerce and shipping services. Also check out Lulu (www.lulu.com).

Archiving Projects for Burning Elsewhere

iDVD provides an archiving feature that saves a project and all of its assets in one self-contained file.

Archiving enables you to author on one Mac, then burn on another. Move projects between home, school, or work. Start a project on a cross-country flight, then archive and transfer your project when you land.

To archive a project, choose Archive Project from the File menu.

If you created customized themes for the DVD—or if you want to be certain that your themes will be available in a future version of iDVD—check the Include Themes box. If you're using standard themes and aren't obsessed about

future compatibility, you can uncheck this box and your archive file will be a bit smaller.

If iDVD has already encoded the DVD's content, you can include those encoded files in the archive by checking the Include

Encoded Files box. Doing so will make your archive file quite a bit larger, however.

After you specify archive settings and click Save, iDVD goes to work, copying everything in your project into a file. You can transfer this file to another Mac using a fast network, an external hard drive, or the FireWire disk mode that Macs provide.

Save As: Gizmo Industries Archived

Where: 📁 Desktop

☑ Include themes   Size: 128 MB
☑ Include encoded files

Cancel   Save

Burning Tips

For many projects, one click of the Burn button is all it takes to commit your work to plastic. But sometimes it's better to take the roundabout route: creating a *disc image* and then using it as the basis for your burns.

If you've downloaded software from the Internet, you're probably already familiar with the concept of disc images. But if you haven't heard the term before, it can seem confusing.

And for good reason: a disc image isn't a disc or an image. It's a file on your hard drive. The bits and bytes in this file are organized in the same way that they would be on a disc. If you double-click a disc image file, the Mac's Finder reads the disc image and creates an icon on your desktop—as if you'd inserted a disc.

iDVD lets you create a disc image for a DVD project. You can then test your DVD on your Mac, or use other software to burn it.

In a bigger hurry? Save the project as a VIDEO_TS folder. You can test your project by opening this folder with the DVD Player program.

Important: If you plan to burn a dual-layer disc, note that Apple recommends burning the disc directly from iDVD, rather than creating a disc image and then burning from that image. To quote from iDVD's online help, "double-layer discs burned from a disc image may cause playback issues in some DVD players, such as freezing during playback."

Creating a Disc Image

Step 1.

Choose Save as Disc Image from the File menu (Shift-⌘-R).

Step 2.

Give your disc image a name and click Save.

iDVD compresses your video, encodes your menus, and then saves the resulting data in the disc image file. The file's name ends in .img.

Testing a Disc Image

To test your DVD using Mac OS X's DVD Player program, begin by double-clicking the disc image file to create an icon on your desktop.

If you double-click this icon to examine its contents, you'll see two folders: AUDIO_TS and VIDEO_TS. (If you added DVD-ROM content to the DVD, you'll see a third folder.) Those awkward names are required by the DVD standard, as are the even more awkward names of the files inside the VIDEO_TS folder.

(The AUDIO_TS folder will always be empty, but don't try to create a DVD that lacks one; the DVD may not play in some players. And if it ever comes up in a trivia contest, TS stands for transport stream.)

To test your disc image, start DVD Player and choose File > Open DVD Media. Navigate to your disc image, select its VIDEO_TS folder, and click Choose or press Return. Now press the spacebar or click DVD Player's Play button, and your faux DVD will begin playing back.

Burning a Disc Image

If you found a problem when testing your disc image—a typo, for example, or a missing piece of content—you haven't wasted a blank DVD. Simply trash the disc image, make your revisions in iDVD, then create and test another disc image.

And if you're ready to burn? If you're burning a single-layer DVD, don't bother with iDVD's Burn button—use the disc image instead.

First, start up Mac OS X's Disk Utility program. (It's located in the Utilities folder within your Applications folder.) Next, click the Burn button in the upper-left corner of Disk Utility's window. In the dialog box that appears, locate and double-click the disc image file. Disk Utility displays another dialog box. Before you click its Burn button, click the little down-pointing arrow to expand the dialog box.

What's the hurry? You can get more reliable burns—and increase the chances that your DVD will play in other players—by burning at your drive's slowest speed.

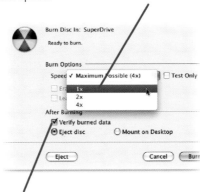

In a hurry? If you uncheck Verify Burn, your disc will be ready sooner. On the downside, you won't know if data was written inaccurately until you try to play the disc.

Other Ways to Burn

If you have Roxio's Toast Titanium software, you can drag your disc image's AUDIO_TS and VIDEO_TS folders into Toast and burn your disc there. If you've installed Toast's Toast It shortcut menu, the job is even easier: Control-click on your disc image icon and choose Toast It from the shortcut menu. (Use Toast's Preferences command to install the Toast It shortcut menu plug-in.)

You can also use Toast to fine-tune any DVD-ROM content you've added— for example, removing the raw versions of the photos that you've included in a slide show (see page 274).

Toast also gives you a choice of burning speeds. For critical projects where you need the broadest compatibility, burn at 1x speed.

Encoding Insights and Tips

You don't have to know how iDVD encodes MPEG-2 video, but if you're curious, here are the details.

High Quality. When you choose High Quality in the Encoder Settings area of the Preferences dialog box, the bit rate depends in part on how much media is in your project. Data rates will vary from a low of 3.5 megabits per second (Mbps) to 7 Mbps. With high-quality encoding, iDVD uses variable bit rate (VBR) encoding: the bit rate of a video stream changes according to the complexity of the scene. Motion-intensive scenes get a higher bit rate, while scenes containing little motion get a lower rate.

Professional Quality. Professional Quality performs the same VBR calculations as High Quality, but it does the job in two passes.

Best Performance. When you choose Best Performance, iDVD encodes at a fixed bit rate of 8 Mbps.

Tip: If you've burned a DVD using high-quality or professional-quality encoding and you delete some content from the project, you may be able to improve the video quality of the remaining content by having iDVD encode it all over again. Choose Delete Encoded Assets from the Advanced menu, then burn the project again.

iDVD Tips

Make It Last

Burned discs don't last forever. To improve their reliability and longevity, don't use peel-and-stick labels. If a label isn't perfectly centered, the DVD will be off-balance when it spins, and that could cause playback problems. If you want to label your DVDs, use an ink-jet printer that can print on DVD media.

Label discs with a Sharpie or other permanent marker. Write small and be brief—the solvents in permanent ink can damage a DVD's substrate over time.

Keep burned DVDs in jewel cases, and store them in a cool, dark place. Be careful to never flex the disc—a DVD is comprised of several different layers, and flexing a disc can cause the layers to separate. To remove a disc from a jewel case, press the center button of the case, then lift the disc out—don't simply pull the disc by its edges. (This advice applies to all optical media, by the way.)

Which Movie Formats Work with iDVD?

You can include digital camera movies in an iDVD project—just drag them into the iDVD window. If the movies are in your iPhoto library, you can use iDVD's photo or movies browsers to access them.

Indeed, you can burn nearly any kind of QuickTime movie onto a DVD, including

movies you've downloaded from the Web or copied from an old CD-ROM.

If a movie is smaller than the DVD standard of 720 by 480 pixels, iDVD enlarges it to fill the screen. This results in a loss of sharpness, but enlarged movies can still look good when viewed on a TV. It's better to have shared a blurry movie than never to have shared at all.

You can't use movies stored in MPEG-1 or MPEG-2 formats. Sony digital cameras use the MPEG format for their movies, and many of the movies that have been posted on file-sharing networks are in MPEG format.

There are free or cheap utilities that enable you to convert MPEG movies into a format that iDVD (and iMovie) can use. I've written up instructions on my site; see www.macilife.com/imovie. You can also use Toast Titanium's Export Video command, as described at right.

Incidentally, this MPEG prohibition does not apply to MPEG-4 movies created by digital cameras. Those movies work just fine in iDVD.

Reverting Your Project

You've made some modifications that you don't like. Many programs, including GarageBand, have a Revert command that lets you get back to the last version

you saved. iDVD lacks a Revert command, but you can simulate one: just reopen the project by choosing its name from the Open Recent submenu in the File menu. Click Don't Save when iDVD asks you if you want to save changes before reopening the project.

Extracting Video

You burned some cherished video to a DVD, then lost the original tape—and now you want to edit it in iMovie.

You can extract video from a DVD and convert it into DV format, but you will lose some quality in the process. If you have Toast Titanium, click its Video button and drag your DVD's VIDEO_TS folder into the Toast window. Locate the clip you want to extract, select it, and click the Export button.

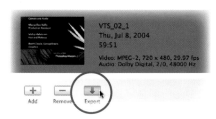

You can also extract video using any of several free or cheap utilities. Video guru Matti Haveri has published a fine tutorial on his Web site; I've linked to it at www.macilife.com/iDVD.

Get more iDVD tips.
www.macilife.com/idvd

Project Management Tips

When you add a movie or set of images to iDVD, the program doesn't actually add those files to your project file. Rather, iDVD simply links to the existing files on your hard drive.

If you need to move a project from one Mac to another, create an archive of the project using the Archive Project command in the File menu. As described on page 277, this command copies all of the project's assets into one file.

If you copy just the project file—or if you delete an asset that you added to the project—iDVD displays broken-link icons for buttons whose assets are missing.

When you open a project containing broken links, iDVD displays an error message.

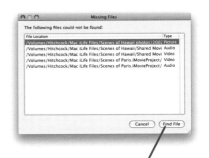

If you've moved a file to a different folder or drive, you can aim iDVD in the right direction: click Find File, then locate and double-click the file.

You can avoid the hassle by not moving assets once you add them to a project, or by creating an archive of the project to gather all its assets in one place.

To get the big picture of a project, choose Project Info from the Project menu.

Use these options to change a project's video format and encoding settings.

To reconnect to a missing file, double-click its entry, then locate the file and double-click its name.

You can change the DVD's name here. This doesn't change the name of your project file; rather, it changes the name of the final DVD. The DVD specification doesn't permit a disc name to have spaces in it; iDVD replaces any spaces with underscores, as in HAWAII_SCENES.

The Project Info window displays a list of the project's assets; its Status column indicates if any assets are missing (Ø).

More iDVD Tips

Copy and Paste Drop Zone Contents

If you've assembled a great set of photos for a drop zone and you'd like to use that same set elsewhere in the project, it's easy to duplicate it. Control-click the drop zone and choose Copy Drop Zone Contents from the shortcut menu. Then, go to the destination drop zone and choose Paste Drop Zone Contents from the shortcut menu.

Browsing Other Folders

You can use the Preferences command to tell iDVD to search other folders and hard drives when displaying its movie browser (page 258). You can expand your browsing options for audio and photos, too. Just drag a folder from the Finder into the appropriate media browser.

This also works for the movie browser—and it's a handy alternative to the Preferences dialog box.

Hacking iDVD Themes

Previous versions of iDVD stored the themes within the application itself, but starting with iDVD 6, Apple moved them to a more sensible location: Computer > Library > Application Support > iDVD > Themes.

Each theme (which ends with the text .theme) is also a *package*—to explore it, Control-click on its icon and choose

Show Package Contents from the shortcut menu. Double-click the Contents folder and then the Resources folder, and you'll find background movies and audio loops. To extract an item—for example, to grab the background audio from the Revolution-Main theme—press Option while dragging the item's icon out to the desktop. This makes a duplicate of the item, leaving the original theme unchanged.

Take care to not throw away or alter any resources whose purpose you don't understand, lest you have to reinstall the iDVD application.

From PDF to DVD

An iDVD slide show isn't restricted to the JPEG image format. A slide show can display numerous graphics formats, including PDF.

iDVD's PDF support means that you can display just about any document in a slide show. Want to put a Microsoft Word document or a Web page in a slide show? Create a PDF version of the document: choose Print from the File menu, then click the Save as PDF button. Drag the PDF into the iDVD slide show editor, and iDVD creates a slide containing the contents of the PDF's first page. (If you have a multi-page document, save each page as a separate PDF or use the Preview application to extract specific pages, as described in the following tip.)

Before making a PDF of a document, you might want to choose the Page Setup command and click the landscape-orientation button. That way, your PDF will have the same horizontal orientation as a slide. If you make the PDF in portrait orientation, your slide will have black borders on either side of the page.

Think twice about using a PDF that contains lots of text, especially in font sizes below 14 point. Small text looks fuzzy on a TV screen.

From iPhoto Book to Slide Show

On page 141, I discussed a method for saving an iPhoto book as a PDF and then extracting pages for printing. Here's a variation of that technique that lets you include iPhoto book pages in iDVD slide shows.

After saving your book as a PDF, open the PDF in Mac OS X's Preview program. Next, open Preview's sidebar (choose Sidebar from the View menu). In the sidebar, locate the page that you want to turn into a slide. Select the page and choose Copy from the Edit menu.

Next, choose the New from Clipboard command from the File menu. The Preview program creates a new document and pastes the page you copied into it. Save the page as a new PDF file.

Get links to background animations and other iDVD add-ons.
www.macilife.com/iDVD

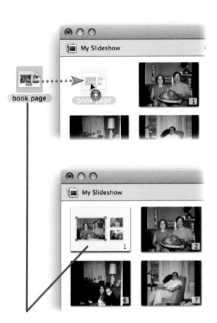

Now add that page to your slide show. Drag the PDF file from the Finder into the iDVD window.

Making Custom Motion Menus

You aren't limited to the motion menus that accompany iDVD. You can make any QuickTime movie a motion menu background: just drag the movie to the Background well in the Menu pane.

If your motion menu movie is smaller than full-screen, iDVD enlarges it to fit. For the best video quality, use a movie whose dimensions are 640 by 480 pixels or 720 by 480 pixels.

As for what to put in your own custom menu, that's up to you. If the star of your DVD is an iMovie production, you might use a two- or three-minute excerpt of your movie. Copy and paste a few clips from your movie into a new iMovie project. Then, use iMovie's Video Adjustments tools to increase the brightness and make the footage appear faint. That way, buttons and text labels will still be easy to read. Share the movie to the Media Browser, return to iDVD, and drag the movie from the Media pane to the Background well in the Menu Info window.

Smooth looping. A motion menu loops until a user chooses a menu option. To avoid a visually jarring loop point, try this: In iMovie, create a still frame of the very first frame of your menu movie. Add this still frame to the very end of the movie, and put a fairly lengthy (say, two-second) dissolve between the end of the movie and the still frame. Finally, trim the clip to make the remainder of the still frame as short as possible. (In the trimmer, drag its right edge to the left until it's right next to the dissolve in the timeline.) Now, when your movie loops, its last frame will appear to gradually dissolve into its first frame.

If you're after something more abstract, you can buy royalty-free libraries of animated backgrounds that you can use as motion menus. Two sources are ArtBeats (www.artbeats.com) and Digital Juice

(www.digitaljuice.com). If you have Final Cut Pro or Final Cut Express, you can use its LiveType program to create rich animated textures.

A motion menu in iDVD can be up to 15 minutes long. But keep in mind that menu video uses disc space just like any other video clip.

Automating iDVD

iDVD provides thorough support for AppleScript, the automation technology that's built into Mac OS X. iDVD's AppleScript support enables you to create scripts that automate the creation and layout of DVDs.

In Mac OS X 10.5 (Leopard), you can use the Automator program to build *workflows* that put iDVD on autopilot. For example, you could create a workflow that prompts a user for a movie and some photos, then builds a DVD containing the results.

To learn more about Automator, visit www.automator.us.

Back to the Top

If you have a DVD containing several levels of submenus, you might want to offer your viewers a button that lets them get back to the uppermost, or title, menu. To do so, choose Project > Add Title Menu Button.

GarageBand:
Music, Podcasts,
and More

The Macintosh
iLife '09

GarageBand at a Glance

GarageBand is a music school, a rehearsal space, and a recording studio—all wrapped into one.

New to music? Use the Learn to Play feature to, yes, learn to play. Take basic guitar or piano lessons for free. Then visit the Lesson Store to buy master classes with major-league artists ranging from Norah Jones to Sting to Ben Folds and more.

In the mood to jam? Fire up Magic GarageBand, and let GarageBand build songs for you on a virtual bandstand. Choose a tune in one of nine genres, pick an instrument for yourself, and play along.

Want to create your own songs? Step into your recording studio. Tap into GarageBand's library of pre-recorded musical phrases, called *loops*. Assemble loops you like into a tune. Plug in a music keyboard, a guitar, or a microphone, then add your own performance. Edit and refine, and send the result to your iTunes library and your iPod. You can even turn your song into an iPhone ringtone.

Want to reach the world with your own Internet radio show? Turn to the podcast-production features in GarageBand. Record your message. Add music, sound effects, graphics, even Web links. Then use iWeb to share it with the rest of us.

If you aren't a musician and you've overlooked GarageBand in the past, give GarageBand '09 an audition. You'll find that it has evolved into a beautiful showcase for all things sonic.

Learn

With Learn to Play, you can learn basic guitar and piano right out of the box—and then go beyond the basics (pages 288–291).

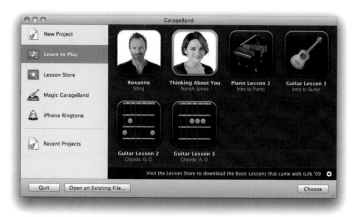

Watch video to see correct techniques for fingering and strumming.

Visit the Lesson Store to buy detailed lessons featuring major artists.

Play

Use Magic GarageBand to explore different musical styles and play along (pages 294–297).

Choose from nine musical genres.

Customize the musicians on your virtual bandstand, choosing the instrument styles you want.

Play along, recording your performance if you like.

Produce

Turn your musical ideas into finished songs by recording your performances, combining loops, or both (pages 298–345).

Tap into a library of thousands of loops: rhythm beds, bass lines, symphonic violins, and more.

Have something to say? Join the podcasting revolution and produce your own Internet radio (pages 346–353).

Learn to Play

You've always wanted to play the piano or the guitar. Maybe you've noodled around on one or the other and wished you had some formal instruction.

Your music teacher has arrived. With the Learn to Play feature, you can learn piano or guitar basics in—caution! cliché ahead—the privacy of your own home.

Each Learn to Play lesson elegantly combines video, music notation, animation, and GarageBand's audio features. Jump around within a lesson, repeating sections when you need to. Play along by attaching a music keyboard or guitar to your Mac.

No musical experience? No problem. The lessons begin at the beginning: in the Intro to the Piano lesson, your teacher starts by pointing out that a piano keyboard has black keys and white keys. Now *that's* the beginning.

If you already play, check out Apple's Lesson Store, which features lessons from major recording artists. It's one thing to figure out the chords to Sting's *Roxanne*. It's another to have him teach you.

In each artist lesson, the artist also performs the entire song. And one click displays an on-screen mixer that lets you silence, or *mute*, certain parts. Mute the guitar player so you can play along yourself. Or mute the vocal so you can sing. You can even slow the tempo without changing the pitch.

Try *that* with your Guitar Hero video game.

Music Lesson Essentials

GarageBand includes one basic piano lesson and one basic guitar lesson. Each lesson teaches one practical skill—for example, some chords or a particular type of rhythm, such as shuffle. Each lesson has multiple chapters, and you can move between chapters and have them repeat. As you learn, you might adjust the tempo, customize the way the song's music notation appears, and more.

Each lesson also has a song that you can play back and play along with, recording your performance, if you like.

Get connected. When learning piano, it helps to have one. If you don't, you can connect a music keyboard to your Mac and play GarageBand's built-in piano instrument; see page 310.

Learning acoustic guitar? Use your Mac's built-in microphone to get in tune and record yourself; see page 290. Have an electric axe? Connect it using the instructions on page 316.

Get the rest. Each set of piano and guitar lessons has eight more parts that are free downloads from the Lesson Store. To grab them, click the Lesson Store item in GarageBand's New Project window. When the Lesson Store window appears, click the Basic Lessons button, then click the Download button for the lessons you want.

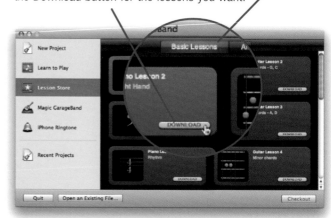

Music Lessons at a Glance

Here's how to get started with a Learn to Play lesson.

Step 1. To open a lesson, double-click it in the New Project window.

Step 2. To begin the lesson, click the Play button.

Notes and Tips

Switch between learn and play. Each lesson has a song that you can play back and practice along with, recording your playing, if you like. To switch between learn and play modes, move the mouse pointer within the video area, then click Learn or Play.

The learning process. You can take a lesson in any way you like. Go from start to finish: click the Play button and watch and listen, strumming your guitar or playing your music keyboard as you go. Or learn in random order: drag the playhead around to watch parts of the lesson. Or begin at the end: have GarageBand play the lesson's song to get a feel for what you'll learn.

Along the way, you might use the Settings button to customize how GarageBand displays the video, the guitar fretboard or piano keyboard, and music notation. And you might record yourself playing along with the song or part of the lesson. For lessons on those topics, turn the page.

Exit the lesson (keyboard shortcut: Esc).

Open the guitar tuner (page 290)

Control display options and other settings (page 290).

Adjust volume levels of the band members when playing back lesson songs (page 293).

Guitar Lesson 1   Intro to Guitar   Tuner   Setup   Mixer

Change Lesson   half speed   normal   Open in GarageBand

Your teacher appears here, along with close-ups showing instrument technique.

Chapter names appear along a horizontal timeline. To skip to a chapter or repeat it, drag the playhead.

Fingering aids help you play chords.

Tick, tick, tick: use the metronome to have your Mac tap the beat.

Adjust the playback tempo (page 291).

Play the lesson or song.

Record yourself as you play along with the instructor or song (page 292).

Adjust playback volume.

Use *cycling* to have part of a lesson repeat over and over—perfect for practicing (page 292).

Open the lesson's song in GarageBand's production view (page 293).

Music Lesson Techniques

When taking music lessons, you might want to customize your learning experience. Venture into the Settings screen to customize how GarageBand displays musical notation, chords, and video.

For example, you can have guitar music displayed in standard notation, as tablature, or as chord grids. You can have piano music displayed as chords (Am, D7) or as standard music notation (with left and right hands displayed separately, if you like).

Don't read music? Just have GarageBand show you which guitar strings or keys to press. And if, like Jimi Hendrix, you're a left-handed guitarist, switch the video display to show a left-handed stringing.

As you progress through a lesson, you might want to repeat a tricky section or skip over an easy one. To navigate though a lesson's chapters, drag the playhead left or right. Want to repeat a chapter over and over so you can do that practice-makes-perfect thing? Just click the Cycling button.

A great (if sometimes humbling) way to assess your progress is to listen to yourself perform. When you're ready for your recital, click the Record button, then play along. If you've clicked the Cycling button, GarageBand even creates a separate *take* for each repetition. When you're done, you can open the song in GarageBand's production view and then listen to and work with each take.

Suffice it to say these instructional luxuries were not provided by the chain-smoking piano teacher who tormented my youth.

Adjusting Display Options

To adjust display options, click the Setup button near the upper-right corner of any lesson. To choose a setting, click it or press the number-key shortcut to its right. When you're finished, click Done.

For Piano

Teacher knows best: GarageBand uses the notation and appearance settings programmed into the lesson.

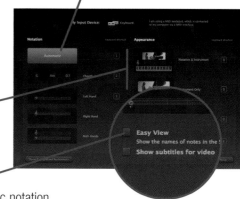

Customize the classroom: Turn music notation off if you don't read music or want to see a larger video window. More experienced? Consider turning off the on-screen keyboard and just viewing notation.

With Easy View, note names appear on the piano keyboard and in music notation.

For Guitar

Notation and appearance settings for guitar lessons are similar. Here's what's different.

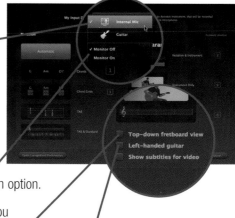

You can use your Mac's built-in microphone to record your acoustic guitar and access GarageBand's tuner. Play electric? Use an audio interface to connect your guitar's output jack to your Mac; see page 316.
Tip: To hear an electric guitar, choose the Monitor On option.

Display the fret board as if you were looking straight down on it instead of at the usual playing angle.   Play as a lefty? Click here.

Tuning a Guitar

You'll want to make sure your axe is in tune, especially if you plan to play along.

Step 1. If you haven't already, use the Settings screen to choose your Mac microphone (for an acoustic guitar) or an audio interface (for an electric guitar or for an acoustic guitar and an external microphone).

Step 2. Click the Tuner button.

Step 3. Using the on-screen fret board, click on the string you want to tune, then pluck that same string on your guitar.

The tuner shows whether the string is sharp or flat, and instructs you to loosen or tighten it accordingly.

Step 4. Repeat Step 3 for the remaining five strings, then click Done.

Repeating a Chapter with Cycling

To have GarageBand repeat a chapter of a lesson over and over, click the Cycling button.

Next, head for the timeline and click the name of the chapter you want to repeat. It highlights in yellow.

When you click the Play button, GarageBand begins playback at the highlighted region, and repeats it. To turn off cycling, click the Cycling button again.

Tip: When you record with cycling on, GarageBand records a separate take each time through. For details, see the next page.

Adjusting Tempo

Not so fast! If you're learning a difficult part, you might want to slow the playback tempo. It's easy: drag the tempo slider to the left.

If you're playing an artist lesson, GarageBand mutes the artist's singing when you slow the tempo. Because Sting refuses to sound liiiike thiiiis.

Tips for Notation Views

When viewing music notation, you have additional treats in store.

Scrubbing. To move around within the song, drag the little down-pointing playhead that appears above the music staves.

You can also move in one-beat increments by pressing the left-arrow and right-arrow keys.

Cycling. When notation is displayed, you can cycle in one-measure increments. Turn cycling on, then click the measure you want to cycle; GarageBand highlights it.

To cycle more than one measure, press Shift while clicking on adjacent measures.

Recording and Mixing Music Lessons

Recording Your Playing

To judge your progress, record yourself playing along with a music lesson. It's a great way to practice your timing—and to borrow from Tim, GarageBand's guitar and piano teacher, accurate timing is just as important as hitting the right notes.

If you're working with the artist lessons, recording gives you the opportunity to sit in with a major leaguer. Play Sting's guitar part in *Roxanne*. Record a solo in Norah Jones' *Thinkin' About You*. Jam with Ben Folds or John Fogerty.

Again, all this differs significantly from the elementary school auditorium recitals that your humble author dreaded.

To Record

Step 1. Move the playhead to the spot where you want to begin recording. To begin at a specific chapter in a lesson, click the chapter's name.

Step 2. Click the Record button.

Keyboard shortcut: press R.

Step 3. Make us proud of you.

Step 4. To stop recording, click the Play or Record buttons, tap the spacebar, or press the R key.

Accidentally record over a performance? Sorry you recorded anything at all? Undo your recording: press ⌘-Z.

You can also delete a recorded region: select it and press the Delete key.

Recording Multiple Takes

With cycling on, you can record a section over and over. Each time through, GarageBand creates a separate take.

Click the Cycling button and select the chapter or measures you want to cycle. (See page 291 for a cycling refresher.) Then, record as described above. When GarageBand reaches the end of the cycling region, it jumps to the beginning and records a new take. This repeats until you stop recording.

Managing multiple takes. When you've recorded multiple takes, GarageBand puts a tiny badge on the recorded region.

To switch between takes, click the badge, and choose a different take.

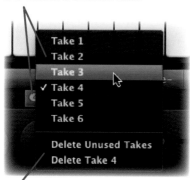

You can also delete one or more takes using this pop-up menu.

Future Concepts

When you record a performance, GarageBand shows your recording below the timeline. The *way* in which GarageBand depicts the recording differs for a guitar or a piano, and for some important reasons.

And this is a good place to introduce important concepts you'll encounter when working in GarageBand's production environment. You don't have to know this stuff to use the Learn to Play lessons, but you'll need to know it if you plan to plumb GarageBand's production features.

Guitars are real. When you record a guitar, a waveform appears below the timeline.

GarageBand records your guitar in a *real instrument* track. This is the type of track GarageBand uses to store audio, whether a vocal, a guitar, or a saxophone.

Keyboards are soft. When you record a keyboard, you see its note data.

GarageBand records your keyboard performance in a *software instrument* track. This is the type of track used for instruments whose sound GarageBand generates: pianos, electric pianos, synthesizers, and much more.

You can learn more about these types of tracks on page 302.

Using the Mixer

With each Learn to Play lesson, you can also learn to mix. Use the Mixer to adjust the relative volumes of each instrument in the song that accompanies a lesson. Make the bass louder or softer. Mute the guitar player and take his place.

Experimenting with the mixer is a great way to prepare yourself for mixing in GarageBand's full production environment. The Mixer is particularly fun with the artist lessons: mute all the instruments to just hear the artist's vocal. Or take the opposite approach: mute the vocal and sing it yourself.

To open the mixer, click the Mixer button near the upper-right corner of the screen.

Here's how the Mixer looks with the Norah Jones *Thinking About You* lesson.

The band members vary depending on the lesson. Try muting and soloing them and listening to the impact that has on the mix.

Mute, solo, and adjust the volume of recordings you've made in this lesson.

Mute, solo, and adjust the volume of your keyboard or guitar.

To close the mixer, click anywhere outside the mixer.

Opening a Song in GarageBand

As I mentioned on page 288, each of the piano and guitar lessons has a song that you can play (and record) along with. You can open these songs in GarageBand's production environment—to customize their instruments, record additional tracks, or just start learning GarageBand's most sophisticated features.

To open a lesson's song, click the Open in GarageBand button near the lower-right corner of the screen.

Note: You can't open the song in an artist lesson, alas.

The instructor's voice and instrument appear on the top tracks.

To mute (silence) a track, click the speaker. To solo a track (mute the other tracks), click the headphones.

To show or hide each member of the band, click the triangle. To restore the original mix, click Reset.

Adjust track volume.

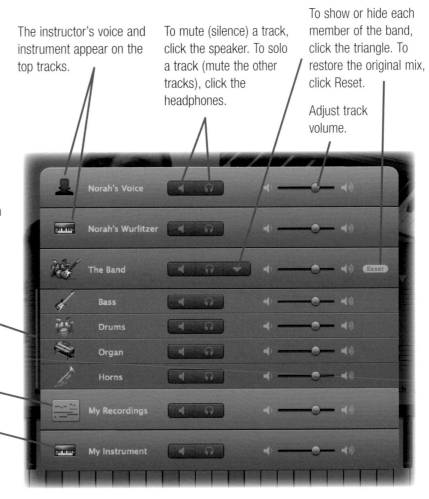

Instant Music: Magic GarageBand

Learning is great, but sometimes you just want to jam. With Magic GarageBand, you can—and in any of nine genres.

Choose a genre, such as blues. Use a virtual bandstand to customize the instrumentation of your song, choosing between different guitar, bass, drum, and keyboard combinations.

Then start playback and start playing. Record your performance, if you like. Adjust the volume of each player. Change instrument settings to experiment with different sounds.

All done? Move on to a different genre. Or take your jam to the next level: click the Open in GarageBand button, and GarageBand builds a project for your song, complete with any recordings you made. Modify the project, adding additional tracks or changing effects settings. Refine the mix. Then send your final effort to iTunes so you can play it on your iPod or iPhone.

Along the way, you'll learn some essential GarageBand concepts: working with tracks, choosing instruments, adjusting levels, and more. So it turns out that Magic GarageBand isn't just a good way to jam; it's also a good way to learn.

Using Magic GarageBand

Step 1. In the New Project dialog box, select Magic GarageBand.

A list of genres appears. To preview a genre's song, point to it and click the Preview button.

Step 2. To choose a genre, double-click it (or select it and click the Choose button).

The bandstand appears, and this is where the fun happens. Move the mouse pointer over each instrument. When you do, a spotlight illuminates it. Click an instrument to customize it, adjust its volume, and more.

Step 3. Go crazy: change instruments, play the song, play along, record your performance, and more (see opposite page).

Notes and Tips

The endless jam: snippets. Each Magic GarageBand tune has several parts—for example, an intro, one or more verses, and an ending. You can have GarageBand play just part of a song over and over: click the Snippet option, then, in the arrangement track, click the part you want to repeat.

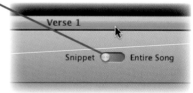

Why bother? Jamming, baby. Open up a blues, click Snippet, then select one of the verses (or select more than one by Shift-clicking). Start playback, and jam the night away. It's a lot like the cycling feature discussed on the previous pages—but with a back-up band.

If you record while playing, GarageBand creates a separate take for each pass; see page 296.

Open up. Your adventures with Magic GarageBand may go no further than experimenting with genres and jamming along with them. But you can also open the song you've created in GarageBand's production environment: just click the Open in GarageBand button. For some tips on what to do then, see page 297.

Magic GarageBand at a Glance

At front and center: you. Each genre gives you a choice of keyboards. To choose a different instrument, click Customize. To play and record a guitar, vocal, or acoustic instrument, use the My Instrument pop-up menu. See the tips below.

Each band member's icon matches its instrument. To change a band member's instrument or adjust its settings, point to it and click.

You can mute, solo, and adjust the volume of each band member. To access the controls, click the instrument, then click the triangle.

Zoom the window to fill your screen—perfect for jam sessions.

To navigate the song, drag the playhead left and right on the arrangement track. To select a snippet of the song, click it.

Record, Play, and adjust the song's playback volume.

Choose between playing the entire song or just part of it, as described on the opposite page.

You're off the gig: to remove an instrument from the band, select the instrument and click No Instrument.

Instrument Notes

Customizing instruments. Each genre provides a choice of keyboards that go nicely with that genre. But you aren't locked into those choices. Click the Customize button, and you can choose from dozens of GarageBand's software instruments: strings, synthesizers, and more.

If you play electric guitar, you can play it through your Mac and have GarageBand apply its guitar amp and effects simulators to it. Connect the guitar as described on page 316, then choose Guitar from the Instrument pop-up menu. To tune up, click the tuning fork button. The tuner here works like the one described on page 291.

You can also use your Mac's internal microphone to record a vocal or acoustic instrument: choose the Internal Mic option from the My Instrument pop-up menu.

Or connect a mixer to your Mac's audio-input jack, then plug a high-quality external mike into the mixer. To avoid applying guitar distortion to your vocal, click the Customize button, then choose one of the settings from the Vocals category. (I like the Live Performance setting.)

Shuffling instruments. Want to roll the instrumental dice and come up with a new band? Click an empty part of the bandstand, then click the Shuffle Instruments button that appears. GarageBand picks a random selection of the instruments available for each part.

Magic GarageBand Recording and Arranging

Recording Yourself

You can record yourself playing along with Magic GarageBand. Click the Record button (or press the R key). Playback starts at the beginning of the song, with record mode turned on.

To stop recording, click the Play or Record buttons, tap the spacebar, or press the R key.

Notes and Tips

In midstream. Want to start recording partway through a song? Begin playback, then click the Record button or tap the R key when you want to record.

Never mind. Unhappy with that recording? Undo it: press ⌘-Z. You can also delete a recorded region: select it and press Delete.

Multiple takes. If you've selected a part on the arrangement track, such as a verse, GarageBand records a separate take for each pass. A little badge appears to indicate multiple takes. To switch between and delete takes, click the badge and choose commands from the pop-up menu; see page 292.

Combining Solos: Playing Magic GarageBand

Here's my second-favorite Magic GarageBand tip. Each song has solos played by the Melody part—the virtual dude on the far right of the virtual bandstand. But only one solo can play as a song plays back. For example, you can't have Verse 1 of the Slow Blues play with a Chicago guitar solo, and Verse 2 play with the Harmonica solo.

Ah, but you can. The trick is to click. Select the Melody part and assign an instrument to it. Start playback. As the playhead approaches a new verse or chorus, click a *different* instrument for the Melody part.

GarageBand takes a moment to switch solos, so you might miss a few notes. But it works, and it's fun. Try selecting just one verse of a blues, starting playback, and then working through each of the Melody instruments. You're "playing" Magic GarageBand as though it were an instrument. In a way, it is.

Combining Solos: Copy and Paste

Here's my favorite Magic GarageBand tip. This trick lets you combine solos from each Melody part into a lengthier, richer song. This tip also gets you working in GarageBand's production environment, so it's a good way to get your mouse feet wet.

Strike up the band. Start as usual: pick a genre and your band members. I love the Slow Blues genre, so let's use it. For the Melody part, choose the Chicago guitar.

Then, click the Open in GarageBand button to create a project containing the song.

Add a verse. Next, you need to create another verse to hold a harmonica solo. Click the Verse 1 heading, hold down the Option key, and drag to the right. Pressing Option tells GarageBand to duplicate that verse; notice GarageBand makes room for the new copy as you drag.

(By the way, you're working with an *arrangement region* here; you can learn more about these regions on page 326.)

Get ready for the new solo. When you duplicated Verse 1, you also duplicated 12 bars of a guitar solo. It's time to delete that to make room for Harmonica Johnny. In the area named Verse 1 Copy, click the region named Chicago 1.1, then tap the Delete key. Now, B. B. GarageKing will step aside when that verse plays.

Save your project.

Hire your harmonica. Here's the trickery. Return to Magic GarageBand: choose File > New, select Magic GarageBand, and double-click Slow Blues. Now, select the Melody part, and choose the Harmonica instrument. Finally, click Open in GarageBand.

You now have a new project with a harmonica solo. You're going to copy that solo, then return to your original Slow Blues project and add the solo to it.

In the Verse 1 area, select the region named Harmonica.2, then choose Edit > Copy. Now return to your original Slow Blues project: go to File > Open Recent, and choose its name.

Paste that harmonica, son. With your original project open, drag the playhead to the start of Verse 1 Copy. The LCD should read 14.1.001: the start of measure 14.

Be sure the Chicago track is selected (click anywhere around the guitar icon). Finally, choose Edit > Paste.

There's your harmonica solo. Play it back.

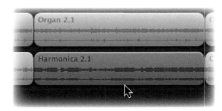

Cool, no? By duplicating verses and then copying and pasting Melody parts, you can create lengthy, rich tunes from Magic GarageBand's building blocks.

The other point is this: you can copy and paste any region from a Magic GarageBand tune into songs you're creating. Across all nine genres are some great solos, bass lines, horn hits, and drums—use them!

Next Steps

What next? Here are a few ideas.

Get acquainted with GarageBand. Adjust levels, and mute or solo some tracks (page 306). Pan instruments to change their position in the stereo mix (page 330). Change effects settings (page 328). Export to iTunes (page 332).

Change the tempo and key. Get familiar with GarageBand's LCD (see the sidebar below). Choose the Project option, then choose a key. Speed up the tempo or slow it down.

Add to your loops. Magic GarageBand regions also make great Apple Loops. Add some to your loop library to expand your musical options; see page 338.

Get to Know the LCD

GarageBand's LCD is a counter and control center. Use its pop-up menu to switch between functions.

Time. Shows the playhead's position in absolute time (hours, minutes, seconds, and fractions thereof). Ideal for podcasting and movie scoring, where beats and measures are less important than minutes and seconds.

Measures. Shows the playhead's position in bars and beats. Ideal for music projects.

Chord/Tuner. See chords as you play them (page 335), or use the instrument tuner (page 317).

Project. View and change a song's key, tempo, and time signature.

To change numeric values in the LCD, drag across them or double-click them, then type.

For example, to jump to measure 33, you can drag up or down on the bar readout, or double click the readout (its numerals flash) and then type *33* and press Return.

Production View at a Glance

GarageBand's production view is where you can tap the program's most powerful music- and audio-production features. It's what turns your Mac into a multitrack recording studio.

Feeling creative? Explore GarageBand's library of pre-recorded musical phrases, called *loops*. Assemble the loops you like into a tune. For extra credit, change the pitch of some loops by *transposing* them.

If you play the piano, plug a music keyboard into your Mac and go to town—GarageBand's *software instruments* enable your Mac to mimic instruments ranging from pianos to guitars to drums and beyond. Use loops to create a rhythm section, and then play along. Edit your performance to make it shine.

If you sing or play an instrument, connect a microphone, electric guitar, or other audio input to your Mac and hit the Record button. Create a three-part harmony by laying down vocal tracks one at a time. Or record multiple tracks at once.

As you compose, you may want to enhance certain tracks with *effects*. Refine your mix as you go. When you're finished, export to iTunes or burn a CD.

Here's how to become a one-Mac band.

The Loop Browser

To locate and audition loops, use the loop browser. Find loops by clicking buttons or typing search terms, such as *conga* (page 305).

To hear a loop, click its name.

The Track Editor

Refine your performance using the track editor.

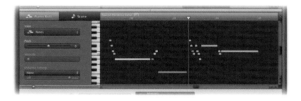

Editing notes. With the track editor for software instruments, you can edit individual notes, either in piano-roll format (above) or in standard music notation (below); see page 312.

Editing audio. With the track editor for real instruments, you can modify recordings (page 323).

Each track is a member of your virtual ensemble. Each track has controls for muting, adjusting volume, and more.

Use the track mixer to adjust a track's overall volume and left-right stereo position (page 330).

Use the Arrange track to define different sections of a song (page 326).

The moving playhead shows the current playback location; drag the playhead to move around within a song.

The *beat ruler* shows beats and measures. To move the playhead to a specific spot, click the ruler.

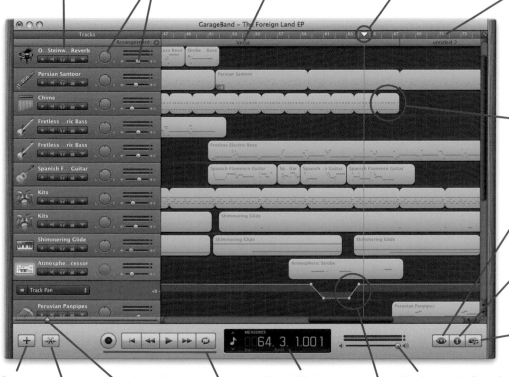

By repeating and modifying loops in the *timeline*, you can assemble everything from rhythm sections to entire arrangements (page 304).

Display the loop browser (opposite page).

Display the Track Info pane (pages 310, 317, and 320).

Display the media browser, for accessing your other iLife media (pages 348 and 354).

Create a new track.

Display the track editor (opposite page).

Drag the zoom slider to zoom in and out on the timeline.

The LCD displays the position of the playhead and more (page 297).

Transport controls: record, play, rewind, and cycle playback (page 307).

Monitor and adjust the overall song volume.

To control volume and panning over time, create automation curves (page 330).

Podcasts, too.
You can also use GarageBand to produce podcasts (see page 346).

How to Be a Songwriter

How you use GarageBand depends on your musical experience and your musical tastes. Here's a look at a few different paths you can take. And note that you aren't restricted to just one route—you might move from path to path as a song comes together.

Start a New Project

Step 1. Choose File > New (⌘-N).

The Project window appears.

Step 2. Double-click the type of project you want to create (see opposite page).

Step 3. Specify the key, tempo, and time signature for your song.

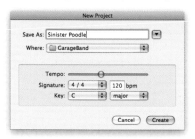

You can change any of these details later. You can even adjust tempo while your song is playing back.

Composing with Loops

Use the loop browser to locate a loop that sounds interesting (page 304).

Playing a Keyboard

Create a software instrument track and choose the desired software instrument (page 310).

If you like, customize the instrument to create a unique sound (pages 328 and 342).

Recording Guitars and Other Audio

Create a guitar track (page 316) or a real instrument track (page 320).

Adjust volume levels to get a loud, but not distorted, signal (pages 317 and 320).

Use the Instrument tuner to get in tune (page 317).

Drag the loop into the timeline to add it to your song; drag the loop pointer to repeat the loop as desired (page 305).

Refine as desired: split and transpose regions (page 308), edit them (pages 312–315), and change the track's effects (page 328).

Record your performance, using GarageBand's Count In command and metronome to keep you in tempo (page 310).

Refine and arrange: modify and move regions (page 306), apply effects (page 328), and fix mistakes (pages 312–315).

Record your performance, laying down multiple takes if you like (page 324).

Edit your recording—rearrange it, change its effects, enhance its tuning or timing, or combine the best parts of several takes into a single track (page 323).

Starting Points

Name	Description
Piano	One Grand Piano software instrument track.
Guitar	One guitar track, ready to apply amplifier and effects simulators.
Vocal	Two real instrument tracks: one for a male vocal, one for a female vocal.
Loops	No preconfigured tracks. The loop browser is open, awaiting your exploration.
Keyboard Collection	Seven software instrument tracks, each assigned to a different keyboard instrument: piano, electric piano, organ, synths, and more.
Acoustic Instrument	One real instrument track with no effects applied.
Songwriting	A vocal track plus a four-piece rhythm section, with a drum loop already added.

Head Starts: Song Templates

To save you time, GarageBand provides *templates* for common songwriting projects. You can customize any project after starting it, adding tracks and changing instruments and effects as needed. But if a template gives you a head start, use it.

Mix

Adjust each track's volume levels and panning, optionally adding a set of final-mastering effects and a fade-out (page 332). When you're finished, export the song to your iTunes music library.

Two Types of Tracks

When you compose in GarageBand, you work with two very different types of tracks: *real instrument* tracks and *software instrument* tracks. The loops that GarageBand provides also fall into these two broad categories: loops with a blue icon are real instrument loops, and loops with a green icon are software instrument loops.

But what's the difference between a real instrument and a software instrument? The answer lies in the fact that today's Macs are powerful enough to generate sound using more than one technique. In fact, GarageBand is able to generate sound using multiple techniques *at once*.

Here's a look a how GarageBand makes its noise—and at what it all means to you.

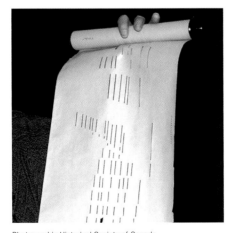

Photographic Historical Society of Canada

Real Instruments: Recorded Sound

A real instrument track holds a digital audio recording—a riff played by a bass player, some strumming on an acoustic guitar, a phrase played by a string section, or a vocal that you record.

A real instrument track is blue, and a real instrument loop has a blue icon ▦. Notice that the track and the icon depict a waveform—a graphical picture of sound, similar to what we saw back on page 220.

Variations. When you record an audio source, its regions are purple. If you import an audio file, its region is orange. See page 323 for all the colorful details.

Software Instruments: Sound on the Fly

A software instrument track doesn't hold actual sound. Instead, it holds only *data* that says what notes to play and how to play them. The sounds you hear when you play a software instrument track are being generated by your Mac as the song plays back.

A software instrument track is a bit like the music rolls that a player piano uses—just as the holes in the music roll tell the piano which notes to play, the bits of data in a software instrument track tell your Mac which notes to generate.

A software instrument track is green, and a software instrument loop has a green icon ▣. Instead of depicting a waveform, a software instrument region shows individual notes—why, it even looks a bit like an antique player piano roll (see photo, left).

The Guitar Track Difference

Guitar players deserve a special place in the world. So say my guitar player friends, anyway. GarageBand seems to agree: it provides a special type of real instrument track designed for holding audio recordings of electric guitars.

It's called a *guitar track*, shockingly enough. Deep down, a guitar track is a real instrument track: it holds audio recordings, as opposed to the note data held by software instrument tracks.

But on top of that foundation are some fantastically cool virtual electronics. When you record to a guitar track, you can tap into a warehouse of amplifier simulations and effects.

The amp simulations use sophisticated math to mimic the sound of the amps you wish you could afford: Fenders, Marshalls, and others. The effects simulate the stomp boxes that guitarists keep at their feet to add distortion, chorus, flanging, and more.

Thanks to guitar tracks, you don't need a room full of back- and budget-breaking amps and other gear. You just need your Mac.

Beyond guitars. Just because a guitar track is *designed* for a guitar recording doesn't mean you can't use it for other sounds, too. You can record any audio—or drag any loop—into a guitar track and apply amp and effect simulations to it. Keep that in mind as you explore your sonic options.

Comparing Approaches

Each type of track has advantages and capabilities that the other lacks.

The real advantage. When it comes to realism, you can't beat real instrument tracks. Listen to the Orchestra Strings loops that come with GarageBand. They don't just sound like a string section—they *are* a string section. Compare their sound to that of the software instrument loop named 70s Ballad Strings 02.

Another advantage of real instrument tracks is that they can hold *your* digital audio. When you plug a microphone into your Mac and belt out *My Way,* your voice is stored in a real instrument track.

The software advantage. The primary advantage of software instrument tracks is versatility. Because software instrument tracks store individual note data, you can edit them in almost any way imaginable. You can even change the instrument entirely. Want to hear how your bass line would sound when played by a synthesizer instead of an electric bass? Just double-click on the software instrument track's header and choose a synth.

On the down side, software instrument tracks make your Mac work harder than real instrument tracks—it's harder to generate sound on the fly than it is to play back a recording.

Common ground. Although real instruments and software instruments work differently, you can do many of the same things with both types of tracks. You can repeat loops within both types of tracks, and you can apply effects to both types. You can even transpose both types of tracks, including audio that you've recorded. However, you can't transpose audio regions across as wide a range as you can software instruments—they'd sound too artificial.

By supporting audio recordings (real instruments) and also being able to generate sound on the fly (software instruments), GarageBand gives you the best of both worlds.

Working with Loops

For many GarageBand musicians (including yours truly), a composing session often begins with some loops: a bass line, some percussion, a repeating synthesizer riff, or maybe all three.

The gateway to GarageBand's library of loops is the loop browser, whose buttons and search box let you quickly home in on loops of specific instruments or specific styles.

Once you find a loop that sounds interesting, you can add it to your song by dragging it into GarageBand's timeline. Once that's done, you can repeat the loop over and over, edit it, and transpose it.

GarageBand lets you audition loops even as your song is playing back—simply click on a loop in the loop browser. This is a great way to hear how a particular loop will fit into the arrangement you're building.

Working with loops is as easy as clicking and dragging. But as you master GarageBand, there's a powerful subtlety behind loops that you may want to take advantage of. Specifically, you can use software instrument loops in real instrument tracks in order to lighten the load on your Mac's processor.

If that makes no sense to you now, don't worry. When your arrangements become complex and you want to wring every bit of performance out of your Mac, you'll find all the details on pages 341 and 344.

Adding a Loop to a Song

To display the loop browser, click 👁 or use the ⌘-L keyboard shortcut. To add a loop to a song, drag the loop into the timeline.

Creating a new track. When you drag a loop into an empty area of the timeline where there is no existing track, GarageBand creates a new track for the loop. The vertical bar indicates where the loop will begin playing. To move the loop after you've added it, drag it left or right (if the loop is too tiny to drag, zoom in).

Adding to an existing track. You can add a loop to an existing track. Mixing loops within a track is one way to add variety to a song.

Tip: You can drag a software instrument loop into a real instrument track, but not vice-versa. For more details, see page 341.

Variations. Many loops include several variations, and are named accordingly. To change to a different loop from the same family, click the tiny arrows in the upper-left corner of the loop, then choose a different loop.

Looping a Region

When you add a loop to a track, you create a *region* that you can modify without changing the original loop. The most common kind of modification you'll perform is to loop a region so that it plays repeatedly.

The notches show the beginning and end of each repetition of the loop.

To loop a region, point to its upper-right corner and drag it to the right.

Using the Loop Browser

Switch between column view, music loop view (shown here), and podcast sounds view (page 348).

Resets the loop browser, clearing any search text and deactivating any keyword buttons you've clicked.

Click the keyword buttons to home in on specific instruments or styles.

To audition a loop, click it. To hear how the loop sounds with the rest of your song, begin playing the song before you click the loop.

To search by keyword, type some text and press Return. You can search for instruments (for example, *piano* or *guitar*) or styles (*jazz, funk*).

If you're auditioning a particular loop and it's overwhelming the rest of your arrangement, use this slider to turn down the loop browser's volume.

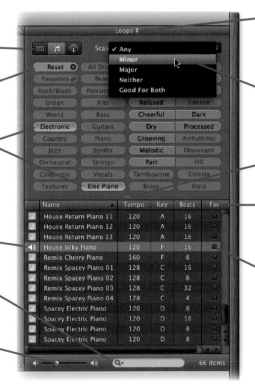

Have lots of loops? Use the Loops pop-up menu to focus on specific collections (page 339).

Many loops use major or minor scales. You can use this menu to filter the list of loops to only those that complement your song.

To resize the keywords area, drag up or down.

To sort the loop list, click any column heading. To resize the columns, drag the vertical borders.

Love that loop? Click the Fav check box to add it to your Favorites list. To display your favorites, click the Favorites button (it's under the Reset button).

Working with Tracks and Regions

Tracks can be a lot easier to work with than musicians. Tracks never show up late for a gig, they always play in tune, their sense of timing is impeccable, and they never trash the hotel room.

Nonetheless, there are some important points to know about working with tracks and the regions that they hold. (A *region*, you'll recall from previous pages, is a set of notes or a snippet of sound. When you drag a loop into the timeline or record a performance, you create a region.) For starters, when creating multitrack arrangements, you should rename tracks so you can tell at a glance which parts they hold: the melody, a solo, an alternate take of a solo.

As you compose, you may want to silence, or *mute*, certain tracks. Maybe you've recorded a few versions of some background strings, each on its own track, and you want to audition each one to hear which sounds best.

On the other hand, there may be times when you want to *solo* a track—to mute all the other tracks and hear only one track. Soloing a track can be useful when you're fine-tuning a track's effects settings or editing a region in the track.

A big part of creating an arrangement involves copying regions within a track or from one track to another. And as you move regions around, you often have to work with the beat ruler at the top of GarageBand's timeline. By fine-tuning the ruler's *snapping* feature, you can have your regions snap into place on exactly the right beat.

Here's how to get along with the members of the band.

Soloing, Muting, and More

The *track header* contains the track's name and controls.

Your turn: enable the track for recording (pages 310, 316, and 320).

Lock up: prevent changes and help performance (page 344).

Quiet: mute the track. Keyboard shortcut: M.

Only you: solo the track. Keyboard shortcut: S.

Over time: create volume and pan curves (page 330). Keyboard shortcut: A.

Renaming a Track

Normally, GarageBand names a track after the instrument you've assigned to it. When you have multiple tracks that use the same instrument, it's hard to tell the tracks apart. Give your tracks descriptive names, such as *Third Verse Strings*. To rename a track, click its name in the track header, hold the pointer over the name for a moment, and, when the name is highlighted, type a new name.

Track Tips

You can move tracks up and down by dragging their headers. Consider grouping related tracks together— put all your rhythm section tracks together, then all your solo tracks, and so on.

When a track header is selected, you can use your keyboard's up- or down-arrow keys to select the track above or below the current track. This shortcut teams up nicely with those described above.

Play It Again: Cycling

When you're rehearsing, mixing, or recording, it's often useful to have part of a song play over and over. To do this, click the Cycle button and then drag in the area just below the beat ruler to indicate the region that you want to repeat.

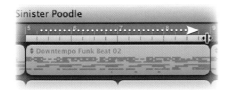

The yellow region repeats until time comes to an end or your parents pull the plug, whichever comes first. To resize the region, drag its left or right edge. To move the region, drag it left or right.

When cycling is on, playback always begins at the start of the cycle region.

Turning cycling on is also the first step to using GarageBand's multiple-take recording feature (page 324).

Duplicating a Track

You can make a duplicate of a track: a new, blank track with the same instrument and effect settings as the original. Select the track's header, then choose Duplicate from the Track menu (⌘-D).

Duplicating a track is another way to record multiple takes of a part: record each take in its own track, then copy and paste the best parts into a single track.

Copying Regions

Copying a region is a common task, and GarageBand provides a couple of ways to accomplish it. You can copy and paste: select a region, choose Copy, move the playhead to the destination, and paste. You can also press the Option key while dragging the region you want to copy.

Note: If you want to copy a region to a different track, the tracks must be of the same type. You can't copy a software instrument region to a real instrument track, or vice-versa.

Zooming tip: When you're moving regions over a large distance, use GarageBand's zoom slider to zoom out for a big-picture view. And use the keyboard shortcuts: Control-left arrow zooms out, while Control-right arrow zooms in.

Copying Versus Looping

You can repeat a region by either looping it or copying it. So which technique should you use? Looping is the fastest way to repeat a region over and over again: just drag the loop pointer as described on page 305.

The advantage of copying a region is that each copy becomes an independent region that you can edit without affecting other copies. With a repeating loop, if you edit one note in the loop, that edit is present in each repetition.

Snap to the Beat

When moving a region, you almost always want to move it to the exact beginning of a particular measure or beat. GarageBand's *timeline grid* supplies this precision: when the grid's snapping feature is active, GarageBand automatically snaps to beats and measures as you drag regions, move the playhead, drag loops to the timeline, and perform other tasks.

Normally, GarageBand adjusts the sensitivity of its grid to match the way you're viewing your song. If you're zoomed all the way out, GarageBand assumes you're performing fairly coarse adjustments, such as dragging a region from one part of a song to another. In this case, GarageBand's grid will snap to the start of each measure.

If you're zoomed all the way in, GarageBand figures you must be making precise adjustments, so it adjusts its grid to snap in sixty-fourth-note increments.

You can override GarageBand's automatic grid sensitivity: just choose the desired value from the grid menu.

Click the timeline grid button to display the grid menu.

The "swing" options delay every other grid point. This lets you maintain a swing feel when dragging regions. The amount of delay is greater with the "Heavy" options.

Every other grid point is delayed slightly.

Transposing and Creating Chord Changes

Unless they're from the soundtrack of *Wayne's World*, most songs aren't built around just one chord. Most songs contain chord *changes* or *progressions*—variations in key that add harmonic interest. Chord changes can be simple, such as those of a 12-bar blues, or they can be complex, such as those of Billy Strayhorn's jazz classic, *Lush Life*.

You can build chord changes in a couple of ways. For fast results, use the master track to create a *pitch curve* that transposes every track in your song (with two exceptions, noted at right).

When you want more control, transpose individual regions as described on the opposite page. This approach lets you be selective about what you transpose. For example, you can transpose some piano or guitar chords while keeping your bass track at the root key of your song. You can also edit individual regions to better fit your song's chord changes.

Transposing with the Master Track

Creating a pitch curve in the master track is the fastest way to "program" chord changes.

Step 1. Choose Show Master Track from the Track menu (⌘-B).

Step 2. In the master track header, choose Master Pitch from the pop-up menu.

Step 3. In the timeline, click at the point where you want to create a chord change—for example, at the beginning of a measure.

Step 4. Drag the control point up or down to transpose in increments of one *semitone* (one half-step). For example, to program the first chord change in a blues, drag up five semitones.

Notes and Tips

Audio limitations. A pitch curve will *not* transpose any audio regions that you recorded (purple regions) or imported (orange ones). To transpose purple regions, see the opposite page. To transpose orange regions, convert them into purple ones first; see page 323.

Changing a change. To remove a control point, select it and press the Delete key. To change its pitch, drag the control point up or down. To change the point when the chord change occurs, drag the control point left or right.

Adjusting precision. The point in time when GarageBand places control points is determined by the current timeline grid setting (see the previous page). If you want more precision in placing or adjusting a control point's position in time, zoom in or choose a smaller note value from the timeline grid button.

Unlock first. If you've locked any tracks (page 306), you can't adjust the pitch curve. If you try, GarageBand displays a dialog box that lets you unlock all locked tracks.

Transposing Individual Regions

This method is more work than creating a pitch curve, but as I noted on the opposite page, it offers more options and creative control.

The fastest way to use this technique is to repeat a loop for the entire duration of a verse (for example, 12 measures), split the loop at each point where you need a chord change, and then transpose the appropriate regions. This is a quick way to lay down a bass track.

If you'd like to follow along with the steps below, create a new song in GarageBand and add the loop named Woody Latin Bass 01 to it.

Step 1. Drag a loop into the timeline and use the loop pointer to drag it out to the desired length.

Step 2. Split the loop at the start of the change.

Drag the playhead to the beginning of the measure that needs to be transposed, then choose Edit > Split (⌘-T).

Step 3. Split the loop at the end of the change.

Drag the playhead to the *end* of the measure that needs transposing, and choose

Split again. You now have an independent region that you can transpose.

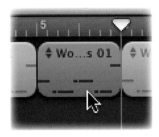

Step 4. Prepare to transpose.

Select the region you just created and open the track editor by clicking the track editor button. Shortcut: Double-click the region to open it in the track editor.

Step 5. In the track editor, drag the Pitch slider or click the numeral, then type a number.

You can transpose in one-semitone increments. In the timeline, GarageBand indicates how far you've transposed a region.

Notes and Tips

Editing a region to fit the changes.
Building a bass line from software instrument loops? You can build a better bass line by editing regions so that they complement your chord changes. For example, if you're going from F to C, you might make the last note of the F measure a C# or a B. That way, the bass will "lead in" to the new chord change. Edits like these can also take some of the repetitiveness out of tracks built from loops.

First, double-click the region you want to edit. Then, in the track editor, drag the last note of the region up or down to the desired note. GarageBand plays the note as you drag it, making it easy to determine where the note should be.

For details on editing software instrument tracks, see pages 312–315.

Transposing real instrument regions.
You can also transpose regions in real instrument tracks, but within a narrower range: one octave in either direction, as opposed to three octaves for software instrument tracks. And although you can't change individual notes as you can with software instrument tracks, you *can* perform some edits to regions in real instrument tracks; see page 323.

Recording Software Instruments

When you connect a music keyboard to your Mac, you unlock a symphony's worth of software instruments that you can play and record. There are pianos and keyboards and guitars of all kinds. There are synthesizers, strings, a flute, and some horns. And there are some drums you just can't beat.

As the following pages describe, you can edit your recordings and use effects to refine your tracks. You can even create completely new instruments of your own design.

If you don't have a music keyboard and don't want to spend a fortune on one, check out the offerings from M-Audio (www.m-audio.com). Its Keystation 61es is a 61-key (five octave) keyboard that sells for under $200. Its "semi-weighted" action gives it a piano-like feel, and its keyboard is *velocity sensitive:* it measures how hard each key is pressed. Most of GarageBand's software instruments respond to this velocity information, changing their loudness and other characteristics to allow you to play (and record) with expression.

You can also use a costlier keyboard that requires a separate MIDI interface. (MIDI stands for *Musical Instrument Digital Interface,* and is a standard for interconnecting electronic instruments and computers. Think of it as USB with a music degree.) Pricier keyboards often provide *weighted action*—their keys respond like a piano's instead of like an organ's, and thus feel more natural to experienced pianists. You'll also find more keys—up to 88 of them.

Recording a Software Instrument

Step 1. Create a new track. Click the New Track button (➕) or choose New Track from the Track menu (Option-⌘-N).

Step 2. In the New Track dialog box, click Software Instrument, then click Create or press Return.

Step 3. Select a category, and then select an instrument.

Tip: You can use the up- and down-arrow keys to move from one instrument to the next.

You can use the pop-up menu to choose from a specific instrument collection (see page 339).

Optional: choose an icon to appear in the track header.

Tip: You can try out the selected instrument by playing keys on your music keyboard or by clicking the on-screen keys in GarageBand's Keyboard or Musical Typing windows (see page 335).

Step 4. Get ready. Position the playhead a few measures before where you want to begin recording. To give yourself time to get ready, choose Count In from the Control menu.

Step 5. Hit it. Click the Record button (⏺) or press the R key. To stop recording, press the spacebar or click the Play button (▶).

Notes and Tips

Watch your playing. As you record, GarageBand displays the new region (and its notes, in piano-roll style) in the timeline. Display the track editor for the current track, and your performance appears as you play—even in music notation.

Recording in an existing track. The instructions at left assume you're starting a brand-new track. You can, of course, also record in an existing software instrument track. Just select the track's header to enable it for recording. To change the track's instrument—before or after you record—double-click the track header to display the Track Info pane.

Multitrack recording. You can record one software instrument track and some real instrument tracks at the same time: record a vocal while you play, or record a couple of acoustic instrumentalists. For details, see page 322.

Multiple-take recording. By turning cycling on, you can record take after take, and then choose the best one; see page 324.

Anatomy of a Music Keyboard

Like many keyboards, M-Audio's Keystation 61es contains no sound-generating circuitry. When you play, the keyboard transmits MIDI data that describes which keys you pressed, how hard, and for how long. Keyboards that lack sound-generating circuitry are often called *controllers*.

Most keyboards can accept an optional foot pedal that plugs into the back of the keyboard and acts like a piano's sustain pedal. If you frequently play piano software instruments, you'll want a pedal. Some keyboards also accept a volume pedal that many software instruments respond to, giving you more expressive options.

On the Keystation 61es, the volume slider controls the volume of the currently selected software instrument track.

All music keyboards provide two controls that allow for more creative expression when you play.

A *pitch bend wheel* lets you do something no acoustic piano permits: bend notes the way guitar players do. The pitch bend wheel pairs up well with guitar and synthesizer instruments.

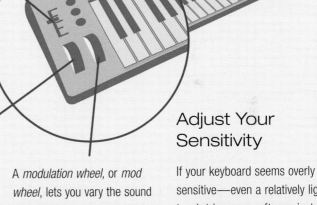

A *modulation wheel,* or *mod wheel,* lets you vary the sound of an instrument, usually by adding a vibrato-type effect. In Apple's Symphony Orchestra Jam Pack, the mod wheel also lets you obtain different articulations (see page 339).

Adjust Your Sensitivity

If your keyboard seems overly sensitive—even a relatively light touch triggers a software instrument's louder sounds—use the Audio/MIDI portion of the Preferences dialog box to turn down the sensitivity. Conversely, if you have to really pound to get louder sounds, increase the sensitivity.

Keyboard Sensitivity:

Less   Neutral   More

Editing Software Instrument Regions

We've already encountered one form of software instrument region editing: transposition (page 308). That's just the beginning. There's almost no end to the ways you can edit MIDI data, and unlike when you're onstage, you can always undo any disasters.

You can edit regions you record or regions that you create by dragging loops from the loop browser. And you can edit in either of two views: the piano roll-style *graphic* view or music-notation view. In either view, you can change notes, modify their duration, change their velocity values, draw new notes, and more. And in notation view, you can print a track's music.

To switch views, click the Piano Roll or Score buttons in the track editor.

Tip: To play a region over and over, click the tiny Play button near the top of the track editor. It's a handy way to audition your edits.

Selecting Multiple Notes

You often need to select multiple notes— for example, prior to duplicating them or adjusting their velocity. To select more than one note, Shift-click on the notes or drag a selection rectangle around them.

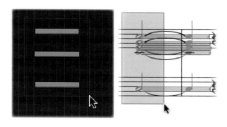

Editing in Graphic View

Editing is easy in the graphic view's piano-roll display.

Fixing wrong notes. To fix a wrong note, drag it up or down until it becomes the right note. If the note is very high or low, scroll the track editor or make it taller by dragging the horizontal divider bar above it.

If you fumbled and accidentally hit two keys when you meant to hit just one, delete the extra wrong note: select it and press the Delete key.

Notes and Tips

Improving expression. By editing the velocity values of some notes, you can improve expression and realism. This is especially true for software instruments, such as Classical Acoustic, that change dramatically depending on how hard you play a note.

To edit a note's velocity, select it and then drag the Velocity slider or type a number next to it. To change the velocity of a range of notes, select the notes first.

Velocity values can range from 1 (quiet as a hoarse mouse) to 127 (way loud). To give you a visual hint of a note's velocity, GarageBand uses shading:

Soft			Loud
Under 32	33 to 63	64 to 95	96 to 127
			(maximum)

Moving a note in time. To move a note backward or forward, drag it left or right. To zoom in for more precision, drag the track editor's zoom slider to the right. You may also want to adjust the track editor's grid sensitivity by using its grid ruler button. Or turn the grid off entirely (⌘-G).

Changing a note's duration. To make a note longer or shorter, drag its right edge to the right or to the left.

Drawing a new note. To draw a new note, press ⌘ and then drag within the track, using the little vertical piano key legend (and your ears) as guides.

Tip: To see a note's velocity, click it and hold the mouse button down.

C3, Velocity 43

Chords in a hurry. You can create chords by duplicating notes: press the Option key, click on a note, and then drag up or down by the desired note interval. This also works on a range of notes: select the notes, then Option-drag them.

Tip: Want to create a cinematic string section? Record a series of single notes, then duplicate them and drag the duplicate up seven semitones (a musical fifth). For some heavy metal action, try this with the Big Electric Lead guitar instrument. Just warn me first.

Editing in Notation View

Read music? Want to learn? Notation view is for you. It's also an ideal place to draw new notes and edit or create sustain-pedal information.

The techniques on the opposite page also apply to notation view, with the following differences.

Adjusting grid precision. When working in notation view, you'll want to use the grid ruler pop-up menu in the track editor to specify the degree of precision you want. For example, to move a note in quarter-note increments, choose 1/4 note. If you choose a small grid increment, you may see a lot of strange and small note or rest values, such as sixty-fourth notes.

Using the arrow keys. You can move notes by selecting them and pressing the arrow keys on your keyboard. To move selected notes back or forward one full measure, press Shift-left arrow or Shift-right arrow. Similarly, to transpose notes up or down one octave, press Shift-up arrow or Shift-down arrow. You can also drag notes with the mouse.

Changing a note's duration. To change a note's duration, select the note, then drag the green duration bar left or right. The duration bar works exactly like the piano roll-style notes in graphic view:

drag to the left to shorten the note, and drag to the right to lengthen it.

Drawing new notes. To draw a new note, choose the note value you want from the Insert pop-up menu.

Then, press ⌘ and click within the staff to create the note. You can also draw in pedal symbols: choose the pedal symbol from the pop-up, ⌘-click where you want the pedal-down symbol, then drag to where you want the pedal-up symbol.

Enlarging the notes. To make the notation view larger, make the track editor taller: drag the horizontal divider bar above it upwards. Similarly, to increase the horizontal spacing between notes, drag the track editor's zoom slider.

Notation Notes

Choosing a clef. Normally, notation view displays both the bass and the treble clef. That makes sense for instruments with a broad note range, such as piano. But for instruments with a narrower range—such as bass or piccolo—you may not need to see both clefs.

To make a choice appropriate to the instrument, click the clef at the left edge of the notation display, then choose the clef you want.

Here's a bass line as it should appear.

Printing music. You can print a track's contents as sheet music. Select the track's header, then be sure that the note grid is displayed at a setting that makes sense for hard copy. If you have it set for a very fine, sixty-fourth-note resolution, for example, you'll have strange-looking notation with lots of short-duration notes. To adjust the resolution, use the grid ruler pop-up menu in the track editor.

To control how many measures appear in each row of music, drag the zoom slider in the lower-left corner of the track editor. Generally, you'll want to drag the slider to the left and zoom out.

To print the music, choose File > Print. To preview the sheet music first, click Preview in the Print dialog box. GarageBand adds little niceties to your hard copy: the song name at the top of the page, the tempo, instrument name, and your name (as it's stored in the My Info portion of the Preferences dialog box).

More Region Editing Techniques

More Controller Editing Options

Modulation and sustain (opposite page) are just two forms of MIDI controller data that you can edit. Here's a look at more controller editing options.

Pitch bend. A music keyboard generates pitch bend data when you move its pitch bend wheel. You can edit this data or draw your own.

Expression. True to its name, expression data lets you increase or decrease the loudness of a region. You might draw in expression data to create a crescendo or decrescendo. Try recording a chord with a horn section instrument, then adding an expression curve to it.

With Apple's Symphony Orchestra Jam Pack, moving the pitch bend wheel generates expression data.

Tip: If you have a volume (expression) pedal connected to your music keyboard, you can have GarageBand respond to and record the data it transmits. Be sure your keyboard is transmitting the pedal's data as expression data (MIDI controller #11), not volume data (MIDI controller #7).

Foot control. Apple's Symphony Orchestra Jam Pack uses foot control data to control articulation for some of the orchestral instruments, such as strings.

Doubling a Track

You can create a duet by duplicating a region in a different track. Create another track of the same type (software instrument or real instrument), then Option-drag the region into that track. (You can also copy and paste.) To start with the same instrument and effect settings, duplicate a track: select it and press ⌘-D.

Next, refine your duet. If it's a software instrument track, experiment with different instruments. You might also transpose one of the tracks to create a harmony or put each part an octave apart. You might also experiment with different effects, panning, and volume settings.

Tip: One way to add richness to a duet is by very slightly offsetting the second track's region. Turn grid snapping off (⌘-G), zoom in on the region, then nudge it ever so slightly to the left or right. This way, the regions won't play back at exactly the same time, strengthening the illusion of multiple musicians.

Importing MIDI Files

GarageBand can also import files created in standard MIDI format. Most sequencers can create MIDI files, and thousands of them are available on the Internet. (Jazz lovers: check out www.thejazzpage.de. Classical buffs: go to www.classicalarchives.com, especially if you have Apple's Symphony

Orchestra Jam Pack. Downloading a MIDI file usually involves Control-clicking on it and choosing Download Linked File from the shortcut menu.)

A standard MIDI file's name ends with *.mid.* To import the file into GarageBand, simply drag it into the timeline. GarageBand reads

the file, creates tracks, and assigns instruments to them.

You may have to fine-tune the results of an importing session. I often have to transpose the bass track up by one octave and reassign software instruments.

Still, importing a MIDI file is a great way to move a song

created in a different sequencer into GarageBand. It's also a fun way to practice and create songs: download a MIDI file, drag it into GarageBand, then remix it, change its tempo, or play along.

Fixing Timing Problems

You can have GarageBand *quantize* a region—move its notes so that they fall exactly on the beats in the beat ruler.

Before quantizing a region, choose a note value from the Enhance Timing pop-up menu in the Advanced area of the track editor. If you're quantizing a walking bass line in 4/4 time, try the quarter-note (1/4 Note) setting. If you're quantizing a more nuanced performance, use a higher resolution. For jazz or other syncopated styles, try one of the swing settings.

With all settings, you can "dial down" the quantization by dragging the Enhance Timing slider to the left. Experiment with different settings. If the results sound strange, try again or choose Undo.

You can also quantize individual notes within a region: select the notes, then perform the above steps.

Quantizing can be a mixed bag; it works well with extremely mechanistic music styles (such as dance and even some classical), but expect disappointing results when quantizing a jazz piano solo or any musical form that plays somewhat fast and loose with beats. Experiment. If you don't like the results, choose None from the pop-up menu to turn quantizing off.

Tip: You can also quantize a track as you record it. Select a track but don't select any notes or regions in the track. Choose a note value from the pop-up menu to have GarageBand quantize to that value as you record. This is handy for drum parts.

Editing Controller Information

Not all MIDI data deals with notes. A keyboard's pitch and modulation wheels also generate data, as does a sustain pedal. You can edit and create this *controller data* in the track editor's graphic view.

Editing controller data involves working with *control points* similar to those of pitch, volume, and panning curves. By adjusting this data, you can change the expressiveness applied by a pitch or mod wheel, adjust your pedal work, and more.

Say you have a software instrument whose sound timbre "sweeps" when you move the modulation wheel (examples include Star Sweeper, Aquatic Sunbeam, Cloud Break, and Falling Star). If you want that sweep to change over a specific number of measures, create a *modulation curve*.

To edit or create controller data, choose the controller type from the View pop-up menu in the Piano Roll track editor. ⌘-click to create control points, then drag them as needed.

You'll find an example of this on my Web site, at www.macilife.com/gbandexamples.zip. Expand the archive by double-clicking it, then open the folder. Check out the GarageBand project named Modulate Me. It contains two regions, each playing the identical note. But in the second region, I drew a modulation curve to create a precisely timed sweep.

As for editing sustain data, you can clean up sloppy pedal work by fine-tuning the position of the control points that represent each pedal push: just drag the control points left or right.

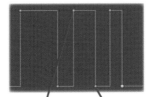

Pedal is pressed   Pedal isn't pressed
(sustain is on).   (sustain is off).

And if you don't have a sustain pedal, you can draw your own sustain data. Check out the project named Add Sustain in the aforementioned examples folder. I recorded the first region without using my sustain pedal. Then I duplicated the region and added sustain data to the duplicate.

Press the pedal: ⌘-click to create a control point.

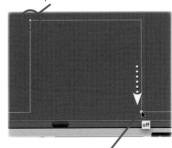

Release: ⌘-click where you want the pedal release, then drag down to the bottom of the grid. Drag control points left and right as needed to fine-tune timing.

I wouldn't want to draw in sustain data for a Billy Joel ballad, but for the occasional sustained arpeggio, it works.

Recording Electric Guitar

Question: How many electric guitar players does it take to change a light bulb? Answer: Five. One to change the bulb, and four to discuss how Eric Clapton would have done it.

You can laugh about electric guitarists (just Google *guitar jokes*), but they get their due in GarageBand. A special type of real instrument track, called a *guitar track*, is designed for recording that electric axe of yours.

What makes a guitar track special? The same thing that makes an electric guitar special: the amplifier. The stuff to which an electric guitar is connected has a huge bearing on your sound. That's why guitarists have bank- and back-breaking collections of amps and effects *stomp boxes*—each combination of amp and effects colors the guitar's sound in its own way.

When guitarists debate one player's sound over another's—something that usually happens after the light bulb is changed—you can bet they're talking about amps and effects as much as guitars themselves.

This outboard gear also gets its due in GarageBand. When recording to a guitar track, you can choose from five guitar amp simulators that use sophisticated math to mimic classic amps, with frightening realism. You can also tap into ten virtual stomp boxes that add distortion, chorus, fuzz, and more.

We'll tour the amps and stomp boxes on the following pages. First, let's look at the nuts and bolts behind recording your strings and frets.

Make the Connection

Your first step in recording an electric guitar is to connect it to your Mac. Few guitars put out a signal strong enough to allow for a direct connection to the Mac's sound-input jack. You'll need audio hardware that amplifies the signal.

If you have a big budget, then, well, you probably aren't a guitarist. Regardless, a large selection of audio interfaces is available; I discuss some on page 320. Such gear can accommodate not only a guitar, it can also connect to microphones.

You can also use an external mixer as your guitar pre-amp: plug the guitar into the mixer, then connect that mixer channel's "send" line to the Mac's audio-input jack.

But if you don't have such gear and you're on a typical musician's budget, consider a USB guitar interface, such as IK Multimedia's StealthPlug. This tiny marvel lets you plug an electric guitar directly into any USB port. The StealthPlug also has a jack for headphones.

Tip: After connecting your guitar, you may need to tweak a setting to have GarageBand use the StealthPlug for audio *input* and your Mac's built-in audio for audio *output*. Choose GarageBand > Preferences, then click Audio/MIDI. From the Audio Output pop-up menu, choose Built-In Output.

Recording an Electric Guitar

Step 1. Create a new track: click the New Track button (the plus sign) or choose Track > New Track.

Step 2. In the New Track dialog box, select Electric Guitar, then click Create or press Return.

Step 3. Pick your poison: choose a guitar preset from the pop-up menu at the top of the Track Info pane.

Step 4 (optional). Customize amp and effects simulators as desired (see the following pages).

Step 5 (optional). Configure your input: double-click the amp in the Track Info pane, then use the controls at the bottom of the pane.

Choose the input you're using.

To hear your guitar as you play, choose On or On with Feedback Protection. The latter option is potentially better for your ears.

Adjust your guitar's volume and the Recording Level slider to get a strong signal (see page 321).

Step 6. Get ready.

Move the playhead a few measures before where you want to start recording, or choose Control > Count In to have GarageBand give you a few beats to get ready.

Step 7. Click the Record button or press the R key, and shred that thing.

Because a guitar track is just a special kind of real instrument track, all the editing options described on pages 322–325 are also available.

Get In Tune with the Instrument Tuner

Another lame guitar joke: How can you tell if an electric guitar is out of tune? See if the strings are vibrating.

Let GarageBand help you get in tune. The instrument tuner listens to the audio coming into a real instrument track and displays its note value.

(This works with single notes only, not with chords. However, the LCD can display chords that you play using a software instrument; see page 335.)

To use the instrument tuner, select the track for the instrument you want to tune and make sure that its Record button is enabled. Then, click the icon on the left side of the LCD and choose

Tuner, or choose Control > Show Instrument Tuner (⌘-F).

The tuner displays the note you're playing.

If the note is flat, the indicator moves to the left of center. If the note is sharp, the indicator moves to the right. When you're in tune, the indicator is centered, as shown here.

Guitar Amps and Effects

Amps on Tour

Each of the amps available in a guitar track simulates, or *models*, a popular guitar amp. Apple doesn't mention any brand names, but the name and appearance of each virtual amp provide strong clues. Here's the rest of the story.

Small Tweed Combo

Fender Tweed Deluxe, a classic blues amp from the 1950s.

Blackface Combo

Another Fender classic, this one from the 1960s. Includes models such as Pro Reverb and Twin Reverb. Dreamy for jazz.

English Combo

The Beatles, Pete Townshend, The Edge, Bono, Jeff Beck: all fans of Vox amps, known for biting high end and distortion.

Vintage Stack

One word: Marshall. Okay, two more words: Jimi Hendrix. Enough said.

Modern Stack

Mesa/Boogie's Dual Rectifier, a line of ear-bleeding distortion machines. The guitar track preset named Big Hair Metal uses this amp. Again, enough said.

Working with Amps

The easiest way to tap GarageBand's guitar and effects simulators is to use the menu of more than 35 presets at the top of a guitar track's Track Info pane.

Tip: Here's a fun way to audition the presets. Create a guitar track, then bring up the loop browser and add the Acoustic Noodling 08 and Acoustic Noodling 02 guitar loops to it. (Together, they provide a nice range of low to high notes.) Next, turn on cycling to repeat those loops. Turn the playback volume down so you don't burst your eardrums. Start playback and switch presets, turning up the volume as desired.

Adjusting settings. Each amp provides a set of virtual knobs that control bass, treble, reverb, gain (crank it up for distortion), and more. To twiddle the dials, click an amp's graphic in the Track Info pane, then drag the knobs.

Note: I'm sorry, Spinal Tap fans, but no setting goes up to 11.

Switching amps. To switch from one amp to another, click the arrows on either side of an amp.

Older amp simulations. GarageBand provides an effect, named Amp Simulation, that you can apply to software and real instrument tracks alike. This effect has been around for a couple of GarageBand versions, and while fun, it can't hold a capo to the amp simulations described on this page. Still, you can use it with GarageBand's guitar software instruments—something a guitar track's amps don't permit. For details on effects, see page 328.

Stomp Boxes

What's at the feet of almost any great electric guitarist? No, not groupies—stomp boxes. These rugged metal wonders color the sound by adding distortion, swirling chorus, fuzz, and more.

Each guitar track preset employs one or more stomp boxes. You can customize their settings, and add or remove boxes. You can choose from a collection of ten virtual stomp boxes, and use up to five on a single guitar track.

Read up on effects chains.
www.macilife.com/garageband

Adjusting a box. To twiddle the knobs on a stomp box, select it in the Track Info pane, then click and drag on the knobs.

To turn a stomp box off or on, click the virtual stomp switch at the bottom-center of the box.

Adding and removing a box. To add a stomp box, double-click an existing stomp box on the stage. Your box collection appears. **Tip:** For a brief description of each, point to it.

Phase Tripper can add either subtle coloration or head-spinning effects.

Next, drag the stomp box you want into one of the empty slots on the stage. To replace an existing box, drag the new box to it.

To remove a stomp box, drag it off the stage. When you release the mouse button, the box disappears in a puff of smoke. This makes GarageBand one of a dwindling number of venues where smoking is still permitted.

Reordering stomp boxes. GarageBand applies stomp box effects in left-to-right order, and the order of the boxes can greatly affect your sound. To change the order, double-click any stomp box, then drag boxes left or right. Many guitar players have their favorite order of effects. For links to some ideas, see macilife.com/garageband.

Syncing. Many stomp boxes have a Sync button. Click it, and the stomp box's effect—for example, vibrato—is synchronized with your project's tempo.

Tips for Amps and Stomp Boxes

Adding Automation

Here's something you can't do with a real guitar amp or stomp box: automate its settings so they change over time. Have a guitar's reverb become stronger during your song's bridge. Or kick the distortion up for a solo. Or have an amp's tone change gradually during a long chord.

To add automation, edit the guitar track's automation curve. See "Automating Effects" on page 336.

Creating Presets

When you customize an amp's setting or the arrangement of stomp boxes, you can save your new settings for future use. Click the Save Setting button at the bottom of the Track Info pane, and give your setting a name.

Settings you create appear at the bottom of the presets pop-up menu.

Recording Other Audio Sources

Connect a microphone or other sound source to your Mac, and you can record a performance in a real instrument track.

Most mikes and guitars don't produce a loud-enough signal for the Mac, which works best with a *line-level* signal like that of a cassette deck, for example. No problem—products aplenty await your wallet. M-Audio, MOTU, and others sell first-rate audio interfaces for the Mac. Cash-starved guitarists and bassists might use a device such as IK Multimedia's StealthPlug (page 316). For vocals and acoustic instruments, another option is a USB microphone such as those made by Blue Microphones, Audio-Technica, and Samson.

As the previous pages showed, GarageBand lets you apply effects to audio that you record. A large selection of effects is available for real instrument tracks. But your audio is always recorded and saved with no effects—unprocessed, or *dry*. GarageBand applies its effects as your music plays back, so you can experiment with effects settings.

Before recording a real instrument track, be sure your audio hardware is properly configured. You may need to visit the Sound system preference and GarageBand's Preferences dialog box to ensure that the audio input is set to the hardware you plan to use. And be sure you have plenty of free disk space before you start—your recording will use 10MB per minute for a stereo track.

Recording to a New Track

Step 1. Create a new track. Click the New Track button (+) or choose New Track from the Track menu (Option-⌘-N).

Step 2. Click the Real Instrument button and click Create or press Return.

Step 3. Choose an instrument.

When you select an instrument, you're choosing a set of effects that GarageBand will apply when playing back the track. You can change this setting later if you like: double-click the track header and choose a different setting in the Track Info pane.

Select a category, then select an instrument within the category.

Don't want to apply any effects to the track? Select No Effects.

If you've connected a stereo microphone or device, choose Stereo 1/2. Otherwise, choose the channel that your sound source is connected to (see page 322).

To monitor or not? See opposite page.

To adjust recording levels, use the Recording Level slider. To have your Mac adjust levels for you, click Automatic Level Control.

Explore some audio-interface and microphone options.
www.macilife.com/garageband

Step 4. Adjust recording levels.

Sing or play some notes, and watch the level meters in the track's header. If the clipping indicators light (see below), ugly distortion looms. Lower the volume of your input source—for example, lower the Recording Level slider in the Track Info pane, or, if you're using a mixer or audio interface, adjust its volume controls.

Step 5. Get ready.

Move the playhead a few measures before where you want to start recording, or use the Count In command in the Control menu to give yourself time to get ready.

Step 6. Press Record (●) and make us proud.

The meters should illuminate fully during loud passages, but the two clipping indicators (the tiny circles) shouldn't light up. If they do, lower the input volume as described above.

Tip: When the clipping indicators light, they stay lit until you click them. This is GarageBand's way of telling you that clipping occurred while your eyes were closed as you belted out *My Way*.

When you're setting levels, this *isn't* the volume control to use. This slider adjusts the track's playback volume, not its recording input level. See for yourself: turn down the track volume while singing or playing, and you'll see that the meters still move. Here's the rule: To adjust *playback* volume, use the track mixer. To adjust *record* volume (technically, input gain), follow the instructions in Step 4, above.

Notes and Tips

Monitor or not? If you're using a microphone and you turn monitoring on, you're likely to hear loud distortion. Indeed, that's why GarageBand provides another option: On with Feedback Protection. Choose this option, and GarageBand warns if it detects feedback and offers to turn monitoring off.

Generally, if you're using a microphone, it's a good idea to leave monitoring off unless you're wearing headphones while you record (a very good idea). There's less risk of feedback with a guitar or bass, particularly if you're far enough away from your speakers.

Just the basics. To quickly create a real instrument track with no effects, choose Track > New Basic Track.

More Audio Techniques

Multitrack Recording

GarageBand is a great tool for musicians who labor alone. But what if you want to record a couple of musicians simultaneously and put each performer on a different track? Or what if you'd like to record yourself singing a vocal while strumming a guitar or playing a MIDI keyboard?

If your Mac has a basic stereo input, you can record two real instrument tracks simultaneously, *plus* one software instrument track: two singers and some GarageBand piano, for example. Connect multichannel audio hardware, and you can record up to eight real instrument tracks and one software instrument track: a real garage band.

Here's how to record two simultaneous audio tracks using your Mac's built-in audio input. These basic steps apply to more ambitious multitracking tasks, too.

Get jacked up. Your Mac's built-in audio input can accommodate two signals: left channel and right channel. When multitrack recording, forget left and right: you're using one channel for one audio source (say, a mike), and the other channel for another source (for example, an electric guitar).

Use a splitter cable or Y-adaptor that has a ⅛-inch stereo miniplug on one end and two audio jacks on the other. Those two audio jacks can be RCA phono jacks, ¼-inch mike jacks—whatever meshes with the gear you plan to connect.

Connect each audio source to one of the splitter's input jacks.

Assign channels. Next, assign one input channel to one track and the other channel to a different track. Double-click a real instrument track's header (or create a brand-new track), and use the Input pop-up menu in the Track Info panel to assign the input to Channel 1. Adjust your audio device's level to get a good input level as described on the previous page.

Input Source: Mono 1 (Built-in Input)

Next, repeat this process for the other track, assigning it to Channel 2.

Input Source: Mono 2 (Built-in Input)

Arm the tracks. Make sure that the two tracks are enabled for recording: click the red Record button in their track headers. If you want to record a software instrument along with the two real instrument tracks, now's the time to create that track and enable it for recording, too.

Get down. Set up the metronome and count-in as desired, and record.

Notes and Tips

Panning your tracks. The technique I've described here creates two mono audio channels. And yet when you play your recording, you'll hear each channel coming from *both* speakers. To control each track's position in the stereo field, use the track's panning knob in the track mixer. For panning advice, see page 331.

Hard drive labor. Recording two simultaneous audio tracks puts your Mac's hard drive to work, especially if you're also playing back some existing real instrument tracks. If you have a slower Mac—or a laptop Mac or Mac mini, all of which have slower hard drives—you might need to mute some existing real instrument tracks to lighten the load on your hard drive and to avoid an error message.

The same applies to software instrument tracks that you've locked (see page 344): if GarageBand displays an error message while recording, try muting those tracks.

Multi-take recording. GarageBand's multi-take recording feature works with real instrument tracks, too. In fact, it even works when you're doing multitrack recording. Turn on track cycling, and each band member gets as many takes as he or she needs to get the part right. For details on multi-take recording, see page 324.

Working with Real Instrument Regions

You can modify real instrument regions —either ones you've recorded or those you created by dragging blue loops into the timeline—in several ways.

Copy, paste, and dupe. You can duplicate a region by copying and pasting or by simply Option-dragging it. Duplicating a lengthy region doesn't use any additional disk space.

Digital splicing. You can also do some basic editing. Maybe you belted out a *yeah* that sounded more like Howard Dean than James Brown. Double-click on the region to open it in the track editor.

Drag across the offending utterance (zoom in and turn off grid snapping for more precision), then choose Delete from the Edit menu.

You can also copy and paste part of a region: select it in the track editor, then choose Copy. Now paste it at a different position or in a different real instrument track.

Tip: To "double" a vocal and add a richer sound, offset the duplicate slightly using the technique on page 314. And pan each member of your chorus to a different position (see page 330).

Enhancing tuning and tempo. Singer sour? Drummer dragging? Use the track editor's Enhance Tuning or Enhance Timing slider. Every track is different, so drag the slider until things sound good.

When adjusting pitch, you can have GarageBand limit enhancement to the song's key (check the Limit to Key box) or to the chromatic scale (uncheck the box). And to try your hand at an effect first popularized by Cher back in the last century, crank Enhance Tuning all the way up.

Track editor tips. Want to turn a selection into an independent region? Just click within the selection.

And with some strategic mouse positioning, you can move, resize, and loop regions directly within the track editor— no need to journey up into the timeline. To move a region, position the pointer near its upper-left corner. When the mouse pointer changes to a ◀▶, drag left or right.

To resize a region within the track editor, point to its lower-left corner and drag. To loop a region, point to its upper-right corner and drag.

Orange Loops: Imported Audio and More

You can import audio from iTunes and the Finder: just drag the audio file into the timeline. GarageBand accepts AIFF, WAV, Apple Lossless, MP3, and AAC formats.

(You can't import a song purchased from the iTunes Store. The workaround: burn the song to a CD, then rip it back into iTunes and import that version.

This limitation doesn't apply to iTunes Plus purchases.)

GarageBand displays imported audio regions in orange.

You can't shift the tempo of orange audio regions, nor can you transpose them—at least not without a little trickery. If you

know that your song's tempo and key match those of the orange region (or if you don't care—maybe you just want to slow down a solo to figure it out), here's the secret: select the orange region, press Control-Option-G, and then click elsewhere in the timeline. GarageBand "stamps" the region with your project's key and tempo settings and turns the

orange region into a purple one. Now you can transpose it and stretch its tempo. This is great for doing remixes of iTunes tracks.

Incidentally, if you open a project created in GarageBand 1.x, its once-purple regions will be orange. Use the Control-Option-G trick to convert them.

Recording Multiple Takes

Sometimes it takes more than one try to get a performance just right. If you're like me, it may take dozens of tries. If at first you don't succeed, GarageBand makes it easy to try, try again. With the multi-take recording feature, you can record a passage over and over again—without having to start and stop, or click buttons, between attempts. GarageBand records each try as a separate *take*.

Multi-take recording is easy to set up, and as I mentioned on previous pages, it works with software instruments and real instruments alike. Indeed, you can even do multi-take recording when you're doing multi*track* recording—each member of the band gets multiple takes. (Keep in mind that recording multiple takes on multiple real-instrument tracks will gobble up disk space.)

After you record multiple takes, you can switch among them and choose the one you like best. The process is much like its counterparts in the Learn to Play lessons and in Magic GarageBand. And, armed with the region-editing skills you picked up on previous pages, you can pick and choose the best parts of each take and edit them into a perfect performance.

Here's how to keep on trying.

To Record Multiple Takes

Step 1. Turn cycling on by clicking the 🔄 button.

Step 2. Adjust the size of the yellow cycling bar to match where you want the recording to start and end.

For more details on cycling, see page 307.

Step 3. Enable one or more tracks for recording, then start recording—and start playing.

When the playhead reaches the end of the cycling region, it returns to the beginning and GarageBand starts recording another take.

It's that easy. Keep recording takes until your hands fall off, your voice turns into gravel, your hard disk fills, or you never want to hear the song again, whichever comes first.

Then what? When you stop recording, check out the region that you recorded: the tiny number in its upper-left corner shows how many takes you recorded.

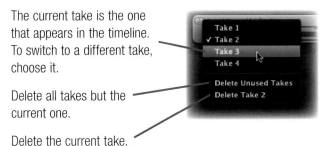

The region displays the very last take you recorded. To switch to a different take, click the tiny number and choose the take you want.

The current take is the one that appears in the timeline. To switch to a different take, choose it.

Delete all takes but the current one.

Delete the current take.

Notes and Tips

Regions and takes. When you use multi-take recording, each region in a track can have its own set of takes. Indeed, if you use the Split command to split a region containing multiple takes, you'll see that each region retains all the takes. This makes possible some slick take-management tricks. For example, you can split a multiple-take region into two regions, and then delete all but one of the takes from one of the regions.

Merging takes. When you're recording multiple takes on a software instrument track, you have an additional option: the ability to merge each take into a single region.

This option is great for building up a drum track. Record the bass drum on your first take, the hi-hat on the second take, ride cymbal on the third, snare on the fourth, and so on. When you're done, you'll have a full drum track contained in one region.

To activate this option, choose GarageBand > Preferences, click the General button, and click the oh-so-wordy option named Automatically Merge Software Instrument Recordings When Using the Cycle Region.

Note: You must activate this option *before* recording the takes.

More Multiple-Take Options

Multi-take recording is great, but it doesn't let you pick and choose parts of each take to build a single track containing the best parts. To do that, you have a few options.

Record on separate tracks. Use the Duplicate Track command to create multiple duplicates of a track, and record each take on its own track. Then, use the region editing techniques covered on previous pages to copy and paste the best parts of each track into one.

Splitting a multi-take region. Say you like the first part of Take 1 and the last part of Take 3. Display Take 1, then move the playhead to the spot just before it goes bad. (If you need extra playhead precision, zoom in and use the Control menu to turn off grid snapping.) Choose Edit > Split; GarageBand splits the region into two. Finally, in the second region, use the tiny pop-up menu to display Take 3.

Multiple takes to one track. Use the multi-take recording feature to record as many takes as you like. Next, use the Duplicate Track command to create *one* duplicate of the track. Now return to the track containing all the takes, and switch from one take to another, copying and pasting the best parts into the duplicate track.

Max Headroom for Sound: The 24-bit Advantage

Back on page 89, I talked about the advantages of 16-bit imaging: it captures a scene more accurately and gives you more headroom to make adjustments without sacrificing image quality.

There's a similar advantage in the audio world. Normally, GarageBand records in 16-bit mode—it uses 16 bits of data to describe each of the 44,100 snapshots of sound that it takes every second.

Many audio interfaces support 24-bit audio. Those extra eight bits make a difference: instead of being able to represent roughly 65,000 different volumes, a 24-bit recording can measure over 16 million.

If you have an audio interface that supports 24-bit audio, you can have GarageBand record at this higher resolution. Choose GarageBand > Preferences, and click the Advanced button. From the Audio Resolution pop-up menu, choose Better or Best. Both options record at 24-bit resolution. If you choose Best, GarageBand also *exports* songs at 24-bit resolution. (At the Better setting, GarageBand exports 16-bit audio.)

Make space. Note that recording in 24-bit mode uses roughly 50 percent more disk space. (Remember, this applies to real instrument tracks only.) Is the extra disk space worth it? Do some tests and let your ears decide. But, in general, more bits are always better in the computer biz, so if your audio hardware supports 24-bit recording, you might as well take advantage of it.

Adding Structure with the Arrange Track

Songs typically have structure: an introduction, verses, a chorus or bridge, and an ending. You can see this in the Magic GarageBand songs and in the tunes that are part of most Learn to Play lessons.

With GarageBand's arrange track, you can create *arrange regions* that define these elements in your projects. Once you do, you can perform all manner of arranging tricks. Build the arrangement for a verse—the rhythm tracks, chords, background vocals, and so on—and then copy it as many times as needed throughout your song. (You can edit each copy, too, to add variety.)

By adding structure to your song, you also have more opportunity to experiment. Should the chorus repeat twice at the end of the tune? How about a different intro treatment? Without the arrange track, questions like these are harder to answer, requiring a lot of copying and pasting and dragging of regions.

With the arrange track, the creative answers you seek are a few clicks away.

Using the Arrange Track

To work with arrangements, start by displaying the arrange track: choose Track > Show Arrange Track.

Defining Arrange Regions

Step 1. In the arrange track, click the Add Region button (⊕).

GarageBand creates an eight-bar region.

Step 2. To change the duration of the arrange region, drag its left and right edge.

Step 3. To name the region, double-click it and pause until the name is highlighted, then type a name.

Notes and Tips

You can also create an arrange region by simply dragging within an empty area of the arrange track—no need to click the little plus sign first.

To resize an arrange region, drag its left or right edge. But note that if you lengthen a region, the region that follows it will be shortened accordingly. For example, if you add four bars to an intro that is followed by a verse, the verse is shortened by four bars. To avoid that, move the adjacent region to create some empty measures between it and the one you want to lengthen.

Working with Arrange Regions

After you've defined one or more arrange regions, you can work with them in several ways.

Moving a region. To move an arrange region to a different spot in your song, click its heading and then drag left or right in the arrange track. When you move a region, everything in the region—notes, automation curves, and so on—moves accordingly.

Swapping two arrange regions. Want to swap Verse 1 and Verse 2? Drag Verse 1 until it's directly over Verse 2. (Verse 2's regions highlight.) When you release the mouse button, GarageBand swaps the two arrange regions.

Replacing a region. To replace one region with another, press ⌘ while dragging the region you want to keep. For example, to replace Verse 3 with Verse 1, ⌘-drag Verse 1 directly over Verse 3.

Duplicating a region. To duplicate a region, press Option and drag the region elsewhere in your song. If you position a region between two existing ones, the region to the right moves to accommodate the region that you're dragging.

Tip: Get in the habit of renaming duplicates after you create them, lest you end up with region names like *Verse Copy Copy Copy*—a great name for the Xerox corporate anthem, but not all that descriptive otherwise.

Deleting a region. Don't want that second chorus after all? Click the arrange region's header to select the region, then press Delete.

This deletes all the music in that region, but leaves the region itself in place—your song has a gap in it.

If you'd prefer to delete the region's notes *and* the region itself, select the region's header, then press ⌘-Option-Delete. GarageBand deletes the region, and regions to the right snuggle in to fill the empty space.

Splitting regions. To split an arrange region into two, select the region, position the playhead at the point where you want to split the region, then choose Edit > Split (⌘-T).

Joining regions. You can also join adjacent arrange regions. Shift-click on each region's header to select it, then choose Edit > Join.

Selecting multiple regions. You can duplicate, move, or delete more than one region at once: just Shift-click on each region before using the techniques on this page.

To select every single region in the song—maybe to add the intro that you just decided your tune needs—click the track header of the arrange track; it's the blank area directly below the word *Tracks*.

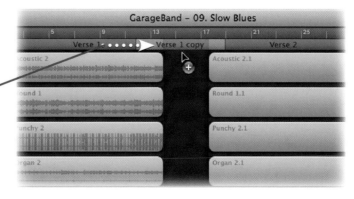

Refining Your Sound with Effects

Effects can be just as important to your final arrangement as the notes you play. With effects, you can add richness to a track—or brain-liquefying distortion, if that's your idea of fun. You can add some spice to a track, or change it beyond recognition.

Effects alter the "color" of sound. Some effects simulate real-world phenomena, such as reverberation and echo. Other effects let you sculpt your sound to enhance certain frequencies. Still other effects process (and sometimes mangle) audio in ways that could only exist in the digital world.

Recording studios have racks of hardware effects boxes. GarageBand's effects exist in software: by applying complex math to your sound, GarageBand can simulate the reverb of a concert hall, the characteristics of an old guitar amplifier, and much more. Best of all, you can customize GarageBand's effects in a limitless number of ways to create sounds that are yours alone.

We've already encountered some of GarageBand's effective talents—the amp and stomp box simulators that you can apply to guitar tracks. Here's a look at the effects that you can apply to software instrument and real instrument tracks.

And as I've said previously, GarageBand never alters your original audio; effects are applied as your song plays. This lets you experiment with effects until you arrive at just the right amount of sonic seasoning.

Effects Basics

All of GarageBand's software instruments employ effects to some degree. Similarly, when you create a real instrument track and choose an instrument, GarageBand assigns a collection of effects to that track (page 320). A song's master track can also apply effects to your entire song (page 332).

To examine and change a track's effects settings, double-click the track header, then click the Edit tab in the Track Info pane.

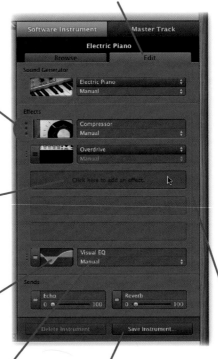

You can drag effects up and down to change the order in which GarageBand applies them (see page 334).

To add an effect, click an empty slot, then choose from the pop-up menu. To remove an effect or use a different one, click the effect's name.

To create your own settings for an effect, click the icon (see opposite page).

Choose effect presets from these pop-up menus.

Like what you've come up with? You can save the customized version of the instrument and use it again in future songs (see opposite page).

For software instruments, standard effects include Compressor, Visual EQ, Echo, and Reverb. (Real instrument tracks provide these same effects, and they add a *noise gate* effect, which removes noise from silent portions of a recording.)

The Fab Four

Compressor, Visual EQ, Echo, and Reverb are mainstay effects, the salt and pepper of sonic seasoning.

Compressor. A compressor is a kind of automatic volume control that adjusts volume thousands of times per second. Most popular music is heavily compressed, and FM radio stations often compress it even more. Compression can add punch to drum tracks and vocals, but too much compression can add an annoying "pumping" quality to sound.

Visual EQ. Visual EQ is a sophisticated equalizer for adjusting bass, mid-range, and treble. It's described on page 334.

Echo. Also called *delay,* the echo effect simulates evenly timed sound reflections.
Tip: GarageBand's echo repeats at a rate that matches your song's tempo. Try applying echo to vocal or synthesizer "stabs" in a dance, electronica, or hip-hop tune. To have different echo rhythms on each track, use the Track Echo effect.

Reverb. A distant cousin to echo, reverb consists of thousands of randomly timed sound reflections. Reverb simulates the sound of an acoustic space: a concert hall, a small lounge, a stadium. GarageBand provides a reverb effect that is controlled by the master track (page 332). A separate Track Reverb effect lets you apply different reverb to a specific track.

Customizing Effects

You can customize effects in several ways.

Turn them off. Maybe you love GarageBand's Arena Run synth, but you don't like the way it echoes every note. Just turn off the Echo effect by unchecking its box.

Turn them on. Explore the pop-up menus and change or add effects. Want to add a rich, swirling texture to a track? Try Flanger, Phaser, or both. Want to liquefy your listeners? Unleash Distortion, Bitcrusher, or Amp Simulation. Want a track to continuously pan between the left and right channel? Try the Tremolo effect's Circular Structure setting. Want to turn a male

singer into a female—or a chipmunk? Try the amazing Vocal Transformer.

Automate them. You can automate an effect so it changes as your song plays— have the reverb get stronger, increase and decrease the amount of tremolo, and so on. For details, see page 336.

Try different presets. Many of GarageBand's effects have an assortment of presets that you can apply with a click.

Create your own presets. Click the effect's icon, and a window appears where you can adjust the effect's parameters.

To create a new preset containing the current settings, open the pop-up menu and choose New Preset.

Each effect has a unique set of parameters that you can adjust.

Saving Instruments

When you change a track's effects, you're customizing the way GarageBand has defined that software or real instrument. If you switch to a different instrument or effect preset, GarageBand asks if you want to save the changed instrument before switching.

If you click Continue (or just press Return), GarageBand discards your settings. If you think you'll want to use them again, click Save As, then type a name for your newly customized instrument.

If you like tinkering with effect settings and you don't want GarageBand pestering you about saving them all the time, check the Do Not Ask Me Again box. You can also use GarageBand's Preferences command to control this paranoia mode.

For more details on creating instruments, see page 342.

Refining the Mix: Volume and Panning

A good song has a pleasing mix of melody, chord changes, and maybe lyrics. A good *recording* of a song has a pleasing mix between instruments. It's possible to have a poorly mixed version of a great song, and as a spin of the radio dial will confirm, it's also possible to have a well-mixed version of a lousy song.

As a GarageBand-based recording engineer, the job of mixing is yours. Adjust each track's volume so all the tracks mesh—no single instrument should overwhelm the others, but important instruments or voices should be louder than less important ones.

And to create a rich stereo field, pan some instruments toward the left channel and others toward the right. You'll find some tips for panning on the opposite page.

To adjust a track's playback volume level and panning position, use the Mixer area of GarageBand's window.

To have a track's volume or panning change as the song plays, create a *volume curve* or *panning curve*—a set of control points that tell GarageBand how to change volume or panning over time.

Note: If you've edited a track's volume or panning curve, you can't drag the volume slider or turn the panning knob. Instead, make volume or panning adjustments to the curve.

Adjusting Volume

To adjust a track's playback volume, drag the slider.

To avoid distortion, lower the volume if the clipping indicators light.

Editing a Volume Curve

To create fades, add expression, or mute a track for part of a song, edit the track's volume curve.

Step 1. Click the triangle next to the track's Lock button or select the track header and press the A key.

Step 2. Choose Track Volume from the pop-up menu and click the little box at the left edge of the pop-up menu to turn on the curve for editing.

Step 3. The horizontal line represents the track's volume. Click the line to create a control point where you want the volume change to begin.

Step 4. Click at a different point on the line to create a second control point, then drag it down to lower the volume, or up to raise it.

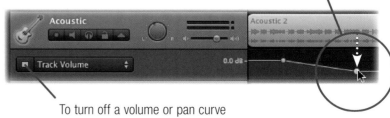

To turn off a volume or pan curve without deleting its control points, click the little blue indicator.

Adjusting Panning

To pan a track, drag its pan knob to turn it clockwise (toward the right speaker) or counterclockwise (toward the left). To return to dead center, Option-click the knob.

Editing a Pan Curve

To pan a track from one channel to the other as the song plays, edit the track's pan curve. Display the track's curve by clicking its triangle or pressing A. Then, choose Track Pan from the pop-up menu and click the little box at the left edge of the pop-up menu to turn on the curve for editing.

Next, create control points and drag them. To pan toward the left channel, drag a control point up. To pan toward the right, drag a control point down.

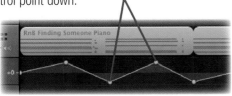

Tips for curves. To adjust a control point's location in time, drag it left or right. To delete a control point, click it and press the Delete key. To delete or move multiple control points at once, select them by Shift-clicking or dragging across them. To duplicate control points, Option-drag them.

If you move regions within your song, any curves you created for them don't move along with the regions. To fix that, choose Control > Lock Automation Curves to Regions. Now, when you move a region, any automation curves beneath it will go along for the ride.

Mixing Tips: Panning

By sweating the details of your stereo mix, you can make your song more aurally interesting. Two ears, two speakers—take advantage of them.

Sit right. Your position relative to your speakers will affect how you hear a stereo mix. When refining your track panning, sit directly between your speakers. Test your mix with headphones if you like, but don't rely exclusively on them—your listeners won't.

Panning hard. Think twice about panning tracks *completely* to the left or right. In the real world, sound reaches both ears even when a musician is at the far side of the stage. Of course, some songs have little to do with the real world, so feel free to bend this rule.

Panning for realism. If you're after a realistic stereo mix, visualize your ensemble and pan accordingly. In a jazz combo, the drums might be slightly to the left, bass in the middle, piano slightly to the right, and sax further right.

Panning a duet. If your song contains a vocal duet or two instruments that trade solos, pan one of the vocalists or instruments somewhat left (about 10 o'clock on the pan wheel) and the other somewhat right.

To simulate backup singers, record each part on a separate track and

pan the tracks near each other on one side of the stage—for example, one track at 9 o'clock and the other at 10 o'clock.

Panning similar instruments. If your song contains multiple instruments that have a similar frequency range—for example, a solo guitar and a rhythm guitar—pan each instrument to the opposite side of center. The 10 o'clock and 2 o'clock positions are good starting points.

Consider your effects. If you've applied an effect that enhances a track's stereo—for example, Chorus, Flanger, or Tremolo—think twice about panning that track heavily to one channel. You'll lose many of the benefits of the effect.

Panning percussion. If you've built up a drum kit by recording different drums and cymbals on different tracks, pan the tracks to increase realism. Put the snare and kick drum dead center. Pan the hi-hat slightly right, and the ride and crash cymbals slightly left. If you're using tom-toms, pan them according to their pitch: high-pitched toms slightly right, low-pitched toms slightly left. This layout mirrors the typical layout of a drum kit: the hi-hat is on the drummer's left and the floor tom is on his or her right.

Creating the Final Mix

In a recording studio, once each track has been recorded and refined, the final mix takes place. Everyone settles into the control room and takes a seat between monitor speakers as a golden-eared recording engineer adjusts the levels and left-right panning of each track.

Then they make decisions about the entire song. If it is to fade out, at what point should the fade take place, and how long should the fade be? Which effects should be applied to the entire mix to add punch and clarity?

The producer and everyone involved with the song listens, tweaks, and listens again. When the song is mixed to their satisfaction, it's released.

In GarageBand, these jobs are yours. But GarageBand helps. It contains dozens of mastering presets aimed at most every musical genre. Use a preset as is, and you've applied a golden-eared engineer's knowledge to your work. Or customize it to suit your ears.

When that's done, you can release your tune by exporting it in a variety of formats. With the Share menu, you can burn your project to a CD. You can also export the project, post it on your iWeb site, add it to your iTunes library, and more.

Have fun at the release party.

Echo Presets

Reverb Presets

Working with the Master Track

GarageBand's *master track* is a special kind of track that doesn't hold notes or regions, but instead controls certain aspects of your entire mix. Specifically, you can transpose the entire song (page 308) and you can apply effects to the master track and create a volume curve to have your song fade in or fade out.

To show the master track, choose Show Master Track from the Track menu (⌘-B).

Applying mastering presets. GarageBand includes dozens of final-mastering presets for common musical genres. To use them, display the Track Info pane, click the Master Track tab, then click the Browse tab. You can customize the presets and create your own final-mix presets using the techniques I've described on previous pages.

Creating a fade. To fade a song, choose Track > Fade Out. GarageBand adds a multi-point volume curve to the master track. **Tip:** To create a musically appealing fade, edit the volume curve so that the fade *ends* at the very beginning of a verse or measure. Don't have a fade end in the middle of a measure—it feels abrupt.

Customizing reverb and echo. As described on page 329, GarageBand provides reverb and echo on both a master level and a track level. To adjust the echo and reverb parameters that GarageBand applies to an entire song, use the master track's Track Info pane.

GarageBand's dozens of reverb and echo settings (shown at left) are worth exploring. The reverb presets are spectacular—everything from a living room to a large cathedral, with some offbeat stops in between. Explore them to add just the right sonic ambience to your track. And if you're into dance and electronic music, you can while away a weekend trying out and customizing GarageBand's echo presets.

Exporting Your Project

Optimizing loudness. Before exporting your project, adjust GarageBand's master volume slider to get loud (but not distorted) playback levels. Play back the loudest parts of your project, and make sure the master volume slider's clipping indicators don't light. Check the levels of individual tracks while you're at it (page 330).

To have GarageBand optimize loudness levels of the exported project, choose GarageBand > Preferences, click Advanced, then check the Auto Normalize box. GarageBand will export the project at an optimum level (a process, incidentally, that's identical to the Normalize Clip Volume option in iMovie's Audio Adjustments window).

Exporting techniques. When you export a project, GarageBand mixes your tracks down to two stereo channels. What happens next depends on your destination.

To CD. To burn an audio CD of a song, choose Share > Burn Song to CD, then insert a blank CD.

Tip: Normally, GarageBand burns a project as one CD track. To define multiple tracks, choose Track > Show Podcast Track and add a chapter marker at each spot where you'd like a new track to begin. For details on chapter markers, see page 351.

To disk. Choose Share > Export Song to Disk to export a project in any of a few audio formats (see below).

To iTunes. Export a project to iTunes, and you can add it to playlists and burn CDs—and sync it to your iPod, iPhone, or Apple TV. Choose Share > Send Song to iTunes. Edit the song information if you like (see "Customizing Tags," at right).

Format options. To export an uncompressed AIFF file, uncheck the Compress box. For a smaller file size with great audio quality, choose the AAC Encoder and Higher Quality options.

Notes and Tips

Customizing tags. To customize how your song is categorized in iTunes—artist name, album name, and so on—use the My Info portion of GarageBand's Preferences dialog box.

Exporting an excerpt. At times, you may want to export only part of a song. Maybe you want to email it to a collaborator or mix it down in order to bring it back into GarageBand (see page 345). To export a portion of a song, turn on cycling and then resize the yellow cycling region in the beat ruler to indicate the portion you want to export.

Exporting a Ringtone

Why buy ringtones when you can make your own? Record your kid saying, "Hey, your phone's ringing." Use a loop or one of the podcast jingles (page 346). Sing or play an instrument. Or search the Internet for a free sound snippet from your favorite TV show, then drag it into GarageBand (page 323). Use any sound you like. A ringtone can be up to 40 seconds long.

To give you a head start in creating ringtones, GarageBand provides ringtone project templates. Choose File > New, select the iPhone Ringtone item in the New Project dialog box, then choose a template.

Before exporting your project as a ringtone, turn cycling on, and resize the yellow cycle region to cover the part of the project that you want to be the ringtone. Then, choose Share > Send Ringtone to iTunes. GarageBand mixes down the project, compresses its audio, and shuttles it to iTunes, where it appears in your Ringtones list—ready to sync to your iPhone.

GarageBand Tips

A Closer Look at Visual EQ

GarageBand's Visual EQ is a powerful four-band equalizer for optimizing the bass, mid-range, and treble portions of a track or your entire project. With Visual EQ, you can add punch to bass parts, add brightness and clarity to vocals, reduce sibilant "S" sounds, and much more.

Visual EQ lives in the Effects area of the Track Info window. Like other effects, it sports a pop-up menu containing a large selection of presets aimed at specific sonic enhancements. And as with other effects, you can customize the presets and create your own.

To do that, click the icon for the Visual EQ effect. The Visual EQ window appears.

Choose a preset from the pop-up menu, and notice how the window changes: the graph depicts how certain frequency ranges will be boosted or attenuated.

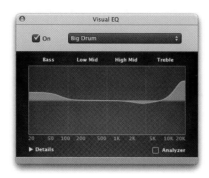

Here's the fun part: drag across the graph, and you can adjust the EQ curve. Drag up and down to increase or attenuate a certain frequency range, and left or right to define which frequency range you want to change.

Here's the even-more-fun part: you can make these adjustments while your song plays back. Try it.

If your heart can take even more joy, click the Analyzer checkbox during playback. Visual EQ displays a real-time graph that depicts the frequency curve. Besides being cool, the curve can help you determine which frequency ranges may need boosting or attenuating. **Tip:** The analyzer uses a lot of processor power, so turn it off when you aren't using it.

To make precise adjustments, click the Details triangle. You can then drag up or

down on the frequency and decibel values to change them, or double-click them and type exact values.

As with many effects, you can apply Visual EQ to individual tracks, to the master track, or to combinations of both.

Changing Effects Order

Speaking of effects, GarageBand lets you rearrange the order in which some effects are applied to a track. By changing the order of the *effects chain* or *signal chain,* as engineers call it, you can obtain different sounds. For example, if you place the Distortion effect *after* the Track Echo or Chorus effect, you get a very different sound than if you place Distortion before those effects. Give it a try and you'll immediately hear what I mean.

GarageBand's effects chain goes from top to bottom in the Track Info window: the effect at the very bottom is applied last, and thus affects every effect that precedes it. To change the order of the effects chain, drag effects up or down in the Track Info window.

The Web contains some useful articles on effects chains. I've linked to some on www.macilife.com/garageband.

Compacting a Project

If you have a project containing real instrument recordings you've made, you can reduce the disk storage requirements of the project by compacting it. You'll sacrifice some sound quality, but the resulting project file will be smaller—helpful if you're collaborating with someone and emailing project files around.

Choose File > Save As, and in the Save dialog box, check the Compact Project box. Choose an audio quality option from the pop-up menu.

What Chord?

When a software instrument track is selected, you can have GarageBand show you what chord you're playing on a music keyboard. In the LCD, choose Chord from the pop-up menu, or choose Control > Show Chord in LCD. Now play a chord, and GarageBand tells you what it is.

If you like the chord display, check out Wonder Warp Software's SimpleChord, an inexpensive and incredibly powerful chord utility.

Playing GarageBand's Keyboards

GarageBand provides two on-screen keyboards that let you audition (and even record) software instruments without having to reach for (or even have) a music keyboard.

Keyboard window. To view this simulated piano keyboard, choose Window > Keyboard (⌘-K).

The current track's instrument appears here.

Musical Typing window. Play notes by pressing keys on your Mac's keyboard. Choose Window > Musical Typing (Shift-⌘-K).

Note: When the Musical Typing window is visible, some of GarageBand's keyboard short-cuts—such as pressing Home to move to the beginning of the song—aren't available.

Play chords by pressing more than one key at once.

Add pitch bend, modulation, or sustain by pressing the number keys or Tab key.

Change the octave range by pressing Z or X or by clicking the little keyboard at the top of the window.

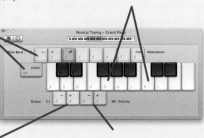

C3 is middle C on a piano.

To display a different range of notes, click the little keyboard.

Scroll and resize the Keyboard window.

The keyboard is velocity sensitive: the closer you click to the bottom edge of a key, the louder the note.

Change velocity by pressing C or V.

Arranging Tips

More Ways to Work with Regions

I've already mentioned the most common tasks you're likely to perform with regions: looping them, moving and copying them, splitting them, transposing them, and editing them.

There's more. Here are a few additional ways you might work with regions.

Resizing a region. To extend a region—make it longer—point to its lower-right corner and drag to the right.

Why extend a region? Say you recorded a riff that you want to loop. If your recorded region doesn't end at the proper measure boundary, the region won't loop properly. By extending the region, you can have it loop.

Another reason to extend a region is to be able to draw in additional notes or controller data using the track editor. Yet another is to add some silence before a region's content repeats.

To make the region shorter, drag its lower-right corner to the left. You might shorten a region in order to "crop out" some unwanted notes—possibly as a prelude to rerecording them. When you shorten a region, you don't delete the notes in the hidden portion of the region. To restore the notes, lengthen the region.

You can also resize a region from its beginning by dragging its lower *left* corner. This enables you to add silence to the beginning of a region (drag to the left) or to crop out audio from the beginning of a real instrument recording (drag to the right).

Joining regions. You've transposed a set of loops using the Split technique from page 309, and now you want to transpose the entire verse to a different key. Select all the loops and choose Join from the Edit menu (⌘-J). GarageBand turns all the regions into one region that you can transpose.

When you join real instrument regions that you've recorded, GarageBand combines those regions into a single audio file.

Adding Variety

When you're working with loops, it's easy to create overly repetitious arrangements. Fortunately, it's also easy to add variety.

Vary loops. Many of the bass and drum loops that come with GarageBand and Apple's GarageBand Jam Packs have variations that sound similar but not identical. Rather than relying on just one loop for a bass or drum track, switch between some different but similar-sounding ones. To switch loops within the same family, click on the tiny arrows in the upper-left corner of a loop region, then choose another loop (see page 304).

Edit some loops. Make your own loop variations. Make a copy of a software instrument loop and edit it—delete a few notes or transpose others. For real instrument loops, select part of the loop, copy it, and then paste it elsewhere.

Another way to edit loops is to change the instrument played by a software instrument loop. Try assigning an electric piano or clavinet to a bass loop.

Record your own bass track. Use bass loops to sketch out an arrangement and choose instruments, then replace the loops with your own bass line.

Take breaks. Add a *drum break* now and then—silence your drums for the last beat or two of a measure or for an entire measure. You can split the region and then delete part of it. Or you can edit the region if it's a software instrument drum track. Or leave the region alone and create a volume curve that plunges the track's volume down all the way, then brings it back up.

Add fills. Don't want to edit a drum loop? Create a new track that uses a software instrument drum kit. Use this track to hold drum fills, such as an occasional cymbal crash or tom-tom fill. Want a kick drum to mark the beat during a drum break? Put it in this track.

Vary the percussion. Add one or more percussion tracks to some verses—shakers, tambourines, claves, congas, bongos.

Add a pad. A *pad* is a note, a series of notes, or a chord that forms a sonic background for a song. It's often a lush string section or an atmospheric synthesizer that plays the root note or a fifth (for example, G in a song written in C).

One way to add variety to an arrangement is to have a pad play throughout one verse. Stop the pad at the start of the next verse, or add another track with a pad that uses a different instrument.

Add Tempo Changes

A song doesn't have to have the same tempo throughout. Add a *ritard* (a gradual slowing of the tempo) to the end of a song, or kick up the beat during a solo.

To add tempo changes, use the master track. Choose Tracks > Show Master Track. In the master track header, choose Master Tempo from the pop-up menu, then add control points and drag them up (to increase the tempo) or down (to decrease it). As you drag a control point, GarageBand displays its tempo, in beats per minute.

GarageBand applies tempo changes gradually. For a sudden tempo change,

add two control points and position one directly above or below the other.

For more details on working with control points, see page 331.

Automate Effects

Another way to add variety is to change how an instrument's effects sound over time. For example, you might want a synthesizer solo to start out mellow, then get more gnarly as the solo builds in intensity. One way to do this is to add the Distortion effect to the track, then automate it.

To add automation to a track, click the triangle in its header (■), or select the header and press the A key. From the automation pop-up menu, choose Add Automation. A dialog box lists the types

of items that you can automate, given the instrument and effects in use. Click the triangle in the dialog box to show automation options, then check the one you want to automate.

Next, choose those options from the track automation pop-up menu, and add control points.

You can also automate the amps and stomp boxes in guitar tracks (page 318).

Saving a Preview

You can save an audio "preview" along with a project. A preview is simply a stereo mix of the song, stashed inside the project file.

Saving a project with a preview makes possible a couple of tricks. For one thing, you can access the project using the media browsers in the other iLife programs—use a song in

an iPhoto slide show or in an iMovie project, for example.

Another benefit to saving a preview along with the project is that you can import one song into another, as described on page 345. Saving a preview also lets you preview the song in the Finder's Quick Look feature and in Time Machine.

To have GarageBand always create a preview when you save a project, choose GarageBand > Preferences, click General, and check the Audio Preview box.

This feature greatly increases the time required to save a project, since GarageBand must create a stereo mix of your song.

For this reason, you might want to leave this feature turned off as you're working on a song— a time when you are (or should be) using the Save command all the time. Then, when you've finished the tune, turn on the preview feature and save the project again.

Expanding Your Loop Library

For a GarageBand musician, loops are like groupies: you can't have too many. A large loop library is a source of creative inspiration. A few minutes of clicking in the loop browser is often all it takes to get the song-writing juices flowing.

There's no shortage of loop collections for GarageBand. Apple offers several great collections of its own: the GarageBand Jam Pack series includes not only thousands of loops, but some ear-stunning software instruments and effects, too (see the opposite page).

Many other companies have also created loop packages for GarageBand; you can sample many of them through GarageBand community sites, such as iCompositions (www.icompositions.com).

GarageBand can also work directly with loops in the ACID format. (ACID is a pioneering loop-based music program that debuted on Windows computers back in 1998.) There are more ACID loops available than you can fit on your hard drive.

GarageBand also lets you create your own loops. Record a riff or edit an existing loop, then—with a few mouse clicks—turn it into a new loop. Try it—create a Magic GarageBand project and turn your favorite regions into loops that you can use in your own songs.

Creating Your Own Apple Loops

You can turn any region into a loop with a few mouse clicks.

Step 1. If necessary, resize or split a region to make it the proper length of your custom loop.

Step 2. Drag the region to the loop browser or select it and choose Add to Loop Library from the Edit menu.

Step 3. Specify information about the loop, then click Create.

For rhythmic regions, choose Loop; this enables GarageBand to shift the loop's tempo to match the song in which it's used. If the region won't require tempo shifting—maybe it's a recording of a single dog bark—choose One-shot.

Type a name for the loop. Here, I'm adding one of the great drum loops from a Magic GarageBand slow blues.

Assign as much information to the new loop as you like. The more information you specify, the easier it will be to locate the loop in future searches.

Narrowing Down Your Choices

If you've installed multiple Jam Packs and other loop collections, there may be times when you want to browse for loops from one specific collection.

To focus on a specific loop collection in the loop browser, point to the word Loops (), hold down the mouse button, and then choose a collection.

To switch back to browsing your entire loop library, choose Show All. To view GarageBand's original, factory-installed loops, choose GarageBand.

As I've described previously, GarageBand provides a similar feature when you're assigning an instrument to a track.

Importing ACID Loops

To add ACID loops to your loop library, simply drag a folder containing the loops into the loop browser. The loops remain in ACID format, but GarageBand indexes them in a way that lets you search using the loop browser's buttons and search box.

Jam Packs: More than Just Loops

Here's an overview of each Jam Pack; you can learn more at www.apple.com/garageband.

Remix Tools. If the turntable on the box doesn't give it away, the sounds will: this Jam Pack is aimed at dance, hip-hop, and electronica composers. Its loops lean toward drum beats and bass lines, synthesizer patterns, and special effects (including, of course, vinyl scratches). Several vintage drum machine software instruments and a sizzling assortment of synthesizers round out the collection.

Rhythm Section. Let the beating begin: this two-DVD set contains roughly 1,000 drum loops in a variety of styles, as well as another 1,000 bass lines and

guitar and keyboard loops. Software instruments include drum sets ranging from jazzy brushes to steel drums, as well as basses and guitars of all kinds—from acoustic to electric, and from Dobro to banjo.

Symphony Orchestra. iPhoto and iMovie have the Ken Burns effect; Symphony Orchestra gives you the John Williams effect. It's a jaw-dropping collection of symphonic orchestra loops and software instruments—the most ambitious Jam Pack of them all.

Its beautifully recorded symphonic loops are an aural feast, but what really sets this Jam Pack apart are its software instruments. By moving the

modulation and pitch-bend wheels of your music keyboard—or by creating controller data in the track editor—you can vary the way an instrument plays to obtain amazing realism. To create crescendos and decrescendos of a sustained note or chord, move the pitch bend wheel. To obtain different articulations, such as staccato or legato, adjust the modulation wheel. And don't miss the accompanying PDF documentation, which includes interesting backgrounders on orchestral history and arranging.

World Music. Go global: this Jam Pack includes a collection of ethnic percussion, wind, and string instruments—from tabla drums to bagpipes to Native

American flutes, Peruvian panpipes, Persian santoors, Spanish Flamenco guitars, and much more. Completing your travels are over 3,000 loops recorded by pros from around the planet.

Voices. Sing it: the Voices Jam Pack adds 1,500 vocal loops, mostly in the R&B, blues, and hip-hop genres. Also included are a variety of vocal software instruments: choral ensembles, choirs, shouts, and more.

Apple Loop Tips

Getting the Loops You're Due

It pains me to say it, but not everyone who uses iLife uses GarageBand. iPhoto and iMovie are by far the most popular iLife programs, and in that order.

Because a lot of people never even explore GarageBand's majesty, Apple doesn't install every single loop and instrument that it has created for the base version of GarageBand. Why use up someone's hard drive space for loops that may never get a chance to loop?

Ah, but you—you're different. You realize how amazing GarageBand is, and you want everything that Apple has created for you. That means installing those extra goodies. It's easy.

When you're roaming the loop browser and you see a loop with a right-pointing arrow next to it, click that arrow.

GarageBand displays a message telling you that the loop you selected isn't installed.

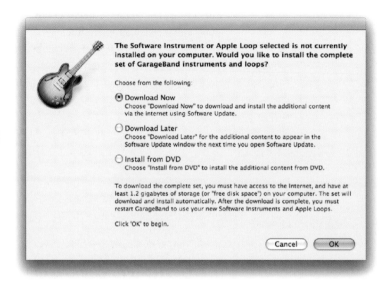

You *can* download the additional content via the Internet and Mac OS X's Software Update tool. You can also empty a swimming pool with a saucepan. But if you have the iLife '09 installation DVD, use it instead; it's a lot faster.

Be sure you have plenty of free hard disk space—the new stuff will use about 1.2GB. Click the Install from DVD option, have your iLife '09 DVD at the ready, then click OK.

Now your copy of GarageBand will be firing on all cylinders.

Customizing the Loop Browser

You can customize the loop browser buttons. To reorganize buttons, drag them around.

To change a button's keyword, Control-click on the button and choose a keyword from the pop-up menu. To restore the original buttons, use the Preferences command.

How Apple Loops Work—and How to Make Them Work Harder

If you've played with GarageBand, you've experienced the program's ability to adjust the pitch and tempo of loops to fit your song. Here's how that works.

Apple Loops contain more than just sound. They also contain *tags*—tidbits of data—that describe the sound, starting with the key and the tempo in which the loop was originally recorded. The tags also contain information about the transients in the recording. A *transient* is a spike in volume—such as occurs when a drumstick slaps a drumhead. Transients denote where beats occur, and GarageBand uses this information when changing the playback tempo of an Apple Loop.

When GarageBand transposes an Apple Loop to a different key, it's performing a process called *pitch shifting*. When GarageBand changes a loop's tempo, it's *time stretching*.

Apple Loops also contain descriptive tags, such as Guitar and Jazz. These tags are what you use to sift through loops by clicking on the buttons in the loop browser.

The green loop difference. Finally, it's important to know that software instrument loops (the green ones) contain more than just "piano roll" note data. They also contain audio, just as real instrument loops do. This lets you use them in real instrument tracks—and

thus lighten the load on your Mac; see pages 344.

To see this for yourself, drag a green loop into a real instrument track—instead of the usual piano-roll notation within a green region, you'll see a waveform display within a blue region.

Two in one. How does this work? A software instrument loop is really two loops in one. It contains not only the MIDI note data that can be used by a software instrument track, but also a rendered version of the loop—an actual audio recording, complete with effects.

Here's another way to see this for yourself. Use the Finder's Find command to locate a software instrument loop, such as Southern Rock Guitar 01. You'll notice that the loop's file name ends in .AIF—it's an audio file in AIFF format. You can open and play this file using QuickTime Player or iTunes. You can even drag the file into iMovie or iDVD. But embedded within the AIFF file is MIDI note data that GarageBand can use.

The fact that software instrument loops also contain audio data has an important ramification: As I mention on page 344, if you plan to use a software instrument loop as is, you can lighten the load on your Mac's processor by using the loop in a real instrument track.

If you haven't yet created the track for the loop, take advantage of the following shortcut: press the Option key while dragging a green loop into the timeline, and GarageBand creates a real instrument track for it.

Here's another reason to take advantage of the dual personality of software instrument loops: guitar tracks. You can apply the great amp and stomp box simulations provided by guitar tracks to any software instrument loop. Just add the loop to a guitar track.

Tip: If you frequently use software instrument loops without changing them, you can use the Loops portion of the Preferences dialog box to have GarageBand always create real instrument tracks when you drag green loops into the timeline.

The downsides. There are some downsides to using a green loop in a real instrument track. You can't edit individual notes or change instrument or effect assignments, since all these things are part of the audio recording. Also, you can't transpose an audio region over as large a range. But for those times when you want to use a green loop as is, adding it to a real instrument track is a great way to improve GarageBand's performance.

Creating Your Own Instruments

In GarageBand, a software instrument is based on a foundation called a *generator*, and every generator has settings that you can tweak. You can create your own software instrument by picking a generator and then adjusting its settings.

For example, say you want to create an instrument that has a funky electronic synthesizer sound. Here's one way you might approach the task.

Step 1. Create a new software instrument track, and pick an instrument—any instrument.

Step 2. Double-click the track's header, click the Edit tab, and examine the Sound Generator pop-up menu.

Some generators are based on short recorded *samples* of actual instruments, such as piano and guitar. Other generators create their sound "from scratch," based on sound synthesis techniques.

Step 3. Choose a generator.

Step 4. Examine the generator's presets. Try them out—you might find one you like.

Step 5. Click the icon to the left of the generator's pop-up menu. This displays the settings that apply to the generator you chose.

Many generators let you customize what's often called the *ADSR envelope*. You can dramatically change a sound's percussive qualities by changing its envelope.

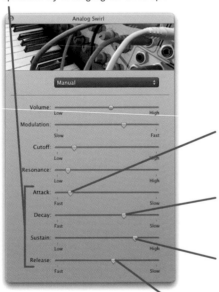

Tip: To get a feel for the kinds of settings each generator provides, drag the settings window so that you can see it and the Track Info pane at the same time. Then paw through the generators and their presets, and watch the settings window change.

Step 6. Play with the settings until you arrive at a sound you like. While you're at it, adjust effects as desired—they're stored along with the generator settings.

Step 7. Click the Save Instrument button in the Track Info pane and type a name for the new instrument. GarageBand saves the instrument settings on your hard drive (see the sidebar on the opposite page).

How quickly should the note sound when a key is pressed? A piano has a fast, or *sharp*, attack (as the hammers hit the strings). A flute has a slower attack.

How quickly should the sound volume fade or drop to the sustain level?

Should the sound sustain when a note is pressed and held down? A piano note decays over time; an organ note doesn't.

What happens when the key is released? With a fast release, the sound ends immediately. With a slower release, the sound fades gradually after the key is released.

Adding Audio Unit Instruments

You can expand GarageBand's sound-generating and effects capabilities with software plug-ins called *Audio Units.* Some absolutely stunning software instruments are available in Audio Unit format. My favorite is Native Instruments' B4, which mimics the legendary Hammond B3 organ with frightening realism. And yes, it runs within GarageBand.

I'm also a big fan of Pluggo from Cycling '74 (www.cycling74.com).

Pluggo is a collection of more than 100 synthesizers and effects, and it lets you run software instruments that use other plug-in formats, such as the popular VST format.

High-end software instruments like B4 cost several times what iLife '09 costs. If you don't want to spend that much, there are some great-sounding Audio Unit instruments and effects that don't cost a dime. To explore what's available, go to www.icompositions.com or do a Google search for *audio units*. Don't expect to get any work done for a while.

Where they live. Commercial Audio Unit plug-ins usually include an installer program that puts things where they belong, but some free Audio Units don't have these installers. So for the record, Audio Units are stored in Library > Audio > Plug-Ins > Components. They can also reside in your home directory, in the same path.

Adding Effects

There's also a large selection of Audio Unit effects, and the aforementioned sites are great places to find them.

You might also explore ChannelStrip from Metric Halo (www.mhlabs.com). This legendary set of mastering effects has long been popular among recording professionals, and now it's available for GarageBand.

And while most people think of Apple's Jam Packs as being primarily a source of loops and software instruments, they're also a source of effects.

If you have a Jam Pack and would like to see what additional effects it provides, double-click any track's header, then choose the Jam Pack's name from the pop-up menu at the top of the Track Info pane. Next, choose an effect and explore its pop-up menu of presets.

How GarageBand Stores Instruments

GarageBand stores a software instrument as a file with a name that ends with .cst—for example, if you named your instrument *Wacko*, its file will be Wacko.cst. GarageBand stores its instrument files deep inside your hard drive's Library folder.

Tip: To put your custom instrument in a different category in GarageBand's Track Info pane, move its file into the appropriate category folder. For example, to move an instrument from the Synth Leads category to the Bass category, move its file from the Synth Leads folder to the Bass folder.

- Bass
- Choir
- Drum Kits
- Guitars
- Horns
- Mallets
- Organs
- Pianos and Keyboards
- Strings
- Synth Basics
- Synth Leads
- Synth Pads
- Woodwinds

Optimizing GarageBand's Performance

With apologies to the great James Brown, GarageBand is the hardest-working program in show business. It synthesizes sound, plays back audio tracks, generates effects—and never skips a beat.

Of course, this assumes that your Mac is fast enough. On slower Macs—for example, older G4 iMacs or iBooks—GarageBand can stumble and display an error message if it isn't able to perform its duties. GarageBand works hard to avoid stopping the music. For instance, if your Mac starts working up a sweat during playback, GarageBand defers scrolling the screen and updating its time readout.

To let you know how hard it's working, GarageBand changes the color of its playhead: from white (don't worry, be happy) to yellow (I will survive) to orange (the thrill is gone) to red (the sound of silence). If you see the red playhead, anticipate an error message—GarageBand is on the verge of maxing out your Mac.

But as I tell my guitar player friends, don't fret. You can do a lot to bring the music back—besides buying a faster Mac.

Performance Tips

Lock tracks. If your song has numerous software instrument tracks or real instrument tracks that use a lot of effects, locking some tracks should be your first step. For details, see the opposite page.

Add memory. A memory upgrade will improve your Mac's overall performance.

Quit other programs. Let your Mac devote all its attention to GarageBand.

Quit and relaunch. Clear GarageBand's head: quit the program and then launch it again.

Use the audio in software instrument loops. If you plan to use a software instrument loop as is (that is, you aren't going to edit the loop or change its instrument or effects assignments), you can lighten the load on your Mac by dragging the loop into a real instrument track. For more details, see page 341.

Tweak preferences. Choose GarageBand's Preferences command and click the Advanced button. There you can examine and change settings that GarageBand normally makes automatically. Try reducing the number of voices per instrument. Note that this restricts the number of simultaneous notes you can play.

Simplify your song. Mute some tracks and turn off some effects. The Amp Simulation effects are particularly power hungry. You *can* greatly lighten GarageBand's burden by unchecking Reverb and Echo in the Master Track's Track Info pane, but doing so will eliminate the ability to use these effects in your song. Still, you might find this a worthwhile price to pay for extra tracks. You can always transfer your song to a faster Mac to get the polish that good reverb provides.

Use an external drive. A high-performance external FireWire hard drive may be able to keep up with multiple real instrument tracks better than your Mac's built-in drive, especially if you have a laptop Mac or Mac mini.

Optimize laptop performance. If you're using a laptop Mac, open the Energy Saver system preference and choose Highest Performance from the Optimize Energy Settings pop-up menu.

Turn off FileVault. Mac OS X's FileVault feature can dramatically slow the reading of data from the Home directory of your hard drive. Turn off FileVault using the Security system preference, or store your songs outside your Home directory.

Bouncing to Disk

If the measures I've described here don't do it for you, there's still hope: an update of a technique that us old fogies—people who grew up with analog multitrack recording—know about all too well.

Back in the analog multitrack days, when you approached the limit of your four-track cassette deck, you would mix down the three tracks you had already recorded and put them on the fourth track. After the mix-down, you could erase and re-use the original three tracks.

This technique was often called *bouncing*, and it's alive and well in GarageBand. Say you've laid down a sweet rhythm section groove—some drums, some bass, and maybe a keyboard or synthesizer pad.

You want to play a synth solo over this, but your PowerBook doesn't have the power.

Solution: save your project with an iLife preview (page 337), then add the project to a new GarageBand project.

Fine-tune your mix. Adjust every setting—panning, volume, effects, everything—until your mix sounds exactly as you want it.

Save with preview. Use the Preferences command to activate the save-with-preview feature, as described on page 336. Then, save the project. GarageBand creates a stereo mixdown of your tune and saves it along with the project.

Start over. Start a new GarageBand project. Be sure to set the key signature and tempo to match your song's settings. Locate your song in the GarageBand media browser, then drag it into the new project.

Add tracks and have fun. Because your rhythm groove is now one audio track—not a whole bunch of different, system-taxing tracks—your Mac can devote its energy to the new tracks.

Making changes. If you decide to change your rhythm groove, just open up your original project, make your changes, and save again. Because GarageBand maintains a link between the two projects, your changes will be incorporated in the second project when you reopen it.

The Key to Locking Tracks

If your Mac is choking during playback, try locking one or more tracks. To lock a track, click the padlock button in the track's header. Then, play the song from the beginning. GarageBand renders the locked track to disk: it creates an audio file containing the track's audio.

When the song begins playing, GarageBand plays back that audio file instead of making your Mac's processor do the heavy lifting involved in generating sounds and effects in real time.

Locking candidates. The best candidates for locking are software instrument tracks (particularly ones that use the Symphony Orchestra Jam Pack) and real instrument tracks containing complex effects, such as the guitar amp simulators.

Harder on the hard drive. Alas, locking tracks makes your hard drive work harder. If you have a laptop Mac or a Mac mini—computers that have slower hard drives than other Macs—you may find that locking a lot of

tracks causes playback problems. When you lock tracks, your project also uses more disk space.

Extracting a locked track. You can use the Finder to extract the audio from a locked track. Control-click on your project's icon and choose Show Package Contents from the shortcut menu. In the window that appears, open the Freeze Files folder: it will contain the audio files that GarageBand has rendered. You can open these files

in other programs (including iTunes), but you can't import them into GarageBand.

To avoid corrupting a project, don't rename or delete any files in the project's Freeze Files folder.

Unlocking a track. You can't edit a locked track or change its instrument or effects settings. (You can make volume and panning adjustments, however.) To change a locked track, unlock it by clicking the padlock button again.

Creating a Podcast at a Glance

You can use iTunes and your iPod to listen to podcasts of all kinds. With GarageBand, you can go from listener to producer.

GarageBand turns your Mac into a radio studio—with broadcast engineer. Connect a microphone to your Mac or use the built-in mike that most Macs provide. GarageBand contains audio filters that optimize the sound produced by a built-in Mac mike.

Record your rants, vacation dispatches, family interviews—whatever you like. You can even record remote interviews with iChat users. Your audio is recorded into real-instrument tracks, so you can edit it using the same techniques described earlier.

Need theme music? Compose your own or use one of the many royalty-free music jingles included with iLife. Use the *ducking* feature to have GarageBand automatically lower and raise the music volume when you start and stop talking—just like the radio.

But don't stop there. Consider creating an *enhanced podcast*. Add chapter markers that enable listeners to conveniently jump around through your show. Add artwork that appears during playback in iTunes and on any iPod that can display photos. And add Web URLs that let iTunes users jump to specific Web pages as your show plays.

When you're finished, send your completed production to iWeb for publishing on the Internet. Here's how to become a podcaster.

Pick a Background

Use the loop browser to explore and choose from more than 100 jingles, including many sets that provide the same song in lengths of 7, 15, and 30 seconds. You can also choose from hundreds of sound effects and music

stingers—and even use the Musical Typing window to play them as you do your show (page 335).

Add Visuals

Use the media browser to add photos (page 350) or movies (page 354). Use the search box to quickly locate what you need.

Add Web Connections

Want your listeners to be able to jump to Web pages that relate to your subject? Add Web addresses (URLs) to your markers (page 351).

When you create a new podcast, GarageBand gives you a standard set of tracks for common elements. You can customize these tracks and add more.

Use the *podcast track* to view and edit marker regions— for example, to synchronize a piece of artwork with a specific section of your show (pages 350–351).

Control how a track's volume is affected by the ducking feature. Click the down-pointing arrow for a background music track (page 349). Customize the ducking effect if you like (page 352).

Specify episode information, which appears in iTunes and iWeb.

Drag an image here to add *episode artwork* to your podcast (opposite page and page 351).

Create, edit, and manage the markers in your enhanced podcast (page 351).

Preview the appearance of your enhanced podcast as it plays back (page 349).

Switch between displaying the Media browser (opposite page) and Track Info pane, where you can refine your sound.

Podcast Production Techniques

Plan

There are as many types of podcasts as there are types of songs. But no matter what topic you cover, you have a common set of planning and production options to consider.

Script (or at least sketch). You don't have to script every word of your podcast, but at least sketch out the structure of your show. And because they're the critical bookends for your barking, consider scripting your introduction and conclusion.

How long? Around 20 to 30 minutes is a good balance between depth and reasonable download times, not to mention listener attention span.

How much? You can record one non-stop rant, but I'm unlikely to listen to it. Consider covering several topics, limiting each to five minutes or so.

What's the theme? Start your podcast with an introductory music jingle. Compose your own or use the ones that come with GarageBand. To explore them, display the loop browser, then click the ▣ button.

GarageBand's jingles come in several durations. Consider using a 30-second version for your intro and a seven-second version as a separator, called a *bumper*, between topic segments.

Tip: Don't waste time by letting your intro music play and play. Your listeners want to hear *you*, so let the music play for just a few seconds, then start your intro. Use GarageBand's automatic ducking feature to lower the music's volume when you start talking.

Who else? Will you have guests? A variety of voices makes for more interesting listening. You can record guests via phone or iChat (page 352) or, ideally, in person, with a second microphone.

Produce

Get started. As shown on the previous pages, when you click Podcast when creating a new GarageBand project, you get a set of tracks for male and female voices. You also get jingles and radio sounds, such as sound effects and *stingers*, which are short, sonic spices of the kind you hear on the radio before traffic and weather reports.

If you'll need additional tracks—perhaps to record a guest with a second microphone, or some music using a software instrument and your music keyboard—add the tracks using the techniques described earlier in this chapter.

Prepare for recording. Record in a quiet location and with the best microphone you can use. (For advice on obtaining good sound, see page 218.) If you're using multiple mikes or audio sources, assign inputs to each track (page 322). Adjust your recording levels (page 321).

Cue the band. When should you add music to your podcast? I recommend waiting until after you've recorded and refined the core content of your podcast. Save the music for the post-production phase. The way GarageBand lets you drag audio regions around makes it easy to time where you want the music to come in.

On the air. To begin recording, click the Record button or press the R key. Make a mistake? Pause for a second or two, then pick up at a point before your blunder. You can edit out the flub later using the techniques on page 323.

Polish

Optional: Adjust effects. The male and female tracks that GarageBand provides in a new podcast project are fine for most efforts. But you might want to open the Track Info pane and explore some of GarageBand's effects and audio-enhancement options. Double-click on the track header for the track you want to tweak, then click the Edit tab in the Track Info pane.

The Speech Enhancer effect can sweeten a voice in several ways. Explore the presets in the pop-up menu, then click the pencil button to view all your options. If you're using the mike built into your Mac, you can choose options that will optimize sound quality. You can also apply a noise-reduction filter.

To add punch to a spoken voice, apply the Compressor effect, but don't go overboard.

Add music and refine timing. Now's the time when I like to add theme and bumper jingles and refine the timing of my podcasts. To take advantage of GarageBand's volume-ducking feature, be sure the down-pointing arrow is active in the Jingles track (or other music tracks you may have added) and the up-pointing arrow is active in your primary voice track or tracks.

Optional: Enhance your podcast. If you're creating an enhanced podcast—one with artwork, chapter markers, URL markers, or any combination thereof— add those items now. See the following pages.

Publish

Preview and proofread. Before exporting the final podcast, play it all the way through. If you've added artwork, chapter, or URL markers, use the Podcast Preview window to verify that they appear when they should. Click any URL markers to ensure that they go to the proper Web address. (If the Podcast Preview window isn't visible, click its button in the track header for the Podcast track.)

Make sure there are no odd audio glitches caused by editing. Adjust volume levels as necessary to deliver a strong signal with no clipping. Adjust ducking settings for the best balance of voice and background (page 352).

Export your podcast. Use the Share menu to send your podcast to iWeb or iTunes, or save it to disk. Choose the MP3 or AAC formats, and choose an audio quality setting.

You can also burn your podcast to an audio CD. For details, see page 333.

Enhancing Your Podcast

With enhanced podcasts, your options go beyond sound to include photos, chapter markers, and URL markers. You can use just one of these enhancements in your podcasts, or you can use all three.

By adding images to the podcast track, you can add photography and artwork that appears in the iTunes window or on photo-capable iPods. Create a training podcast that illustrates the steps involved in performing a task. Or an art history podcast that shows famous works as you talk about them. Or a vacation travelogue that shows your stops.

With chapter markers, you can add convenient navigation to your podcast. When your podcast is played in iTunes, a chapter menu appears that allows listeners (and viewers) to jump to sections of interest. When playing your podcast on an iPod, your audience can navigate the chapters using their click wheels or touch screens.

With URL markers, you can add the immediacy of the Internet. Create links to pages that relate to your subject. The link appears in the iTunes window, and your podcast's audience can jump to the link's URL by clicking it.

The one downside to an enhanced podcast is that you must deliver it in the AAC audio format, which means that the podcast will play only in iTunes and on iPods and Apple TV. If you're planning to deliver your podcast in MP3 format to reach the broadest possible audience, keep your podcasts unenhanced.

Adding Artwork

Step 1. Display the media browser by clicking its button.

Step 2. In the media browser, click the Photos button, then locate the photo you want to add.

Step 3. Drag the photo to a location in the podcast track.

Step 4. To fine-tune the amount of time the artwork appears, drag the edges of its region left or right.

You can also drag the entire artwork region left and right, just as you can other GarageBand regions. **Tip:** To have regions snap toward each other as you drag, choose Control > Show Alignment Guides. This helps prevent you from accidentally replacing part of a region by dragging another region over it.

Notes and Tips

Editing art. To adjust an item's zooming and cropping, double-click the item's thumb-nail in the Artwork column. Use the Artwork Editor to zoom in and adjust which part of the art is visible, then click Set.

You can also replace an image by dragging a new image to the editor.

Art from elsewhere. You can also add an image to the podcast track by dragging it from the Finder. You can even add an image from a Web page by dragging it from the Safari browser.

More than just art. An artwork region can also represent a chapter marker and a URL marker. For example, maybe you'd like a chapter to begin when a particular image appears. In the podcast track, select the image. Next, in the podcast track editor, click in the Chapter Title box and type a name for the chapter. For more details, see the opposite page.

Adding Chapter Markers

Step 1. Position the GarageBand playhead at the point where you want the marker to appear, then click the Add Marker button in the podcast track editor.

Tip: You can click Add Markers to add markers as your podcast plays back.

Step 2. In the podcast track editor, select the marker's *Chapter Title* placeholder text in the Chapter Title column, then type a title.

In iTunes, a Chapters menu appears in the menu bar when the podcast plays.

Tip: As noted on the opposite page, you can use an artwork region as a chapter marker by simply typing a title in the region's Chapter Title box.

Adding URL Markers

As with chapter markers, you can assign a URL to a region that contains artwork; just skip to Step 2 below.

Step 1. Position the playhead at the point where you want the marker, then click the Add Marker button in the podcast track editor.

Step 2. In the podcast track editor, type the URL title and address.

Type the address of the Web page here. You can also copy an address from the Safari location bar and paste it here.

The URL title is displayed in the artwork area of the iTunes window.

Adding Episode Artwork

Episode artwork is a single image that appears in iTunes while your podcast is playing. iWeb also uses episode artwork when you add a podcast to a Web page (page 381). You might use episode artwork to display your company logo, a favorite photo from your vacation podcast, or a graphic created in Photoshop or Photoshop Elements that contains a few words about the podcast's topic.

If your podcast also contains artwork regions as described on the opposite page, the regions replace the episode artwork as the podcast plays back. When those artwork regions end, the episode artwork reappears.

To add episode artwork, drag an image from the media browser (or elsewhere) to the Episode Artwork well at the left edge of the podcast track editor. To tweak the cropping of the artwork, double-click it in the Episode Artwork well, then use the Artwork Editor as described on the opposite page.

odcasting Tips

Adjusting Ducking

GarageBand's ducking feature makes it easy to create a podcast in which you talk over background music. Activate ducking, and GarageBand lowers the volume of the music when you talk, then brings it up again during pauses. There's no need to manually create volume automation curves that adjust the music's volume.

But the ducker may not always lower the volume as much as you'd like—and as any boxer will tell you, partial ducking just isn't enough.

If your voice is still getting a left hook from your background music, adjust the ducker. Display the Track Info pane, click the Master Track button, then click the Edit tab and choose one of the presets from the Ducker pop-up menu.

The presets let you choose how quickly music volume is lowered and restored, and to what degree. You can also create a custom preset by clicking the ducker's icon, next to the pop-up.

Stamp Your Podcast

Many podcasters like to begin each episode with a very brief announcement of the podcast's name and date: *This is The Digital Hub, Episode 3, for August 17, 2008.* This little "stamp" is handy for listeners who are using iPods. It lets them immediately verify that they're listening to the right episode—without having to take their eyes off the road.

Music Rights and Wrongs

Thinking of doing a music podcast? Note that you can't legally publish a podcast containing commercial recordings—at least not without paying for the rights to do so.

To learn the latest about the frequently changing world of digital music licensing, do some Google searches for *podcast music licensing* and *podcast music rights.*

Tune Into Magnatune. You might also investigate music sources that permit rebroadcasting and podcast use. A great stop is Magnatune (www.magnatune. com), which has refreshingly simple policies for free for non-commercial use, and very cheap for commercial use.

And you have to love a record label whose corporate slogan is "We are not evil."

Recording iChat Interviews

You can use Apple's iChat conferencing software to record audio interviews with distant guests. GarageBand stores each participant's voice in its own track. And if you're conducting a video conference, GarageBand grabs a still shot of each participant when he or she begins speaking and adds that image to the podcast track.

To record iChat interviews, you must initiate the audio or video conference—that is, *you* must be the one to invite the other guests to the conference. Do that, and then chat with your guests for a minute or two to make sure that your Internet connection, and the Internet as a whole, are behaving themselves. I've had best-laid interview plans shattered by Internet difficulties that were out of my control. Use this testing time to remind your guests that you'll be recording them.

When you're ready to begin recording, click GarageBand's Record button or press the R key. GarageBand asks if you want to record the chat.

Click Yes, and GarageBand begins recording. Now grill your guests and grill them hard.

In my experience, you need a fairly fast Mac to get good results when recording iChat conferences. My old 1.67GHz PowerBook G4 sometimes stumbles, but a G5 or Intel Duo system does a good job. And needless to say, a fast Internet connection is a must, particularly for multi-guest interviews.

Recording Using iChat

If you and your chat victim—er, participant—are both using Mac OS X 10.5 (Leopard) or a later version, you can use iChat to record both the audio and video of a chat. When you're finished, you have a movie that you can drag into GarageBand.

After starting the chat, choose Video > Record Chat in iChat. iChat notifies the participant that he or he is about to be recorded.

When you're done, iChat adds the movie to your iTunes library, stashing it in a playlist named iChat Chats. Locate the movie and drag it into GarageBand.

Tip: If you recorded a video chat but you want only the audio, simply choose Track > Show Podcast Track after you import the video. GarageBand discards the video but keeps the audio.

If you want to record within iChat but your chat participant isn't using Leopard, check out Ecamm Network's Conference Recorder, an iChat add-on that can record audio and video chats conducted with pre-Leopard iChat versions—and even with Windows audio-video chat programs.

Recording Phone Interviews

iChat interviews can be fun, but you might prefer to back away from the cutting edge and conduct your interviews the way many radio stations do: via telephone.

You have a few options for recording a telephone call. Radio Shack sells several phone-recording adaptors for under $30. Connect the adaptor to your phone and attach it to your Mac's microphone jack, and you're underway.

The problem with inexpensive recording devices, though, is that *your* voice also sounds like it's coming over the phone (which, from your Mac's standpoint, it is). What you want is for your voice to be recorded by that high-quality microphone that you were smart enough to buy. For this, you need a specialized piece of hardware called a *telephone hybrid.*

A telephone hybrid is a box that contains jacks for the telephone line and your microphone. Connect your mike and your phone to the hybrid, then connect the audio output of the hybrid to your Mac's microphone jack. Some hybrids also have volume knobs that let you adjust the mix between your mike and your guest's phone.

A good source for telephone hybrids is JK Audio (www.jkaudio.com). The company's least expensive device, the AutoHybrid, sells for under $200. A Google search for *telephone hybrid* will yield more sources.

The Skype angle. If you use the Skype software to make Internet phone calls, you can conduct interviews via Skype and record the results. You can use Rogue Amoeba Software's Audio Hijack Pro to record Skype calls, but many podcasters swear by Ecamm Network's Call Recorder, a simple and inexpensive utility designed specifically for the task.

Scoring Movies with GarageBand

iMovie's audio features are adequate for many projects, but your soundtrack options don't end there. You can bring video into GarageBand and apply GarageBand's audio and music-making features to the movie's soundtrack.

GarageBand's video features aren't for editing the picture; that's a job for iMovie. Rather, you bring a finished edit into GarageBand for additional sonic seasoning. Punch up the sound with GarageBand's effects. Record and edit narration with more precision than iMovie provides. Or compose your own music soundtracks by using loops and by recording your own performances. When you're finished, send the final movie to iTunes, iWeb, or iDVD.

You might also use GarageBand's video features to create a *video podcast*: a podcast that adds the dimension of motion. As with GarageBand's audio podcasting features, you can add chapter and URL markers to the video. When you're done, you can send your final product to iWeb or save it for manual uploading to a Web server.

You'll need a fast Mac with a fast hard drive for movie scoring. If you have playback problems, consult the advice on page 344 to optimize GarageBand's performance.

Refining an iMovie Soundtrack

Step 1. In iMovie, finish your edit, then share the movie to the media browser (Share > Media Browser; see page 240).

Step 2. In GarageBand, display the media browser, click the Movies button, then locate your movie and drag it into the tracks area of the GarageBand window.

iMovie imports the movie and displays it in the video track (opposite page).

Step 3. Enhance to your ears' content: add tracks, record narration, apply effects, or add chapter and URL markers for a video podcast.

Step 4. Use the commands in the Share menu to send your finished movie to iTunes, iWeb, or iDVD, or to export it as a QuickTime movie (opposite page).

Notes and Tips

Chapters for iDVD. iMovie lets you create chapter markers for a DVD, but you can also use GarageBand to do the job. In iMovie, share your project to the media browser, choosing the Large quality setting. Bring the movie into GarageBand as described above.

Next, select the movie track and click the track editor button. Use the track editor to add chapter markers. Give each chapter a title—iDVD will use it to label each chapter's button.

Finally, choose Share > Send Movie to iDVD. iDVD creates a new project and adds the movie to it, creating a Scene Selection menu for accessing the chapters.

Movies from elsewhere. In addition to using the media browser to add a movie to GarageBand, you can also simply drag a movie's icon from any location on your hard drive into the GarageBand window.

Working with Movies

When you've brought a movie into GarageBand, here's what you see—and what you can do.

Your movie's video frames appear in the video track. The more you zoom in on the timeline, the more sequential frames you see. When you want to position a region (for example, a sound effect) so that it begins when a specific frame appears, zoom in until you see that frame.

The video track editor works much like the podcast track editor: you can add chapter markers and URL markers.

Creating a video podcast? Use this area to type a description for the podcast.

Your movie's soundtrack appears as an imported audio region. You can add filters or effects to this track using the techniques described earlier in this chapter.

To view the movie, display the preview window: click its button in the movie track header.

Tips for Video

Enhancing narration. If you've recorded a voice-over or other narration in GarageBand (or, for that matter, in iMovie), consider applying GarageBand's audio effects to it. For example, use the Compressor effect to add punch to a narration. Use the Speech Enhancer filter to reduce noise and optimize male or female voices.

Exporting your final effort. When you've finished refining a movie's soundtrack, you can use the Share menu to send your final effort to iTunes, iWeb, or iDVD.

You can also export the project as a QuickTime movie. Choose Share > Export Movie to Disk, and choose a quality setting from the pop-up menu.

To customize export settings, choose the Expert option, then adjust the settings in the subsequent dialog box. Your options are identical to those described on page 241.

iWeb:
Your World on
the Web

iWeb at a Glance

With iWeb, you can put your world on the Web. You can create Web sites containing text, photos, movies, podcasts, and more. iWeb insulates you from Web publishing technicalities, such as markup languages and servers.

Start by choosing one of the site design *templates* that are built into iWeb. Many of those designs have counterparts in other iLife programs. For example, the Travel template in iWeb resembles the Travel theme in iPhoto and iDVD. Thus, you can create a Web site about your vacation and have it match your iPhoto books and calendars, and the DVD containing your video and travel slide shows—a consistent visual identity, as the marketers would say.

Each iWeb template provides several types of pages. As you create a site, you simply add new pages as needed to accommodate what you want to publish.

Decided on a design? Just add content. Replace the placeholder photos and text with your own. Use the page design as is, or use iWeb's formatting tools to customize it to your own liking. You can add maps and ads from Google, as well as MobileMe galleries, with a few clicks, too. If you've used Apple's Pages or Keynote software, you'll feel at home with iWeb's formatting features.

iWeb also simplifies creating blogs and podcasts. Creating a new blog or podcast entry is as easy as creating a new email message. iWeb also manages the chores of creating archive pages and RSS feeds.

When you're finished, one click publishes your site.

A Gallery of Web Pages

Each iWeb template provides eight page styles, each aimed at a specific type of content. Not shown here: the Blank style, which shares the template's background and color scheme, but lacks placeholder text and graphics.

Welcome

An introductory home page, ideal for welcoming visitors and stating the purpose of your site.

About Me

A good place to describe yourself, your business, your organization—whatever your site is about.

Photos

A photo album, with small photo thumbnails and a button for displaying photos as a slide show. You can also create a photos page from within iPhoto (page 372).

My Albums

An index page that acts as a gateway to photos and movie pages. Drag iPhoto albums and movies here to quickly publish them (pages 372–377).

Movie

A page designed to present a QuickTime movie (page 391).

Blog

Your blog's main page, with links to individual blog entries. You can also create a blog entry from within iPhoto (page 378). A similar page style holds podcasts.

The *sidebar* lists the sites you create and their pages. You can create multiple sites with iWeb, and even move pages between sites.

Change the theme of the current page.

As you create pages, iWeb creates a *navigation menu* that your site's visitors will use to get around. iWeb updates your navigation menu as you rearrange and expand your site.

Create your pages on the *webpage canvas*. Drag text and graphics around, add and remove text boxes and photos, type and format text, add shapes, and more.

Add photos from your iPhoto library or another source (page 372).

Open the Adjust panel (right) for image tweaking, such as in iPhoto (page 367).

Open the Inspector (right) for precise formatting, linking, and more.

Adventures in Paris

Two Weeks in the City of Lights
Paris! Food, museums, shopping, food, history, culture, and food.

We're heading to the City of Lights soon, and will be using this site to keep in touch with friends and family—with photos, movies, and more-or-less daily dispatches. So join us!

And did we mention that there's great food?

Open the Media browser (right) for accessing photos, movies, and music.

Add a new Web page (page 361).

Send the site to MobileMe (page 386).

Open the published version of the site in your Web browser.

Add text boxes (page 364) and shapes (page 368), and refine layouts (page 366).

Add a *hit counter* to count the visitors to your site, and an email link to allow visitors to contact you (page 390).

Creating a Web Site

What do you want to publish? A few iPhoto albums? The occasional movie? A podcast? Or a full Web site containing numerous pages as well as photo albums, a blog, and a podcast?

iWeb can handle any of these tasks. If you're planning an ambitious site, though, consider sketching out the site's structure on paper before you start. You might want to draw an organizational chart, with the home page at the top and other pages beneath it—much like the DVD menu diagram on page 266. This kind of advance planning can help you map out your site and organize your thoughts.

After you've planned your attack, perform it. Start by creating a new site and choosing a page template for its design. Then replace the placeholder content with your own text and graphics. Tweak the text formatting if you like, but be careful—the "wrong" kinds of formatting can cause iWeb to create large pages that load slowly (page 364).

As your site comes together, you'll add additional pages and create links to connect them. You might also create links to other sites on the World Wide Web. You'll add graphics and adjust their appearance, and maybe add a widget or two. And then you'll publish your site on Apple's MobileMe service or elsewhere.

I cover each of these phases, and more, in the pages that follow. Here's how to get started.

Creating a New Site

First Time Here?

The first time you start iWeb, it presents its list of templates and page styles.

Step 1. Choose the template that best matches what you have in mind for your site. Remember, you can customize your pages.

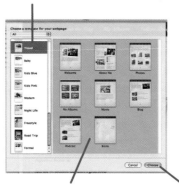

Step 2. Choose a page style. The Welcome and About Me styles are good starting points for general-purpose pages, while the remaining styles are tailored for specific tasks (page 358).

Step 3. Click Choose or press Return.

Repeat Customer?

You can create multiple Web sites and switch between them with the click of a mouse. When you want to create a new site, choose New Site from the File menu (Shift-⌘-N), then choose a template and page style as described above.

Renaming Sites and Pages

To change the name of a site or page, double-click it in the sidebar, then type a new name.

Creating a Page: The Basics

After you choose a page style, iWeb gives you a page filled with placeholder graphics and text. By replacing this placeholder content with your own, you can create an attractive Web page.

Here's a look at the basic techniques behind iWeb page design. In the following pages, I describe how you can tailor a page design to your tastes.

Replacing placeholder text. To replace a section of placeholder text, select it and begin typing.

Replace placeholder photos. To replace a placeholder photo with one of your own, drag the photo from the media browser or from any folder on your hard drive to the placeholder photo.

Brevity rules. Unless you specify otherwise (page 363), iWeb adds a navigation menu link for a new page. If you use a wordy page name, the link may not display correctly—and it will definitely look hokey.

Kill the advertising. To remove the "Made on a Mac" graphic, select it and press the Delete key.

Creating Additional Pages

To add a new page to a site, choose File > New Page or click the Add Page button. Choose a template and page style as described on the opposite page.

Off the menu. Normally, iWeb includes a new page in your site's navigation menu. In some cases, you may not want this—maybe you plan to use a text link or other button to provide access to that page. Use the Inspector to remove a page from the navigation menu; see page 363.

Where iWeb Stores Your Sites

iWeb stores all of your sites and their pages in one place: a file named *Domain* tucked deep within your hard drive. Specifically, the Domain file lives in your home directory, within Library > Application Support > iWeb.

Get in the habit of backing up the Domain file now and then. Time Machine, part of Mac OS X, will automatically back up the Domain file unless you specifically exclude a folder that contains that file.

Page Design Basics

If you aren't a tailor, it's better to buy off the rack than to try to make your own suit. And if you aren't a Web designer, it's a good idea to stick with the built-in page styles that each iWeb template provides.

But the temptation to tinker may beckon. Maybe a certain page style requires a few more graphics to meet your needs, and maybe one of those graphics could use some work. Maybe you'd like to use a different type font, or adjust the line spacing of some text. Maybe a page needs another block of text, or a different background color.

You can perform many design tweaks directly on the webpage canvas. Click and drag blocks of text or graphics to move them around. Resize an item by selecting it and then dragging one of its selection handles.

For other design tasks, you'll turn to iWeb's Inspector. This small floating window is actually numerous control panels in one; you display the Inspector you need by clicking a button at the top of the Inspector window. With the Inspector, you can specify paragraph formatting, add and remove page backgrounds, create special graphics effects, and more.

For still other tasks, you'll use menu commands and the tools at the bottom of the iWeb window. Add additional text boxes to a page. Add shapes, such as lines and boxes. Control how objects overlap, specify colors and fonts, insert Web widgets, modify images, and more.

Here's a tour of your design studio.

Moving an Object

To move an object (for example, a text box or a graphic), click and drag it to the desired location.

iWeb displays *alignment guides* when an object you're dragging is centered on the page or aligned with another object on the page. To customize the alignment guides, use the Preferences command (page 391).

As you drag an item, iWeb displays its location on the page, in pixels. Here, the photo is 91 pixels from the left edge of the page and 203 pixels from the top.

Notes and Tips

Go straight. If you press the Shift key while dragging, iWeb constrains the item's movement to horizontal, vertical, or a 45-degree angle.

Keyboard control. To nudge an item in one-pixel increments, select the item and then press one of the arrow keys on your keyboard. To nudge in 10-pixel increments, press Shift along with an arrow key.

Have another. To duplicate an item, press the Option key while dragging the item.

Resizing an Object

To resize an object, select it and drag one of its selection handles. If you resize a text box, its text reflows to fit the new size.

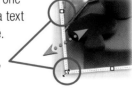

To resize an item in just one direction, drag a side handle.

Tip: To avoid changing the proportions of a text box or shape when resizing it, press the Shift key while dragging.

Anatomy of a Page

Each page style in an iWeb template has four regions. Each region serves its own purpose, and by changing the dimensions of the regions, you can change the appearance and dimensions of a Web page.

To see each of the four regions, choose Show Layout from the View menu (Shift-⌘-L). iWeb displays faint gray lines between each region.

Some page styles use some regions, but not others. For example, the page styles in the Travel template lack header regions. You can add those regions, however, by using the Page Inspector as described at right.

The *header* appears at the very top of the page.

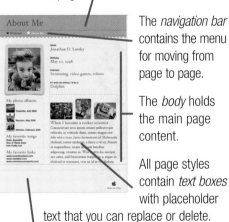

The *navigation bar* contains the menu for moving from page to page.

The *body* holds the main page content.

All page styles contain *text boxes* with placeholder text that you can replace or delete. You can also add additional text boxes.

The *footer* is at the very bottom of the page and typically holds the "Made on a Mac" graphic along with other optional elements, such as page counters and "email me" buttons (page 390).

Introducing the Inspector

The Inspector is the gateway to many design and formatting tasks in iWeb. To display the Inspector, click the ⓘ button near the lower-right corner of the iWeb window, or choose Show Inspector from the View menu (Option-⌘-I).

If you don't want a page to appear in your site's navigation menu, uncheck this box.

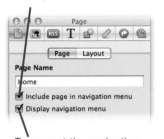

To prevent the navigation menu from appearing on the page, uncheck this box.

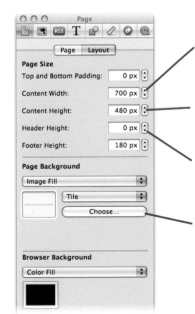

Changing Pages: The Page Inspector

iWeb's page styles tend to have short pages that your site's visitors can scroll through with just a click or two. That's convenient, but maybe you have more content than will fit within a page's confines. As long as your design is uncluttered (and your content interesting), there's nothing wrong with having a longer Web page.

To change a page's dimensions, use the Page Inspector. Display the Inspector, then click 📄 to display the Page Inspector.

The Page Size values determine the dimensions of a page and each of its regions.

You can make a page wider by increasing the value in the Content Width box, but don't go overboard: you don't want your site's visitors to have to scroll horizontally to read the entire page.

To make a page longer, increase the Content Height value by clicking the arrows or typing a new value. (The values are in pixels.)

Want to add a header region to a page style that lacks one? Specify a value here.

With many page styles, you can customize the page background here (see page 370).

Working with Text

To state the obvious, text plays a large role on Web sites. iWeb gives you plenty of text control. You can use the fonts that Apple has used for page templates, or you can summon the Fonts panel and format as you prefer.

But there's a peril to this typographic freedom. If you use fonts that aren't commonly available on Macs and Windows PCs, or if you perform some non-standard formatting (as I describe on the opposite page), iWeb renders that text as a graphic. Instead of getting a full page of fast-loading text, you get a large "picture of text" that makes your Web page load slowly. And because the text won't *really* be text, if your site's visitors try to print the page, they'll get poor-quality hard copy.

The best way to avoid this problem is to format large passages of text conservatively: stick with the fonts in iWeb's templates, or with fonts that are common on Macs and Windows PCs, such as Verdana. If you want a headline in a fancy font, create a separate text box for it.

Finally, because Web sites aren't Web sites without hyperlinks, you can turn a word or series of words into a link that whisks your visitors off to another page—elsewhere on your site or elsewhere in the world.

Text Basics

Mind your placeholder. iWeb's page styles have placeholder text boxes, but you don't have to fill every box with text. If you don't need a particular box, select it and press the Delete key. Note that you can't delete the text boxes on the blog and podcast page styles.

You can always recognize a text box that iWeb won't let you delete: when you select it, its selection handles are gray. On objects that you *can* delete, selection handles are white.

tempor fermentum.
ndisse nulla pretium,
por placerat.

arcu aliquam maecenas li
tempor fermentum. Ligula
nulla pretium, rhoncus tem

Adding a text box. You can also add a new text box to a page by clicking the Text Box button or choosing Insert > Text Box.

Linking to another page. It's easy to turn a word or phrase into a hyperlink that connects to another Web page. Select the word or phrase, then turn to the Link Inspector. Click the ⓘ button, then, in the Inspector, click ⊙.

Check the box. (To turn a hyperlink into ordinary text, uncheck the box.)

You can link to another page on your site, a page elsewhere on the Web, a file, or an email message (page 390).

For an external link, type the Internet address here. If you don't type the *http://* part of the address, iWeb adds it for you.

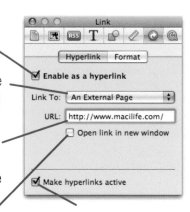

If this box is checked, the link will open in a new browser window.

When this box is checked, hyperlinks work as they will when you publish your site. To be able to click on text for editing, uncheck this box.

Text Formatting Techniques

Formatting characters. To change your text's font, size, and style, use the Fonts panel. To display the panel, click the 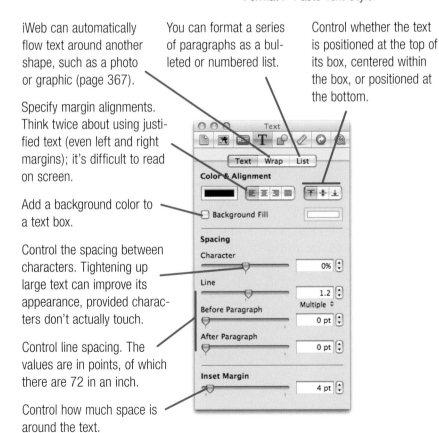 button or choose Format > Font > Show Fonts (⌘-T). Select the text you want to format, then use the Fonts panel to do the job. **Important:** Avoid using the text shadow feature available in the Fonts panel. Adding a text shadow to even one character causes iWeb to render the entire text box as a graphic.

iWeb can automatically flow text around another shape, such as a photo or graphic (page 367).

Specify margin alignments. Think twice about using justified text (even left and right margins); it's difficult to read on screen.

Add a background color to a text box.

Control the spacing between characters. Tightening up large text can improve its appearance, provided characters don't actually touch.

Control line spacing. The values are in points, of which there are 72 in an inch.

Control how much space is around the text.

Formatting paragraphs. You can also apply paragraph-level formatting: line spacing, alignment, and so on. For these tasks, use the Text Inspector. Click the button, then, in the Inspector, click.

Copying and pasting style. To copy one text box's formatting to another, select the formatted text and choose Format > Copy Text Style. Then select the text you want to format and choose Format > Paste Text Style.

You can format a series of paragraphs as a bulleted or numbered list.

Control whether the text is positioned at the top of its box, centered within the box, or positioned at the bottom.

Lose the text, keep the style. You may prefer to write your text in a word processor, then paste it into iWeb when you're done. At the same time, though, you may want to retain the existing font formatting of some placeholder text. No problem. After copying your text to the Clipboard, switch back to iWeb, select the text box where you want your new text to reside, then choose Edit > Paste and Match Style. iWeb pastes the new text but gives it the formatting of the old.

Resizing and rotating. You can resize text boxes using the mouse or the Metrics Inspector. You can also use the Metrics Inspector to rotate text, but note that iWeb will turn the text into a graphic.

Opacity and more. To change the opacity of text—for example, to make it appear faint—use the Graphics Inspector (page 366). You can also add a solid or dotted border around a text box.

Formatting links. To format the text links on your page, use the Format portion of the Link Inspector. Removing underlining from text links can make your page's text easier to read. I like to disable underlining except when the mouse is pointing at a link (the rollover state). Just be consistent across your site.

Working with Graphics

Essential Photo Techniques

Words are important, but a picture can be worth at least few of them. iWeb makes it easy to add images to your pages. Just drag them from the media browser (or from any location on your hard drive) to the webpage canvas.

Then, you can modify the photos—make them larger or smaller, crop them, and more. You can also use iWeb's layering controls to change how the photos stack with other objects on the page.

Chances are most of the images you'll be adding will be photos, but you might also add non-photo graphics: your company's logo, an elaborate headline created in Photoshop, and so on.

Basic formatting. You can resize an image by dragging its selection handles (see page 362). For more precision, click the Inspector's ✐ button. This summons the Metrics Inspector, where you can specify exact pixel dimensions. (To squish or squeeze a photo, uncheck the Constrain Proportions box.)

You can also use the Metrics Inspector to rotate images and specify their exact location on the page. And you can use the Graphic Inspector to add shadows, reflections, borders, and more. To make the image faint so you can superimpose text over it, use the Graphic Inspector's Opacity slider.

Fixed versus inline. When you add a photo to a page, its location is fixed at the point where you drag it. However, you can also insert a photo *inside* a text box. That's called an *inline graphic*, and because it lives among the letters, it moves when you move them. It also moves within the text box as you edit and format.

Use inline graphics for images that need to stay close to specific pieces of text—a photo of a business executive next to her biography; or the photos or illustrations in a report, an educational page, or a lengthy travelogue.

To add a photo as an inline graphic, press the ⌘ key while dragging the photo into a

text box. As you drag, position the vertical insertion point where you want the graphic to appear—for example, just before the first letter in a paragraph. When you release the mouse button, iWeb inserts the photo, which you can resize as needed. You can also cut (⌘-X) a photo that's already on a page, click the insertion point in a text box, and paste (⌘-V).

You can also use the Text Inspector to have iWeb wrap the text around the graphic (see the opposite page).

Replacing a placeholder image. iWeb's placeholder images remind me of those photos of strangers that are tucked inside new wallets. To replace an iWeb stranger, drag a photo to the place-holder photo.

Make it link. You can turn a graphic into a button that, when clicked, takes your site's visitors to another Web page. Select the graphic, display the Link Inspector, and specify the link details (see page 364).

Forward and Backward: Layering Controls

As you add items to a page, you may have objects that overlap. For example, in the Travel template's Welcome page, two photos overlap each other, and the photos themselves overlap a couple of design elements (the passport stamps).

When you add a new object to a page, it appears at the top of the "stack." You can control how objects overlap by using the Bring Forward and Send

Backward commands in the Arrange menu.

For example, to change the layering order so that a dog photo appears atop a cat photo, select the dog photo and choose Bring Forward,

or select the cat photo and choose Send Backward.

I guess you can tell: I'm a dog person.

A Gallery of Image Techniques

Cropping a Photo

In iWeb's world, cropping is called *mask-ing*. To crop out part of an image, you must adjust the size of the image's mask. (You can also mask an image with a shape; see page 368.)

Step 1. Select the image.

Step 2. Click the toolbar's Mask button or choose Format > Mask.

Beneath the image, the sizing and mask editor appears.

Step 3. Click Edit Mask.

Drag the mask and its selection handles to indicate the part of the image you want to retain. You can also nudge the mask using the keyboard's arrow keys and zoom the photo in and out by dragging the slider.

Step 4. When you're finished, click outside of the image, press Return, or click Edit Mask again.

iWeb hides the portion that was outside of the mask. To remove the cropping, click the Unmask button in the toolbar or choose Format > Unmask.

Adjusting a Photo

iWeb's Adjust panel works much like its counterpart in iPhoto, with one big exception: your original photo isn't altered. iWeb simply applies your adjustments to the copy of the photo that you add to the page.

Tip: Windows computers often display photos darker than Macs do, so you might consider using the Adjust panel to lighten dark photos slightly so they don't appear too murky when viewed on Windows computers.

Wrapping Text Around a Photo

For inline graphics, you can set up a *text wrap* so that text flows around vertical and horizontal boundaries of the photo.

After adding a photo as an inline graphic, as described on the opposite page, select the photo and open the Text Inspector. Click its Wrap button, and check the Object Causes Wrap box.

The object can appear at the left or right edge of a paragraph.

You can add extra space around the image.

Reflections, If You Must

In some of iWeb's page styles, photos have a reflection effect, as though they're suspended over a piece of frosted glass.

You can apply the reflection effect to photos that you add, too—but don't overdo it.

Select the photo, then display the Graphic Inspector ( ). Check the Reflection box. To adjust the intensity of the reflection, drag the slider.

To remove the reflection in an iWeb template that uses it, select the graphic and uncheck the Reflection box.

Stroke and Frame

You can add a stroke (a line) around a graphic or add a faux picture frame. In the Graphics Inspector, use the Stroke pop-up menu.

More Graphics Techniques

Rotating Images

In some iWeb page styles, photos are slightly askew to add visual interest. You can rotate photos you add: press the ⌘ key while dragging a photo's corner handle.

For more precision, type a value in the Metrics Inspector. You can also twiddle the little Rotate dial in the Metrics Inspector.

Behind the scenes, iWeb creates a new version of the image, with transparency enabled to let the background show through. iWeb also creates a separate image for a reflection if you've added one.

Adding Shapes

With the Shapes pop-up menu, you can endow a page with anything from straight lines to comic-book speech bubbles.

You can turn a shape into a hyperlink, and you can resize and modify shapes using the Graphic Inspector, the Color window, and the techniques discussed throughout this chapter.

Some shapes have settings panels for specifying details, such as the number of points in a star.

Inline shape. To insert a shape as an inline graphic, first click within a text box at the spot where you want the shape to live.

Text in a shape. You can type text within a shape: double-click in the shape, and start typing. If you type more text than will fit in the shape, a little plus sign (+) warning appears at the bottom of the shape.

Masking a photo with a shape. When you add a photo to an iWeb page, the photo has a mask—a rectangle. You can use other shapes to mask a photo, however, and doing so gives you more creative options for breaking away from all the rectangles and straight lines that you see on Web layouts.

To mask a photo with a shape, select the photo, then choose Format > Mask With Shape > *the shape you want.*

Adjust the mask and the photo's position within it using the techniques described on the previous pages.

If you've already added a photo and a shape to a page, you can marry the two: select both (Shift-click on each one), then choose Format > Mask with Selected Shape (⌘-Shift-M). Finally, drag the photo to the shape.

Don't want the mask shape after all? Select the masked photo and click the Unmask button (or choose Format > Unmask or press ⌘-Shift-M).

Using Instant Alpha

With Instant Alpha, you can selectively remove the background of an image. Instant Alpha (which is also part of Apple's Pages program) replaces the often tedious process of painting out the background of an image.

You might use Instant Alpha when you want to seamlessly blend an image into the background or have part of an image appear over or behind some text. You can also combine two photos to remove a background and place the subject of the photo into another scene.

Instant Alpha is easy to use: just drag across the color you want to remove. As you drag, iWeb masks out similar colors. The phrase "similar" is key: you'll get the best results with large areas of solid color. It's easier to remove a blue-sky background than a crowded city street background.

Step 1. Drag a photo onto a page or select a photo that's already on the page.

Step 2. Choose Format > Instant Alpha.

A crosshair pointer appears when you point to the photo.

Step 3. Slowly drag across the area you want to remove.

As you drag, the selection grows to encompass areas that use the same color.

Tip: For more precision, make the photo temporarily larger: drag one of its selection handles. When you're finished making your alpha mask, you can restore the photo's previous size.

Step 4. To remove a differently colored area, repeat step 3. Each time you click, you get a new selection, and can select more color.

Step 5. When you're finished, press Return.

The page background now shows through the areas you've masked.

Notes and Tips

Removing Instant Alpha. To remove Instant Alpha, select the photo to which you've applied it, and choose Format > Remove Instant Alpha.

Creating a new background for a photo. To create a different background for a photo, use Instant Alpha to remove the background of one shot, then position that shot over another one, using the Forward and Backward buttons as needed to have the photos stack properly.

Original photo

With Instant Alpha

With a new background

Customizing Page Backgrounds

Many of iWeb's page templates have background images or patterns. By using the Page Inspector, you can customize the backgrounds of Web pages in several ways. Open the page that has the background you want to customize, then display the Layout portion of the Page Inspector. Choose one of the following options from the pop-up menu in the Page Background area.

Color Fill. Give the page a solid background color. After choosing Color Fill, click the color well (located below the pop-up menu), then choose a color.

Gradient Fill. Add a *gradient* (a gradual shift from one color to another). After choosing this option, use the controls below the pop-up menu to fine-tune the gradient.

Specify the start and end colors of the gradient. To swap the two colors, click the double-headed arrow.

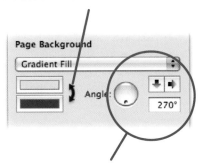

Control the angle of the gradient by dragging the Angle dial, by clicking the arrows, or by typing a value.

Image Fill. Add a photo or other graphic to the background. Use the controls below the pop-up menu to fine-tune the fill (see "Using Background Images," at right).

Tinted Image Fill. Similar to Image Fill, this option lets you add a color tint to the background image. To make the color more or less transparent, use the Opacity slider in the Colors window.

Changing the Browser Background Color

At the bottom of the Page Inspector are options for customizing the background color of the browser window. This is the area outside the dimensions of your Web page: if you imagine your Web page as a sheet of paper, the browser background color is the color of the desk on which the paper rests.

Visitors to your site who have relatively small displays may not even see the browser background color, but those lucky folks with 30-inch Apple Cinema Displays are quite likely to.

Normally, the browser background color is white, but you can change the color. Choose Color Fill from the pop-up menu, click the color well, and pick a color.

Tip: To pick up a color that is present elsewhere on your Web page, click the magnifying glass in the Colors window, and then click on the color you want to match. This trick works in any Mac program that uses the Colors window.

Background Textures

Web browsers have a cool capability: they can repeat, or *tile*, a small image so that it completely fills the background of the Web page.

Web designers take advantage of tiles to create page backgrounds that have interesting textures or patterns. Because a Web browser can tile a small image, the Web designer doesn't have to worry about creating a massive background graphic that's big enough to accommodate any size of browser window.

You can download an astronomical quantity of free page-background textures from a variety of Web sites. Do a Google search for *web page backgrounds*, and prepare to spend a lot of time exploring.

Once you've found a pattern you like, drag it to your desktop. In the Page Inspector, choose Image Fill from either the Page Background or Browser Background pop-up menu, depending on which background you want to change. Finally, drag the image into the Page Background or Browser Background image well.

You'll find a lot of garish, busy background patterns out there. Avoid them— they'll make your page look amateurish and will impair the legibility of your text.

Using Background Images

Adding a background image or texture to a Web page can be a nice way to dress it up—provided that the image or texture doesn't impair the legibility of the page's text.

To add a background image to a page, choose Image Fill from the Page Background or Browser Background pop-up menu in the Page Inspector. Then add the image and specify how you want iWeb to display it.

Here, I'm dragging a photo from the media browser, but you can also drag an image from any location on your hard drive. You can also click the Choose button and locate the image in the subsequent dialog box.

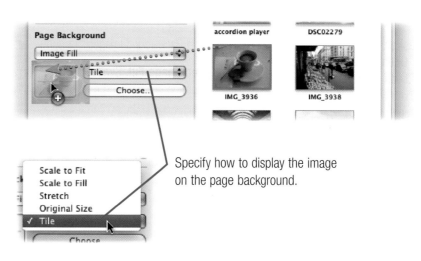

Specify how to display the image on the page background.

Here's a look at each image-fill option; note that only the Original Size and Tile options are available for the browser background.

Scale to Fill. iWeb enlarges the image to fill the page dimensions; the outer portions of the image are cropped off. This is the most useful option when you want an image to fill a page.

For this example, I added a solid white shape to the navigation bar so that its text didn't appear superimposed over the image.

Scale to Fit. iWeb displays the entire image, with no cropping. With horizontally oriented images, this option is likely to leave large borders above and below the image.

Stretch. iWeb fills the page with the image, altering the image's proportions to avoid any cropping. The image is likely to have a squished or stretched appearance.

Original Size. iWeb displays the image at its original size. For large images, such as digital camera photos, you're likely to see only a small part of the image on the page.

Tile. iWeb repeats the image across the background. Use this option to create background textures, as described on the opposite page.

Creating a Photos Page

With iWeb photos pages, you can create online photo albums with a few mouse clicks. The album pages contain rows of small thumbnail images that your visitors can click to see larger versions. They can also view a slide show. You can even allow visitors to add comments.

Thanks to the way the iLife programs work together, you can start your foray into photos pages in either iPhoto or iWeb. In iPhoto, stash some photos in an album and then sequence them in the order you want them to appear. Then use the Share menu to send the photos to iWeb.

Prefer to start in iWeb? Create a new page and choose a Photos page style. Then drag photos into the placeholder area, or better yet, drag an entire event or album from the media browser. Have lots of photos pages? Create a My Albums page to act as a table of contents for all of them (see page 376).

iWeb places a caption beneath each thumbnail image. And here's another good reason to use iPhoto to assign titles to your photos (page 38): iWeb uses a photo's title as its caption.

A photos page in iWeb can contain up to 500 photos. You can customize numerous aspects of a photos page: how many columns of thumbnail images to display; how much room to leave for text captions; the kind of frame you want to appear around each thumbnail; and more. And you can apply all the other design techniques described earlier in this chapter: add text, change backgrounds, and tweak formatting.

Creating a Photos Page within iPhoto

Step 1. Stash the photos you want to publish in an album. If you're lazy, you can also simply select a series of photos in your library. Or select a faces tile on the Corkboard or browse to a place in Places.

Step 2. Choose Share > Send to iWeb > Photo Page.

Step 3. In iWeb, choose a template, then click Choose or press Return.

Creating a Photos Page within iWeb

Step 1. Choose File > New Page or click the Add Page button in the lower-left corner of the iWeb window.

Step 2. Choose a template, then select its Photos page style, and then click Choose or press Return.

Step 3. Drag photos into the thumbnails placeholder area. Here, I'm using the media browser to add an entire iPhoto album.

Notes and Tips

Mix and match. You can mix and match approaches: create a photos page using iPhoto, then switch to iWeb to add additional photos to the existing page. You can't take the opposite route, however—when you send photos from iPhoto to iWeb, the photos are always added to a *new* photos page.

Rearrange and refine. To change the order of the photos in a photos page, simply drag the photos. To remove a photo, select it and press the Delete key. To change a photo's caption, click it and start typing.

Photos Page Tips and Techniques

Photos page or MobileMe gallery?

iPhoto creates lovely galleries (page 108), so why bother with photos pages? Control. Photos pages offer far more formatting options, and they allow visitors to comment on your photos.

Want to share some photos quickly and enable other iPhoto users to subscribe to them? Create a Web gallery album. Want full control over your design, along with goodies like comments, fancy slide show options, and RSS support? Create a photos page.

And it isn't an either/or proposition. You can publish the same iPhoto album or event as *both* a Web gallery album and a photos page. And as the following pages describe, you can add Web gallery albums that you've already created to your iWeb site.

Movies, too. Don't let the name fool you: a photos page can also hold movies. Just drag movies from the media browser or any location on your hard drive into the thumbnail grid.

How it Looks and Works

When visitors click a thumbnail on a photos page, they see a *detail page*. This page contains a large version of the photo, as well as controls for downloading the photo and displaying other photos in the album. If you've enabled photo comments (see the following page), a link appears that allows visitors to add their two cents' worth.

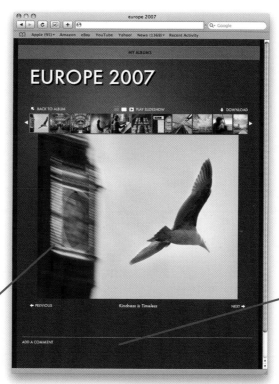

A visitor can weigh in on the photo and include an optional name and web site. The security text prevents spammers from using your site to do their dirty work.

Comments appear below the photo.

Customizing a Photos Page

iWeb's photos pages look great right off the rack, but if you'd prefer to tailor your photos pages, here's your sewing machine.

Customizing the thumbnail grid. To customize the grid of thumbnail photos on a photos page, select any thumbnail. The Photo Grid window appears.

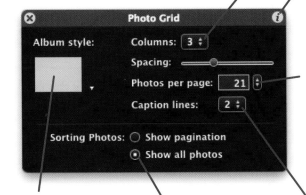

Frame shop: choose the frame style you want.

Choose your view: if your settings result in a multi-page album, you can choose to view the actual pages in iWeb or to see every single photo on just one page. The latter option is handy when you're sequencing photos and writing captions. (If all your photos will fit on a single Web page, these two options don't appear.)

Specify how many columns of thumbnails you want and the spacing between thumbnails. I like a two-column grid; its thumbnails are larger.

Display the Photos Inspector (right).

How many photos per page? If the number of photos in the photo grid exceeds this value, iWeb creates additional pages for you, complete with navigation buttons that let visitors move from page to page.

Specify how many lines of text you want to allow for each caption. Don't want captions? Choose 0.

Customizing the page. With the Photos Inspector, you can customize the photos page and its slide show.

To enable visitors to subscribe to a photos page in their RSS newsreaders, check this box. (For background on RSS, see page 10.)

Visitors can download photos; choose the size you'd like to offer here.

Customize or disable the slide show (see opposite).

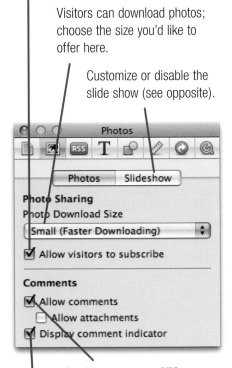

As shown on page 373, you can allow visitors to comment on your photos. You can also allow them to post attachments—for example, to share their version of a scene you photographed.

To have a tiny badge appear on photos that have comments, check this box. The badge lets visitors know someone had something to say about the photo.

Customizing the slide show. To customize (or disable) the slide show, click the Slideshow button in the Photos Inspector.

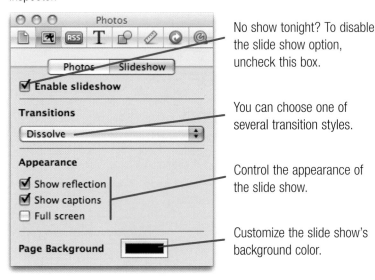

No show tonight? To disable the slide show option, uncheck this box.

You can choose one of several transition styles.

Control the appearance of the slide show.

Customize the slide show's background color.

Customizing captions. To customize the appearance of the captions beneath photo thumbnails, use the Text Inspector and the Fonts panel. For example, you can have the captions be left-aligned beneath each thumbnail instead of centered, and you can change the font.

To be sure that iWeb applies your formatting changes to every caption, select the thumbnail grid but not any thumbnails within it. Click near one of the edges of the grid. If you end up selecting a thumbnail, too, ⌘-click it to deselect.

Customizing photo borders. By selecting the photo grid and then displaying the Graphic Inspector, you can add a drop shadow behind photo thumbnails, customize the color of the border around the thumbnails, and more.

Managing Comments and Attachments

If visitors comment on your photos, how do you know? Choose File > Check for New Comments. If someone commented on a photo, iWeb adds the comment to the photo's detail page.

Sometimes, you might want to delete a comment. Maybe someone posted a large attachment, and you don't want it taking up space on your iDisk. Or maybe someone posted something inappropriate.

You can delete a comment in two ways.

In iWeb. Use the sidebar to go to the page containing the comment. Scroll down until you see the comment, then click the X that appears in its upper-right corner. If you're connected to the Internet, iWeb deletes the comment immediately; you don't have to republish the site.

In Safari. Fire up Safari, go to the page containing the comment, and click the lock icon.

Manage Comments

☐ Select All

☑ **Bill Gates**
Great capture!

A page appears asking for your MobileMe name and password. Supply them, and the Manage Comments page appears, where

you can select individual comments for deletion, or delete all comments on that photo.

Creating a My Albums Page

If you like to publish photos on your iWeb site, you'll quickly create a lot of photos pages. If you're into iMovie, you'll create a lot of movie pages, too. You could let iWeb create a link in your site's navigation bar for every single media page that you create, but your navigation bar will get big and unwieldy.

A book has an index that lets people find and jump to the page they need. iWeb provides *My Albums* pages that perform the same role. A My Albums page is an index page, a jumping-off point that consolidates access to your media pages.

A My Albums page can have up to 99 albums on it. You can create as many My Albums pages as you like—one for your vacation photos, another for your vintage family photos, and another for movies. Each albums page provides elegant animation effects, including a skimming feature that lets visitors preview the photos in a photos page. You can let visitors subscribe to the page in their RSS newsreaders, and you can customize the look of the page.

You can create an albums page after you've published a lot of media pages, or before. In fact, if you anticipate creating a lot of media pages, you can save yourself some time by creating an albums page first. Then, you can create new photos pages or movie pages by simply dragging photos or movies to the My Albums page.

Creating a My Albums Page

Step 1. Choose File > New Page or click the Add Page button.

Step 2. Choose a template, then select its My Albums page style.

Step 3. Click Choose or press Return.

iWeb names the page My Albums, but you can rename it in the sidebar.

Now What?

You can build your albums page in any of several ways.

Adding existing media pages. If you've already created some photos or movies pages, you can add them to the albums page by dragging them within the sidebar.

You can also click the My Albums page, and then drag photos or movies pages from the sidebar into the albums page.

Creating new media pages. To create a new photos page and add it to the My Albums page all in one step, display the My Albums page, then drag photos into it.

iWeb creates a photos page and adds it to the My Albums page. To customize the photos page, see page 374.

You can also create a blank photos page: select the albums page in the sidebar, then create a new photos page.

To create a new movies page, the drill is similar: drag a movie from the media browser or any location on your hard drive to the My Albums page.

Customizing the My Albums Page

You can customize the look of your My Albums page using many of the same techniques described on previous pages.

Tweak the grid. Each photos page and movies page on a My Albums page has its own thumbnail. To customize the grid of thumbnails, click one of the thumbnails. The Media Index window appears.

Choose how you want each thumbnail to be framed. There are 17 styles available, and even more in the Graphic Inspector.

You can choose to show or hide the name of each media page (which you can edit on the page) and, for photos pages, and the number of photos.

To not offer an RSS subscription option for your My Albums page, uncheck this box.

Display the Graphic Inspector, where you can choose more frame styles.

Choose how many columns of thumbnails you want and the space between them. Like large thumbnails? Choose a 1-column format.

Each thumbnail animates when a visitor points to it. The skim animation is the most useful: it lets visitors preview your photos. To disable animation, choose None.

Customizing Notes and Tips

Offering a subscription option. You can let visitors subscribe to your My Albums page in their RSS newsreaders or in Safari. Indeed, if you frequently add photos pages to your site (or change existing ones), it makes more sense for folks to subscribe to your My Albums page than to individual photos pages.

iWeb adds the Subscribe link automatically. If you'd rather not offer a subscription option, uncheck the box in the Media Index window or in the Photos Inspector's Photos tab.

Customizing the album frame. If you don't like the faux album frame styles,

you can turn the frame off. In the Media Index window, choose the upper-left style from the Index Style pop-up menu.

To have a line as a border, select the album region, open the Graphic Inspector, and choose Line from the Stroke pop-up menu. You can choose a color, style, and thickness. The Graphic Inspector also offers a wider set of frame choices.

Reorganizing albums. You might want to change the order of the album thumbnails in the My Albums page. Easy: Just drag the thumbnails. You can also change their order by dragging your media pages up and down in the iWeb sidebar.

Formatting flexibility. As with any iWeb page, you can change the font formatting of a My Albums page. The techniques are identical to those described on page 365.

Adding a Web Gallery album. If you've published some MobileMe galleries using iPhoto (page 108), you can add them to your My Albums page, too. Display your My Albums page, then choose Insert > Widget > MobileMe Gallery > *the album you want*.

Creating a Blog

The term *blog* sounds like something that would make you reach for the stain remover, but it's actually a corrupt contraction of the words *Web log*.

My *Webster's* defines *blog* thusly: "A personal Web site that provides updated headlines and news articles of other sites that are of interest to the user; also may include journal entries, commentaries and recommendations compiled by the user."

I'll build on that definition to add that a blog's contents, called *postings* or *entries*, are generally presented in reverse chronological order: the most recent entry appears first. I'll also add that blogs almost always use RSS to let readers subscribe and have new postings delivered to their RSS newsreaders.

And I'll amend the definition to remove the word *personal*. It's true that blogs are often personal journals. But businesses of all kinds have embraced blogging, too, relying on blogs to conduct conversations with their customers and engage in a dialog that's often more honest than the public relations people would like (see *Publish & Prosper: Blogging for Your Business*, by DL Byron and Steve Broback, New Riders, 2006).

iWeb makes it easy to create a basic blog. Apple's MobileMe service even allows visitors to leave comments and search your blog.

The process of publishing podcasts is nearly identical to that of publishing blogs; simply choose the Podcast page style instead of Blog. For details on podcast production, see the previous chapter.

Creating a New Blog

Step 1. Choose File > New Page or click the Add Page button.

Step 2. Choose a template, click its Blog page style, then click Choose or press Return.

The Entries page appears.

To add a new blog entry, click Add Entry. iWeb creates a new page, which appears below the list of entries.

Take it back: to delete a blog entry, select the entry and then click Delete Entry. Change your mind? Choose Undo to resurrect it.

Each blog entry appears here. To edit an entry, select it. To change an entry's title, double-click it.

Create your blog entry here. You can replace placeholder text and graphics and perform all the other design tasks described earlier in this chapter.

To resize the list of entries, drag the horizontal separator up or down.

The Elements of a Blog

In the course of managing a blog, iWeb creates and manages three types of pages.

Blog Page

The blog page is the main lobby for your blog. Visitors see excerpts of up to 50 of your most recent entries, and each excerpt has a link that lets them read the full entry. (You can customize the number and size of excerpts as described on the following pages.)

In the sidebar, the main blog page has the name *Blog*, although you can rename it as you can any iWeb page.

Entry Page

An *entry page* contains one blog posting: your rant of the day (or the hour). Each entry page also contains links, labeled *Previous* and *Next*, that allow your site's visitors to step through each of your blog entries. You can delete these links if you'd prefer that your visitors use your blog and archive pages to navigate.

Notes and Tips

Today's the day. It's common for each entry in a blog to be stamped with the day of its posting. When you create a new blog entry, iWeb gives it the current date.

However, you can bend time to your will. To change the date of a blog entry, double-click

Archive Page

The *archive page* is the dusty newspaper morgue where old back issues live; that is, it's where visitors can access all of your blog posts, not just recent ones.

the entry's date—either in the list of blog entries or on a blog entry page itself—then choose a new date (and date format, if you like).

Room for everyone. You can have as many blogs and podcasts within a Web site as you like. Have several family members (or colleagues) with something to say? Each one can have his or her own blog.

Customizing Your Blog

As with all of the pages that iWeb creates, you can use blog pages as they are or customize them to suit your tastes and needs.

Some of your customizing options involve the structure of the blog: how many excerpts appear on the main page, for example, whether an RSS subscription button is available, and whether you want to allow visitors to comment on your blog entries and to search your blog.

Other customizing options are design-oriented. With the Blog Summary window, you can customize many aspects of your blog's layout.

Here's a look at your blog customizing options.

Customizing the Main Page

You can use the Blog & Podcast Inspector to specify how many excerpts appear on your blog's main page as well as the length of each excerpt.

In the sidebar, select the blog's main page, then display the Inspector and click its RSS button.

You can show as few as one excerpt or as many as 50. To avoid creating a huge, slow-loading page, think twice about showing more than five or 10 excerpts.

Control how much of each entry iWeb excerpts. If you drag the slider all the way to the left, your visitors will see only the entry title and the *Read More* link.

Tip: Want to reduce the amount of clicking your visitors must do to read your latest dispatch? Show only one excerpt, and drag the Excerpt Length slider all the way to the right. Your latest entry will appear by itself, in its entirety, on the blog's main page.

Create a two-way conversation by enabling visitors to leave comments. You can also let them add attachments to their comments.

Tip: To check for and manage comments, use the techniques described on page 375.

To allow visitors to search your blog (a nice convenience), check this box.

The RSS Angle

Normally, iWeb adds a Subscribe button to your blog's main page. Visitors to your site can use this button to subscribe to the RSS feed that iWeb creates for your blog. If you don't want to offer an RSS subscription option, delete the Subscribe button.

Excerpts and RSS. The excerpts that iWeb creates for each entry are also what subscribers see when they update your subscription. If you want to deliver the entire blog post to your subscribers—a nicety that many newsreader users appreciate—drag the Excerpt Length slider all the way to the right.

Note: Your blog must be hosted on MobileMe in order to provide comments and searching.

Customizing Your Blog's Layout

You can customize the layout of your blog summary page (the main page that visitors to your blog see).

To begin, select your blog's name in the iWeb sidebar. The Blog Summary window appears.

Choose from several different layouts; each one positions the photo differently in relation to the text.

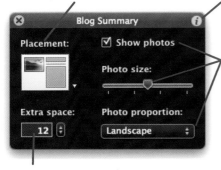

Add or remove space between the photo and text.

Customizing Entry Page Formatting

You can also customize the formatting of your blog entry pages. Don't like the font or size that an iWeb template uses? Change it. Want shorter lines of text so you can place photos in the margins? Resize the text box that holds the entry's main text.

Display the Blog & Podcast Inspector, described on the opposite page.

Photo controls. To omit photos from the summary page, uncheck the box. To control the size of photos, use the slider. To choose a photo proportion, use the pop-up menu. (Some proportions may cause photos to appear cropped on the summary page.)

To change the formatting of an item on an entry page, display that entry page, select the item, then use the Fonts panel as described on page 365. You can also add graphics and other embellishments using the techniques described earlier in this chapter.

If you change formatting in one entry page, iWeb does *not* change other entries in your blog. So what if you want to use your new design for all future blog entries? It's easy. When you're ready to create a new blog entry, select the entry with the formatting you modified, and choose Edit > Duplicate. iWeb makes a duplicate of the entry. The duplicate is now your newest blog post: just edit its date (page 379) and update its content.

Each time you want a new blog post, duplicate one of your specially formatted entry pages.

The Podcast Angle

As I mentioned on page 378, publishing a podcast with iWeb is similar to creating a blog. In the template chooser, pick the Podcast page style. Then, drag the podcast that you exported from GarageBand into the entry page.

The Blog & Podcast Inspector does provide some podcast-specific options. To see them, click its Podcast button.

To submit your podcast to the iTunes store, be sure that the Allow Podcast in iTunes Store box is checked, then choose File > Submit Podcast to iTunes. In the dialog box that appears, specify copyright and category information, then click Publish and Submit.

Maps, YouTube, and More: Web Widgets

With Web widgets, you can endow your site's pages with special features: Google maps, Google ads, YouTube videos, MobileMe Web gallery albums, and more.

With the Google Maps widget, you can insert a map of any location you choose. Provide directions to your business, show the address of the park where you took your latest photos, or share a satellite view of your favorite tourist spot. You can customize a map's appearance, scale, and size.

With the Google AdSense widget, you can add advertisements to your site. Google uses its industrial-strength search technology to match ads that it thinks are appropriate to the content of a given page—and when visitors click an ad on your site, you make a tiny sum.

What other wonders do widgets allow? Add YouTube videos to your pages. Snap a photo or shoot a movie clip using your Mac's built-in iSight camera, then add the results to a page. Use RSS to add content to your site. Add a fun countdown clock.

And if you're an HTML jockey, you can write your own code to add effects or features that are difficult or impossible to create with iWeb's built-in features.

Widget Essentials

Adding a Widget

You can add a widget in one of two ways. With either technique, adding a widget has two phases: add the widget itself, then specify details about it: for example, the address and display options for a Google map.

From the Media browser. Click the Show Media button, then click Widgets. Drag the widget you want into your page.

When you drag the widget's icon into the page, the icon blooms into a content box that will hold the widget's content (for example, a Google map or YouTube video). Position the box where you want it, then use the floating window below the box to specify the options required for that widget.

From the Insert menu. Choose Insert > Widget > *the widget you want*. A content box appears in the middle of your page, with the widget's option window below it.

Which method is best? It doesn't much matter, though sometimes the Insert menu is more efficient, as I describe later.

Customizing a Widget

Besides actually specifying what the widget will display, you can also customize its appearance on your page using the same techniques described earlier in this chapter.

To resize a widget, drag its corner handles. To move the widget, drag it on the page.

For widgets that display text, such as the RSS widget, you can customize the text's font formatting. Select the text in the widget's content box, and use the Fonts panel as described on page 365.

Learn more. Each widget's options window has a Learn More button; click it to display detailed online help for that widget.

See iWeb widgets in action.
www.macilife.com/iweb

Adding a Google Map

Step 1. Add the Google Maps widget to the page.

A placeholder appears on the page, and the Google Maps window appears above it.

Step 2. In the Google Maps window, type an address and click Apply.

The Google map appears on your page. You can place as many maps as you want on a page.

Customizing Tips

To resize the map, drag its selection handles. To hide the address bubble and zoom controls, uncheck their boxes in the Google Maps window. To fine-tune the area shown by the map, drag within it. To switch between map, satellite, and hybrid views, click their buttons in the map.

Adding Google AdSense Ads

Google's AdSense program lets you display ads on your site. You can choose from three categories—text ads, text and image ads, and text links—and each category provides several sizes of ads.

Step 1. Add the Google AdSense widget to a page.

Step 2. If you already have an account with Google, click I Already Have an Account and follow the steps provided. No account yet? Enter your preferred email address, then click Submit.

The Google AdSense Ad window appears.

Step 3. Choose an ad format and color.

Note: You can't resize AdSense ads.

Adding YouTube Clips

Step 1. In your Web browser, go to the YouTube page containing the video you want to add.

Step 2. Copy the page's address: select it in the browser's address bar and choose Edit > Copy. You can also get the address from the little URL box to the right of the video window.

Step 3. In iWeb, add the YouTube widget to a page.

Step 4. Paste the address into the YouTube widget's options window, then click Apply.

The YouTube video loads and appears on the page.

Tip: Even though YouTube videos are movies, you don't have to use the Movie page style. The Movie page style is for QuickTime movies; YouTube videos are delivered in the Adobe Flash format.

Your World on Widgets

These days, many of us have outposts throughout the World Wide Web. We post photos on Flickr and keep track of our contacts' shots. We post movies on YouTube and subscribe to movies from our favorite 'tubers. And we have favorite blogs and news sites that we visit all the time.

You've already created a personal site in iWeb. Why not create a page or two that collects content from your various Web stopping points and puts it in one place?

In the past, the answer to that question might have been, "Because it's too hard." It's easy now, thanks to iWeb and the fact that most major Web sites (and many minor ones) provide RSS feeds for their content. By combining those feeds with iWeb's RSS widget, you can add content from other sites to your pages. (For an introduction to RSS, see page 10.)

How might you use this? Put feeds from your Flickr contacts and favorite YouTube categories on your page. Add headlines from your favorite blogs or newspapers. Have you created a site for your business? Add a news page that collects headlines from relevant news sources.

Major portals, such as Google and Yahoo, have provided these kinds of niceties for a long time. Now you can do it on your iWeb site. Here's an overview of the process, along with a look at the rest of iWeb's built-in widgets.

Sampling the Possibilities

In this example, I've used the RSS widget and the HTML widget to create a page containing a list of my most recent Flickr posts, a box for my YouTube channel, and a feed containing headlines from Macworld.com.

By just visiting this page, I—and, more to the point, anyone who visits my iWeb site—can get an at-a-glance look at some of things that matter to me. It's a simple example, but it shows how you can use iWeb and RSS to "aggregate content," as Web-business types like to call it, from other sites.

How it works. RSS, baby. When a site provides an RSS feed for its content, you can tap into that feed and shuttle it into iWeb's RSS widget. iWeb subscribes to the feed and displays its up-to-the-minute content on your site.

Using the RSS Widget

Here's how to use the RSS widget to add your most recent Flickr uploads to your iWeb page.

Step 1. On Flickr, scroll to the bottom of your photostream's home page, then locate the feed icon ( ). Control-click on it and choose Copy Link from the shortcut menu.

Step 2. In iWeb, add the RSS feed widget to a page.

A content box appears along with the widget's options window.

Step 3. Click inside the Subscription URL box, choose Edit > Paste, then click Apply.

iWeb displays the feed's content.

See a World Wide Widget example.
www.macilife.com/iweb

Customizing a Feed's Appearance

You can resize and reposition the feed's content box and use the Fonts panel to format its text. The RSS Feed options window gives you even more options.

Choose from seven layout styles for each entry. (In this Flickr example, an "entry" is one photo. On other sites, it might be one blog post or one news story.) Many styles display a photo, too, if the entry has one.

How many entries should appear in the content box? If you're showing only headlines, you might boost this number to show more entries.

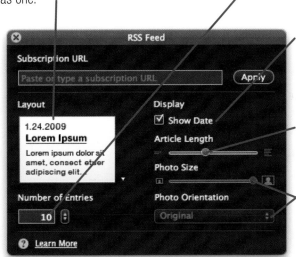

Show or hide the date of an entry.

To show just headlines (as with the Macworld.com headlines on the opposite page), drag the slider all the way to the left.

If you've chosen a layout that provides photos, use these controls to specify size and orientation.

Using the HTML Widget

Here's how to use the HTML Widget to add a box for your YouTube account.

Step 1. On YouTube, go to your profile page and locate the *Connect With* box along the left-hand side.

Step 2. At the bottom of the *Connect With* box is a box labeled *Embed This Channel*. Click the code in the box, then choose Edit > Copy.

Step 3. In iWeb, add the HTML widget to a page.

Step 4. Click in the large box in the HTML Snippet window, and choose Edit > Paste.

The YouTube code appears in the box.

Step 5. Click Apply.

The Rest of the Widget Family

MobileMe Gallery. To insert a MobileMe Gallery album on any page, add the MobileMe Gallery widget to a page, then choose a gallery. **Tip:** It's faster to use the Insert menu than the media browser—the menu lets you directly choose the gallery you want.

An animated thumbnail of the gallery appears. You can change the thumbnail's position, but not its size.

iSight Photo and iSight Movie. Have a camera in your Mac? Use these widgets to shoot a photo or movie and add it to a page. Replace the photo or movie any time: just click its content box and shoot another. For movies, use the QuickTime Inspector (page 391) to tweak appearance. **Tip:** To turn off the three-second countdown each widget provides, press Option while clicking the camera icon.

Countdown. Creating a site for an upcoming event? Add a countdown to the page. It's gimmicky, but fun.

Publishing Your Site

When your site is ready for its debut, you'll *publish* it on Apple's MobileMe service. Click iWeb's Publish button, and iWeb translates your designs into HTML (Hypertext Markup Language, the coding language used to describe the appearance of Web pages). iWeb also prepares your graphics, and then transfers everything to Apple's servers, which dish it out the world.

Similarly, when you change your site— create a new blog entry, fix a typo, or add an entire set of pages—you must publish it in order for your changes to become available. When you publish a site that you've updated, iWeb transfers only those pages that changed since the last time you published the site.

Normally, the sites you publish are available for anyone to see. But you can also post a guard at the door: you can specify a user name and password that visitors must specify before they can see your site.

iWeb meshes best with MobileMe, but you can also transfer a site to another Internet provider. And you can publish your sites to a folder on your hard drive. For details, see pages 388–389.

Have more than one site? You can combine approaches: publish your personal site to MobileMe, and your business site to an Internet provider. iWeb doesn't much care whose servers dish out your pages.

Important: As mentioned on previous pages, in order to have comments, blog and podcast searching, password protection, and hit counters, your site must be hosted on Apple's MobileMe service.

Publishing on MobileMe

Publishing your site on MobileMe couldn't be easier: just click the Publish Site button near the lower-left corner of the iWeb window. If you've created more than one site, mosey over to the sidebar and select the site you want to publish before clicking Publish Site.

iWeb publishes the site while you get onto other tasks, and then alerts you when it's done. You can then choose to visit the site or send an announcement email containing the site's address.

Tip: To visit a specific page, select it in the iWeb sidebar, then press the Option key while clicking the Visit button.

In the sidebar, published pages have blue icons ( ). Pages that you've created or modified since you last published have red icons ( ). That's iWeb's way of telling you that you need to publish the site to make those changes available to the world.

Assigning a Password

To protect a site with a password, click the site's name in the sidebar to display the Publishing Settings window. Check the *Make my published site private* check box, then type a user name and password in the boxes.

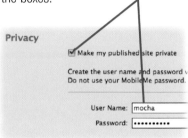

Then give that information to everyone who needs to access the site. (You can use the Announce button that appears after you publish to do this.)

Note that you can't create a separate user name and password for each person. Every visitor will have the same user name and password.

Change your mind? To unprotect a site, opening it to the world, return to the Publishing Settings window, delete the user name and password text, then click the Publish Site button again. Similarly, you can make a public site private by sprinting to Publishing Settings, typing a user name and password, then clicking Publish Site.

Publishing Tips

Where Your Sites Live

iWeb stores your sites on your iDisk, the virtual storage locker that is included with your MobileMe subscription. To view your iDisk, switch to the Finder, then choose Go > iDisk > My iDisk.

Within your iDisk is a folder named Web, and within that folder is folder named Sites. Your iWeb-created sites are in the Sites folder.

Publish Everything

When you publish to MobileMe, iWeb transfers only those pages that you added or changed since you last published. However, you can force iWeb to transfer everything: choose File > Publish Entire Site.

If you notice that links between your iWeb sites aren't working, try this technique to fix the problem.

Clear Your Cache

You've changed a page and published it, but the page looks the same when you visit your site. That's probably because your Web browser has retained the previous version of the page in its *cache*. A browser keeps recently loaded graphics in its cache to avoid having to load them again should you revisit a page.

If you're using the Safari browser, you can empty the browser cache by choosing Safari > Empty Cache. If you'd rather not empty the entire cache, you can force Safari to reload the entire page by pressing the Shift key while clicking Safari's ⟳ button.

Your Own Domain Name

Normally, when you publish your site on MobileMe, your Web site's address begins with web.me.com. However, if you've registered your own domain name (for example, www.jimheid.com), you can set up MobileMe to use your domain name. It adds a professional touch to your Web site.

To set up a personal domain name in iWeb, choose File > Set Up Personal Domain. Your browser will take you to MobileMe. Log in to your account, and click the Personal Domain button, and follow the instructions.

The process involves modifying your domain information with the company where you registered your domain—for example, Domain Direct. It's a straightforward process that usually involves visiting the company's site, logging in, and adjusting a setting called CNAME. If you get stuck, contact your domain registrar's technical support department.

When you set up a personal domain, your site is still being published on MobileMe. You simply set up an alias that lets your domain name point to your pages on MobileMe.

Need more help? Apple has published step-by-step instructions for setting up a personal domain. I've linked to them at macilife.com/iweb.

More Publishing Options

Publishing to a Folder

You can have iWeb publish a site on your hard drive. Instead of transferring your site's pages to MobileMe or another Web server, iWeb simply saves them in a folder on your drive.

To make it happen, click the site's name in the sidebar to display the Site Publishing Settings window. From the Publish To pop-up menu, choose Local Folder.

Normally, when you publish to a folder, iWeb saves the site in the Sites folder within your home folder. If you'd rather the site live somewhere else, use the Folder Location area to specify a different folder or hard drive. After that's done, click the Publish Site button.

Why would you even want to publish a site on your hard drive?

Testing. One reason might be to test it and see exactly how the site will look in a browser. After publishing the site, open it in your browser. If all looks well, switch the publishing option back to MobileMe or FTP, and publish the site for all to see.

From iWeb to iDVD. Here's a reason that's more fun: Use iWeb to create a site that complements some photos or movies that you plan to burn to a DVD using iDVD. Publish the site to a folder, and then include it in the DVD-ROM portion of the DVD (page 274).

Imagine that you've created a lavish iMovie project, and some iPhoto slide shows, to celebrate a cross-country road trip. And maybe you used iWeb to publish a blog as you journeyed, along with iWeb photo pages and Google maps. Publish that site to a folder, then burn it, along with your movies and photos, to a DVD. Glue the DVD's envelope into the back of a companion iPhoto book, and you've made a multimedia extravaganza.

Local serving. A more obscure reason you might publish to a local folder is to use Mac OS X's Web sharing feature. Use the Sharing system preference to turn on Web sharing, and your Mac becomes a Web server. (Geek note: Unless you have a static Internet protocol address, it's

generally impractical to have your Mac serve your site. If you have a typical DSL or cable modem connection to the Internet, you probably don't have a static IP address. And if all this is Greek to you, forget that I even brought it up.)

Publishing via FTP

FTP stands for *file transfer protocol*, and it's a method of sending files around on the Internet. When you're having a Web site served by an Internet hosting provider other that MobileMe, you can have iWeb transmit your site's pages to your hosting provider via FTP.

To set it up, select the site in the sidebar to display the Site Publishing Settings window. From the Publish To pop-up menu, choose FTP Server. Then, peck the necessary details into the FTP Server Settings area.

The address of your Web server; check with your hosting provider to get the address you'll need to supply.

The user name and password for the account that you have with your provider.

If you want to stash the site in a specific folder on your server, type the folder's path here. Be sure to get the forward slashes right; some providers require a slash at the end of the path, while others don't. Check with your provider for specifics.

In most cases, you'll use ordinary FTP, as shown here. And don't edit the Port number unless your provider tells you to.

Use the Test Connection button to verify your settings. iWeb attempts to connect to the server and upload a tiny test file.

If your test connection was successful, you're all set. Click the Publish Site button to upload your site.

As these instructions show, transmitting something via FTP is trickier than beaming it to MobileMe. It's a good idea to consult your hosting provider to get the necessary technical specifics before you even try.

About the Website URL Box

When publishing to a folder or to an FTP server, the Publishing Settings Window contains a text box labeled Website URL.

URL: http://www.acmecoyote.com

Your site's root URL. Used for creating links and RSS feeds.

You can leave this box empty when you're publishing to a folder for local viewing (for example, to burn the site on a DVD, as described above).

When you're publishing to an FTP server, type the base URL of your site in the box. iWeb uses this address to craft links to and between the site's pages and to create RSS feeds on pages such as blog entries and photo albums.

Facebook and Site Publishing

If you're on Facebook, you might want to let your Facebook friends know when you've published updates to a site. Head into the Site Publishing Settings window for the site and check the box labeled *Update my Facebook profile when I publish this site.*

A window appears asking for your Facebook login information. (It's the same window we encountered back on page 112.) Supply your login information and click the Login button.

That site is now linked to your Facebook account.

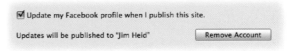

☑ Update my Facebook profile when I publish this site.

Updates will be published to "Jim Heid"   [Remove Account]

When you publish the site, iWeb adds an activity notice to your Facebook wall.

RECENT ACTIVITY

🖼 Jim's iWeb Site Acme Coyote Supplies has been updated.

If you change your mind about letting your Facebook friends know every time you fix a typo and republish a page, return to the Site Publishing Settings window and uncheck the Update box. The site is still linked to your Facebook account, but iWeb won't send up a flare every time you make a change. When you're ready to let your friends know about changes again, check the box.

To completely sever the ties between your site and Facebook, click the Remove Account button.

iWeb Tips

Adding Goodies

If Google maps, ads, RSS feeds, iSight photos and more aren't enough, there are a few more goodies you can add to your pages.

It's a hit. A *hit counter* is a Web odometer that displays how many times a particular page has been viewed. To add a counter to a page, choose Insert > Button > Hit Counter. iWeb inserts the hit counter.

You can position the hit counter wherever you like, but be sure it fits entirely within the webpage canvas.

Notes: A hit counter works only if you serve your site through Apple's MobileMe service. To reset the hit counter to zero, delete the hit counter, publish the page, then add a new hit counter and publish the page once more.

Keep in touch. Want to provide a convenient way for your site's visitors to email you? Add an Email Me button: choose Insert > Button > Email Me. When a visitor clicks that button, his or her email program will open a new message addressed to you.

To specify your email address, select the site in the sidebar. In the Site Publishing Settings window, complete the Contact Email field.

If you want incoming email messages to go to a different address, create a text or graphic hyperlink and, in the Link Inspector, choose An Email Message from the Link To pop-up menu. Specify the address and subject for the email in the boxes that appear.

Date and time. It's common for a Web page to contain a date listing when the page was last modified. When you want to date-stamp your pages, don't look at your calendar—let iWeb do the work. Click within a text box to create a blinking insertion point, then choose Insert > Date & Time. A dialog box appears giving you a choice of date and time formats. Select the one you want, then click Insert or press Return. If you'd like the date and time to be updated when-

ever you launch iWeb, check the Automatically Update box.

If you've worked on a page and would like to update its date or time stamp, Control-click on the date and time and choose Update Date & Time Now from the shortcut menu. You can also double-click the date and time to change its display format and the date and time shown.

Playlists. Want to share a list of your favorite tunes with your site's visitors? Drag an iTunes playlist from the media browser into the webpage canvas. iWeb creates a set of links for each song.

When visitors click song links (or their link arrows), they'll be taken to those songs on the iTunes Store, where they can buy, buy, buy.

By the way, you can also link to any item on the iTunes Store by simply dragging the item from iTunes into the webpage canvas.

Get more iWeb tips and resources.
www.macilife.com/iweb

Your iTunes widgets. Make that My iTunes widgets. Whatever. You can create flashy widgets that list your most recent iTunes purchases, favorite artists, and reviews.

In iTunes, choose Store > View My Account, and sign in. Click the Manage My iTunes button, then choose the widgets you want. iTunes supplies their HTML code, which you can paste into iWeb's HTML Snippet widget (page 385).

Beyond Apple's Templates

Want to go beyond the templates that are built into iWeb? Go visit Suzanne Boben. She's a designer who has created her own line of templates—some of which are free.

Check out her amazing contributions to the iWeb world at www.11mystics.com.

Customize Your Guides

With the Preferences command, you can customize the alignment guides that iWeb displays as you drag items on the webpage canvas. You can change the color of the guides and you can have iWeb display guides at the edges of an object as well as at its center.

Activating this second option can make it easier to align items. (Apple's iWork '09 programs provide a similar convenience.)

From iWork to iWeb

Speaking of iWork, it's worth noting that you can paste elements created in Keynote or Pages into iWeb. Need a chart or a price list table on your Web page? Create it in Pages or Keynote, then select it, copy it, and paste it into iWeb.

Adding QuickTime Movies and Audio

Each iWeb template provides a page style designed specifically for holding a QuickTime movie. But you aren't restricted to just that page style. You can add a QuickTime movie to any iWeb page: simply drag it from the media browser or any location on your hard drive. If the movie is larger than 10MB,

iWeb warns you that it may take a lifetime to download on slower connections.

As with graphics, movies can stand alone on a page or they can be in line with text. You might format a movie as an inline object if you want to have text wrap around it. For details on working with inline objects, see page 366.

If you drag a movie to the image placeholder in a blog entry, the movie becomes a video podcast.

Controlling movie display. To customize how a movie plays, select the movie and open the QuickTime Inspector. You can control the start and stop point and pick the poster frame that appears before the movie plays.

To have the movie play when the page loads, check the Autoplay box. To have it play over and over, check Loop. Don't want to give your visitors any playback controls? Uncheck the Movie Controller box. But think twice about this measure—friendly Web sites give visitors control.

Audio only. You can also add an audio file to a Web page by dragging it from the media browser or any location on your hard drive.

Index

Index

Index

Index

Index

Index

Index

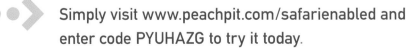